NAVIGATING PUBLIC OPINION

Russell Brooker
414-382-6243

NAVIGATING
PUBLIC OPINION

Polls, Policy, and the Future of American Democracy

Edited by
JEFF MANZA
FAY LOMAX COOK
BENJAMIN I. PAGE

OXFORD
UNIVERSITY PRESS
2002

OXFORD
UNIVERSITY PRESS

Oxford   New York
Auckland   Bangkok   Buenos Aires   Cape Town   Chennai
Dar es Salaam   Delhi   Hong Kong   Istanbul   Karachi   Kolkata
Kuala Lumpur   Madrid   Melbourne   Mexico City   Mumbai   Nairobi
São Paulo   Shanghai   Singapore   Taipei   Tokyo   Toronto

and an associated company in Berlin

Copyright © 2002 by Oxford University Press, Inc.

Published by Oxford University Press, Inc.
198 Madison Avenue, New York, New York 10016

www.oup.com

Oxford is a registered trademark of Oxford University Press

Library of Congress Cataloging-in-Publication Data
Navigating public opinion : polls, policy, and the future of American democracy / edited by
Jeff Manza, Fay Lomax Cook, and Benjamin I. Page.
p.   cm.
Includes bibliographical references and index.
ISBN 0-19-514933-5; ISBN 0-19-514934-3 (pbk.)
1. Public opinion—United States.   2. Public opinion polls.
I. Manza, Jeff.   II. Cook, Fay Lomax.   III. Page, Benjamin I.
HN90.P8   N385   2002
303.3'8'0973—dc21   2002020128

1 3 5 7 9 8 6 4 2

Printed in the United States of America
on acid-free paper

PREFACE

At the tail end of the Clinton administration, on the late-night television show *Politically Incorrect* (a show that brings together a random group of celebrities nightly to talk about the news), a discussion began about Bill Clinton's allegedly excessive reliance on polls in making policy decisions. Toward the end of the segment, the host of the show, comedian Bill Maher, cynically remarked that maybe we shouldn't think of this as such a bad thing after all, because at least by using polls, the government is listening to the American people. The audience broke into wild applause at his ironic comment.

The tensions captured in that moment are real. The relationship between citizens' preferences and what governments (and politicians) do is at the core of democratic governance. In the last few years, a new level of sophistication in research on these topics has entered into debates over these classical questions. Analysts have developed new theories and methods for assessing the impact of public opinion, the role of elites in shaping public opinion, and how we measure and conceptualize public opinion in the first place. This volume aims to incorporate these frequently spirited debates, juxtaposing diverse positions in dialogue with one another with the hopes of providing readers with a sense of the state of the art, and the issues that remain open for further investigation. We have entitled this book *Navigating Public Opinion* to try to capture the diverse ways in which the authors in this book suggest that political actors engage public opinion: some view public opinion as creating waves that move the ship of state; others see the waves of public opinion as buffeted by the forces generated by politicians or other elites; still others are concerned with the instruments used to gauge it in the first place.

This volume emerged from a conference on the theme "Polls, Policy, and the Future of American Democracy," sponsored by the Institute for Policy Research at Northwestern University, and held on Northwestern's Evanston campus in May 2000. We thank our fellow conference organizers—Dennis Chong, Susan Herbst, Lawrence Jacobs, and Charles Manski—for putting together that event on a modest budget. The other program participants (Scott Althaus, Paul Quirk, Richard Sobel, Richard Longworth, Amy Searight, David Axelrod, and Kenneth Abbott) provided thoughtful commentaries and other significant contributions to the conference. We are indebted to several sources for support at Northwestern: the Institute for Policy Research, the Program on American Studies, the Deans of Speech and the Weinberg College of Arts and Science, the Center for International and Comparative Studies, and the Departments of Political Science and Sociology.

This book and the conference which preceded it were both made possible by the superb administrative efforts of Audrey Chambers and Ellen Whittingham of the Institute for Policy Research at all stages of the project. Capable research assistance was provided by Michael Sauder and Marcus Britton. Several people provided additional advice or other help with this project: in particular, we thank Clem Brooks, Robert Shapiro, and John Tryneski. We also thank our editor at Oxford University Press, Dedi Felman, for arranging absolutely stellar anonymous reviews of the first draft of the manuscript and providing very helpful guidance in reshaping the manuscript for publication. We also thank those anonymous reviewers for their careful and informative suggestions. Last, but not least, we want to publicly thank all of the contributors to this volume for (mostly) getting their chapters in on time, with minimal prodding from the editors, and also for the quality and seriousness of purpose reflected in what they have written.

Evanston, IL   *Jeff Manza*
September 2001   *Fay Lomax Cook*
                                                                          Benjamin Page

CONTENTS

PART II. HOW POLITICAL ELITES
USE PUBLIC OPINION

PART III. MEASURING PUBLIC OPINION

PART IV. CONCLUSION

      Democracy..315
      HUMPHREY TAYLOR

18.   The Semi-Sovereign Public 325
      BENJAMIN I. PAGE

      References 345

      Index 373

CONTRIBUTORS

JASON BARABAS is assistant professor of political science at Southern Illinois University. His research in political behavior focuses on public opinion, political psychology, deliberation, and public policy. His work has been published in *International Studies Quarterly* and *Political Analysis*.

PAUL BURSTEIN is a professor of sociology and adjunct professor of political science, University of Washington, Seattle. He is the author of *Discrimination, Jobs, and Politics: The Struggle for Equal Employment Opportunity in the United States since the New Deal* (University of Chicago Press, 1998) and articles on public opinion, social movement organizations, and policy change. His current work focuses on how public opinion, the party balance, interest groups, and social movement organizations affect congressional action on proposals for policy change.

FAY LOMAX COOK is the director of the Institute for Policy Research and professor of human development and social policy in the School of Education and Social Policy, with a joint appointment in the Department of Political Science, at Northwestern University. She conducts research on the relationship between public opinion and social policy, the politics of public policy, and the dynamics of public support for social programs. She is the author or coauthor of *Who Should Be Helped? Public Support for Social Services* (Sage Publications, 1979); *The Journalism of Outrage: Investigative Reporting and Agenda Building in America* (Guilford Publications, 1991, with David Protess and others); and *Support for the American*

Welfare State: The Views of Congress and the Public (with Edith J. Barrett, Columbia University Press, 1992). She is past president and a fellow of the Gerontological Society of America and a member of the National Academy of Social Insurance.

G. WILLIAM DOMHOFF is a research professor in sociology at the University of California, Santa Cruz, where he teaches a course on power, politics, and social change. He also has taught at the University of California, Santa Barbara; the University of Paris; and Colgate University, where he was a Lindsay O'Connor Chair in American Institutions in 2001. Four of his books are among the top fifty best-sellers in sociology for the years 1950 to 1995: *Who Rules America?* (Prentice-Hall, 1967); *The Higher Circles* (Random House, 1970); *The Powers That Be* (Random House, 1979); and *Who Rules America Now?* (Simon and Schuster, 1983). His empirical refutation of Robert A. Dahl's *Who Governs?*, published under the title *Who Really Rules? New Haven and Community Power Reexamined* (Transaction Books, 1978), was a runner-up for the C. Wright Mills Prize awarded annually by the Society for the Study of Social Problems. More recently he is the author of *The Power Elite and the State* (Aldine de Gruyter, 1990); *State Autonomy or Class Dominance?* (Aldine de Gruyter, 1996); and *Who Rules America: Power and Politics, 4th Edition* (McGraw-Hill, 2002). He won the Distinguished Contributions to Scholarship Award from the Pacific Sociological Association in 1999.

ROBERT S. ERIKSON is a professor of political science at Columbia University. He has won the Heinz Eulau Award of the American Political Science Association and the Pi Sigma Alpha Award of the Midwest Political Science Association. He has coauthored *American Public Opinion: Its Origins, Content, and Impact* (6th ed., 2001), *The Macro Polity* (Cambridge University Press, 2002), and *Statehouse Democracy* (Cambridge University Press, 1993).

MARTIN GILENS is an associate professor of political science and associate director of the Institute for Social Science Research at UCLA. His interests include public opinion and mass media, the American welfare state, racial attitudes, and survey methods. His current research examines the forces that shape Americans' public policy preferences and the consequences of those preferences for government policymaking. Professor Gilens is the author of *Why Americans Hate Welfare: Race, Media and the Politics of Antipoverty Policy* (University of Chicago Press, 1999) and has published on media, race, gender, and welfare politics in the *American Political Science Review,* the *American Journal of Political Science,* the *Journal of Politics,* the *British Journal of Political Science, Public Opinion Quarterly,* and the *Berkeley Journal of Sociology.*

SUSAN HERBST is a professor and chair of the political science department at Northwestern University. She is author of several books on public opinion, most recently *Reading Public Opinion* (University of Chicago Press, 1998) and coauthor of the textbook *Public Opinion* (Westview Press, 1999).

PHILIP E. N. HOWARD is completing his Ph.D. in sociology at Northwestern University. His dissertation research is an ethnographic and network study of the political campaign consultants who specialize in new media and communication technologies. He has published several articles and book chapters on the use of new media and polling technologies in politics and is editing a book about the Internet and American life.

LAWRENCE R. JACOBS is a professor of political science, adjunct professor in the Hubert H. Humphrey Institute at the University of Minnesota, and associate director of the Institute of Social, Economic, and Ecological Sustainability. In addition to articles in the *American Political Science Review, Comparative Politics,* and *World Politics,* his books include *Politicians Don't Pander: Political Manipulation and the Loss of Democratic Responsiveness* (University of Chicago Press, 2000, with Robert Shapiro), which won book awards from the Kennedy School at Harvard University, the American Political Science Association, and the American Sociological Association; *The Health of Nations: Public Opinion and the Making of Health Policy in the U.S. and Britain* (Cornell University Press, 1993); and *Inequality and the Politics of Health* (coedited with James Morone and Lawrence D. Brown) (Westview Press, 2002).

STEVEN KULL is director of the Program on International Policy Attitudes, a joint program of the Center on Policy Attitudes and the Center for International and Security Studies at the University of Maryland, and a member of the faculty at the University's School of Public Affairs. A political psychologist specializing in the study of public and elite attitudes on public policy issues, he has conducted numerous nationwide polls and focus groups. He is regularly interviewed by the media, and briefs officials in the government in the United States and Europe, NATO, and the UN on the U.S. public. His most recent book, coauthored with I. M. Destler, is *Misreading the Public: The Myth of a New Isolationism* (Brookings Institution Press, 1999). In the 1980s, at Stanford University, he carried out a study of defense policymakers that resulted in his book *Minds at War: Nuclear Reality and the Inner Conflicts of Defense Policymakers* (Basic Books). Later, he carried out a study of Soviet "new thinking," publishing his findings as *Burying Lenin: The Revolution in Soviet Ideology and Foreign Policy* (Westview Press). Dr. Kull is a member of the Council on Foreign Relations and the American Association for Public Opinion Research.

TAEKU LEE is an assistant professor of public policy at Harvard's Kennedy School of Government. He is author of *Mobilizing Public Opinion* (University of Chicago Press, 2002), and has written on the role of identity, language, information, trust, stereotypes, and discrimination in shaping racial attitudes and racial politics. Lee is also currently at work on projects that examine the politics of obesity and the role of elite influence on public support for health care reform.

MICHAEL B. MacKUEN is Burton Craige Distinguished Professor of Political Science at the University of North Carolina at Chapel Hill. He has won the Heinz Eulau Award of the American Political Science Association and the Pi Sigma Alpha Award of the Midwest Political Science Association. He has coauthored *The Macro Polity* (Cambridge University Press, 2002), *Affective Intelligence and Political Judgment* (University of Chicago Press, 2000), and *More than the News: Two Studies of Media Power* (Sage Publications, 1981).

CHARLES F. MANSKI has been Board of Trustees Professor in Economics at Northwestern University since 1997. He formerly was a member of the faculty at the University of Wisconsin–Madison (1983–98), the Hebrew University of Jerusalem (1979–83), and Carnegie Mellon University (1973–80). Manski's research spans econometrics, judgment and decision, and the analysis of social policy. He is the author of *Identification Problems in the Social Sciences* (Harvard University Press, 1995) and *Analog Estimation Methods in Econometrics* (Chapman & Hall, 1988), coauthor of *College Choice in America* (Harvard University Press, 1983), and coeditor of *Evaluating Welfare and Training Programs* (Harvard University Press, 1992) and *Structural Analysis of Discrete Data with Econometric Applications* (MIT Press, 1981). Manski has served as director of the Institute for Research on Poverty (1988–91) and as chair of the Board of Overseers of the Panel Study of Income Dynamics (1994–98). At the National Research Council, he has been chair of the Committee on Data and Research for Policy on Illegal Drugs (1998–2001) and a member of the Committee on National Statistics (1996–2000) and the Commission on Behavioral and Social Sciences and Education (1992–98), among other activities.

JEFF MANZA is an associate professor of sociology and political science and a Faculty Fellow at the Institute of Policy Research at Northwestern University. His research and teaching interests are in political sociology, social stratification, and social policy. He is the coauthor of *Social Cleavages and Political Change: Voter Alignments and U.S. Party Coalitions* (Oxford University Press, 1999), which received a distinguished book prize from the political sociology section of the American Sociological Association, and *Locking Up the Vote: Felon Disfranchisement and American Democracy* (Oxford University Press, forthcoming).

PETER V. MILLER is associate dean for external programs in the School of Speech and associate professor of communication studies at Northwestern University. His research has focused on interviewer and mode effects in survey research, audience measurement, political polling, and mass media effects. He is coeditor of two collections of essays on preelection polls in presidential campaigns. He has served two terms on the Executive Council of the American Association for Public Opinion Research, one as Standards Chair and one as Conference Chair. Miller was appointed editor of *Public Opinion Quarterly* in 2001, having served as associate editor for the journal's Poll Review section for several years.

BENJAMIN I. PAGE is Gordon Scott Fulcher Professor of Decision Making in the Department of Political Science at Northwestern University. He is the author or coauthor of eight books, including *Who Gets What from Government* (University of California Press, 1983), *Who Deliberates* (University of Chicago Press, 1996), *The Rational Public* (University of Chicago Press, 1992), and *What Government Can Do* (University of Chicago Press, 2000).

CLAY RAMSAY has been research director of the Program on International Policy Attitudes (a joint program of the Center on Policy Attitudes and the Center for International and Strategic Studies at the University of Maryland) since 1999, and senior fellow since 1993. He has coauthored numerous reports and articles on the program's work (notably *The Foreign Policy Gap: How Policymakers Misread the Public*, with Steven Kull and I. M. Destler, 1997) and currently the on-line reference "Americans and the World" Web site (www.americans-world.org). He is also a historian of modern Europe and the author of *The Ideology of the Great Fear* (Johns Hopkins). He received his Ph.D. in history from Stanford University and has taught at Oberlin College.

ROBERT Y. SHAPIRO is a professor of political science and the current chair of the Political Science Department at Columbia University. He specializes in American politics with research and teaching interests in public opinion, policymaking, political leadership, the mass media, and the applications of statistical methods. Professor Shapiro has published numerous articles in major academic journals and is coauthor of *The Rational Public: Fifty Years of Trends in Americans' Policy Preferences* (with Benjamin I. Page, University of Chicago Press, 1992). His recent book, *Politicians Don't Pander: Political Manipulation and the Loss of Democratic Responsiveness* (with Lawrence R. Jacobs, University of Chicago Press, 2000), was the winner of the Goldsmith Book Prize (of the Press/Politics Center, John F. Kennedy School of Government, Harvard University) and also awards from the American Sociological Association and American Political Science Association.

JAMES A. STIMSON is Raymond Dawson Distinguished Professor of Political Science at the University of North Carolina at Chapel Hill. He has won the Heinz Eulau and Gladys Kammerer Awards of the American Political Science Association, the Chastain Award of the Southern Political Science Association, and the Pi Sigma Alpha Award of the Midwest Political Science Association. He is the author of *Public Opinion in America: Mood, Cycles, and Swings* (2nd ed., Westview Press, 1999) and the coauthor of *The Macro Polity* (Cambridge University Press, 2002), and *Issue Evolution: Race and the Transformation of American Politics* (Princeton University Press, 1989).

HUMPHREY TAYLOR is the chairman of The Harris Poll, a service of Harris Interactive. He has had overall responsibility for more than 8,000 surveys in 80 countries. He writes a weekly column syndicated in over 100 newspapers. He has been a guest lecturer at Harvard (the Kennedy School and the School of Public Health), Oxford, NYU, and UCSF. He is the author of the chapters on opinion polls in two of the leading textbooks on marketing research in both the United States and Europe (published by ESOMAR and the AMA). He is a two-time winner of the Market Research Society's silver medal for the best paper published in 1997 and 2000. He conceived and managed the world's first daily tracking polls (for the Conservative Party in Britain) in 1970. While in Britain, Mr. Taylor conducted all of the private political polling for the Conservative Party and was a close adviser to Prime Ministers Edward Heath and Margaret Thatcher.

R. KENT WEAVER is a Senior Fellow in the Governmental Studies Program at the Brookings Institution. He is the author of *Ending Welfare As We Know It* (Brookings, 2000), *Automatic Government: The Politics of Indexation* (Brookings, 1988), and *The Politics of Industrial Change* (Brookings, 1985) and the coauthor and co-editor of several other books, including *Looking Before We Leap: Social Science and Welfare Reform* (Brookings, 1995) and *Do Institutions Matter?: Government Capabilities in the U.S. and Abroad* (Brookings, 1993).

JAMES WITTE is an associate professor of sociology at Clemson University. Areas of interest include the sociology of the Internet, economy and society, and survey research methods. Witte was the principal investigator for the National Geographic Society's Web-based survey, Survey2000 and is also principal investigator for the National Science Foundation funded follow-up study, Survey2001. Survey2001, which includes a number of methodological experiments and a parallel telephone survey, was hosted on the National Geographic Society Web site in the fall of 2001.

NAVIGATING PUBLIC OPINION

Navigating Public Opinion

An Introduction

JEFF MANZA, FAY LOMAX COOK,
AND BENJAMIN I. PAGE

The responsiveness of political institutions to citizens' preferences is central to democratic theory and practice. The rapid growth of opinion polling since the mid-1930s, and politicians' and policymakers' increasing use of polls and other measures of public opinion in recent decades, suggests that the *potential* for public opinion to directly contribute to political outcomes has increased dramatically. This was certainly the optimistic hope of some of the early pioneers of survey research. Writing in 1940, at the dawn of the modern polling era, George Gallup suggested that soon politicians "will be better able to represent ... the general public" by avoiding "the kind of distorted picture sent to them by telegram enthusiasts and overzealous pressure groups who claim to speak for all the people, but actually only speak for themselves" (Gallup and Rae 1940, p. 266; for similarly hopeful speculations about the impact of opinion polling on the operation of government, see Truman 1945).

However, research and theory about the impact of public opinion on policymaking since then has produced decidedly mixed views. Some analysts have found a strong, persisting impact of public opinion on public policy. Yet others reject the idea that the public has consistent views at all, or even if it does, that those views are independent of manipulation by elites and/or exercise much influence over policymaking. Still others view the relationship as more mixed, with public opinion having greater influence in some contexts than others.

Normative aspects of the opinion/policy link are also controversial. While some analysts have seen new mechanisms for including ordinary citizens' views into policy debates through increased polling, others decry the same processes for their potential to encourage politicians to "pander" to the public. For example, political commentator Elizabeth Drew (1998, p. 29) argues that "people tend to think that the politicians in Washington are 'out of touch' with their constituents, but if they were any more in touch, their ears would never leave the ground. The politicians of today are, on the whole, a highly reactive breed . . . reflecting the momentary mood of the public." Similarly Arianna Huffington (2000, pp. 73, 77) deplores the development of "poll driven leadership" and asserts that "today's new poll-happy pol has replaced the old fashioned leader—one unafraid to make difficult, unpopular decisions." Politicians running for office now often emphasize their ability to provide "leadership" beyond mere pandering to polls. For example, in announcements of their candidacies for the presidency in 2000, both George W. Bush ("I've learned to lead. I don't run polls to tell me what to think") and Bill Bradley ("I'm more interested in leadership than polls and politics") made a point of such explicit declarations.

A number of scholarly analysts (Blumenthal 1980; King 1997; Ornstein and Mann 2000) and political operatives (Morris 1997) have suggested that the increased use of polling is linked to the emergence of a "permanent campaign" in which the divide between governing and campaigning is increasingly eroding. The "permanent campaign" idea emphasizes institutional developments (including the declining capacity of parties to recruit politicians, the steadily rising importance of money and interest group activity, and new political and communications technologies) that, taken as a whole, have prompted elected officials toward ever growing reliance on public relations and polling. As Hugh Heclo (2000, pp. 17–18) describes it,

> The permanent campaign can be described as our unwritten Anti-Constitution. The written Constitution would keep the citizenry at arm's length from the governing process. The Anti-Constitution sees all efforts at deliberation outside the public eye as conspiratorial. The Constitution would normally consider the people as the sum of localities linked to government through representatives who take counsel with each other. The Anti-Constitution sees a largely undifferentiated public where one representative is interchangeable with another so long as he or she takes instructions. The Constitution would submit the results of governing to the people at regular intervals in many different election venues. The Anti-Constitution prescribes instant responsiveness to the continuous monitoring of the people's mass opinions and mood.

In the world of the permanent campaign, political strategists and pollsters claim increasingly important roles as mediators between citizens and their government.

The debate about possible changes in the relationship between public opinion and policy reflects underlying (and often contradictory) social, technological, and political changes of the past few decades. Among these are rapid advancements in polling techniques and technologies, along with an ever-growing number of public and private polls; the rapid growth of media outlets and changes in the form and content of political reporting using poll data; and the increasing availability of money and other resources (such as sophisticated advice from professional political consultants) that enable political actors to strategically craft policy messages. Such institutional and organizational changes have simultaneously increased the measurement and reporting of public attitudes (thus potentially increasing public influence) while providing political elites with new avenues to shape or direct those attitudes.

Finally, there is the question of what exactly is being measured when polls and surveys query the views of the public. Debates about the opinion-policy link have, to this point, proceeded largely independently of the rapidly changing world of polling and survey research. Yet methodological innovations can improve understanding of public opinion, for example, by moving beyond forced-choice responses to questions interviewers pose to respondents. Such innovations include a wide range of survey experiments and (in the near future) use of Internet polling.

This book explores these issues. The range of topics it covers on the linkages between public opinion and public policy can be viewed as a funnel, starting from broad questions about the extent of responsiveness to public opinion in the political system as a whole, to more focused investigations of how political elites use and understand public opinion in particular policymaking contexts, and finally to the question of how public opinion itself is measured. The contributions in this volume move progressively through this funnel. Part 1 of the book begins with the global question of the link between public opinion and public policy, and whether that relationship has changed over time. Part 2 focuses on how political actors "read" and use public opinion. Part 3 reconsiders some aspects of the problem of measuring public opinion in contemporary polling and survey research. The concluding essays in part 4 return to the broad questions, asking about the role of public opinion in the context of democratic politics, and examining the limits of our current knowledge.

Given the vigorous scholarly debates over the questions posed in this book, we have explicitly included a range of views about how and when public opinion matters. Deep disagreements about how best to measure and assess the impact of public opinion divide scholars and analysts. Although the contending positions in these debates are not resolved here, the range of views demonstrates the lines of division and the questions that should be examined in the future.

PUBLIC OPINION AND PUBLIC RESPONSIVENESS

The issues treated in part 1 of this volume address long-standing scholarly controversies over the relationship between public opinion and public policy. In chapter 1, Jeff Manza and Fay Lomax Cook examine current debates. They identify three images of the policy impact of public opinion and their development in quantitative, historical, or case-study investigations. The first image posits significant, enduring effects of public opinion on policymaking. Quantitative studies have frequently reported strong correlations between majority opinion on an issue (or changes in public attitudes on an issue) and policy outcomes. Case studies of policy change within particular policy domains have also frequently highlighted the role of public opinion. The second image finds only limited connections between public opinion and policy outcomes. Some versions focus on the capacity of elites to manipulate, control, or direct public opinion, thus rendering any correlation between opinion and policy spurious. Others deny that public opinion is sufficiently coherent to produce an independent causal impact. The third image admits contingency: in some contexts, public opinion moves policy, but in others it does not. Contingency analysts have sought to explain the sources of variation in responsiveness between policy domains, or over time.

Following this overview, the next four chapters analyze responsiveness empirically. The boldest recent articulation of the large effects view of the impact of public opinion can be found in the work of James Stimson, Robert Erikson, and Michael MacKuen (see, e.g., Stimson, MacKuen and Erikson 1994, 1995; Erikson, MacKuen and Stimson 2002). Their earlier work established a central pole in the contemporary debate over responsiveness, analyzing the association between changes in public "mood" (see Stimson 1999) and policy outcomes (see especially Stimson, MacKuen and Erikson 1995). In their chapter here, Erikson, MacKuen, and Stimson present an updated version of their time-series analyses of the global linkages between domestic policy mood and governmental outcomes. "Mood" is measured by condensing available public opinion across a wide range of policies into a single broad global indicator. The dependent variable distinguishes liberal and conservative domestic policy activity or laws adopted in each year. They report strong evidence of a link between mood and policy, and emphasize the feedback processes through which policy changes influence later public opinion. They also outline a broader systems model of policymaking, noting that public opinion is linked to other elements of the political system, including feedback through elections, changes in partisanship, or approval or disapproval of the party in office.

Erikson, Stimson, and MacKuen's work over the past decade provides one type of evidence in favor of the large effects image of public opinion. The systems model they sketch in chapter 2 situates the dynamics of opinion (mood) and policy into a comprehensive framework for understanding the ebb and flow of American political life. Their conclusions, however, have not gone unchallenged. Lawrence Jacobs and Robert Shapiro, in chapter 3, suggest a different image of the opinion-policy link. For Jacobs and Shapiro, institutional developments over the past half-century have combined to make it easier for politicians to use public opinion constructively, through the strategic use of polling and what they call "crafted talk" (see Jacobs 1993; Jacobs and Shapiro 1994b, 1995b, 2000). In their contribution here, Jacobs and Shapiro develop a contingency model of the influence of public opinion, starting from evidence of declining responsiveness to public opinion in recent years. They then suggest historical and institutional factors responsible for this declining responsiveness, noting especially the increasing importance of political activists within party organizations and the rapid growth in interest group activity. The development of crafted talk and the strategic use of public opinion, they argue, have interacted in recent years with institutional developments that encourage politicians to ignore public opinion. They conclude their chapter by contrasting their views with those of Erikson et al., suggesting that global measures of mood and policy obscure important changes in the link between opinion and policy. In chapter 4, Erikson, MacKuen, and Stimson reply to Jacobs and Shapiro.

The next two chapters develop case studies of how public opinion shapes policymaking within individual policy domains. In chapter 5, Paul Burstein examines the relationship between public opinion and congressional action on equal employment legislation from 1942 to 2000. By focusing on a single policy issue over a long historical period, Burstein is able to examine its changing salience in a way that most studies that examine shorter periods may miss. He finds that, for the most part, congressional action on labor market opportunity has been consistent with shifts in public opinion. Such responsiveness seemed to exist even when the policy alternatives being debated were not very salient to the public.

In chapter 6, Kent Weaver examines the relationship between public opinion and welfare reform, seeking to understand the role of public opinion in the Personal Responsibility and Work Opportunity Reconciliation Act of 1996, a landmark in social legislation that replaced the sixty-year-old Aid to Families with Dependent Children (AFDC) program with a new block grant program, Temporary Assistance to Needy Families (TANF). Weaver shows that public opinion played an important role in helping to push welfare reform onto the policy agenda: the public's increasing lack of support for the existing welfare system led both President Clinton and congressional Republicans to believe that political opportunity would result from a dramatic change to AFDC. However, public attitudes played a much more mixed role in promoting specific solutions to the welfare problem. The final TANF legislation contained some provisions with strong public support and some provisions without it. Notably, however, Weaver's analysis points out that the final legislation contained no provisions that the public opposed.

The case studies of Burstein and Weaver are broadly consistent with the Erikson et al. model in affirming the strong impact of public opinion, but—as both authors note—case studies usually show that public opinion on any issue is rarely sufficiently detailed to provide more than very broad general guidance to policymakers. It may be a contributing factor for policy change, but it is clearly not sufficient. Weaver's focus on the opinion-priming role of competing political elites on issues for which public opinion is fairly amorphous (like welfare) moves closer to the Jacobs and Shapiro model. Further, Burstein suggests that policy outputs do not necessarily fit a liberal-conservative dichotomy as in the Erikson et al. model implies. This point is also raised by Jacobs and Shapiro and revisited by Benjamin Page in the conclusion.

If the case studies of Burstein and Weaver provide critical but nuanced support for a strong effects view, in chapter 7, G. William Domhoff develops a more fundamental critique that takes as its starting point the organizational capacity of political and business elites to shape public opinion. Domhoff argues that public opinion moves policy only within constraints established by the dominant political agendas of powerful elites. In a body of work developed over the past thirty years, Domhoff has pursued the question of how elites create and maintain such influence and shape political system responsiveness (e.g., Domhoff 1967, 1990, 1998). His "power elite" model of the policy process examines how elite organizations seek to shape public opinion through (1) the creation or mobilization of policy organizations, (2) think tanks, (3) "citizens' " groups, and (4) direct lobbying and financial contributions. In his contribution here (chapter 7), Domhoff provides a concise summary of this model in dialogue with the other authors in this section, drawing upon his earlier empirical investigations. He claims that in focusing narrowly on the movement of public mood over time, Erikson, MacKuen, and Stimson see the trees but miss the forest. The success of power elite organizations in limiting the range of legitimate public opinion, or shaping it directly, Domhoff contends, stymies many policy ideas from ever being considered in the first place.

HOW ELITES USE AND INTERPRET PUBLIC OPINION

Domhoff's work offers a broad view of how elites treat public opinion, but his focus on mechanisms of elite influence hardly exhausts the range of possibilities for investigation. This is particularly true with regard to the day-to-day activities of politicians and policymakers, who must think about what public opinion actually is (rather than what it might be) in their day-to-day activities. Political actors must find ways of gauging, interpreting, and maneuvering within or around public opinion.

Part 2 of the book, then, raises the issue of how elites "read" or "use" public opinion. Fay Cook, Jason Barabas, and Benjamin Page ask, in chapter 8, how policy actors involved in the Social Security debate (notably the president, members of Congress, experts, and interest group leaders) "invoke" public opinion when making policy appeals. Systematic examination of this "invoked" public opinion raises rather sharp doubts, however, about the kinds of claims made about the public. The most frequently cited invocation of public opinion on Social Security is that young people are more likely to believe in UFOs than to believe they will receive Social Security when they retire. Yet this claim rests on extremely misleading polling data and has been overturned by subsequent surveys with more adequate tests of the UFO claim. Nonetheless, this "fact" of public opinion has been repeatedly cited in political debates over Social Security. Policy elites may invoke public opinion as registered in polls, but they also frequently *construct* public views to advance policy positions.

In examining a widely debated and contested national political issue, Cook, Barabas and Page consider a case for which political elites have access to a wide range of polling data. What happens when polls and polling data are less widely available? Susan Herbst's study (chapter 8, drawing on her earlier work [Herbst 1998]), examines how state-level politicians and their staffs "read" public opinion when opinion data are sparse. As she notes in her chapter introduction, most policymaking in the decentralized political system of the United States takes place at the state level. But few state opinion polls are taken; those that are tend to focus on future elections. This does not mean that state politicians are unconcerned about public opinion; rather, they must construct the views of the public through other means than reading poll data. So how do they do it? The policy managers Herbst studied in Illinois perused media—the newspapers, in particular—and attended closely to the arguments of interest groups. Although scholars do not typically interpret media content or interest group opinion as synonymous with public opinion, those who work in the trenches at a state legislature often do. Perhaps most strikingly, Herbst finds that political actors are largely unconcerned about the potential biases of these sources, because they believe that opinion polling has problematic biases as well.

Most of the scholarly analyses of the opinion-policy link have focused on domestic policy domains such as Social Security, welfare, or civil rights. Policy debates over foreign and defense policy questions are frequently less salient for the mass public, and the public is generally less well informed about policy choices. Yet as Robert Shapiro and Lawrence Jacobs show in chapter 10, time-series analyses have shown that public opinion about these issues appears to be as closely associated with policy outcomes as public opinion on domestic issues. For example, a significant number of studies have shown a connection between levels of defense spending and public support for increases or decreases in spending, as well as in relation to other foreign policy issues.

Shapiro and Jacobs incisively summarize the state of knowledge about the opinion-policy link in regard to foreign and defense policy. As they found in chapter 3 on domestic policy responsiveness, they report evidence of an overall declining responsiveness on foreign and defense issues. They also summarize their own work on presidential polling on foreign policy, providing clear evidence that presidents since John F. Kennedy have relied widely on private opinion polling about foreign policy issues. Surprisingly, they report that responsiveness began to decline during the Jimmy Carter presidency, in spite of Carter's stated openness to public involvement in foreign affairs. This pattern continued through Ronald Reagan's administration, perhaps most notably in its refusal to budge on its commitment to nuclear weapons modernization and defense budget increases despite a revived peace and growing antinuclear movements. Since the end of the Cold War, declining media coverage of foreign issues (and the absence of a concise policy frame for it) has made the public voice more confused, and has given political leaders greater opportunity to engage in "crafted talk" about foreign policy.

In chapter 11, Steven Kull and Clay Ramsey, by contrast, examine the relationship between elite perception of public opinion and the actuality. They find that elites badly misunderstand the nature of public attitudes, by often assuming that public views are strongly isolationist. Kull's earlier interviews with foreign policy practitioners from Congress, the executive branch, and the media provide further confirmation of this (Kull and Destler 1999). Among these allegedly isolationist sentiments is opposition to the United Nations and to increases in U.S. foreign economic aid. To test the proposition systematically, they fielded a new survey, containing items tapping isolationist sentiments, to sample national opinion and that of four congressional districts deemed especially prone to isolationist sentiments. The results showed, as have earlier national surveys, that the public is considerably more internationalist and supportive of programs designed to aid poor foreign countries than the experts think.

Kull and Ramsey's findings relate to both Cook et al.'s findings on Social Security and Herbst's work on state-level domestic policymaking. Herbst's findings show one way in which policymakers may misperceive public sentiments: they receive flawed inputs. Cook et al. suggest a second way: policymakers invoke public opinion to support positions they already hold. Kull and Ramsey suggest a third way—deeply held assumptions about public views are simply taken for granted, even when they are at odds with the facts. Kull and Ramsey also suggest a certain irony about foreign policymaking and political leadership. Assuming isolationism on the part of the public, politicians and national security officials seek to "lead" by rejecting the (perceived) isolationism of the American public. Often the internationalist agendas they pursue in fact have quite a bit more support from the public than policymakers perceive, thus sharply reducing the actual political costs.

MEASURING PUBLIC OPINION

If "true" public opinion is to influence policymaking, it obviously has to be measured and reported in ways that approximately reflect the actual views of citizens. This is a demanding requirement. Representative samples of citizens must be drawn and poll questions employed that probe the complexities of attitudes. Both of these requirements prove problematic in practice, for different reasons, but the authors in part 3 focus most of their attention on issues relating to polling methodology and survey content. Opinion and issue polling over the past seven decades has generally used closed-ended survey questions in which respondents answer an identical battery of items administered to the entire sample, with limited (or no) probes for contradictions or ambiguities in responses. Although the limitations of such survey design have been apparent for some time (see, e.g., Schuman and Presser 1981), canned surveys continue to be the dominant mode of measuring public opinion among nonacademic pollsters.

Peter Miller's overview and discussion of the historical background of the

issues surrounding contemporary polling and survey research (chapter 12) provides a point of departure from which to reconsider these issues. Unlike other
ways of identifying public opinion, polls gather information in ways that permit
replication and error measurement. Emphasizing the power of probability sampling methods and standardized opinion measurement procedures, Miller urges
caution in abandoning traditional methods. Yet he also notes that there are many
methodological innovations that have the potential to improve our understanding
of public attitudes. These innovations can be seen as reflecting both how public
opinion is measured through question design (the issue treated in different ways
by Gilens and Manski), and through new ways of measuring of public opinion
in the first place (Witte).

Gilens argues for the utility of survey experiments as a way of exploring the
complexity of citizens' attitudes more fully. Experimental designs can incorporate
and test multiple "framings" of a particular policy proposal or controversy within
the overall design of the survey. Gilens (1999) has shown in other work another
important advantage of experiments: their ability to capture largely hidden
sources of the public's beliefs about a particular issue. Americans have much
stronger resistance to welfare when they perceive it as a handout to blacks; for
example, Gilens's (1999: chap. 4) experimental work shows that willingness to be
generous to the poor drops considerably when it is a single *black* mother who is
being helped, as opposed to a single *white* mother (cf. Sniderman and Piazza
1993; Kinder and Sanders 1996). In his contribution here, Gilens examines a wide
range of experimental designs, providing telling examples in which experiments
produce a substantially different picture of attitudes than one gets from a conventional cross-sectional survey. Although experimental work has generally accompanied academic surveys, which are more demanding and expensive to conduct, in principle some of these applications could be incorporated into
conventional polling practices.

One of the most common opinion poll is the preelection poll. In chapter 14,
Charles Manski makes a case for the advantages of probabilistic polling in the
preelection context. He notes that asking respondents about which candidate they
are likely to vote for corresponds to asking about future expectations of behavior.
He argues that other work on future expectations—including his own extensive
work on future economic expectations and behavior (e.g., Manski 1990, 2001)—
suggests that a probabilistic approach (in which respondents are asked about the
probability of a future event or behavior), as opposed to a yes/no response dichotomy, provides a more robust basis for assessing likely voting intent than
standard verbal questions with response categories limited to major party candidates or undecided.

The Manski approach has several possibly important implications. First, although preelection polls taken right before an election have become increasingly
precise over the years, they nonetheless sometimes have difficulty, even in presidential elections when voters are most knowledgeable about the candidates and,
presumably, their own preferences (see, e.g., Converse and Traugott 1986). In the

early stages of a campaign, when voters may be more uncertain about their final choice, probabilistic questions better capture that uncertainty. Strong third party candidates also create problems for conventional polls. For example, both the 1992 presidential vote for Ross Perot and the 1998 Minnesota gubernatorial vote for Jesse Ventura were significantly underestimated in conventional polls. A probabilistic approach might better capture the prospects for a third-party breakthrough by indicating the uncertainty in support for the major party candidates in the run-up to the election. Survey houses use different conventional techniques, resulting in divergent outcomes; standardization with probabilistic methods would reduce those differences.

Second, a probabilistic approach potentially strengthens the capacity of media analysts and campaign strategists to assess the strength of support for a particular candidate, as opposed to its magnitude. Vaguely defined response categories may miss the uncertainty that actual voters feel about their choices. Polling that captures such uncertainty should strengthen analyst's ability to distinguish races in which support is strong for one or both of the major party candidates from those in which it is weaker and would give voters more information about the chances of third-party candidates. Finally, estimating who is likely to vote is probably strengthened by a probabilistic approach. Survey respondents are reluctant to admit that they will not vote when offered only a forced-choice format, but may be much more willing to admit *some* uncertainty when asked about their likelihood of voting (from 0% to 100%). Manski notes that systematic empirical work employing probabilistic approaches to election polling has not widely been attempted. Manski's own small-scale experiment using probabilistic questions during the 2000 presidential election provides evidence that they do produce more information than conventional methods.

The final innovation in public opinion research that we consider in this volume concerns the role of the Internet in assessing public opinion. A number of observers have expressed enthusiasm for the possibility that in the future, Internet polling could improve how we measure public preferences. James Witte and Philip Howard have carried out one of the first social scientific Internet polls, Survey2000, a Web-based survey completed by more than 50,000 individuals in 1998. Their chapter here considers the methodological and empirical issues this type of survey raises. They begin by noting major advantages of web surveys: low cost, quick turnaround, a potentially lower burden for respondents (who can complete surveys when they choose), and greater potential to incorporate experimental designs into standard attitudinal surveys. Growing problems with conventional telephone surveys (as discussed by Miller as well) provide a further reason to consider the potential of Internet surveys. As Internet usage becomes universal in the years to come, Internet surveys will become increasingly common; indeed, some major polling houses are beginning to use Internet polls.

Yet extensive problems, including selection bias (both self-selection and sample bias), hinder Internet polling. Whether these problems can be overcome remains to be seen. Witte and Howard address sample bias issues by comparing the results of Survey2000 with another major Internet poll Norman Nie recently conducted. Working through the different findings of the two surveys, Witte and Howard show how sample bias operates in different directions in the two surveys. They suggest that these early, pioneering Internet efforts highlight the issues— and problems yet to be resolved—that future research will have to address.

Finally, in chapter 16 Taeku Lee takes a look at the broader question of how we understand public opinion in the first place, and the implication of that understanding for thinking about the opinion-policy link. His argument builds important bridges between critical theories of public opinion (e.g., Blumer 1948; Bourdieu 1979; Herbst 1993) and mainstream social science work. He provides a compelling reexamination of the rise of survey data to "sovereign status" as the dominant measure of public opinion, showing that alternatives models of opinion have been largely squeezed out of existence. This is not an unproblematic development. He notes that in some crucial cases, such as changing racial attitudes in the 1950s and 1960s, conventional survey research and opinion polling developed relevant questions (and hence information about public opinion) long after important changes in citizens' attitudes had taken place. He outlines an alternative way of investigating opinion change in a dynamic context by systematically examining letters to public officials (a project developed at greater length in his recent book [Lee 2002]).

CONCLUDING ASSESSMENTS

Controversies over the impact of public opinion on public policy raise crucial questions about the character and practice of American democracy. The chapters in this book represent the challenge and intensity of these debates. The two concluding chapters, by Harris Poll chairman Humphrey Taylor and Benjamin Page, encourage us to examine the larger picture. Taylor argues that polls—especially preelection polls—prevent governments from resorting to the temptation to fix elections. A preelection poll showing the opposition winning an election (combined with a global environment in which democratic government is increasingly the norm [Markoff 1996]) makes it difficult for incumbents to remain legitimately in power through fraud. The stunning recent electoral changes in Mexico, Yugoslavia, and elsewhere exemplify such a dynamic. Some analysts have called for abolishing preelection polls, or sharply limiting them, a practice partially adopted in France and elsewhere. Critics of election polls claim that such polls may skew the outcome. Taylor's chapter suggests that the cost of such restrictions is too high, and he counsels strongly against it.

Taylor's observations hold considerable significance for developing democracies, where the institutionalization of fair and competitive elections is less than certain. But we should not be complacent about the more established democracies. History teaches us that although democracy is currently the predominant form of governance around the world, new antidemocratic waves (such as in the 1920s and 1930s) may reappear. His argument constitutes a vitally important restatement of the importance of polling, and the institutionalization of the pre-election poll, for democracy.

In the final chapter, Benjamin Page sums up what we have learned from the preceding chapters about when, how much, and under what circumstances public opinion affects policymaking. He reminds us of the methodological difficulties the relationship entails and points to topics for future research.

The analyses and arguments presented in this volume are unlikely to resolve the complicated debate about government responsiveness to public opinion in the United States. But they reveal that the core questions about the impact of public opinion, either globally or in particular policy domains, can be systematically addressed. Future improvements in the way we measure or conceptualize public opinion may increase responsiveness. To be sure—the expression of powerful interests or institutionalized policies can subvert the prospects for responsive government. Some of the contributors here speak specifically about declining responsiveness in view of such factors. While debates will continue, it is clear that understanding the nature and limits of public opinion in the American political system will remain central to the practice of democracy proceed.

Part I

DOES POLICY RESPONSIVENESS EXIST?

1

The Impact of Public Opinion on Public Policy

The State of the Debate

JEFF MANZA AND FAY LOMAX COOK

At the center of scholarly interest in public opinion is its impact on public policy. In this chapter, we review current debates over the opinion-policy link in the rapidly growing body of research on polls, public opinion, and policymaking in contemporary American politics. Our discussion provides a point of departure for the chapters in the next two parts of this volume.[1]

Three distinct images emerge from the existing literature on the opinion-policy link: those that perceive the effects of public opinion as exerting significant and enduring effects; those that perceive only small, insignificant, or declining effects; and those emphasizing historical and institutional variation in responsiveness. Advocates of the first view have produced both multiple-issue quantitative studies, and more detailed case studies of policymaking within single policy domains. Some of these studies have produced high estimates of the association between majority opinion (or over-time changes in public opinion) and the adoption of new public policies.

By contrast, those who insist the impact of public opinion is "small" express skepticism about the capacity of public opinion to influence policy outcomes. For some, the very concept of a coherent or consistent "public opinion" capable of moving legislators seems unlikely. Others argue that whereas a "public opinion" can be constructed through polls, most citizens hold only weak policy opinions. Thus, they are frequently subject to manipulation by elites in government, the mass media, or business or are likely to be ignored by politicians. Politicians and policymakers may also use polls not as devices to grasp popular opinion but rather as the means to craft legislation or policy rhetoric that will influence the public.

Finally, a number of analysts have proposed a "contingency" image of responsiveness: public opinion varies in how it impacts policy outcomes over time and space, in particular policy domains. Different domains have varying levels of responsiveness, according to contingency arguments, because of the nature of public opinion within the domain or institutional or political factors that mediate the opinion-policy link.

"LARGE EFFECTS" IMAGES OF THE IMPACT OF PUBLIC OPINION

Three distinct types of evidence and arguments support the view that there is a high degree of policy responsiveness to public opinion in American politics. The first comes from quantitatively oriented historical studies of the effects of either national or district majority public opinion, or changes in opinion, on policy outputs. Most of these investigations are based on time-series analyses using measures of public opinion and legislative or executive (or in a few cases, judicial) policymaking. The second set of arguments comes from more intensive examinations of policymaking in one or a few policy domains. Finally, a last set of arguments, more commonly asserted in journalistic treatments of American politics, highlight the importance of the polls and other sources of information in influencing the behavior of politicians and the output of the political system.

General Theories of Responsiveness

Claims that politicians, state managers, or the political system as a whole, are responsive to public opinion ultimately rest on the argument that political elites derive benefit from pursuing policies that accord (or appear to accord) with the wishes of citizens (Downs 1957; Geer 1996; Jacobs and Shapiro 2000, chap. 1). Of course, office seekers or officeholders may really seek nothing more than to represent majority opinion, but few analysts today believe today believe that politicians treat adhering to public opinion as an end in itself. Nonetheless, politicians and state managers may perceive it to be in their interests to minimize the distance between their own positions and that of the public.

Within the strategic (or rational choice) interpretation, both prospective and retrospective models have been advanced to account for the dynamic of responsiveness. In the prospective model, most closely related to the intellectual tradition associated with Anthony Downs (1957), rational office-seeking candidates try to align their issue positions with those of the "median" voter (and parties are said to prefer to nominate candidates who favor such positions). In two-party elections, the winning candidate typically aligns most closely with public opinion on the widest possible number of issues. In this way, elected officials and state managers in democratic societies usually come to reflect the preferences of citizens. Yet voters also evaluate candidates' previous performance (of either the incumbent candidate or his or her party). Retrospective approaches (e.g., Fiorina 1981) extend the classical Downsian model to argue that voters reward or punish politicians for previous policy decisions. Thus, citizens' policy preferences are more indirectly reflected in policy, by steering policymaking toward or away from particular past decisions. Such arguments have also been used to explain the decisions of legislators in office, including their anticipation of future public preferences (cf. Fiorina 1973; Mayhew 1974; Arnold 1990).

Global Studies of Responsiveness

A number of studies have reported high levels of overall responsiveness in the American political system to public opinion. One approach has been to investigate voters' preferences in particular states or districts and the behavior (such as that reflected in roll-call votes) of politicians and policymakers from those regions. The early work of Miller and Stokes (1963), characterized as the "dyadic representation" model, examined the relationship between opinions of voters in congressional districts and the behavior of House members while in office, reporting some modest (though variable) links. Other studies of constituency opinion—employing a variety of methodological assumptions and different measures of opinion and behavior—have extended the foundation Miller and Stokes established, generally reporting stronger evidence of a persisting link (see, e.g., Achen 1975, 1978; Erikson 1978; Page, Shapiro, Gronke, and Rosenberg 1984; Bartels 1991; McDonough 1992).[2] A few studies have used variation in state policymaking to test for an opinion-policy connection. Erikson and his colleagues (Erikson, Wright, and McIver 1989, 1993), for example, conducted a cross-sectional fifty-state analysis of public opinion and public policy. They find that states with more liberal polities will enact more liberal public policies (and conversely states with more conservative citizens enact conservative policies) across a broad range of policy domains, even when a broad range of statistical controls are included (see also Hill and Hinton-Andersson 1995; Hays, Esler, and Hays 1996; Berry, Ringquist, Fording, and Hanson, 1998).

The strongest evidence of the national impact of public opinion appears in time-series analyses in which opinion measured at time t is examined in relationship to policy output at $t + 1$. Research on the opinion-policy link over long historical time periods has often produced evidence that policy reflects public opinion. Stimson, Erikson, and MacKuen (Stimson, MacKuen, and Erikson 1994, 1995; Stimson 1999; Erikson, MacKuen, and Stimson 2002) have examined the association of historical evidence of changes in "public mood" with the output of national legislation and Supreme Court decisions. They presume that although citizens' views on detailed policy controversies may be poorly informed, political elites can nonetheless discern a broad ideological mood that moves toward liberalism or conservatism over time (Stimson 1999).[3] The measure of public mood in these studies standardizes pubic opinion (as reflected on a range of repeated survey questions) and legislative outputs into a single liberal-conservative measure of each.

Stimson, Erikson, and MacKuen have tested for linkages through a time-series analysis of public opinion and lawmaking by Congress, the president, and the Supreme Court since the 1950s. Across the three insitutional arenas, they find in general that, as the public mood shifts to a more liberal position, more liberal legislation is passed into law and vice versa (see especially Stimson, MacKuen, and Erikson 1995). In their dramatic formulation,

> We propose that public opinion moves meaningfully over time, that government officials sense this movement, and that . . . those officials alter their behavior in response to the sensed movement. This is dynamic representation, a simple idea and an old one. Public sentiment shifts. Political actors sense the shift. And then they alter their policy behavior at the margins. . . . Like antelope in an open field, they cock their ears and focus their full attention on the slightest sign of danger. (pp. 543, 559)

They posit two distinct interpretations of the ways in which the elected branches of government can respond to mood changes: electoral turnover (mood changes produce swings in the party balance in Congress or control of the presidency) and rational anticipation (incumbents change their behavior in response to perceived changes in mood before elections).[4] These indirect and direct effects of public opinion produce an exceptionally large coefficient for the impact of policy mood on policy, estimated in the full analysis to be 1.094 (or, as they put it, "there exists about a one-to-one translation of preferences into policy" [1995, p. 557]).[5]

Other researchers have also examined historical data on the opinion-policy link and reached similar conclusions. Monroe (1979) examined the links between majority opinion toward a proposed policy change and legislative outcomes in over 500 cases where new policies were adopted. He found that in 63% of the cases, policy moved in the direction preferred by majority opinion. Page and Shapiro (1983) identified 357 instances of change in public opinion on a particular issue, and measured relevant policy developments one year later and over longer periods. They found that policy changed in ways congruent with public opinion 43% of the time, there was no change in policy in 33% of the cases, and non-congruent change occurred in 22%. Adjusting for policy areas where change was not possible in the direction the public desired and allowing for a longer time horizon, they concluded overall that in about two-thirds of the cases with policy change, the change reflected public opinion.

Finally, public opinion may shape policymaking across many policy domains when popular support for the president or the party in control of Congress erodes. Negative public opinion can have a powerful impact on policymaking. Low standing in the polls may encourage a president to drop an unpopular proposal or to promote new, supposedly more popular proposals. For example, several studies have found that presidents change policy course in response to low approval ratings and change budget priorities accordingly (e.g., Hicks [1984] on deficit spending and Hibbs [1987] on macroeconomic policies). The same logic applies to policy proposals within particular policy domains. Ronald Reagan's proposals to dramatically scale back the federal role in financing social programs in the early 1980s or Bill Clinton's proposal for a national health program in the early 1990s may be associated with their defeat (Cook and Barrett 1992; Jacobs and Shapiro 2000).

Quantitative studies have established a case for the existence of policy responsiveness to public opinion. But because these studies tend to include few other covariates, they may miss factors that mediate or precede the relationship between opinion and policy. To some extent, this potential weakness simply reflects the difficulties of conceptualizing and measuring policy attitudes and policy outputs. But the omission of other policy-relevant variables nonetheless leads to important questions about the magnitude of the effects of public opinion on policy.

Studies of Specific Policy Domains

Case studies of particular issues or domains are especially well suited to developing more comprehensive models of the opinion/policy link. Researchers can account for other politically significant factors and chart detailed policy sequences. In this section we consider briefly some of the research that endorses a "large effects" interpretation of policy responsiveness to public opinion based on case studies.[6]

In domestic social policy, most of the studies that include public opinion (or change over time in public attitudes) report substantial evidence of responsiveness. Building from Erikson et al.'s (1993) work on state liberalism and Stimson's (1999) measures of public mood, Fording (1997) finds that public opinion is a significant factor explaining state-level differences in AFDC program expansion between 1962 and 1980 (cf. Hill, Leighley, and Hinton-Andersson, 1995; Berry et al. 1998). Burstein's (1998b) study of the evolution of equal employment opportunity legislation from the 1940s to the 1970s found that shifting racial attitudes of whites and growing acceptance of the principles of racial equality enabled liberal policy breakthroughs. Jacobs (1993) found strong archival evidence that perceptions of public opinion paved the way for the adoption of Medicare in the mid-1960s. Quirk and Hinchliffe (1998) assert that public opinion influenced the direction of public policy in six policy domains in the 1970s and 1980s (including Social Security, business regulation, tax cuts, and petroleum policy), although the precise routes through which public opinion influenced the direction of policy debates in Congress and in the White House varied.

In foreign policy, many studies have attempted to assess the impact of public opinion on policy (for reviews, see Holsti 1996b; Powlick and Katz 1998; Kull and Destler 1999; Foyle 1999; Sobel 2001; Shapiro and Jacobs, chap. 10). Perhaps the most widely studied question has been whether public opinion shapes defense spending. The general finding has been that the actual level of military effort is associated with majority public opinion (see Jencks 1985; Shapiro and Page 1994; Wlezien 1995, 1996; see also Shapiro and Jacobs, chap. 10). For example, Jencks (1985) found an exceptionally high correlation ($r = .94$) between public opinion and military spending and annual changes in spending between 1973 and 1980. Taking a longer view, Hartley and Russett (1992) find smaller, but still significant, persisting impacts of public opinion on changes in U.S. defense spending (controlling for Soviet military spending and the size of national budget deficit) in the Cold War era between 1965 and 1990 (see also the replication of these findings, adding information about issue salience, in Jones [1994]). Bartels (1991) examined the sources of congressional support for the Reagan military build-up, finding that district opinion exercised significant influence on congressional voting patterns. Sobel's (2001) case studies of four major foreign military interventions since Vietnam indicate that administration efforts to act were frequently "constrained" by public unwillingness to support broader objectives.[7]

The Importance of Polling

A third set of arguments for policy responsiveness to public opinion focuses on the impact of the vast increase in the information available to political actors about public opinion, largely through the rapid growth of polling.[8] Geer (1996) makes a simple but powerful point about this historical shift: political actors are more likely to respond to public opinion when they are confident they know what it is.[9] He notes that while president, George Washington would occasionally mount his horse to ride around the countryside to talk to ordinary citizens to discern public opinion and Abraham Lincoln tried to discern public opinion from reading newspapers and letters from the public. Recent presidents, however, have extremely detailed information about citizens' preferences (Geer 1996, chap. 1). The "public opinion apparatus" (Jacobs and Shapiro 1995b) that presidents since Kennedy have developed includes extensive private polling operations under the direct control of the White House (see also Eisinger 1996). Polls conducted by other political actors and organizations—members of Congress, interest groups, national and state Democratic and Republican parties, and the mass media— provide further sources of information about public attitudes.[10] As Brehm (1993, p. 3) has put it, "There is hardly an aspect of American political life untouched by polling and survey research."[11]

Such vast information, however it is gathered and for whatever purpose, may of its own accord produce higher levels of policy responsiveness. Geer (1996, p. 2) asserts that "well-informed politicians behave differently than their less well-informed counterparts—even when their motivations are the same." He claims that greater information facilitates responsiveness by enabling political leaders to make reasoned judgments about where the public stands. Jacobs (1992a, 1993) argues that although private polling by presidents and other policymakers may be intended to help craft policy and political rhetoric, the information from polls can nonetheless produce a "recoil effect" in which actors alter their behavior in response to opinion.[12]

"SMALL EFFECTS" IMAGES OF THE IMPACT OF PUBLIC OPINION

Some analysts are skeptical about these empirical and theoretical arguments for why and how public opinion matters. Some dismiss the possibility of coherent public views or argue that public opinion is so easily led or manipulated by elites that it cannot constitute an independent causal factor. In either case, there is little reason to think that a direct connection exists between what the public thinks and what policymakers do.

General Theories of Nonresponsiveness

Two different types of assumptions generally underlie arguments that policymaking is not responsive to public opinion. The first emphasizes the autonomy of both elected officials and bureaucrats from the mass public. If theories of responsiveness often invoke some version of a median-voter model, models of nonresponsiveness argue that for a variety of reasons politicians can deviate from mass preferences without fear of retribution.[13] Such deviations may reflect the greater influence of activists and articulate actors, interest groups, party and organizational interests, or the policy and political dispositions of politicians themselves, any of which can lead toward nonresponsiveness. Politicians may prefer to please activists—who provide important sources of money and voluntary labor—instead of general voters, whom they may take for granted (Aldrich 1995; Aldrich 1995).[14] Politicians' and policymakers' own (often strongly held) policy preferences may conflict with public opinion, thereby prompting nonresponsiveness (Cohen 1997; Jacobs and Shapiro 2000, p. 19). Research on "strategic shirking" suggests politicians will vote their preferences whenever they do not fear an electoral backlash (e.g., Kau and Rubin 1993). Politicians also have incentives not to shift away from previously announced policy positions in response to changing public opinion, for fear of appearing inconsistent or untrustworthy, even at the cost of nonresponsiveness (e.g., Lott and Davids 1992).

The second assumption, sometimes related to the first, is that the policy preferences of most citizens are either nonattitudes (in the famous formulation of Converse [1964]) or are weak or contradictory enough to permit manipulation by elites. In this view, "public opinion surveys present only a rough idea of what people generally think because the results are highly sensitive to a number of factors.... Polls may even create the impression of public opinion on questions in which none actually exists" (Domhoff 1998, p. 172).[15] Many analysts have also emphasized that the flow of information from polls and surveys is hardly unidirectional (from mass public to political elites). Polls and surveys can help shape policy proposals or frame policy rhetoric to maximize the "fit" with public opinion. And measured public opinion may result from, rather than cause, the policy activities of politicians.

Empirical Evidence of Nonresponsiveness

Policy is likely to be nonresponsive to public opinion when the public has few clear and consistent views that political leaders might meaningfully follow. Converse's (1964) widely debated thesis drew on analyses of a National Election Study panel in the late 1950s. He showed that most respondents did not maintain ideologically consistent responses to repeated survey questions, and he interpreted such seemingly random responses as reflecting "nonattitudes." Converse's controversial thesis elicited a vigorous but largely unresolved debate (see Brooks 1994). Nie, Verba, and Petrocik (1979; see also Inglehart 1990, chap. 10) attempted to show that rising educational levels and the changing political environment of the late 1960s had improved the ideological and informational capacities of citizens. But claims of declining nonattitudes prompted telling critiques on methodological grounds (Bishop, Oldendick, and Tuchfarber 1978; Sullivan, Piereson, and Marcus 1978). Other scholars, such as Smith (1989) and Delli Carpini and Keeter (1996), have found little substantive support for the claim that voters are becoming more sophisticated. As Ferejohn (1990, p. 3) summarizes the issue:

> Nothing strikes the student of public opinion and democracy more forcefully than the paucity of information most people possess about politics. Decades of behavioral research have shown that most people know little about their elected officeholders, and virtually nothing about the public issues that occupy officials from Washington to city hall. Those attitudes they express to interviewers are usually ephemeral and transient. In what sense, then, can the policies of any government be said to reflect the will of the governed when that will cannot even be said to exist?

There have been various responses to the dilemma Ferejohn poses. Recent work in political psychology has sought to determine how voters and citizens are capable of sophisticated reasoning based on cues and heuristics, *even* in the absence of detailed information or policy understandings (e.g., Sniderman, Brody, and Tetlock 1991; Popkin 1994 [1991]; Zaller 1992). Despite information limitations, cognitive processes may permit reasoned action (see Ferejohn and Kuklinski 1990; Lupia, McCubbins, and Popkin 2000). Other critics of Converse have challenged the view that surveys adequately measure citizen knowledge. Some have suggested that the ambiguities of the questions, or the inherent complexities of the issues, rather than nonattitudes, produce respondent instability (Achen 1975; Zaller and Feldman 1992). Finally, the response instability produced by survey experiments (as Martin Gilens notes in chap. 13) may reflect not ephemeral responses but those underlying complexities. In Zaller's (1992) influential formulation, survey respondents actually sample among the range of possible views they find attractive in response to questions, generating individual-level instability in responses but still permitting informative aggregate-level results. Page and Shapiro (1992) demonstrate that *aggregate* public opinion—and most significantly, changes in aggregate opinion over time—can be characterized as "rational" as it is associated with, and moves in a meaningful way with, events, crises, or economic fluctuations, even if individual survey respondents are poorly informed or ideologically inconsistent.

Sources of Information about Public Opinion

3

Nonresponsiveness may also stem from the sources of public opinion politicians and policymakers draw on. Herbst's (1998) investigation of how state political leaders "read" public opinion is especially instructive in this regard. The dominant approach of the policy managers Herbst studied in Illinois was to examine constituent letters, letters to the editors of newspapers, and the positions taken by organized interest groups as ways to gauge public opinion. Surprisingly, she finds that these three inputs were viewed by these policy managers as "representative" of public opinion because they viewed the results of opinion polling with skepticism. We know less about how national political elites discern public opinion, but Powlick (1995b) and Kull and Destler (1999, pp. 219–21) report evidence from separate studies of the impact of public opinion on foreign policymaking that government officials and members of Congress draw on the media and current state of congressional opinion as reflecting the public opinion. To the extent that such indicators of public opinion may be biases, political elites may pursue policies contrary to public opinion even if they think they are acting with reference to the wishes of the public.[16]

Elite Manipulation of Public Opinion

4

Even if the public has coherent underlying views, political or economic elites may be able to prioritize or reshape those views. Strategic use of the mass media is central to such efforts (see Bennett and Entman 2001). As we noted in the previous section, presidential polling operations have become an institutionalized feature of the White House over the past sixty years, but especially since the Kennedy administration. Whereas these polls may be used to gauge public opinion on a particular issue, they also test the popularity of particular political rhetoric and policy framings through the media in *advance* of public presentation, to improve the reception of particular proposals already decided upon (Jacobs and Shapiro 2000, chap. 2). Each major governmental agency has its own sophisticated public relations operation to promote its activities, and many undertake efforts to understand and shape public views in their domain. The White House Office of Communication continually tries to manage the news and shape citizen perceptions in ways that are favorable to the administration's agenda (Maltese 1994).

Do these efforts have any visible impact on public opinion? Some research suggests that presidents may, under certain circumstances, have special powers to shape or direct public opinion by focusing public attention on particular social problems or policy proposals through prominent speeches or careful use of the mass media (Skowronek 1993; Cohen 1997; but cf. Hill 1998).[17] The power to increase the salience of an issue can alter the impact of opinion, even if policy preferences per se do not change. For example, Beckett's (1997) study of the politics of criminal justice since the 1960s demonstrates the powerful effects of such presidential priming on public opinion. When presidents (or presidential candidates) focus on the "crime problem" or drugs, public concern dramatically increases, and though peak levels of concern cannot be maintained, overall support for anti-crime or anti-drug policies has grown in the 1980s and 1990s (even though crime rates were stagnant or falling during this period).[18]

More rarely, presidents may sometimes succeed in changing public opinion itself (Page and Shapiro 1992, chap. 8; Cohen 1997), although such impacts are often temporary, as their opponents will inevitably challenge such opinion-shaping projects and may eventually return attitudes to their previous level. A prominent recent example of such a dynamic is Bill Clinton's dramatic speech in September 1993 outlining his call for a national health insurance program. This produced a spike in popular support for a public health insurance program, but extensive attacks on the administration's proposals eventually reduced support for the plan (see Hacker 1997; Jacobs and Shapiro 2000).

Other political actors besides presidents attempt to shape public opinion, although their more limited access to the mass media reduces their effectiveness of such efforts (with governors, senators, and large-city mayors having the greatest opportunities, followed by lower-level elected officials and bureaucrats). Business elites and interest groups also seek to influence public opinion. In the power elite literature, the business community's efforts to shape public opinion, notably through the funding of peak business associations, think tanks, and policy organizations, have been documented in considerable detail. Most closely associated with the writings of G. William Domhoff,[19] power elite analysts have argued that the orchestrated efforts of American business have broad influence over public opinion and the making of public policy (see, e.g., Domhoff 1967, 1990, 1998; Akard 1992; Ferguson 1995; Martin 2000; cf. Vogel 1989).[20]

Variation or Weakening of Opinion-Policy Linkages?

Finally, a number of scholars have asserted that responsiveness has declined over time. Monroe (1998) and Jacobs and Shapiro (1997a) report evidence from replications of their earlier studies (Monroe 1979; Page and Shapiro 1983) suggesting declining responsiveness in recent years (see also Jacobs and Shapiro 2000, and chap. 3, this volume).[21] More sweepingly, the research of Ansolabehere, Snyder, and Stewart (2001) reports long-term historical evidence of a variable impact of constituency opinion on candidates' issue and ideological positioning. They find that ideological responsiveness was low from the nineteenth century through the 1930s, rose steadily from the mid-1930s through the early 1970s, but then declined into the 1990s.[22] Other analysts have suggested that the rapid expansion of money in the American political system undermines responsiveness by encouraging loopholes in legislation that appears symbolically responsive, but is actually substantively at odds with public opinion (e.g., Clawson, Neustadtl, and Weller 1998). Increasing polarization in Congress, especially with the erosion of the Southern wing of the Democratic Party and the Northern liberal wing of the Republican Party, has reduced opportunities for bipartisan bargaining that may lead to more responsive outcomes.

"CONTINGENT" IMPACT OF PUBLIC OPINION

If the "large" and "small" effects views represent the two major poles in the debates over the opinion-policy link, a variety of contingent assessments standing between them have been advanced.[23] In an oft-cited passage, V. O. Key asserted in 1961 that

> the anxieties of students about their inability to gauge the effects of opinion rest on an implicit assumption that public opinion is, or in some way ought to be, positively directive of government action. Our analyses suggest that the relationships between government and public opinion must be pictured in varied ways.... Mass opinion may set general limits, themselves subject to change over time, within which government may act. In some instances opinion may be permissive but not directive of specific action. In others opinion may be, if not directive, virtually determinative of particular acts. (p. 97)

Key's approach implies a third, "contingent" view of the opinion-policy link. The image of policy responsiveness implied by contingency approaches sees neither the large or small effects view as providing a useful starting point for understanding of the impact of public opinion. Rather, contingency approaches investigate institutional and comparative-historical variation in the opinion-policy link. In short, the views of the public may or may not matter, depending on factors unique to each political issue or controversy.

Interviews with a representative sample of members of the House of Representatives led Cook and Barrett (1992) to suggest a contingency theory of the link between the desires of the public and congressional responsiveness. Depending on the particular issue, Congress members say they are influenced differently by what the public thinks. For example, when asked how he made decisions, a representative in the survey responded, "I decide based on the three Cs: Constitution, Conscience, and Constituency." Further, he said that the balance among the three factors changes depending on the issue (Cook and Barrett, 1992, p. 235). This mix underlies similarities and differences in the degree of responsiveness of policymakers to the public in any policy domain.

The primary evidence for a contingency model comes from comparative analyses of how and when opinion moves policy in different policy domains or over time (see, e.g., Sharp 1999; Hill and Hurley 1999). There are well-established institutional reasons why responsiveness may vary. Policymaking occurs through legislation, administrative action, or judicial decisions at the national, state, and local level. Where policy gets made matters (e.g., Baumgartner and Jones 1993). Legislative bodies are subject to periodic elections, which potentially raise the stakes of nonresponsiveness. Judges often have permanent appointments and thus need not fear loss of office. Bureaucratic officials' exposure to public opinion depends on the type of policy they are responsible for or the structure of their agency. And the high budgetary cost of responsiveness may reduce the impact of public opinion for some issues (Sharp 1999, pp. 26–27).

The salience of an issue to the public and the coherence and intensity of citizens' attitudes toward it vary widely. The salience of a particular issue for the public may matter both for the possibility of shifts over time in public opinion (Page and Shapiro 1992, chap. 2), and for the likelihood that politicians will listen to the public (e.g., Jacobs 1993; Jones 1994; Burstein 1998b). Some issues are more opaque to the public than others, with important consequences. For example, Page and Shapiro (1992, p. 373) argue that elites' manipulation of public opinion is much more common on foreign than domestic policy. Higher visibility of salient issues means that the costs to politicians of deviating from median preferences are higher (Geer 1996, p. 171). The distribution of attitudes may also matter; when attitudes are bifurcated and there is little room for compromise, such as on abortion, responsiveness is more problematic than when attitudes are more evenly distributed (e.g., Strickland and Whicker 1992).

Another mechanism differentiating responsiveness across policy domains is the structure of each domain (cf. Laumann and Knoke [1987] and Burstein [1991] on policy domains). Some policy domains are crowded with powerful interest groups or have long-established policies that are more difficult (or costly) to alter. In such cases, responsiveness is likely to be low. In other domains, especially those with new or emerging issue controversies or devoid of well-organized interest organizations, responsiveness is likely to be greater.[24] Policy domains where social movements from below generate pressure on state managers for policy reform increase the likelihood of responsiveness (Burstein 1999). Issues that attract a large "attentive public" can increase responsiveness (e.g., Kingdon 1995, pp. 148–49).[25]

CONCLUSION

The three views of policy responsiveness to public opinion in the United States outlined in this chapter reach fundamentally different conclusions that cannot be easily reconciled. For some analysts, the relationship between citizens' opinions and the policy output of governments is strong. Global studies of the opinion-policy link, as well as case studies that have included public opinion as an explanatory variable, usually report significant effects. These findings suggest that a pluralist model of American government may still have life, although not all advocates of this view of public opinion necessarily deem it a healthy relationship for democratic governance. If politicians gain from "pandering" to public opinion, their capacity to exercise leadership that cuts against the latest polling data is correspondingly reduced.

Proponents of the "small effects" view of the impact of public opinion on policy making contest claims of a systematic association between public opinion and policy making. Some argue that a coherent public opinion does not exist outside the polling context, or that the relationship derives from either antecedent or mediating factors ignored or dismissed by the large effects theories. The most important of these factors is the degree to which public opinion can be influenced by political elites. If public opinion is indeed subject to elite influence, its independent causal force in the political system is limited at best.

Contingency approaches, by contrast, emphasize indeterminacy in the relationship, seeing citizens' opinions about some policy questions as inherently easier to shape from above than others because of institutional factors or divergence in the character of public opinion. Variation across policy domains is also produced by the structure of interest group representation and the legacies of path-dependent policy making processes. The relationship also may change over time, introducing historical contingency into the equation.

These viewpoints are extensively elaborated in the chapters that follow. We do not attempt to end the debate here (see Manza and Cook [2002] for our own analysis). It is clear, however, that the vexing question of how much influence citizens have over democratic governments, frequently asked and answered in the past, remains frustratingly unyielding to simple answer. Attempting to understand and map the opinion-policy link will continue to challenge those concerned about democratic theory and practice.

NOTES

1. Space constraints preclude a full-blown review of the relevant literatures on the opinion-policy link. Other reviews that have influenced our discussion include Page (1994); Jacobs and Shapiro (1994b, 2000, chaps. 1 and 2); Quirk and Hinchliffe (1998); Burstein (1998a); Sharp (1999, chap. 1); and Glynn Herbst, O'Keefe, and Shapirs (1999, chap. 9). We develop a broader critical discussion in Manza and Cook (2002).

2. These studies evolved significantly from the original Miller and Stokes work, addressing issues of causal inference (such as the possibility that elected officials may influence the attitudes of their constituents), measurement error, and simultaneity bias.

3. Their analysis of public opinion is complex. They start from the position that the public is rarely if ever informed enough about the details of any particular public policy to express meaningful opinions. Support for "spending more" or "spending less," for example, hardly provides the basis for policy makers to craft legislation. But this does not mean that public opinion has no impact on policy making. Quite the contrary. It is through

changes in the broad public mood (and related impact on election results) Stimson, Erikson, and MacKuen argue, that politicians come to grasp the public preferences, and they translate that into policy. See Stimson, MacKuen, and Erikson (1994).

4. Their analyses suggest that the election mechanism is more important for the Senate and the president, but for the House a rational anticipation interpretation provides a better model. Not surprisingly, the Supreme Court is by far the least responsive institution, with positive but statistically insignificant coefficients for policy opinion and the political composition of the court (Stimson, MacKuen, and Erikson 1995, pp. 555–56).

5. They qualify these strong conclusions in noting that they did not attempt to model the impact of policy outcomes on later public opinion (Stimson, MacKuen, and Erikson 1995, p. 559).

6. Most studies of policy change within a single domain that have considered the role of public opinion have generally found an impact. Reviewing the literature on case studies of the impact of public opinion, Burstein (1998a, pp. 36–41) identifies twenty case studies published in the past two decades, *all but one* of which reports a strong relationship between opinion in the policy domain and policy output. Our discussion in this section is indebted to Burstein's valuable review. More recently, however, Burstein (2001) has made the crucially important point that case studies will always tend to produce exaggerated impressions of the impact of opinion on policy, as such studies typically select policies most likely to have clear indicators of public attitudes from poll data. But many of the issues considered by Congress are neither salient to the public, nor have meaningful public preferences.

7. Although the case for an impact of public opinion on foreign policy appears well established, because foreign and defense policies are often event- and crisis-driven, there are sharp problems of causal inference. When a foreign crisis changes the context within which the public views a question, rapid changes in public attitudes are possible, which may, in turn, appear to be associated with later changes in policy. But in such cases, it appears likely that the same factors that move public opinion also move elites and the overall direction of policy making. In other words, the apparent correlation may be largely spurious.

8. Overviews of the growth and development of polling and survey research can be found in Converse (1986) and Herbst (1993). On the growth of polling by presidents since Kennedy, see Jacobs and Shapiro (1995b). For comparative evidence showing that the United States is not alone in the growth and wide availability of polling, see Butler and Ranney (1992).

9. V. O. Key made the same point bluntly in 1961:

> In an earlier day, public opinion seemed to be pictured as a mysterious vapor that emanated from the undifferentiated citizenry and in some way or another enveloped the apparatus of government to bring it into conformity with the public will. These weird conceptions . . . passed out of style as the technique of the sample survey permitted the determination, with some accuracy, of opinions within the population. (p. 536)

This passage is quoted in Geer (1996, p. 61).

10. The growth of the "permanent campaign," discussed in the previous chapter, is a significant part of this process. In the permanent campaign, the divide between elections and governing erodes, with political consultants and pollsters providing elected officials with increasingly sophisticated information about how to strategically craft proposals and gauge the state of public opinion. See Ornstein and Mann (2000).

11. Some commentators have argued that the sheer magnitude of the polls and other sources of information available about citizen preferences today has reached the point of overload. See, for example, Yankelovich (1991), Wines (1994), and Ornstein (1996).

12. Many political commentators, however, have decried the growth of polls, arguing that politicians are all too prone to simply "pander" to the public. Jacobs and Shapiro (2000, pp. 3–4), for example, cite a number of examples of journalistic writing about the tendency of modern American politicians to simply cave in to public opinion.

13. The "bringing the state back in" project of political sociologists and political scientists in the 1980s is the most important intellectual contribution here (see, e.g., Evans, Rueschemeyer, and Skocpol 1985). However, much of the "state autonomy" literature often did not explicitly consider public opinion in developing case studies of historical outcomes. See Burstein (1998a) for a critical commentary.

14. Incumbency advantages and high—in recent years, overwhelming—reelection rates, especially in House elections may further contribute to the sense that the policy preferences of the mass public need not necessarily govern politicians' voting decisions.

15. See, for example, Blumer (1948), Bourdieu (1979), Herbst (1993), and Geer (1996) for other discussions of the implications of the rise of opinion polling for the establishment or creation of "public opinion."

16. Alternative measures of public opinion need not necessarily be biased and could, in some cases, actually provide a more authoritative source of opinion than polls. In his study of opinion formation during the Civil Rights era (1948–64), Taeku Lee (2001) argues that the content and character of letters to the president provided a more authoritative source of rapidly changing attitudes toward race than did the opinion snapshots provided by opinion polls.

17. The massive literature on the agenda-setting powers of the media (see, e.g., Iyengar and Kinder 1987; Bennett 1990; Baumgartner and Jones 1993; Zaller 1996) provide evidence for one crucial mechanism that enables presidents—with their privileged access to the media—to manipulate public concerns.

18. For example, when George Bush launched an aggressive campaign against illegal drugs in 1989, an astonishing 64% of respondents in September told Gallup interviewers that drugs were the *most* important problem facing the nation. Similar jumps in public concern about crime followed on the heels of Richard Nixon's 1968 presidential campaign, Ronald Reagan's anti-crime and war-on-drugs campaigns, and Bill Clinton's proposal for a sweeping crime bill in 1994.

19. Domhoff first introduced his power elite model in 1967, in the first edition of *Who Rules America?*, and has elaborated it in a series of works since then (see Domhoff 1967, 1970, 1990, 1998). Domhoff's model does not imply that the power elite seeks to influence or control *all* decisions. Many issues—in particular, social issues—may be very important in other respects but generate no particular stance among the power elite. Second, on some issues the power elite is internally divided and incapable of speaking with one voice. These divisions may arise from either clashing sectoral or firm interests, or even occasional genuine disagreements over the direction of policy in a particular arena. In most cases, power elite consensus is not a given but has to be developed by the various policy organizations and other institutions of the power elite. In this sense, Domhoff's important work in this area has straddled the "lesser effects" and contingency perspectives.

20. Smith (2000) has recently offered a systematic examination of power elite theories of business influence on public opinion and the making of public policy. His analyses suggest that although businesses can shape public opinion through think tank advocacy and the mass media (2000, chap. 8), for the most part this impact is fairly modest (e.g., pp. 210–13). More strikingly, he produces evidence that business unity around some policy questions frequently produces media attention and corresponding backlashes that undermine aggregate corporate political power.

21. Monroe (1998) found that majority opinion on policy questions declined from 63% in the 1960–79 period to 55% in the 1980–93 period. Jacobs and Shapiro (1997a), in a preliminary investigation, found that policy responsiveness to public opinion in welfare, crime, Social Security, and health care fell from 67% in 1984–87 to just 36% during the first half of Bill Clinton's first term in office.

22. Ansolabehere et al. (2001) analyzed racial issues separately from other issues, to avoid confounding the peculiarities of racial politics among the Southern congressional delegations before the 1970s. The details of the story are more complicated than the simple summary here suggests. Beginning with the New Deal, Republicans began responding to constituency opinion, as those running in districts with higher levels of Democratic strength in their districts adopted more "liberal" policy stances. It was not until the mid-1960s that Democratic candidates became responsive to the level of Republican strength in their districts. Responsiveness began to decline in the mid-1970s, but among Republicans more than Democrats. We thank Stephen Ansolabehere for making a pre-publication draft available to us.

23. For our own work on the development of a contingent model, see Cook and Barrett (1992) and Manza and Cook (2002). Sharp's (1999, chap. 1) thoughtful overview of the logic of contingency approaches has informed our discussion of these issues.

24. Domhoff's (1998) observation that power elite organizations have varying degrees of concern about different issues (ranging from intense concern on something like labor law to nonexistent concern on something like gay and lesbian rights) provides another reason to expect a variable impact of public opinion across policy domains.

25. Concrete comparisons across policy domains unsurprisingly indicate differences in levels of responsiveness. For example, Sharp's (1999) analysis of the dynamics of public opinion and policy change on six issues (criminal justice, affirmative action, pornography, abortion, welfare, and Social Security) suggests wide variation, with some policy domains such as Social Security and welfare significantly more responsive than on issues such as affirmative action or abortion.

2

Public Opinion and Policy

Causal Flow in a Macro System Model

ROBERT S. ERIKSON, MICHAEL B. MACKUEN,
AND JAMES A. STIMSON

In a democracy such as the United States, policy is supposed to flow from the preferences of the public. Of the many studies of a possible causal connection from public opinion to policy, almost all are cross-sectional, that is, involving a search for covariance between public opinion and policy across units measured for a constant time period. Although often reporting positive opinion-policy relationships, these studies invite the critique that reported cross-sectional correlations are subject to rival causal interpretations beyond the claim of representative democracy at work.

In this chapter, we again ask whether public opinion and public policy are connected. We do so, however, not with another cross-sectional analysis, but from a time-series perspective. We inquire whether current public opinion predicts subsequent policy activity and actual policy at the national level, and, if so, why.

Much of what we present here briefly restates major results from our fifteen-year investigation of public opinion and policymaking in *The Macro Polity* (Erikson, MacKuen, and Stimson 2002), based on statistical modeling of a conventional sort. It serves to set the stage and define our interest. Then, we turn to thinking about systems of relationships and ask what we can learn by building models of systems in which each part influences the others.

POLICY REPRESENTATION: CROSS-SECTIONAL VERSUS TIME-SERIES EVIDENCE

Does public opinion influence public policy? Start with the evidence one can adduce in cross-sectional analyses. The views of constituents are statistically related to the positions their legislators take. The two are positively correlated. For example, in the U.S. Senate, roll call liberalism correlates with liberal ideological identification in the state (e.g., Wright and Berkman 1986). In the House of Representatives, roll call liberalism correlates with constituency Democratic presidential voting, a good proxy for the liberalism of House districts (Erikson and Wright 2001a, 2001b). In the American states, policy liberalism and the views of governing elites correlate with the state electorates' degree of liberal ideological identification (Erikson, Wright, and McIver 1993). And at the cross-national level, the left-right placement of the governing parties and coalitions correlate with the left-right preferences of national electorates (Powell 2000).

What are we to infer from patterns such as these, evident across numerous political arenas? The obvious answer would be strong evidence of democracy at work, with public opinion influencing public policy. But, if so, how? And can we be sure that some mechanism other than opinion causing policy is not responsible for the correlation?

A best-case interpretation is that the evidence shows democratic representation but fails to discriminate among alternative pathways. When we start thinking about those alternative pathways, the problem gets thornier. Do legislators consciously solicit the views of constituents? Do they take them into account, but only indirectly, making inference from indirect cues such as constituency demographics and constituency voting behavior? Or we might imagine a process where no legislator ever consciously considers the wishes of constituents but nonetheless reflects them because the elections process has molded agreement between constituents and representatives. These different scenarios are all democratic in the fundamental sense that the will of the people is somehow reflected in governance.

But we have not exhausted the possible explanations for the positive correlation between opinion and policy. Suppose the truth was that the voters decide based on reasons that have nothing to do with public policy. Even under this hypothetical circumstance, opinion and policy could correlate in the cross-section, leading to the spurious conclusion that opinion caused the policy. Before making causal claims about democratic representation, we should not rule out alternative mechanisms for generating opinion-policy correlations. We consider three.

First, and most obviously, the representatives and the represented can agree not only because the represented cause their representatives' behavior but also for the opposite reason—because representatives lead or "educate" their constituents. It is possible to think of voters as docile followers, readily susceptible to elite propaganda. To the extent this conceptualization is correct, so that elected leaders can tell their constituents what to believe, the illusion of representation is enhanced.

Of course, voters are not totally passive in such a manner. Still, politicians try to influence voters' opinions because they can gain electorally whenever they convince issue-oriented voters to agree with their views. Elected officials often face the dilemma of acting on their personal convictions or, for electoral survival, the convictions of their constituents. For the elected official, an attractive solution—if it can be accomplished—is to convert skeptical constituents to their own position, thus eliminating the dilemma by converting the two choices into one. (For elaboration of this argument, see Jacobs and Shapiro [2000].)

A second reason why an opinion-policy correlation might not be causal is that people create the correlation with their feet rather than their votes. Such a notion is popular in the literature on taxation and spending in suburban municipalities. Suppose we observe a correlation between communities' taste for taxes and their tax rates—the more they dislike taxes, the lower their tax rates. But why? We might like to believe that municipalities calibrate their tax rates to fit public tastes. But the most plausible explanation may be that tax rates are set exogenously and then attract residents whose preferences match the policy. Similarly, communities with good schools attract residents who care about good schools. School quality could be an accident of exogeneity that generates a correlation between education quality and concern with education, even in the absence of democratic representation.[1]

Of course, this sort of theorizing assumes that citizens are both geographically mobile and sensitive to policy considerations. If people were sensitive to policy considerations when they decide where to reside, would they not also show policy sensitivity when they vote? Still, even at a higher level of government than the local municipality, people can choose their place of residence based on policy considerations, thus somewhat affecting the opinion-policy correlation. In part, liberals live in liberal states and conservatives live in conservative states because liberals and conservatives prefer to live where they find agreeable policies (and agreeable neighbors). Even when we turn to the cross-national context, we recall that emigration and immigration are often political in origin; to some degree this process of national selection must enhance the degree of correlation between national opinion and national policy.

Finally, geography, apart from geographic mobility, affects the opinion-policy correlation. Imagine a nation where there is opinion diversity across geographic constituencies and relative homogeneity within them. Urban residents, dependent on mass transit in their daily lives, like the idea of government subsidy for transit. Those in rural areas have lives tied the quality of highways; they like them wide, straight, level, and smooth, and they will urge government to produce what they want and need. Western ranchers and farmers use guns to kill rattlesnakes and coyotes—and not very often one another. They do not like the idea of government regulating gun ownership and usage. Urbanites perceive guns as weapons for homocide, thinking that they and their loved ones might become targets. They would like to diminish the possibility by greater regulation and restriction. In many areas of policy discourse and conflict, views come to be associated with the areas in which people live.

Given such a scenario, we can elucidate another explanation for observed opinion-policy correlations. Even if the geographic constituencies choose their leaders at random, the fact that the leaders are drawn from the constituencies they represent will ensure some sharing of opinion by the public and its representatives. All that matters is that candidates have relatively uniform views within a constituency. Evidence of representation will emerge even when no voter considers policy views and no representative consciously acts to honor constituent preferences.[2]

When we observe correlation between opinion and policy, our inclination is to see it as evidence of democratic representation at work. However, given the possibilities of alternative causal mechanisms, it is no surprise that cross-sectional opinion-policy correlations are often viewed with skepticism (e.g., Sharp 1999). The skeptic's argument would have particularly strong force if cross-sectional correlations between constituency preferences and representative behavior were the sole evidence for ascertaining the degree of policy representation. By itself, the sharing of preferences by the representative and the represented demonstrates congruence but nothing more. In democratic theory, the aim is a causal dynamic by which the preferences of constituencies cause the behavior of the representatives—beyond what would occur by elite persuasion, voter mobility, or geographic accident.

Fortunately, the case for democratic representation is enhanced by a full consideration of the extensive evidence beyond raw correlations—such as the findings of the considerable literature on policy issues and election outcomes and elite anticipation of the electoral response. Still, if we are to convince the avowed skeptic, the strongest evidence comes from time series. The idea is not that time-series data patterns automatically trump cross-sectional ones, but rather that with time series one can exploit temporal order to infer causal ordering.

Imagine a body of evidence in which current public opinion is significantly related to future policy in a systematic pattern over time, in which opinion change precedes policy change in temporal sequence. Given such evidence, could one easily refute the idea that opinion is the cause of policy? If opinion leads policy—and particular if policy does not lead opinion—one could not comfortably argue that the causal arrow goes from policy to opinion. Given such time-series evidence, could the opinion-policy congruence be due to people voting with their feet? This possibility becomes implausible because it implies vast migrations in and out of the governmental entity (city, state, or nation) in advance of new turns in policy direction. And the mere sharing of opinions by elites and masses is an awkward explanation if public opinion predicts future policy independent of current policy, which presumably reflects current elite preferences. Of course, spurious relationships are always possible in the absence of a true controlled experiment. Thus, our skeptic could argue, for example, that elites change public policy in their desired direction while propagandizing so that the public will accept it as good. But before taking such propositions too seriously, we must ask, why would such powerful elites need to influence public opinion if public opinion was irrelevant to policymaking?

The table is set to examine the dynamic case. Time-ordered relationships are vastly easier to study for evidence of cause and effect. If we are to understand process, it is helpful to observe change in progress. That idea is the starting point for the classic Page and Shapiro (1983) quasi-experimental study of *changes* in opinions and policies. Page and Shapiro observe changes in particular opinions over a span of time and then ask whether policy changes lying between them move also in the same direction. They conclude that the answer is yes. Here we have evidence for representatives responding to changed preferences. Accident or coincidence can be ruled out.

Thinking about the very same question, "If opinion changes, does government respond?" we have moved toward representing the process in the covariation of two time series, rather than the before-after test scenario of the quasi-experiment. The quasi-experimental evidence establishes the fact of representation but offers little guidance for how it might be modeled. That further step motivates our work, both what has gone before and what will appear in this chapter.

MEASURING PUBLIC OPINION:
LIBERAL-CONSERVATIVE "MOOD"

If the issues that government processes were discrete—that is, they arise; get discussed, resolved, or ignored; and then *disappear*—then the idea of representation as a continuous process would be intractable. If, alternatively, individual issues are merely specific cases of a general and continuing issue debate, then we may think of measuring the net liberalism or conservatism of both public opinion and policy, connecting the two. Another way to pose the question is to ask whether opinion has some common element that persists over time and across apparently dissimilar issues. Our traditions on this matter sharply conflict. Policy studies begin with the presumption that all policies are unique. There is education policy, environmental policy, transit policy, gun policy, and on and on, all different. In common parlance and punditry, however, we contradict this view by referring to most (not all) issues is the same reference frame: liberalism and conservatism. If it is meaningful to refer to, say, a liberal position on environment, on education, on guns, and transit, then this "liberalism" must be something common to all; schools must somehow be related to trees, trains, and guns.

Cf beginning of Ch. 7

The matter may be easier in operational terms than as an abstraction. Imagine that we have a technology for solving for the common element(s) of a large array of public attitudes toward distinct issues—a principal components analysis in which issues are variables and time is the unit of analysis. Then the number of dimensions required to adequately account for the variation in the issue array is an empirical question. One dimension might run through all, perhaps one in each policy domain (e.g., education, environment, guns, transit, and all the rest) that ties together more specific controversies, or perhaps each specific issue debate requires its own dimension. We approached the data willing to believe any outcome, without a strong prior belief. We learned (Stimson 1991, 1999; Erikson, MacKuen, and Stimson 2002) that most of the systematic variation in measured policy opinion questions could be accounted for by a single left-right organizing dimension.[3] That dimension we call *public policy mood* and interpret as a generic response to government itself. Mood liberalism taps willingness to expand the size and scope of federal activity in all policy domains. Mood conservatism taps a preference for a lesser federal role.

In retrospect, we should have expected this outcome. We know from scholarship on government policymaking (most prominently Poole and Rosenthal 1997) that it is characterized by low dimensionality, most issues fit nicely within a left-right divide. And we know, of course, that all conflicts have their electoral resolution in a two-party political system, which tends to force issue controversy into a bipolar mode, both for governors and the governed. And when issues arise unaligned with the common dimension, there is great pressure to bend them to fit the ongoing debate (for the racial case, see Carmines and Stimson 1989; for the abortion controversy, see Adams 1997).

Thus, we have the first half of our question "If opinion changes" captured in a single time series, public policy mood. The measurement of mood is too complex to describe in much detail here (see instead Stimson 1991, 1999). Suffice it to say, mood is a composite incorporating virtually all available public opinion surveys that tap the common dimension of government activity. The annual or biennial measures of mood represent a weighted average of the trend, holding constant the specific survey question and weighting items according to their commonality with the dominant dimension. Using the ideological terms in common parlance, periods of high mood indicate a public at its most "liberal," while low scores indicate a public at its most "conservative." By the mood index, the public was most liberal in the early 1960s—just before the liberal Great Society legislation—and most conservative around 1952 (at the start of the series) and around 1980 at the advent of Reagan's conservative revolution. From "high" to "low" points or back again, the amount of change in mood can be considered large—upward from a standard deviation of cross-sectional liberalism-conservatism by our estimates—and encompassing all segments of the electorate (see Erikson, MacKuen, and Stimson [2002, chap. 6] for details).

To answer the representation question then requires also a continuous measure of the second piece, the policy response. The policy response, it turns out, includes two parts: year-to-year adjustments, which are sometimes wholly symbolic and sometimes modify existing policies at the margin (*policy activity* in our usage to come), and the making of law, a matter of more gravity and permanence (*policy*).[4] The former is captured by aggregate measures of position-taking measurable by congressional roll call votes, presidential positions, and the like.

The latter is based on actual legislation passed by Congress (and overriding presidential vetoes).

We now have the two concepts necessary for analysis of government response to opinion. Public policy mood we treat as the current public view of the status quo, the answer to the question "Does government do too little, about the right amount, or too much?" Because the actual reach of government expands and contracts with alternating regimes, we expect public opinion to respond in a thermostatic mode, to say "too much" when government is expansive, creating new programs, taxing more, spending more, and "too little" when conservative regimes cut back and scale down. This would be true even if absolute preferences for the "best" size of government were wholly constant.

DYNAMIC REPRESENTATION: MOOD AND POLICY ACTIVITY

We postulate that rational politicians who wish to succeed in future elections and reelections use current public opinion as leverage in the calculation of which positions are dangerous or advantageous. We model policy activity as a function of previous policy activity and of public opinion (mood), as represented by an equation of the form:

$$y_t = \delta y_{t-1} + \beta x_{t-1} \tag{1}$$

with y_t and y_{t-1} our policy activity construct and x_{t-1} the previous year's public opinion. For the theoretical model, x could equally well be current public opinion. We use the lagged value to ensure correct causal ordering. The parameters δ and β can then be estimated by some form of dynamic regression.

But equation 1 doesn't fully close the loop on opinion influence. A nonzero β tells us that public opinion influences policy activity, but not quite how. Because public opinion influences election outcomes, it alters the composition of government, influencing policy activity by changing the preferences of those who become entitled to be policymakers. Democrats, for example, are more liberal than Republicans, so a public opinion that tilts an election result toward the Democratic Party would tend to produce more liberal policy activity *even if no elected politician took account of public opinion in his or her behavior.*

To sort out the two prevailing pathways to opinion influence, we need to allow the "electoral connection" scheme to work its influence in order to observe whether there is also direct influence of opinion on policy activity. To do so, we add the party composition, z_t, to the difference equation specification:

$$y_t = \delta y_{t-1} + \beta x_{t-1} + \gamma z_t \tag{2}$$

where z_t represents the current party composition, for example, percent Democratic, which is a function of public opinion in the most recent previous election. Simple though it is, equation 2 requires only an occasional control variable to be a complete specification for assessing the impact of public opinion on policy activity. We have estimated the parameters of 2 for various governing bodies and under varying conditions. Table 2.1 is a summary statement, where the policy activity measure is a joint function across House, Senate, presidency, and Supreme Court.[5]

To clarify inference, we estimate the model in two stages, entertaining first a "reduced form" specification that predicts policy activity only from mood, an empirical estimate of the parameters of equation 1. This is a test of whether public opinion influences policy activity, ignoring issues of process and pathway. The answer of table 2.1 is that it does; the modest coefficient (0.18) is statistically significant. The picture is shown in figure 2.1. Here we see a temporal relationship stronger at some times than at others. To understand more fully, we must move beyond the bivariate case.

When we turn to the full model, the evidence is stronger and clearer. It tells us that composition matters (0.88) a lot, a surprise to no one, and that public opinion also matters in addition (0.36). The evidence produces undeniable support for the key assertion: changes in public opinion produce changes in government policy activity. To our question, "If public opinion changes, does government respond?" the answer is an unqualified "Yes."

Table 2.1 Estimations of Global Representation: Predicting Policy Activity, 1956–1996

	Model	
Variables	Reduced Form	Full Model (with Vietnam)
Dynamics (Y_{t-1})	0.77[a]	0.20
	(8.64)	(1.90)
Mood$_{t-1}$	0.18[a]	0.36*
	(2.15)	(4.16)
Composition (average of percent Democratic, House and Senate, Democratic dummy for presidency, percent liberal for Supreme Court)		0.88*
		(5.91)
Cumulative Vietnam deaths		−0.23*
		(−7.05)
Constant	1.13	−29.67*
	(0.17)	(−3.37)
Number of cases	41	41

Note: Policy Activity, the dependent variable of this analysis, is a weighted function of (1) Senate Percent Liberal Wins, (2) Senate Median Liberal Coalition Size, (3) House Percent Liberal Wins, (4) House Median Liberal Coalition Size, (5) Presidential Key Vote Liberalism, (6) Presidential Support Coalition Liberalism, (7) Supreme Court, Civil Liberties Domain, and (8) Supreme Court, Economics Domain. Measurement details are available in Erikson, MacKuen, and Stimson, 2002. *T* values are in parentheses.

*$p < .05$

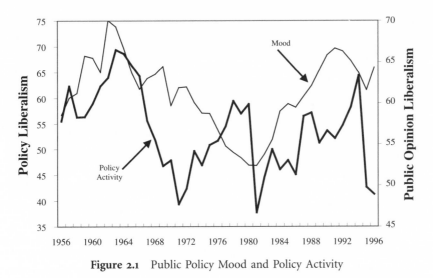

Figure 2.1   Public Policy Mood and Policy Activity

Note that mood affects policy activity two ways. The composition effect is simply that the party composition of government affects policy activity—with Democrats behaving more liberally than Republicans.[6] A key part of the story—discussed shortly—is that the electorate chooses the party composition based on its current mood. The direct effect of mood on policy activity represents only the politicians' response in anticipation of the electorate's potential sanctions. For instance, consider the electorate momentarily in a liberal mood. Democratic politicians become free to engage in their liberal proclivities because the electorate's liberalism lowers the cost of policy liberalism. Republican politicians become compelled to act more liberal than usual because of the political costs of bucking opinion.

DYNAMIC REPRESENTATION: MOOD AND POLICY

On the surface, the daily actions of Congress, the president, and courts appear to translate directly into public policy. Or they might not. One can imagine acts of government that amount to nothing more than posturing. Debates can be held and votes taken on matters of momentary import that amount to nothing. Thus, we ask whether the slow accretions of policy encapsulated in law also move in response to public demands.

"Policy," in this conception, is the body of law that remains in place forever—or until reversed by other permanent changes. Given its cumulative character, policy cannot be a simple response to *current* public demands. Thus, we focus on change, asking what happens in each biennium that leaves a lasting residue. Our measurement strategy is an adaptation of David Mayhew's compilation of important laws—which we have coded for direction (liberal or conservative) and extended in time.

We measure policy as the accumulation of "laws." The laws index is constructed in simple fashion from Mayhew's (1991) compilation as the number of liberal (important) laws minus the number of conservative (important) laws for the Congress (biennium), from 1953–54 through 1995–56. Policy is measured by adding up the laws scores, cumulatively, from 1953–54 through 1995–96. As liberal important laws outnumber conservative important laws by about 9 to 1, we detrend the measure. On average, the net change (laws) is between five and six major laws in the liberal direction, each Congress.[7]

Asking again, "Does government respond to public demands?," we have a model of the pathways to representation similar to the policy activity discussion before. Again looking at all of government output, we are concerned with responses to government composition—now measured as a scale of party control of the three elected branches, House, Senate, and presidency, 0–3 for number in Democratic hands—and with response to public opinion directly. Equation 2 again captures the structure. Table 2.2 presents the equations; figure 2.2 shows the pattern of mood leading laws over time. The story with laws is much the same as we saw earlier with policy activity. The liberalism of laws produced by the U.S. government is very much a function of which party is in control and also of public opinion as measured by mood. Liberal policy comes from Democratic governments. But holding composition constant, what government does is also responsive directly to public opinion, captured in the public policy mood of the previous biennium. With regard to changes in important public policies,

Table 2.2 Policy Change (Laws) as a Function of Mood and Party Control

	Dependent Variable = Δ Policy (Laws)		
Policy Mood$_{t-1}$	0.62*	0.47*	
	(2.99)	(2.10)	
Mean policy mood$_{t-1,t-2}$			0.62*
			(2.92)
Democratic Party control$_t$		2.72*	2.28*
		(2.32)	(2.10)
Laws$_{t-1}$	0.30		
	(1.69)		
Number of cases	22	22	22
Adjusted R^2	.46	.52	.59
RMSE	3.83	3.62	3.40

Note: Biennial data, 1953–1996. Change (Δ) in Policy = Laws. Democratic Party control = the number of the three institutions (presidency, House of Representatives, Senate) controlled by Democrats. *T* values are in parentheses.
  * $p < .05$

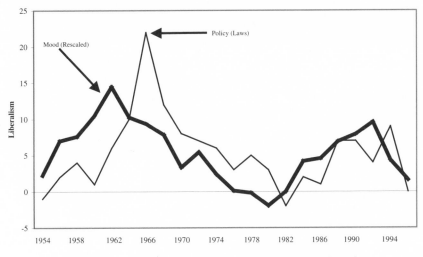

Figure 2.2   Public Policy Mood and Policy Change (Laws)

government is responsive to public opinion, now demonstrated for a second policy construct.[8]

THE FLOW BACK TO OPINION

Our interest in opinion and policy goes beyond how government responds to public opinion, representation. It is also important to understand how people react respond to the government response. We expect citizens to want more government when government in fact does little, to want less when it does much. That implies a negative association between what government does (policy) and how citizens respond (mood). We model such a relationship in table 2.3. We ask in that analysis whether public opinion (mood) responds to changes in policy. We answer the question first in a specification that lets mood be a function only of its previous value and of policy in the previous biennium. The key coefficient of −0.22 tells us that the response is as expected; liberalism in policy in one biennium produces a conservative reaction in opinion in the next and vice versa.[9]

We know from other analyses that mood is a function of economic outcomes also. Thus, that first specification, ignoring that information, is not quite complete. We supplement the analysis by adding inflation and unemployment effects in the second column. The result is a slight reduction of the key policy coefficient (to −0.17), which nonetheless leaves the effect in the predicted direction and quite highly significant. We have asked, "If government policy changes, do citizens respond?" The answer clearly is that they do.

Thus, we complete the loop. Government action and its cumulative residue responds to public opinion and public opinion responds to government action.

Table 2.3 Mood as a Function of Policy

	Only Policy	*Policy and Economics*
Policy$_{t-1}$	−0.22*	−0.17*
	(−4.54)	(−2.85)
Policy mood$_{t-1}$	0.39*	0.41*
	(3.18)	(3.68)
Inflation$_t$		−0.25
		(−1.16)
ΔUnemployment$_t$		1.38*
		(2.50)
Constant	38.26*	37.57*
	(5.09)	(5.34)
Number of cases	22	22
Adjusted R^2	.77	.81
RMSE	2.02	1.82

Note: Biennial data, 1953–96. Policy is cumulative laws, detrended. T values are in parentheses.

* $p < .05$

These two dynamics are related in a system of equations. We start the system with a shock to mood—say, an exogenous "conservative" shock. Politicians immediately become more conservative in their posturing or policy activity; eventually, actual policy becomes more conservative. In appreciation, the public lowers its demand for more conservatism and, barring further disruptions, the system returns to equilibrium.

So far we have said little about the process that makes this work—the voters' behavior at election time. We turn next to the electoral connection. For politicians to respond to mood requires that by doing so they gain—or at least think they gain—an electoral advantage.

THE ELECTORAL CONNECTION

The pivotal link in the chain of requirements for policy representation is that the electorate votes in a policy-oriented fashion. We have seen that for the direction of national policy, party composition matters and so does mood, when party composition is controlled. This mood effect represents the anticipation of elected officials—the belief that heeding public opinion enhances electoral security. This anticipatory response is contingent on the electorate paying a certain degree of attention, or at minimum that elected officials think that they are paying attention. Is the electorate's responsiveness to policy considerations real or does the anticipatory response of politicians rest on an illusion?

Decades of electoral research provide a bleak picture of the political quali-fications of the typical American voter. The typical voter is not particularly in-terested in policy issues and often is shockingly ill-informed. At election time, our typical voter starts with a standing preference based on a long-term party identification but also shows a tendency to defect based on evidence that the in party is governing well or poorly. Is there room for policy voting to emerge, given the state of the typical voter? Perhaps we should be reminded that not too long ago, the central debate of electoral politics was whether the American voter was even "rational."

Two points must be raised to this concern. First, one must distinguish be-tween occasional ignorance and irrationality. Contemporary research claims that although the American electorate may often be uninformed, voters do make in-telligent use of the information that they possess (see, for instance, Page and Shapiro 1992; Popkin 1991; Lupia and McCubbins 1998). Second, and perhaps more important in the context here, the macro-level entity (the American elec-torate) must be distinguished from the micro-level construct (the typical Amer-ican voter). To put it simply, if the typical American voter is (by definition) at the fiftieth percentile of attentiveness to policy issues, the macro-level behavior of the American electorate is heavily weighted by the behavior of the people above the fiftieth percentile of attentiveness. The behavior of the electorate shows more intelligence than our knowledge of the typical voter would suggest.

Is there a degree of policy responsiveness to voting in the United States that is observable with time-series evidence? The statistical question is whether election year mood predicts election results. We show that it does, for three dependent variables: the Democratic vote for president, the Democratic percentage of House seats, and the Democratic percentage of Senate seats among those up for election in the particular year. Our primary control variable is *macropartisanship* (party identification in Gallup surveys) in October of the election year. For the two congressional equations, we add a midterm dummy for the midterm effect. For the House seats equation, we add lagged seats. The statistical efficiency of the two congressional equations is enhanced by using "seemingly unrelated regressions." The results appear in table 2.4.

The results of table 2.4 imply that mood is a considerable influence on national elections. The mood coefficients are all highly significant, at the .01 level or better.[10] To appreciate the size of the coefficients, consider that each percentage point of mood represents an average across-the-board change of 1% on liberal-conservative policy items in opinion polls. The parameter estimates suggest that each percentage point opinion shift carries with it almost 1% of the two-party presidential vote, about two 3 House seats and about two-thirds of a Senate seat.[11]

Clearly, elections are at the center of the representation process. The more liberal the electorate, the more Democratic its voting. The more Democrats elected, the more liberal become the policies. At the same time, politicians antic-ipate this process and the effects of their actions on public opinion.

Table 2.4 Predicting Election Results from Policy Mood and Macropartisanship

	Dependent Variable		
	Democratic Presidential Vote[a]	Democrat Percent of House Seats[b]	Democrat Percent of Senate Seats[b,c]
Mood, election year	0.92*	0.47*	1.81*
	(3.23)	(3.07)	(5.32)
Macropartisanship, October, election year	1.15*	0.56*	1.43*
	(3.98)	(3.45)	(3.94)
Midterm (1 = Dem. Pres, −1 = Rep. Pres., 0 = Pres. year)		−5.57*	−9.17*
		(−5.58)	(−4.23)
Lagged Dem. percentage of House seats		0.71	
		(6.12)	
Constant	−75.05*	−49.04*	−141.01*
	(−2.59)	(−2.45)	(−3.53)
Number of cases	(12)	(23)	(23)
Adjusted R^2	.60	.63	.60

[a] OLS equation. Democratic presidential vote is as a percent of the two-party vote.

[b] SUR (Seemingly unrelated regressions). SUR− R^2 are unadjusted. Seats are measured as the percent of two-party seats.

[c] The Senate seat equation is based on all Senate seats up in the specific election cycle. Seats decided in earlier election years are ignored.

T values (z values for SUR) are in parentheses. Based on all national elections, 1952–96.

* $p < .05$

THE REPRESENTATIVE SYSTEM

The representation system consists not of a single equation but instead a system of interrelated equations. The parameters of these equations are themselves contingent on other variables we have ignored. The size of the mood effect on elections, for instance, is ultimately a function of the ideological attentiveness of individual voters and the diversity of ideological choices presented by the two major parties. Widen the ideological gulf between the parties, for example—or enlighten the electorate—and the parameters capturing the electorate's responsiveness will change.

The anticipatory policy response of elites to mood in turn depends on the degree to which the electorate responds to policy issues. It also depends on their balancing of electoral versus policy considerations in the politicians' optimizing equations. At one extreme, professional politicians striving only to stay elected follow their constituencies at the expense of personal preferences. At the other extreme, elected officials (perhaps when term-limited) follow their preferences and shirk their responsibilities to their constituents.

An important element of the system is the feedback from policy to mood. Liberal policy causes conservative mood and vice versa. We should pause a moment to figure out why this should be. It is not that legislation generates a boomerang of disillusionment. And it is not that politicians spend their capital passing unpopular legislation. (Available poll data show that, although major laws are often controversial, they are usually favored by the median voter.) Rather, liberal policy breeds conservative mood and vice versa because popular liberal legislation lessens the perceived need for more liberal legislation and popular conservative legislation lessens the perceived need for more conservative legislation. To take an example, Johnson's Great Society was popular but lessened the perceived need for further liberalism of the kind that the Democratic Party could deliver. Similarly, Reagan's conservative revolution was popular but lessened the perceived need for further conservatism of the kind the Republicans could deliver.

The mood measure represents the *relative* judgment of the American electorate. When the electorate is in a liberal mood, the people see their policies as more conservative than they want. When the electorate is in a conservative mood, the people see their policies as more conservative than they want. Mood then responds "negatively" to policy because liberal (conservative) legislation lowers the demand for liberalism (conservatism).

This theorizing suggests still another aspect to the system. If mood measures the difference between policy and preferences, we should introduce *preferences* as a further latent (or unmeasured) variable. Mood can change when policy changes, but when it changes in a way not readily attributed to policy, the source might be exogenous changes in the electorate's preferences.

At this point, we push the modeling to the limit. A potentially useful way to model the representation process has mood as a thermostat, with the public opinion registering its view that policy should be "more liberal" or "more conservative" (see Wlezien 1995). The unmeasured preference then is the electorate's set point, but one that can vary over time. Restating the model in the language of time-series statistics, policy equals preferences plus error in an error correction model, where mood represents the error. By this formulation, one can visualize a graph of policy and preferences over time, where mood represents the difference between the two, or the error.[12]

If one pursues this idea to the next step, mood represents a parameter k times the quantity "latent preferences minus policy" where preferences are measured in policy units. The value of k calibrates how many units of major legislation (the policy measure) constitute one unit of mood. That is, one unit of mood is a demand for k major laws. But what is k?

We can offer a speculative answer, based on assumptions of rationality. When modeling representation, we can impute rational expectations to the actors. Rational expectation does not mean the absence of error, but rather the absence of *systematic* errors. Actors do not persist in making the same mistake; they are able to learn. For instance, if voters have rational expectations, they would cast partisan votes based on their personal issue positions (liberals vote Democratic, conservatives vote Republican) only if the political parties actually pursue different policies in office. Similarly, if politicians have rational expectations, they would not

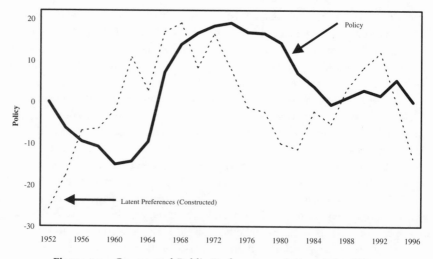

Figure 2.3 Constructed Public Preferences and Cumulative Policy

act *as if* the electorate were paying attention to their policies unless the electorate was paying attention.[13] Finally, if politicians have rational expectations, they learn the magnitudes of the signals sent by the electorate when the electorate changes its mood. This is the key for calibrating mood and policy on a common scale.

Using this rational expectations framework, we see a k value of about 3, meaning that one unit (percentage point) of mood is equivalent to a demand for three major laws. If, say, Congress enacts three extra major liberal laws, mood moves conservative one percentage point. If k is less than 3, according to the pattern of the mood and policy time-series data, the policy response to mood would be too strong—Congress would move policy farther than the public's target, requiring a spiral of overcorrections each direction that would imply that politicians are unable to learn.[14] If k is greater than 3, then the data suggest the policy response to mood would be too weak—Congress would always underestimate the public demand and never reach the public's target. In this sense, a k value of about 3 is just about right.

The potential payoff of this theorizing is the speculative depiction of the time series of public *preferences* overlaid with actual *policy*. Figure 2.3 presents the picture. Here, *mood* equals the *preferences* minus *policy* gap. The greater the gap, the more liberal the *mood*. By this depiction of figure 2.3, *preferences* move quite a bit. The contemporaneous correlation between hypothetical *preferences* and measured *policy* is not great (a mere .30), but *preferences* do correlate at an impressive .83 with *policy* eight years later.[15] Preferences by this model take up to eight years to translate into law. If this is the correct depiction, the response of *policy* (unlike *policy activity*) is slow. This is exactly what we expect, given a Madisonian system of checks and balances. *Policy* responds surely but slowly so that *preferences* sometimes change faster than the system can respond.

THE LARGER SYSTEM: MACRO POLITY

The representation process that we have described is only one part of a larger set of dynamics that compose the macro political system. We have examined the public opinion-policy system of equations as if it were in a vacuum from which other political variables were sealed out so as not to interfere and complicate the analysis. Although this isolation is appropriate as a first step, a complete understanding requires that we place the representation subsystem within the context of the larger system of equations.

In modal social science, we abstract a piece of a larger system of relationships for study. We declare our explanatory focus a "dependent variable" and set about building theoretical and then statistical models to account for it. With this familiar approach, our larger study has modeled presidential approval, macropartisanship, and the economic perceptions that affect them. We have also modeled public policy mood; election outcomes for the presidency and both congressional chambers; policy activity in the House, Senate, presidency, and the Supreme Court; and the production of important laws.

Over time, almost all the "dependent" variables of one analysis become inputs of another. We could start a causal chain at an arbitrary point and consider the consequences. Economic performance, for example (measured as familiar employment and inflation outcomes), moves presidential approval, macropartisanship, and mood in different ways. Each of these three affected variables influences election outcomes and policy activity. Elections sometimes cause shifts in party control, which alter future levels of unemployment and inflation, thereby bringing us back to where we (thought we) started—the economy's performance. This is, in short, a system.

The Cascade of Causality—An Example

To illustrate the properties of the system, we trace in greater detail the impact of a hypothetical increase in unemployment at a particular time. We ask, what are the short-term and long-term ramifications for other variables, including those involving the representation process?

The story begins with a public response in terms of economic perceptions, even be the expectation of the unemployment shock in advance of the realization. The first political response is an immediate decline in presidential approval. Then, both directly and via approval, the public's economic pessimism finds its way into macropartisanship, harming the standing of the party occupying the White House. Already the process is complicated, as the effect on approval decays with a half-life in months, whereas the (smaller) influence on macropartisanship leaves a permanent imprint.

Although these first impacts are contingent on which party holds the presidency, another effect is not. Increasing unemployment causes a surge of support for government programs—a liberalization of the public's mood. Thus, Democratic presidents experience offsetting effects from unemployment—losses of presidential and party standing offset somewhat by gains in support for the party's liberal positions. In contrast, unemployment under Republican administrations produces only negative effects for the ruling Republicans.[16]

Elections for president and Congress are next to feel the effects of our unemployment shock. They are a function of approval, of macropartisanship, and of public policy mood, all of them carrying some of the signal of our unemployment shock. Thus, we leverage the number of seats in Congress and the probable presidential outcome down the temporal road from the initial unemployment shock. The next responses to consider are the changes in policy activity. These stem in part from the personnel changes brought about by the election. But even before the next election, they are generated by elite anticipation of the electoral forces including mood, which, of course, is affected by the unemployment shock that starts the process. Policy activity—the actions of Congress and the president—leads to actual policy, which has a permanent and cumulative character. Laws passed remain in force permanently or until some explicit counter action.

Change in laws (the accumulation of policy) sets off a later effect in mood, now contrary to the original impetus. When the unemployment shock leads to liberal laws, the electorate's mood shifts in the conservative direction. Meanwhile, if the unemployment shock helps to put a Democrat in the White House, the president would be one inclined toward economic initiatives that target unemployment. Thus, one net effect of the hypothetical unemployment shock that started our chain of events is an eventual (and possibly mistimed) reduction of unemployment.

At this point, we might ask the simple question, familiar from the old path-modeling tradition: what is the total effect of the increase in unemployment? Although our cascade of consequences is all based on regression analyses, obtaining an answer is not as simple as just multiplying through the known coefficients to get total effects. Some of the effects are contingent and some are not. Some influence future events only as probabilities (for example, the party of the president) that have an uncertain and nonlinear translation into outcomes. And all of the cascading effects move through the system over time at differing rates. Some decay quickly. Some are permanent. Some, for example, election effects, do not even begin until several months after the cascade begins. Moreover, much of the variance in our variables appears to the observer to be due to stochastic error, detering us from making deterministic predictions.

Computer simulation is one approach we are pursuing to understand the long-term effects of changes in political variables. To simulate from a series of causal equations, one manipulates various aspects of the system by changing some or holding others constant and running the system (in some instances many times) to study the consequences.

Our simulations of the macro polity are a work in progress, with much to be learned. For instance, we can rerun history after inducing simple counterfactuals and observe what "happened." The short-term effects of the counterfactual changes in these exercises are usually and understandably predictable: that is, in terms of policy, mood and party control matter. The long-run effects are often another matter. For instance, in one version of our model when we reelect Carter over Reagan in 1980, the Republicans win control of the House of Representatives in the 1980s rather than in 1994, a triumph that would not be deducible from the equations alone. Similarly, when we induce an artificial liberal boost to mood in 1976, in time for the Ford-Carter election, policy changes in the expected liberal direction, but in the long-run mood shifts in the conservative direction, contrary to the initial inducement of a liberal shock.

Where the simulation yields counterintuitive outcomes, the question becomes, is the problem with the intuition or with the simulations? The answer can be debated, and the model can be tweaked to seek better fits with expectations. Unfortunately, we cannot know whether the changes induced are normal, typical, or representative; we have no sampling theory for systems. But there are unconventional lessons that can be learned. More surmise than inference, they nonetheless are lessons derived from looking at systems as systems.

CONCLUSIONS: THE OPINION-POLICY DYNAMIC

This chapter has focused on the time-series dynamics of policy representation in the United States. Much of our analysis is on short-dynamics within the representation subsystem. The presented evidence to show that not only the liberalism-conservatism of public opinion influences national policy but also that policy alterations in the direction of public opinion shift the public's demand in the reverse direction: liberal electorates cause liberal policies that lower the demand for further liberalism.

The representation process is embedded in a larger series of equations, from which we have explored simulation models with the goal of an improved understanding of long-term processes. Our preliminary simulations suggest an emphasis on the unpredictability of long-run consequences. For instance, what are the policy consequences of the Bush presidential victory in 2000? The short-run consequence is surely a more conservative swing of public policy. But what of the long run? Does policy eventually "correct" to a less conservative course? In the long run, is Bush-beats-Gore "good news" politically for the Republican or the Democratic Party? Our answer must be that we do not know. We still have much to learn.

NOTES

1. The theory of a market of mobile consumers shopping for communities traces to Tiebout (1956). For recent reviews of the evidence, see Dowding, John, and Biggs (1994) and Bickers and Stein (1998).

2. Luttbeg (1968) first identified this process as the "sharing" model (see also Erikson and Tedin 2001).

3. We were, and remain, agnostic about the possibility of a second dimension. The statistical evidence supports it. The interpretative evidence is, however, so confusing and contradictory that we can bring little substantive meaning to it and cannot rule out the possibility that the evidence of a common dimension is an artifact of some real shared covariation that is not substantively meaningful. We can be more confident of what it is not; this is not the "social issue" that is almost uniformly the second dimension of American politics in the views of pundits.

4. And we need to apologize for sowing some confusion on the terms. The measures we called "policy" in our 1995 article directly on this subject (Stimson, MacKuen, and Erikson 1995) have become "policy activity" in our newest work. The new labels for old content was necessitated by our realization that we had to treat the two components separately, even though they share a single name in our literature.

5. In equation (2.2), public opinion is lagged, but composition is not. In reality, the impact of public opinion can be immediate, requiring no delay. Empirically, we model the direct impact of public opinion with a lag to avoid ambiguity about causal direction. See also Erikson, MacKuen, and Stimson (2002, chap. 8).

6. Table 2.1 includes Vietnam casualties (Johnson years only) as a control. This variable acts as a suppressor variable, with the war thwarting liberal activity at a time of liberal public opinion. Note that the coefficient for mood goes *up* in the full model compared to the reduced form model. The major reason is that the dynamic term—the effect of lagged policy activity—dissipates in the full model and the substantive variables compensate. The correlation between independent variables mood and composition is positive, as one would expect, with more Democrats elected when the electorate is in a liberal mood. For further elaboration, see Erikson, MacKuen, and Stimson (2002, chap. 8), and Stimson, MacKuen, and Erikson (1995).

7. See Erikson, MacKuen, and Stimson (2002), particularly chapter 9, for discussion of the policy concept and measure. We use an extension of Mayhew's major laws through 1996 that was compiled by Jay Greene.

8. This is yet a third, which we have not reported here or elsewhere: the content of the budgetary process also responds to both composition and public opinion. Spending on liberal domestic programs goes up when Democrats are numerous and when public opinion demands more spending, going down with Republican composition and with conservative opinion. This supports similar budgetary claims by Wlezien (1995).

9. The significance of the relationship also holds up from a simpler test, regressing current mood change on lagged laws. The more liberal the legislation of one Congress, the more conservative the mood change from that biennium to the next.

10. The midterm effects in table 2.3 are significant and negative, meaning that each party's share of seats decreases at midterms when it holds the presidency. This fact is often treated by itself as evidence of an ideological reaction by the public, with the electorate adding seats to the out-party to ideologically balance the president (see, for instance, Alesina and Rosenthal 1995).

11. The equations of table 2.4 are bare-boned versions of our modeling of election results in *The Macro Polity*. Party platforms also matter for presidential races, although not for congressional elections. Presidential approval and economic prosperity show little direct impact on election results with macropartisanship controlled. See Erikson, MacKuen, and Stimson (2002, chap. 7).

12. Technically, mood would represent the error with a minus sign. A liberal mood means too conservative, not too liberal.

13. The early representation studies by Miller and Stokes (1966; see also Stokes and Miller 1966) were often interpreted to mean that politicians paid far more attention to their constituents than was justified by the public's limited awareness of their actions. Rather than dismiss representatives' preoccupations with constituency as irrational, perhaps stemming from politicians' deluded sense of self-importance, we think it more profitable to ask whether it might be a clue that constituency attention is indeed electorally warranted (see Mayhew 1974).

14. Imagine, for instance, a liberal mood that the government interprets as a more liberal mandate than the electorate intends. Policy then becomes too liberal for the public, whose new mood signals trigger an overly conservative spate of policies, which makes the public ask for more liberalism, etc. The problem with this scenario is that it implies that politicians (and perhaps the public) are not able to learn from past errors.

15. In a related correlation involving observable variables, biennial mood correlates at .89 with policy change over the subsequent eight years.

16. Similarly, the political consequences of inflation are a mixed package for Republican presidents but only bad news for Democratic presidents.

3

Politics and Policymaking in the Real World

Crafted Talk and the Loss of Democratic Responsiveness

LAWRENCE R. JACOBS AND ROBERT Y. SHAPIRO

The public opinion polls that fill newspapers and the offices of government officials and election campaigns have fueled the nearly unquestioned assumption among observers of American politics that elected officials "pander" to public opinion. Politicians, they charge, tailor government policy to polls and other indicators of public opinion.

The presumption that politicians slavishly follow public opinion when they design policy is wrong or, more precisely, less true today than it was two or three decades ago. As a thought experiment, consider some of the most significant government decisions and policy proposals over the past decade or so: committing American troops to driving Iraqi troops from Kuwait; the House decisions to impeach President Clinton; failed campaign finance reform; aborted tobacco legislation; Clinton's proposals in his first budget for an energy levy and an increased tax on Social Security benefits (despite his campaign promises to cut middle-class taxes); the North American Free Trade Agreement (at its outset); U.S. intervention in Bosnia; House Republican proposals after the 1994 elections for a "revolution" in policies toward the environment, education, Medicare, and other issues; President George W. Bush's tax cut, the Bush administration's rejection of the Kyoto agreement on global warming; and President Bush's support for partial privatization of Social Security. On all of these issues (and others), government officials made decisions and offered proposals that defied what most Americans preferred.

This initial inkling that politicians may not be quite as responsive to public opinion when making policy decisions as commonly assumed is corroborated here with more systematic evidence.

The term "pandering" is most commonly associated with the notion that polls and public opinion drive substantive policy choices; this *substantive responsiveness*, we suggest, is on the decline (though it has by no means disappeared). A second form of responsiveness involves the use of polls and focus groups to attempt to manipulate public opinion; this *instrumental responsiveness* is amply present today. Politicians and other political activists spend a fortune on focus groups and public opinion polls to pinpoint the most alluring words, symbols, and arguments for their desired policies; the purpose is to move Americans to "hold opinions that they would not hold if aware of the best available information and analysis" (Zaller 1992, p. 313). Politicians and political activists respond to public opinion in order to craft their presentations of already decided policy. This strategy of "crafted talk" is used to *simulate responsiveness*—political activists' words and presentations are crafted to change the public's perceptions, understandings, and evaluations of specific policy proposals and create the appearance of responsiveness as they pursue their desired policy goals. Although the public's values and fundamental preferences (such as strong and sustained support for Social Security and environmental protection) are unlikely to change, politicians do work to alter the public's perceptions, of specific proposals, such as President George W. Bush's initiative to privatize Social Security or his proposal for greater exploration for oil and gas.[1] Politicians, then, use polls and focus groups not to move their positions closer to the public's (as commonly assumed) but just the opposite—to find the most effective means to move public opinion closer to their own desired policies. Elected officials follow a simple motivation in opting for crafted talk: lower the potential electoral costs to themselves and their supporters of not following the preferences of average voters while increasing the electoral costs to rival politicians. They want the best of both worlds: to enact their preferred policies and to maximize the probability that they and their allies will be reelected and their opponents defeated.

In short, the widespread image of politicians as "pandering" to public opinion when making policy decisions is mistaken. We suggest in this chapter and in our recent book, *Politicians Don't Pander: Political Manipulation and the Loss of Democratic Responsiveness*, that the influence of public opinion on policy decisions has declined since the 1970s. Instead, politicians' own policy goals (and those of their supporters) are increasingly driving their major policy decisions and their public opinion research, which is used to identify the language, symbols, and arguments to "win" public support for their policy objectives. Responsiveness to public opinion and attempted manipulation of public opinion are not mutually exclusive; politicians attempt to manipulate public opinion by tracking public thinking to select the actions and words that resonate with the public. The next section provides evidence of declining responsiveness and situates this trend within larger institutional and political changes in American politics since the 1980s. We, then, compare our conclusions with the systems analysis offered in the previous chapter by Robert Erikson, Michael MacKuen, and James Stimson.

STUDYING PUBLIC OPINION AND
GOVERNMENT POLICY ISSUES

Research on the connection between public opinion and *specific* government policies reveals two key findings: first, political responsiveness has risen and fallen over time; second, and more specifically, it has declined since the 1970s.[2]

Benjamin Page and Robert Shapiro (1983; Shapiro 1982) tracked the variation over time in the congruence of changes in public preferences toward specific policy issues and changes in subsequent government policy. Table 3.1 shows that the degree of congruence between government policy change and opinion change varied noticeably between the 1930s and 1980. The incidence of changes in policy paralleling changes in public opinion declined from 67% in the 1935 to 1945 period (heavily dominated by wartime issues) to 54% during the 1960s, and then increased to 75% during the 1970s. The clear implication of this analysis is that government responsiveness to public opinion has changed over time, with the 1970s as a high point of responsiveness.

In another study using a different methodology, Stephen Ansolabehere, James Snyder, and Charles Stewart (2001) examined the responsiveness of members of the House of Representatives in their policymaking activity between 1874 and 1996. They used the Republican share of the presidential two-party vote within each congressional district as an indicator of constituency opinions and compared it to the ideological direction of the policymaking of each party's candidates for the House of Representatives. Figure 3.1 also shows substantial variation over time

Table 3.1   Variations in Congruence over Time

Time Period	Percentage Congruent	(N)
1935–45	67	(18)
1946–52	63	(59)
1953–60	59	(37)
1961–68	54	(26)
1969–79	75	(91)

Percentages are based on Ns in parentheses, which are the total number of congruent plus noncongruent cases.

Source: Shapiro (1982).

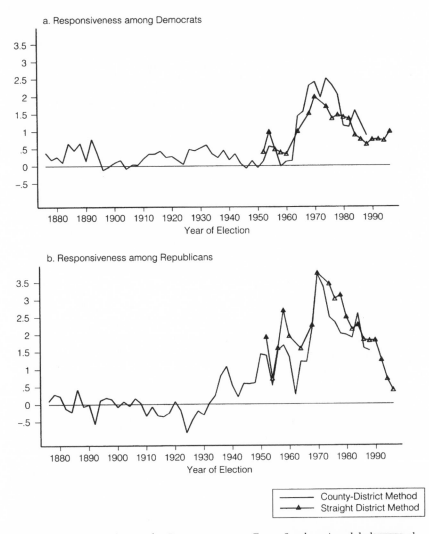

Figure 3.1   Responsiveness by Party, 1874–1996. From Stephen Ansolabehere et al., "Candidate Positioning in U.S. House Elections," *American Journal of Political Science* 45 (2001): 136–59. Reprinted by permission.

in political responsiveness. In particular, they found that the candidates' ideological responsiveness to opinion within their district was weak prior to the 1930s, rose in 1934 and peaked in the early 1970s, then declined into the 1990s (precipitously among Republican candidates). The finding that responsiveness peaked in the 1970s corroborates the results Page and Shapiro's different approach produced. One of the most striking findings in figure 3.1 is the precipitous decline since the high point in responsiveness during the 1970s.

Table 3.2   Opinion/Policy Consistency by Policy Area

	1960–79		1981–93	
	Consistent (%)	n	Consistent (%)	n
All cases	63	327	55	566
By policy area				
Social welfare	63	51	51	45
Economic and labor	67	46	51	156
Defense	52	21	61	49
Foreign policy	84	38	67	150
Civil rights/liberties	59	39	56	61
Energy and environment	72	36	67	27
Political reform	41	34	17	23
Vietnam	71	35	. . .	. . .
Miscellaneous	74	27	40	55

Source: Monroe (1998).

A third methodology for studying substantive responsiveness has also found a decline since the 1970s. Alan Monroe (1979, 1998) investigated whether 500 separate government policies were consistent with the preferences of a majority of Americans. Table 3.2 shows that government policies in the 1980–93 period were less consistent with the preferences of a majority of Americans than during 1960–79. This pattern holds both overall and within eight of nine separate policy areas: the overall consistency of government policies with majority public preferences declined from 63% in the 1960–79 period to 55% in the 1980–93 period, with the steepest declines in the policy areas of social welfare, economic and labor issues, and, especially, political reform.

Monroe's study is partly confirmed by our own preliminary study, which used the approach adopted by Page and Shapiro (1983). We examined the congruence of changes in public preferences and subsequent changes in government policy toward a subset of issues. We found a noticeable decline in the correspondence between opinion and policy changes during the 1980s and especially the 1990s (Jacobs and Shapiro 1997a). Focusing on four areas of social policy (welfare, crime, Social Security, and health care), we found that congruent changes in opinion and policy fell from 67% during Reagan's second term (1984–87) to 40% during the Bush administration (1988–92) and 36% during half of Clinton's first term (1993–94).

In short, the evidence suggests that government responsiveness to public opinion varies over time and has declined over the past several decades. The findings indicate that politicians' policy decisions *do* respond to public opinion but that responsiveness has *fallen off* since the 1970s. The change in responsiveness underscores the most significant feature of government responsiveness: it is not static but rather has changed over time.

A CONDITIONAL POLITICAL EXPLANATION
FOR RESPONSIVENESS

Research on government institutions and political dynamics has shown systemic changes that account for the variation in substantive responsiveness and, in particular, the decline since the 1970s. As a general rule, politicians who enjoy long careers in elected office are skilled at weighing the political costs and benefits of their statements and actions. Their perceptions of the costs and benefits of their behavior affect their motivation and willingness to pursue two distinct goals. The first goal is electoral and suggests pleasing as many voters within their constituencies as possible. The second goal is to enact the policies they and their supporters most desire. Obviously, the skilled politician prefers to take actions that advance both electoral goals and policy goals. But political reality often presents politicians with unpleasant choices. Electoral goals are a constant concern of elected officials, though the intensity of concern increases as election day approaches. But the pressure on politicians to pursue policy goals favored by supporters has varied over time as political and institutional conditions have changed.

A series of significant and widely researched developments in American politics has elevated the expected benefits to politicians of pursuing policy goals that they and their supporters favor. We discuss two here; others are examined more fully in *Politicians Don't Pander* (Jacobs and Shapiro 2000, chap. 1 and 2).

Changes since the 1970s in the organization and balance of power within political parties dramatically increased the power of party activists, as well as core partisan voters who routinely support each party. As a result, control over the selection of congressional and presidential candidates and the platforms of presidential campaigns, shifted from party organizations and a small cadre of party leaders to party caucuses and direct primaries after the 1960s. Instead of winning the party nomination by battling for support among the small cadre of party leaders, candidates since the 1970s have depended on securing the support of party activists, who provide the bulk of the contributions, volunteers, and votes necessary to win the party's nomination and then the general election (Aldrich 1995, chap. 6; Rohde 1991; Verba, Schlozman, and Brady 1995; Davidson and Oleszek 1998, pp. 67–68).[3]

The knighting of political activists as the selectors of each party's nomination has had enormous political consequences since the 1970s. Political activists voice policy positions that are more ideologically extreme than those of the general public or even their fellow (but less active) partisans. The consequence is that each party's nomination requires cementing the support of party activists, which in turn pressures the candidates and officeholders to support ideologically extreme positions that diverge both from those of the opposing party and from centrist opinion (Fiorina 1974; Aldrich 1995; Polsby 1980; Jacobson 1987, p. 20; Wright 1994). ("Centrist opinion" refers to the median voter or citizen in the distribution of public opinion and not to an ideologically fixed "left" or "right.") Indeed, the anticipated reaction of party activists has also influenced which candidates are recruited to run: each party tends to recruit candidates whose own personal attitudes and ideological views about "good public policy" closely mirror those of activists.

The pressure of party activists has produced national Democratic and Republican parties that have become increasingly polarized since the 1970s, as evident in two trends. First, there is greater unity *within* each political party as the proportion of moderates in both parties (but especially the Republican Party) has declined dramatically from the 1970s to the 1990s. Legislators who harbored policy views outside their party's mainstream and regularly voted with the opposing party—like liberal New York Republican Jacob Javits and conservative Arkansas Democrat Wilbur Mills—have been replaced in each party by more ideologically extreme politicians (McCarty, Poole, and Rosenthal 1997; Bond and Fleisher 1990; Fleisher and Bond 1996). The diminishing number of moderates and the decline of intra-party differences are evident in roll call votes on the floor of the House and Senate, which no longer divide each party as they did from 1945 to 1976. Since the mid-1970s, the proportion of close floor votes in Congress on which more than 10% of each party disagreed with a majority of their party has declined. Moreover, the ideological position of each party's members has moved closer together. Poole and Rosenthal's (1997) measures of the distance between the votes of members of the same party in the House and Senate show less division within each party during the 1990s than at any time since 1947. The second trend producing partisan polarization has been the growing ideological distance *between* each party. Poole and Rosenthal's analysis suggests that the distance separating the average House and Senate Democrat from the average Republican increased over time. In addition, roll call votes in Congress were more frequently divided between liberals and conservatives in the 1990s than at any time since 1947, when President Harry Truman faced a contentious Republican-dominated Congress.

Democrats and Republicans became more ideologically homogeneous and polarized by the 1990s and the first years of the twenty-first century (as illustrated by gridlock on economic and fiscal policy). The implications are significant: the combination of fewer legislators outside a party's ideological mainstream and growing policy differences between the parties on social and economic issues has increased the costs of compromising the policy goals of partisans. Responsiveness to centrist opinion becomes less likely if it means an erosion of support from party activists.

The political incentives of the new political order were well illustrated in the impeachment of Bill Clinton. The congressional Republicans' relentless pursuit of impeachment was largely driven by the priority that Republican activists attached to the policy goal (removing Clinton) instead of the electoral goal (appealing to a majority of Americans). Moderate Republicans could not ignore the risk of opposing impeachment—it could lead to a challenge in the next primary election. Put another way, Republican members of Congress disregarded the two-thirds of Americans who opposed impeachment because their electoral goal of responding to a majority of voters was offset by the substantial costs of compromising their policy goals of enacting legislation that Republican activists and other supporters favored.

The second factor that heightened politicians' expectations about the benefits of pursuing policy goals that they and their supporters favored was the rapid growth in the number and diversity of national interest groups that could mobilize particularistic groups within a legislator's constituency and use national political action committees to provide campaign contributions to supporters (Cigler and Loomis 1983; Salisbury 1990; Walker 1991; Heclo 1978). Until the 1960s, interest groups were relatively few in number and those from similar sectors of society came together under relatively strong peak associations such as the American Medical Association, which dominated health policy. The dominance of a few peak organizations aggregated the demands of interest groups and provided a tangible bargaining partner for politicians as they balanced electoral pressure to follow centrist opinion.

After the 1960s, however, indicators—from the number of registered lobbyists to the number of corporations operating offices in Washington—revealed a dramatic growth in the number and variety of organizations engaged in pursuing their interests in Washington. New groups and new coalitions on social, economic, and political issues formed continually. Moreover, once-dominant peak organizations were replaced by associations that specialized in small policy niches or that formed complicated coalitions that cut across formal associations (Cigler and Loomis 1983; Salisbury 1990; Walker 1991; Heclo 1979). The groups increasingly used campaign contributions, grass-roots organizing, and media campaigns to pressure politicians to advance their particularistic policy concerns.

Organized labor—a decisive influence into the 1960s—saw its membership slip from over 30% to 14% of the workforce in just three decades, recording one of the lowest rates of union membership among industrial countries. The AFL-CIO, once the lead voice for organized labor, no longer served as a dominating peak association. Labor's decline combined with intensified business opposition to government social welfare programs has been credited with shifting the political balance to the right and moving the average officeholder's position away from centrist opinion (Rogers and Ferguson; Weir, 1998).

The result was that a relatively small number of powerful interest groups no longer dominated government decision making, in particular policy areas such as health care. The proliferation of narrowly based interest groups increased the pressure on politicians to pursue specific policy goals; politicians could no longer negotiate with a peak organization to gain flexibility on some issues in exchange for supporting an organization's priorities. Greater numbers of interest groups with focused agendas also stimulated volunteers and, especially, contributions (Stein and Bickers 1995).

Incentives to pursue policy goals grew (though perhaps not as extensively as some reformers assume) with the increasing importance of money in politics—in the form of campaign contributions by political action committees (PACs) and well-funded lobbying campaigns during policy debates, epitomized by the $100 million spent by opponents of the Clinton health plan in 1993–94 and by the infamous "Harry and Louise" commercials (West, Heith, Goodwin 1996, pp. 42–43; but cf. Jacobs 2001). Although researchers disagree on the nature and extent of the influence extracted by contributors to campaigns and policy initiatives,[4] there is some agreement that the pressure on politicians to fund media advertising and political consultants has advantaged private interests by disproportionately increasing their access to politicians and the mass public and enabling them to prevent threatened actions by lawmakers (McChesney 1997; Sorauf 1988; West and Loomis 1999; Ferguson 1995).

Since the 1970s, the rise of ideological polarization, the proliferation of interest groups, the increasing importance of campaign expenditures, and other factors have elevated the perceived benefit to politicians of pursuing policy goals that they and their supporters favor rather than responding to centrist public opinion. Responding to centrist public opinion at the expense of policy goals entails compromising their own philosophical convictions and possibly alienating ideologically extreme party activists and other supporters who volunteer and contribute money to their primary and general election campaigns. In contemporary America, designing policy to reflect what most Americans prefer has increasingly become costly to politicians and therefore something that the ambitious politician will avoid. To get the best of both worlds, politicians pursue the policy goals they and their supporters prefer yet try to lower the electoral risks by attempting to manipulate public opinion.

The approach of imminent elections, however, temporarily interrupt the drive of politicians to reach their policy objectives. As the elections approached in the summer of 1996, congressional Republicans and Clinton briefly replaced partisan gridlock with compromise and cooperation to pass legislation that had strong public support, such as the minimum wage law, the Kassabaum-Kennedy reform of private health insurance operations, and, arguably, welfare reform. The clearest evidence for the impact of electoral proximity comes from studies of senators who moderate their earlier positions and increase their responsiveness to their state's median voters as election day neared (Levitt 1996; Kuklinski 1978; Amacher and Boyes 1978; Elling 1982; Wright 1989; Wood and Andersson 1998). Our own analysis found a similar pattern for presidents; comparing the publicly enunciated positions of Lyndon Johnson with his private polling revealed a pattern of rising responsiveness as the 1964 presidential election approached (Jacobs and Shapiro 1993). The heat of an upcoming presidential election and elevated attention from average voters appear to motivate politicians for a short period to respond to public opinion and run the risk of absorbing the costs of compromising their policy goals.

Although the drift of institutional changes over the past several decades have both increased the costs to politicians of compromising policy goals and responding to centrist opinion and raised their benefits of pursuing the policy goals of supporters, standard models of competitive elections predict long-term responsiveness. Particularly under conditions of divided government and narrow electoral margins, competitive elections are expected either to produce an alteration in power that clusters around the median voter (even if it zig-zags from left to right of the median) or to induce compromise that hews to centrist opinion in an effort to avoid electoral punishment (Sundquist 1968). However, the last two decades, as well as the historical record, suggest that responsiveness has remained comparatively low across elections and that elections may not be a self-correcting cure. Three reasons stand out. First, motivated politicians exercise substantial discretion to pursue unpopular policies. Voters lack complete knowledge of their representatives' positions; they cannot always monitor and punish officeholders due to the plethora of considerations that enter into their choices (including non-policy evaluations of personal image), and policymakers' strategic packaging of decisions obscures the costs and responsibility of policy changes (Arnold 1990). Second, muting responsiveness to centrist opinion is electorally expedient for most members of Congress from ideologically homogeneous districts. Third, politicians of both major parties use crafted talk to obscure their *true* policy goals and to appear responsive to centrist opinion through their language and symbolic actions such as candidate Bush's frequent photographs with blacks during the 2000 presidential election even as the African American community thoroughly rejected his policies. The 2000 election also showed both candidates closely hewing to language that embraced tax cuts, smaller bureaucracy, more consumer choice, and expanded social welfare provisions (e.g., establishment of Medicare drug benefit). The policy goals of politicians have diverged even as their rhetoric has converged toward words and presentations that signal an affinity for what the median voter favors.

POLICYMAKING IN ACTION

Our book, *Politicians Don't Pander*, builds a theory and explanation for variations in responsiveness and, in particular, the decline since the 1970s. We intensively analyzed President Clinton's drive for health care reform in 1993–94 and the first Gingrich Congress (1995–96) to explain *why* policymakers were discounting public opinion in fashioning policy decisions. We combined quantitative research with a review of White House memoranda, content analysis of the statements and decisions of leading policymakers, and semi-structured interviews with senior officials. In this section, we briefly outline the political motivations and strategic considerations that led authoritative officials from diametrically opposed ideological perspectives to converge on a similar approach to public opinion.

Clinton Revisionism: Where Is the Great Panderer?

Perhaps the second most common rap on President Clinton—beyond the questions about his private conduct—was that he was poll-addicted. Here was the poster child for the pandering politician. Yet interviews, White House documents, content analysis, and other evidence suggest that during the formulation of Clinton's health reform proposal—the centerpiece of his domestic policy agenda—public opinion was repeatedly discounted in favor of policy goals that arose from the president's own philosophy and policy preferences, interest group pressure, and other factors not directly related to public opinion. Only after the president's plan began to take shape were his pollsters called in to "poll the presentation."

Clinton advisers, both defensive and critical, agreed that the president's New Democratic philosophy and economic considerations regarding universal coverage and other issues were "uppermost in Clinton's mind." Health reform rose to the top of Clinton's agenda during his campaign and his first two years in office because he and his advisers identified it as the means to achieve his overriding goals of economic rejuvenation and deficit reduction.[5] Public opinion toward health care reform did not elevate it on his agenda. One senior aide during the campaign and the administration explained that Clinton promoted health care reform from the start of the 1992 presidential race because "he viewed health care primarily as an economic issue first, and as a social issue second."[6] According to a wide spectrum of Clinton's aides, Clinton's commitment to economic growth and deficit reduction led to his support of universal health insurance.[7] Universal coverage was expected to control government and business costs by ending the rampant practice of shifting the expenses for treating the uninsured to the insured and by focusing Americans on remaining healthy and efficiently using the health system. According to advisers, Clinton's "goal was not a social goal of coverage expansion per se"; he "went in as a way to save and reduce the deficit" and, perhaps, to "finance high priority new initiatives in such areas as education or the environment."[8]

The novel approach to health care reform that Clinton embraced was the offspring of his New Democratic philosophy; it seemed to promise an approach to health care reform that would expand insurance coverage yet avoid a visible government role and massive tax increase. Clinton backed a liberal variant of managed competition that proposed to establish universal access to health insurance by requiring employers to contribute to their employees' insurance and by creating new regional bodies that negotiated with private health plans and monitored competition between them. Clinton viewed his novel approach, according to an aide, as allowing him to "say 'I have a competitive bill, not a regulatory bill' "[9] that would finance health care reform by squeezing waste out of the system rather than imposing enormous direct tax hikes. White House officials, especially Ira Magaziner, who coordinated health care reform, repeatedly assured the president and Mrs. Clinton that by eliminating "waste in the current system, . . . system savings will exceed system costs significantly" and would "cover universal access and possibly contribute to deficit reduction."[10] Managed competition seemed to promise "something for nothing."[11] (The Congressional Budget Office [1994] would later report that Clinton's managed competition approach did not produce greater savings than costs.) By contrast, health policy experts or advocates of a Canadian-inspired single-payer system who proposed direct government

regulation of health care spending were labeled "Old Democrats" and were de-
rided as "Washington people" dependent on the outdated ideas of "direct . . . tax
increases . . . [and] regulatory approaches that the president was not fond of."[12]
Put simply, the president and his senior aides like Ira Magaziner preferred the
liberal variant of managed competition to alternative approaches because of their
strong views of what constituted "good public policy."

Appeasing interest groups and Democratic constituents also drove White
House decisions, especially in designing the framework of the president's managed
competition approach. Long-term care and drug benefits were added, according
to White House documents, to "make the Medicare and Medicaid savings possible
for the American Association of Retired Persons [and other senior and disability
groups] to support"; the early retiree discounts were created to "solidify large
business, labor, senior and state and local government support"; and numerous
other policies were designed to curry favor with small businesses, urban areas,
provider groups, and single-payer advocates.[13] Even on the issue of comprehensive
benefits, for which White House pollster Stanley Greenberg reported strong national support, several administration officials suggested that aggregate public
opinion was not as influential as "a lot of pressure from a lot of seniors." "We
knew," one political adviser recalled, "that if we didn't have long-term care we
wouldn't get the AARP."

In short, within the White House, Clinton officials repeatedly insisted that
their "plan [was] constructed by the policy people" and that "polling didn't drive
the policy decision."[14] They fully accepted, as aides reported, that "the most compelling features of our package in policy terms may *not yield the highest public
support*" (emphasis added).[15] Public opinion was discounted (often explicitly) in
favor of the policy preferences of interest groups, party activists, and the president
himself.

Our intensive case study provides an opportunity to penetrate the black box
of policymaking portrayed in systems analysis and analysis of aggregated data;
the purpose is to investigate how politicians understand, evaluate, and use public
opinion (Jacobs 1992a, b, c, 1993). Studying the strategic calculations of policymakers unravels a perplexing puzzle of the Clinton era: why would Clinton gorge
himself at a sumptuously provided banquet of polls and focus groups yet discount
public opinion in favor of policy goals when designing policy? Why spend a
fortune on researching public opinion when it does not drive your policy decisions?

Our analysis of the Clinton White House's health care operations suggests
that it used polls and focus groups as part of a strategy of crafted talk or, as
White House aides put it, to "craft the communication strategy and the message"
in order to appeal most effectively to the public.[16] White House aides candidly
acknowledged that the purpose of public opinion research was to move Americans
toward supporting what "you care about . . . and believe." Polls and focus groups
were aimed at determining, as one official said, "where people [are] in relationship to where you want them to be, based on your strong beliefs."[17] "We didn't

poll the policy," well-placed aides explained, to discover what "people really wanted policy wise"; rather, "we polled the *presentation* of the policy."[18]

In particular, White House aides most consistently used polls and focus groups to identify the language, symbols, and "arguments that will resonate with people."[19] Pinpointing the "words that people use" in everyday life told the White House staff how to "talk, describe, and sell" the reform package in a manner that effectively appealed to public opinion.[20] The White House staff used public opinion research, then, to identify existing public attitudes and information that supported aspects of the Clinton plan (e.g., universal coverage) as well as unfavorable views (e.g., proposals to control costs and expand government bureaucracy); then, they crafted presentations to prompt Americans to bring attitudes and information favorable toward the Clinton plan into the top of their minds. White House research on Americans' attitudes directed decisions on three aspects of "message" development: its choice of "security for all" as an overriding theme, its emphasis on the personal benefits of reform, and its selection of specific words to describe its plan—such as the word "alliance" to publicly describe the new entities that were to purchase health insurance for consumers (health policy designers referred to them as "health insurance purchasing cooperatives," or HIPCs).

Bill Clinton's policy preferences, philosophy toward government, and political judgments about the policy goals of his supporters drove the formulation of his health care reform plan. Only *after* he and his advisers reached their decisions did they focus on public opinion, and then the strategic objective was to win over the public to their policy positions and thereby induce cooperation from policymakers.

Political Learning: What Gingrich Republicans Shared with Clinton Democrats

The stark policy differences between congressional Republicans (especially in the House after Speaker Newt Gingrich took the gavel) and the Clinton White House produced the Washington version of the "war between the Tates." Even as Washington's political titans squared off during the 1990s, they were driven by common motivations and strategy: they pursued the policy goals that they and their supporters wanted to achieve into the fall of 1996, and they discounted the fact that most citizens did not support some of these desired policies. The Republicans echoed both the public's broad objectives (evident in the supermajorities of more than 70% that favored balancing the budget, cutting taxes, establishing a presidential line-item veto, eliminating "welfare," and passing term limits) as well as the public's philosophical leanings toward individualism and limited government (about two-thirds of Americans consistently tell pollsters that the government does too many things that are better left to business and individuals).[21]

The Republicans' specific proposals to achieve these broad objectives, however, contradicted the public's specific policy preferences. They ran counter to the long-standing public preferences toward Medicare and Medicaid, environmental and safety regulation, school lunches, student loans, Americorps volunteers, education and training, increased defense spending, and other policy areas (Cook and Barrett 1992; Page and Shapiro 1992).[22] Although Americans favored ending "welfare," they did not support either the sharp cuts in government spending for poor people or the punitive approach to children and the poor that the House proposed. During the 104th Congress, majorities of nearly 60% of Americans continued to support government assistance for "poor" people and over 80% believed that the government was spending too little or about the right amount on "assistance to the poor" and "poor children." Moreover, the 104th Congress failed to act on the popular political reforms of term limits and lobbying regulations, despite Republican promises in the Contract with America to enact them.

An intensive analysis of the Republicans' motivations for discounting public opinion points to the importance legislators attached to their own policy goals (what they considered "good public policy"), as well as the demands of party activists and interest groups. The policy decisions of many House Republicans were driven by the fact that—in the words of House Republican Whip Tom DeLay—they were "ideologues [with] . . . an agenda [and] . . . philosophy" (quoted in Drew 1996, p. 116). House Republican Sam Brownback, a leader of legislators who first entered Congress in 1994, agreed that "most of my colleagues are very ideologically driven" and came to Washington committed to making good on a "very aggressive, very ideological campaign . . . [to] reduce the size of the federal government" (quoted in Drew 1996, pp. 124–25).

The views of DeLay and Brownback were repeated in our interviews with staffers; legislators were determined to "do what's best" according to their personal values. One Republican respondent explained: "On policy, beliefs are more important than public opinion." Another explained that the member of Congress "just does what he feels he needs to do. Public opinion is not at all useful in day-to-day policy making." Eighty-eight percent of the legislative staff we interviewed (46 out of 52) acknowledged that public opinion information was used to lobby their offices but argued that it had no influence on the member; their member "stuck" to his or her beliefs and distrusted the results because the "numbers are so easy to manipulate" to serve the interests of the lobbyist, whether an interest group, another legislator, or the White House. The persistent and unequivocal downplaying of public opinion by the staff we interviewed is consistent with the gap between public opinion and Republican positions as well as with the previous research on a member of Congress and his constituents, which suggests that the preferences of a member's constituents has a modest and highly contingent effect on the legislator's voting decisions and electoral prospects.

The policy goals of Republicans were the product of not only legislators' own beliefs but also the preferences of the Republican Party activists and interest groups who supported them, especially the Christian Coalition, the National Rifle Association, and the National Association of Small Businesses (Drew 1996). The standing of the Republicans' allies was reflected in the dramatic rise during the 104th Congress in testimony before congressional committees by conservative advocacy groups, business groups, and others sympathetic to the party's goals (Gormley 1998).

As Republican leaders would discover, legislative proposals that compromised the party's policy goals and responded to centrist opinion faced a potential revolt by rank and file legislators as well as party supporters. Conservative Republicans (especially in the House) were vigilant in protesting what they saw as backsliding on key elements of their agenda, equating "compromise" and "split[ting] the difference" with the abdication of principle (Drew 1996, p. 310). The Christian Coalition and other supporters pressured Republicans to enact their preferred legislation and ominously warned (in one mailing) of retribution for failing to follow its policy goals: "We'll throw you out. We mean it" (quoted in Schneider 1995).

In short, the intensive cases studies of the Clinton and Republican policy initiatives in the 1990s, as well as more systematic research on political responsiveness, point to three findings. First, the responsiveness of government policy to the public is not static but varies over time. Second, it has declined since the 1970s. Third, changes in American political dynamics and institutional developments have increased the perceived political benefits of pursuing policy goals over electoral goals, increasing the incentives for discounting the preferences of centrist opinion when it has diverged from those of party activists and other supporters of ambitious officeholders.

STUDYING VARIATION AND POLITICAL CONFLICT IN SUBSTANTIVE RESPONSIVENESS

The previous chapter by Erikson, MacKuen, and Stimson, as well as their previous work (Stimson, MacKuen, and Erikson 1994, 1995), offers an alternative interpretation of government policy and public opinion in which politicians incessantly follow public opinion.

Stimson, MacKuen, and Erikson base their conclusions on highly aggregated measures of domestic public opinion (or, in their terms, "mood") and government policy. They use global measures of liberalism and conservatism for each year to track the decisions of American government on domestic affairs since the 1950s (such as legislation enacted by Congress). They have similarly condensed available public opinion toward domestic policies into comparably global measures of liberal and conservative public "mood." The researchers then asked: Did changes in government policy in a liberal or conservative direction correspond to changes in public mood for more or less government? In short, their method treats policy decisions and national public opinion as a single dimension of ideological conservatism and liberalism and then compares the public's liberal-conservative "mood" to overarching policy measures.

Based on these highly aggregated measures of public opinion and policy,

CRAFTED TALK AND THE LOSS OF DEMOCRATIC RESPONSIVENESS 69

Stimson, MacKuen, and Erikson (1995) have reported that government policy has followed public opinion as it moved in a liberal direction in the 1960s, in a conservative direction around 1980, and then back toward a liberal course in the late 1980s. These results have heartily supported the assumption that politicians unrelentingly "pander" to public opinion when making policy: for politicians, public opinion is the only signal that matters. Politicians behave "[l]ike antelopes in an open field" (p. 559): "When politicians perceive public opinion change, they adapt their behavior to please their constituency" (p. 545).

The authors' chapter in this volume augments their previous reports of "antelope"-like responsiveness of politicians by conducting "systems" analysis and focusing on the "larger set of dynamics that comprise the macro political system" (chap. 2). Their admirable motivation is to demonstrate the endogeneity of previously disconnected aspects of American politics: economic conditions, public opinion, policymaking, elections, and other factors. The authors' embrace of systems analysis both modifies their treatment of political representation in important respects (partisan composition is now incorporated with public opinion in an analysis of government policy) and raises new questions.

Systems analysis reached its heyday in the social sciences during the decades after World War II and then became the subject of probing questions during the 1970s.[23] In 1970, Giovanni Sartori classified research—in one of the classics of social science methodology—as running along a "ladder of abstraction" between two extremes. At one extreme were descriptive studies that suffered from the "microscopic errors" of exclusively focusing on particular detail and failing to identify common patterns across cases; at the other extreme were global approaches such as systems analysis that attempted to explain everything but committed the "macroscopic errors" of failing to measure accurately the most basic aspects of political reality. Sartori's recommendation was for "middle-level" theorizing that produced empirically grounded but theoretically informed analysis.

Indeed, the critical reaction to systems analysis was an important catalyst for the return to the workings of institutions that is now a prominent part of contemporary political science. Three or so decades ago journals and books chronicled the ways in which government institutions and political conflict produced government activities that defied the predictions of systems analysis. The fashionable catchwords of the day referred to breaking open the "black box" of systems analysis into which inputs flowed and outputs popped out; the aim was to accurately understand policymaking while producing generalizeable "middle-level" theorizing (e.g., Skocpol 1979; Verbal 1971; Tilly 1975).

Although the empirically grounded research by Stimson, Erikson, and MacKuen and, specifically, their *Macro Polity* project avoids the most extreme form of systems analysis, their work does raise two questions posed three decades earlier about systems analysis: the authors rely on a form of overaggregation that creates "macroscopic errors"; they do not study changes in relationships over time that produce temporal variations in responsiveness. The result is that their empirical portrayal of public opinion and policy and their inferences about democratic governance are incomplete: not allowing for strategic attempts to manipulate public opinion leads them to conflate responsiveness to genuine public preferences with possible simulated responsiveness. Their conceptualization of public opinion, the nature of their data, and their research design do not allow them to disentangle variations in responsiveness over time that stem from changing political and institutional dynamics.

Overaggregation

Stimson, Erikson, and MacKuen claim that highly aggregated measures of liberal-conservative trends in public mood and national policy are more accurate and realistic than studying public opinion and policy toward actual policy issues. Their case principally rests on two claims. First, typical citizens, in their view, form only highly generalizeable policy attitudes and "usually fail" to develop specific preferences (Stimson, Erikson, and MacKuen 1994); on the other hand, they are confident that their mood measure identifies the "common element that persists over time and across apparently dissimilar issues" (chap. 2). Second, politicians are preoccupied with the public's general "mood" instead of attitudes toward government policies: "it is the general public disposition, the mood, which policy makers must monitor" (Stimson, MacKuen, and Erikson 1994, pp. 30–31).

The macro, or systems, approach to public opinion and government policy is susceptible to the macroscopic errors Sartori identified in an earlier generation's systems analysis. Most notably, important distinctions that the public makes among different policies do not fit along a single ideological continuum. Americans' thinking about social welfare policies is quite different from their evaluation of social policies (abortion, capital punishment, law and order issues, and different racial issues): Americans may be liberal on social welfare issues even as they express conservative views on social policies.[24] Research on public support for specific policies and on changes in these preferences over time demonstrates that the public consistently draws reasonable distinctions—based on available information—between different government programs (Jacobs and Shapiro 2000, chap. 7; Page and Shapiro 1992; Zaller 1992; Best 1999; Cook 1979; Cook and Barrett 1992; Mayer 1992).

Overaggregation has significant statistical consequences that obscure critical empirical patterns. First, the efforts of Stimson, Erikson, and MacKuen to average a number of diverse issues that move in opposite directions greatly reduces the variance that they have to explain. Second, they limit the variance they do model to a particular trend that fits the model nicely. Their approach is akin to analyzing group means rather than individual behavior: it is much neater and easier but obscures critical patterns in the data.[25] Our point, then, is not for greater particularism and "thick description"; accurate tracking of empirical patterns is necessary to build worthwhile theory, yet the authors' approach masks critical aspects of the data.

Problems with Model Specification

Erikson, MacKuen, and Stimson mis-specify their model because they fail to adequately control for endogeneity and spuriousness, despite their initial acknowledgment of the problem (chap. 2). Research on politicians' calculations, behavior, and strategy reveals that they are not content to rely on global indicators of public opinion. Instead, presidents and other officeholders and political activists devote enormous time, money, and organizational resources to tracking and analyzing public preferences and reactions toward specific policy issues (Jacobs 1992 a, b and c; Jacobs 1993; Jacobs and Shapiro 1995b; Heith 1995). Even a cursory review of presidential archives unearths a veritable warehouse of polling data on specific policy issues. During the 1996 presidential campaign, for instance, Bill Clinton and his advisers tracked the public's preferences toward an array of policy issues from welfare reform to health care and income policy, with many surveys probing voters' reactions to specific options for policy change (Morris 1999, appendix). Clinton decided in 1996 to move simultaneously in a conservative direction by signing welfare reform and in a liberal direction by expanding the government's role in health care and income policy. A global approach to public opinion and policy would have conflated these two quite different sets of public attitudes and mistakenly characterized Clinton's behavior as moving in strictly a conservative direction. Put another way, the systems approach to political representations lacks the micro-foundations to bolster its assumption that politicians follow global mood.

The overaggregation of public opinion and government policy produces a substantial risk: the systems approach may lose sight of politicians' efforts to manipulate public opinion in order to simulate responsiveness. A long (and perhaps dominant) line of research on American politics has documented the substantial efforts of politicians to changing public opinion through "explanations" and orchestrated presentations (Fenno 1973, 1978; Ginsberg 1986; Kernell 1986) or to prevent voters from clearly monitoring their representatives by tracking the costs of particular legislation to a single vote (Arnold 1990). The commitment of politicians to changing public opinion is consistent with much of the research on contemporary government institutions and elections, which point to party activists and other factors as the primary influences on politicians (Aldrich 1995; Rohde 1991; Page 1978; Wittman 1983, 1990; Poole and Rosenthal 1997; Kingdon 1989; Fiorina 1974; Shapiro, Brady, Brody, and Ferejohn 1990).

Focusing on global outcomes runs the risk of obscuring causal connections. Does public opinion drive policy decisions or do politicians make strategic and targeted efforts to alter public opinion? What the systems approach treats as substantive responsiveness may in fact be the product of "simulated responsiveness"—cases in which politicians (with the inadvertent aid of the media) influence public opinion in order to create the *appearance* of responsiveness to public opinion.[26] In short, the study of global ideological trends may both underestimate the strategic behavior of elites to attempt to change (and not simply accept) centrist opinion and overstate the actual level of government responsiveness to the public's relatively autonomous preferences.

Erikson, MacKuen, and Stimson do suggest in the previous chapter that public opinion is affected by government policy but the impact is highly abstract and not animated by political conflict and strategic calculations. Public opinion is scripted by the authors to move mechanically in the opposite ideological direction of policy: "We expect citizens to want more government when government in fact does little, to want less when it does much" (chap. 2). Although the authors investigate the impact of partisan composition on responsiveness, their framework and analysis do not consider directly the impact of partisan policy goals on political strategy and on attempts to manipulate public opinion: their initial acknowledgment of endogeneity remains outside their actual systems model. As we suggested earlier, intense political conflict and dueling ideological commitments during the 1990s motivated rival sets of political elites to adopt crafted talk as a strategy to win public opinion. The product of these dueling campaigns to win public opinion was vividly illustrated in September 1994: Republicans gloated that most Americans got what they wanted when Congress defeated Clinton's proposal; Democrats (who controlled the White House and both chambers of Congress) decided to accept quietly the defeat of the unpopular Clinton health plan. Although the policy decisions of Democrats and Republicans in September 1994 appear to "respond" to the public's evaluation of the Clinton plan (which had declined by twenty percentage points over the past year), that reaction was itself the product of a sustained and well-orchestrated strategy by opponents of health reform and the media's coverage of the political battle.

In short, the macro, or systems, approach to political representation may be confusing substantive responsiveness and simulated responsiveness. The result is that the global approach misses the decline in government responsiveness since the 1970s because it failed to accurately measure public opinion toward policy, government policy itself, and the relationship between the two. The global view obscures the institutional and political dynamics that condition real politicians to discount substantive responsiveness in favor of attempted manipulation. Studying political representation requires analyses that connect public opinion with real institutional and political dynamics.

The Static Treatment of Substantive Responsiveness

Although Erikson, MacKuen, and Stimson have previously characterized their findings as demonstrating "antelope"-like hyper responsiveness by politicians, the results they present in the previous chapter may create the false impression of muted responsiveness. For instance, they note that about a "third of each year's public opinion change is found in next year's policy activity" (chap. 2). Few (if any) students of government responsiveness would be surprised by this result or expect public opinion to have no impact on policy. Their comment, however, focuses narrowly on the *direct* impact of public opinion. Their tables and figures make it clear that public opinion also exerts substantial *indirect* influences as well—namely, a determinative impact on partisan composition (see table 2.1) and Democratic Party control (see table 2.2). The combined direct and indirect impact of public opinion is substantial and consistent with an interpretation of the political system as highly responsive.

The systems approach to political representation outlined in the previous chapter treats substantive responsiveness as stable over time: what is heralded as a dynamic model is, in fact, quite static in important respects. Global aggregation and the omission of direct attention to political conflict and institutional dynamics lead the authors to miss the ways in which changing political and institutional patterns alter the motivations and strategic calculations of politicians as they weigh policy goals and electoral goals. The underlying—and theoretically undeveloped—presumption is that politicians' goals do not vary over time.

But there is a larger point here: the impact of partisan composition varies over time and alters political calculations and thereby the levels of responsiveness. Politicians have been caught in a tug-of-war between wanting the benefits of pleasing voters (as the "median voter" theory predicts) and fearing the costs of displeasing party and interest group supporters. The costs and benefits that politicians attach to pleasing voters by responding to their policy preferences and pursuing cherished policy goals vary over the course of both short-term election cycles as well as longer-term historical cycles of several decades or more. Although the authors acknowledge that "policy will always err in the direction of the ideological position of the party" (chap. 2), they treat this as a fixed rather than changing condition. Indeed, it is precisely the intensification of partisan polarization that has increased the incentives for ambitious politicians to discount public opinion over the past two decades or so. *We need a dynamic theory of political representation that explains rises and falls in substantive responsiveness as a function of real and changing political and institutional factors.*

Let us be clear, then, about our criticism of the approach Erikson, MacKuen, and Stimson use. Their models examine changes in variables over time. Our point, however, is that the structure and parameters of the statistical models Erikson, MacKuen, and Stimson employ are static.

POLITICS AND POLITICAL REPRESENTATION

Political representation is one of the most significant indicators of the health of a working democracy. Popular sovereignty and the notion that government largely follows the wishes of its citizenry is a normative rationale for representative government. Many of the most heavily studied areas of American politics and political science more generally—from elections and interest groups to legislative and executive politics—are the tools for achieving political representation, and their study is intellectually motivated by just this concern with popular sovereignty. Yet the amount and depth of the actual research on political representation lag far behind the importance attached to it. More and better research on the connection between government policy and the wishes of the citizens is a high priority for political scientists.

Perhaps the most significant challenges for future research on political representation are to include real institutions and political dynamics and to identify variation over time. Failing to examine the political costs and benefits that real politicians associate with responsiveness threatens to construct a mere abstraction. The substantive responsiveness of politicians to centrist opinion varies over time. Identifying this variation and developing grounded explanations for it is a daunting but significant challenge for future research.

NOTES

We greatly appreciate the written comments and gentle persuasion of Jeff Manza; Ben Page posed his usual dose of challenging questions that led us to rethink several key points.

1. Rather than attempting to alter fundamental preferences, most politicians pursue a "priming" strategy that focuses on activating already existing advantageous attitudes and considerations. For instance, opponents of President Clinton's health care reform plan highlighted "big" government to activate already established public uneasiness, just as President Bush has accentuated "choice" in promoting Social Security privatization (Jacobs and Shapiro 2000).

2. For a review of research on public opinion and policymaking, see Jacobs and Shapiro 1994b Burstein (1998a), and Glynn, Herbst, O'Keefe, and Shapiro (1999, chap. 9). Our previous research pointed to the influence of public opinion on policymaking, but it also emphasized that policymakers' responsiveness to public opinion was conditioned by political and institutional dynamics, as evident in the variations across policy issues, time periods, and political environment (Jacobs 1992a, b, and c; 1993; Shapiro 1982; Page and Shapiro 1983, esp. p. 188, n. 17).

3. Party activists influence the selection of candidates not only by dominating the nomination process but also by recruiting candidates. Many candidates are drawn to politics by their initial experience as activists and by their attraction to the policy positions of the party and their fellow activists (Aldrich 1995, chap. 6).

4. Disagreements among scholars stem from difficulties in measuring the preferences and contributions of different groups (Domhoff 1996; Sorauf 1988) and disputes over whether money is dispersed to reflect the distribution of influence in American politics (Sorauf 1988) or concentrated in the hands of blocs of business investors to advance (at least since the 1970s) conservative interests (Ferguson 1995). One challenge (requiring additional research) is linking variations in campaign finance to the rises and falls of responsiveness before 1980.

5. For an explanation of Clinton's placement of health care high on his agenda and his adoption of a managed competition approach, see Jacob Hacker's (1997) careful book.

6. Interview with #16 by LRJ, 12/6/94, in person, White House, Washington, DC.

7. Interviews with members of Congress and advisers to the president were conducted on an anonymous basis by Lawrence Jacobs; each interviewee was assigned a random number. Interview with #16 by LRJ, 12/6/94, in person, White House, Washington, DC; interview with #23 by LRJ, 8/2/94, in person, White House, Washington, DC; interview with #23 by LRJ, 6/28/94, in person, White House, Washington, DC; interview with #17 by

LRJ, 8/1/94, in person, in Washington, DC; interview with #22 by LRJ, 6/28/94, in person, Washington, DC.

8. Interview with administration official #7 by LRJ; interview with #24 by LRJ, telephone, 10/8/97.

9. Interview with #21 by LRJ, 8/2/94, in person, Washington, DC.

10. Memo to Mrs. Clinton from Ira Magaziner, 5/3/93, re: "The Policy"; "Preliminary Work Plan for the Interagency Health Care Task Force," by Magaziner, 1/26/93, notes; memo to Mrs. Clinton from Lynn Magherio regarding waste in current system, 9/18/93; memo to the president and Mrs. Clinton Ira from Magaziner, 3/8/93, regarding health care reform and the budget process; interview with #22 by LRJ. The memos cited here and in nn. 13 and 15 were examined on site at the Clinton White House.

11. Interview with administration official #7 by LRJ.

12. Interview with administration official #7 by LRJ; telephone interview with #25 by LRJ, 6/22/94; interview with #17 by LRJ, 8/1/94, in person, in Washington, DC; interview with #10 by LRJ, Washington, DC, 6/19/95; interview with #22 by LRJ, 6/28/94, in person, Washington, DC; interview with #21 by LRJ, 8/2/94, in person, Washington, DC; interview with #16 by LRJ, 12/6/94, in person, White House, Washington, DC; interview with administration official #7; interview with #20 by LRJ, 8/31/94, telephone; Johnson and Broder (1996).

13. Memo to the president and Mrs. Clinton from Ira Magaziner regarding where we are positioned, 10/1/93; "Long-Term Care: Political Context," 6/2/93, by Ira Magaziner.

14. Interview with #2 by LRJ; interview with #26 by LRJ, 6/28/94, in person, Washington, DC; interview with #1 by LRJ, 12/6/94; interview with #16, notes; interview with #10 by LRJ, Washington, DC, 6/19/95; interview with #13 by LRJ, 8/2/94, in person, Washington, DC; interview with #15 by LRJ, 6/28/94, in person, Washington, DC.

15. Memo to Mrs. Clinton from Bob Boorstin and David Dreyer (copies to McLarty, Rasco, and Magaziner), 1/25/93.

16. Interview with #2 by LRJ.

17. Interview with #2 by LRJ.

18. Interview with #2 by LRJ; interview with #1 by LRJ, 12/6/94.

19. Interview with #2 by LRJ; interview with #8 by LRJ; interview with #16 by LRJ; interview with #15 by LRJ, 6/28/94, in person, Washington, DC.

20. Interview with #24 by LRJ; interview with #10 by LRJ.

21. *New York Times*/CBS News poll, February 22–24, 1996; Weaver, Shapiro, and Jacobs (1995a and b); McClosky and Zaller (1984); *Public Perspective* (1995, p. 28).

22. Princeton Survey Research Associates poll, October 25–30, 1995, for the Times Mirror Center for the People and the Press.

23. Jervis (1997) offers a more complex approach to systems analysis—one that addresses its limitations while harvesting its contributions.

24. Stimson (1991) has tried to account for some of these differences by allowing for an additional dimension or two, but important differences remain both across policy issues at one point in time and over time. The Erikson, MacKuen, and Stimson chapter returns to this issue in footnote 3; our point is that even looking for two or perhaps three dimensions does not sufficiently disaggregate the public's policy attitudes.

25. We thank Ben Page for crystallizing our thinking on this point.

26. Politicians may influence public opinion by priming Americans to alter the standards they use in evaluating government policies rather than by literally altering the public's fundamental preferences (Jacobs 2001; Jacobs and Shapiro 2000).

4

Panderers or Shirkers?

Politicians and Public Opinion

ROBERT S. ERIKSON, MICHAEL B. MACKUEN,
AND JAMES A. STIMSON

In chapter 3 and in an earlier award-winning book (Jacobs and Shapiro 2000), Jacobs and Shapiro argue that "politicians don't pander." What does this mean? Jacobs and Shapiro make a compelling case that politicians are more complicated than mere machines seeking reelection. Politicians, they say, are also motivated by policy considerations. Politicians try to create public policies that, from their diverse ideological perspectives, they perceive to be in the public interest. Jacobs and Shapiro assert, moreover, that when facing the dilemma of satisfying public opinion to stay elected or making good policy, politicians often try to educate the public. For politicians, the policy decision comes first, then the crafting of a message to sell it to the public. When politicians successfully nudge the public's policy preferences closer to their own, they improve their chances both for re-election and achieving desirable public policies.

So far, so good. Political scientists are all too timid in acknowledging that elected politicians actually care about the policies they produce. Of course, members of Congress, for example, are not indifferent to the policy implications of their work. And Jacobs and Shapiro's idea that politicians try to "educate" is a refreshing insight. If they were to stop there, what they say would generate little controversy. The trouble is the next step. What they sometimes seem to *really* mean by "politicians don't pander" is that politicians care, that they try to educate, *and* that they don't give a damn about public opinion. "Pandering," in other words, means being slaves to public opinion and the polls. To do the opposite—not to pander—means ignoring public opinion.

In short, Jacobs and Shapiro write as if compelled not only to defend their favorite explanation but also to challenge the relevance of other contenders. The analogy would be if our work that contends that public opinion does matter (chapter 2 of this volume; Erikson, Stimson, and MacKuen 2002) went on to argue that politicians follow only public opinion at the expense of all else. Then we could title our contribution "Politicians Don't Shirk." Like "not pandering," "not shirking" is an awkward phrase that implies a mono-variable explanation. As applied to politicians, to "shirk" means to ignore the interests of their clients, the public.[1] When a politician's actions stray from the preference of the constituency median voter, the politician "shirks."

Do politicians "not shirk" or do they "not pander"? This would be an unconstructive debate that neither side would (or should!) win. Although we have no quarrel with their *Politicians Don't Pander*, they evidently challenge *The Macro Polity*. The last part of their contribution in chapter 3 launches a critique of our research, summarized in chapter 2, which claims to show policy as responsive to public opinion. Does a fundamental incompatibility prevent politicians from responding both to their own policy preferences and the preferences of their constituents?

Jacobs and Shapiro exaggerate our position. They say we say that "politicians *incessantly* follow public opinion" (p. 24, our italics) as if "public opinion is the only signal that matters" (p. 25). Not so. Perhaps more disturbingly, and in a surprise to us, we are guilty of an alleged "enthusiasm for resuscitating systems analysis" (p. 25), by which they mean a defunct theoretical approach that Sartori proclaimed dead over two decades ago.[2] Finally, we are all wrong in our evidence anyway. We "mis-specify" our model because we "fail to control for endogeneity and spuriousness" (p. 28). As no statistical critique follows this remark, some may interpret it to mean that any statistical evidence that public opinion matters is inherently suspect.

Jacobs and Shapiro do not actually claim that public opinion has no impact on public policy. After all, they purport to take seriously the research showing that public policies or policy changes usually agree with majority opinion or change in opinion. Similarly, we grant that they cannot really believe that our modeling assumes that politicians either have no policy beliefs or set aside their personal beliefs when they make policy. For the rest of this chapter, we focus on areas of agreement and disagreement between us and discuss how the differences and misunderstandings might be resolved. Jacobs and Shapiro raise some interesting points that deserve discussion.

ARE *POLITICIANS DON'T PANDER* AND *THE MACRO POLITY* IN LOGICAL CONFLICT?

Suppose, in the abstract, that X causes Y. What does this fact imply about the possible effect of a rival independent variable—call it Z—on Y? Or, again assuming X causes Y, what does this imply about the possible reverse effect of Y on X? Unless there is a rule of nature that each variable can have but one cause or that there can be no simultaneous effects, the answer, of course, is "nothing." For instance, whether the size of the police force affects the crime rate has no logical bearing on the possible effect of poverty on crime. And if the number of officers affects the crime rate, it does not logically follow that the crime rate cannot affect the number of officers. In fact, the truth of one causal statement will often strengthen the case for the plausibility of the other. When cops on the street actually prevent crime, there is more reason to expect that police will be sent to areas with high crime rates.[3]

The application to the current discussion should be obvious. We see a clear compatibility rather than a logical conflict between Jacobs and Shapiro's work (politicians care about policy and try to educate their constituents) and ours (public opinion matters). First, politicians can be strongly motivated to satisfy both public opinion and their own beliefs. Second, if politicians do influence public opinion, it does not logically follow that public opinion therefore cannot influence politicians and their policy making. Indeed, if politicians try to influence public opinion as Jacobs and Shapiro say they do, the only plausible motivation is because public opinion matters at election time. We develop these points in the following section.

The Public's Preferences versus Personal Preferences?

We begin with the assumption that elected politicians want to construct useful policies and to stay elected, if for no other reason than to be able to make more good policies. What politicians must do to stay elected depends on such matters as the attentiveness of the voters to policy issues and the politicians' ability to discern what the voters want. Suppose voters are totally inattentive to policy. Politicians could manufacture policies without regard to public opinion. Or suppose voters are totally attentive and clearly transmit their preferences to politicians. Politicians would need to pander to the median voter as if their political careers depend on it.[4]

The reality of course is somewhere in between. Jacobs and Shapiro are largely silent on electoral sanctions, offering more discussion of politicians' obligations to extremists in their party constituencies than of obligations to the median voter. Our view is that the overall responsiveness of the electorate is strong enough to compel politicians to respect the electoral consequences of ignoring public opinion—but certainly not strong enough to make them abandon their ideological principles. This is no grudging conception that yes, maybe politicians lead as well as follow. Both individually and collectively, the three of us have always incorporated both conceptions of representation. For example, Stimson said it explicitly in a 1991 precursor to this work: "The postulate is this: Politicians engage in representative behavior because they wish to lead, to have influence on the direction of public opinion" (p. 9). The dichotomy of leading versus following however, is a troublesome simplification. Politicians must stay in touch with public opinion in order to exert the leverage to move it.[5]

Policy-driven politicians do not necessarily thwart policy representation. When politicians make policy based on their personal policy preferences, they can actually enhance representation by providing a valuable policy cue that voters. Instead of relying on the cheap talk of campaign rhetoric, voters can use the information that Democratic and Republican politicians have different policy tastes and choose accordingly. Democratic and Republican politicians may both try to follow public opinion somewhat, but the voters know also that when elected, Democratic politicians "cheat" to the left and Republicans "cheat" to the right. Aggregated to the national level, the party composition of Congress reveals most that is needed to know about the net liberalism-conservatism of the membership.

Politicians Responding to Public Opinion versus Politicians Educating the Public?

The inner workings of policy representation are commonly depicted as politicians responding to exogenous policy preferences emanating from public opinion. Jacobs and Shapiro turn this around to show that politicians often decide on a policy program and then try to convince the public of their position. At first glance, it might seem that if politicians try to educate public opinion, public opinion must actually have little influence on policymaking. But the truth is that one depends on the other. Politicians would likely try to educate the public if the public's policy preferences affect the politicians' electoral fates. Voters' policy positions affect their electoral choices and ultimately public policy. If policy issues were essentially irrelevant to voters, politicians would not need to gain the voters' agreement for the policies they are about to institute.[6]

Does it matter whether voters get their ideas from politicians and other political elites? It is possible to misperceive the contention that public opinion matters as an assertion that public opinion implausibly emanates from the exogenous preferences of uninformed voters—the opinions of the lowly "masses," as opposed to worldly "elites." Although we remain neutral on the matter, it does seem unlikely that the shifting currents of public opinion regularly bubble up exogenously from the bottom strata of society. The alternative is that opinion change originates disproportionately from "elites," including Jacobs and Shapiro's politicians.

That opinion change originates with the opinions of informed "elites" is no reason to diminish the causal connection from opinion to policy. Elite ideas may trickle down to the mass public; mass opinion change then might generate policy change. But this is not to argue that elite consensus is then propagandized to a compliant public for its deferential ratification. Political arguments emanate from competing elite points of view, and the public chooses which to endorse.[7]

HEALTH CARE AND THE FIRST REPUBLICAN CONGRESS:
AN ALTERNATIVE INTERPRETATION

Jacobs and Shapiro present two detailed examples of policymaking—Clinton's failed health care plan and Gingrich's aborted "Contract with America." Jacobs and Shapiro inform us of the zeal and idealism with which elected leaders and their staffs promoted these policies not necessarily because of electoral payoff but because they saw them as "good." According to Jacobs and Shapiro, in each instance the leadership initially held a vision of correct policy; when the policy specifics were burnished, they worked to sell it to the public.

We have no reason to dispute the main points of Jacobs and Shapiro's accounts of these policy events. Of course, one can quibble with the details. For instance, was the "Canadian" health care model scrapped because it was supposedly inferior to "Hillary care," or was it abandoned as too "leftist" and therefore less viable with the public? And did the early post-1994 Republican Congress really pursue a mission too important to be constrained by public opinion? The Republican leadership tried to sell its contract as mandated by the Republican succession to power. One can amass evidence that the congressional Republicans had convinced themselves that they had the ear of the people, only to express befuddlement at extensive public opposition to many of the details.

All this is somewhat beside the point, however. In each instance, two important things happened that receive little notice in the Jacobs and Shapiro narrative. First, both the health care initiative and the contract received a rebuke at the polls—when the public turned Congress over to the Republicans in 1994 and when they gave Clinton his easy victory in 1996.[8] After 1994, a major health care initiative was a dead issue. After 1996, there was no hope of passing the content of the contract. And in each instance, even before the electoral rebuke, the politicians realized that the policy initiative had overreached. Already, by summer 1994, "Hillary care" proved so unpopular that it was pronounced "dead on arrival" when placed at the doorstep of a Democratic Congress. In summer 1996, the Republican Congress, realizing its disadvantage with the more moderate president in the eye of public opinion, desperately tried to backtrack from its rightward course, even passing the first increase in the minimum wage in nearly a decade.

In the end, the essentially moderate public was the decisive determinant of the policy agenda of the 1990s. The Clinton administration steered too far left and then the Republican Congress steered too far right, each convinced that the public supported them. The electorate made the call to produce the ideological balance of divided government.

HAS THE ROLE OF PUBLIC OPINION DECLINED?

Has the importance of public opinion declined over the years? Jacobs and Shapiro say that our work is overly "static" because we did not test for this possibility in our work—to test for (in the lingo of time-series analysis) the presence of time-varying parameters. We chose not to do so, partially because of a belief that our slim data were not up to the task and partially because we saw no compelling theoretical argument for the role of public opinion to vary visibly over the post–World War II span of our analysis.

Jacobs and Shapiro are convinced that the impact of public opinion on policy has been in decline at least since the 1970s. Largely, they argue that the parties have become increasingly polarized ideologically, driven by changes in the nomination system that increase the role of party activists. Obviously, the parties have become increasingly polarized, for reasons scholars continue to investigate. But does it really follow that, just because parties are more polarized, public opinion thus plays a lesser role in policymaking? The matter may be too complicated for confident assertions.

Polarized parties do sharpen the choices available to voters. Indeed, a previous generation of political scientists claimed that policy representation was handicapped by an absence of "responsible" political parties; they meant that parties should provide clear policy choices to guide the electorate toward better collective decisions. Polarized parties now provide that choice.

Polarization enforces the bundling of all issues into coherent sets over which disagreement occurs along party lines. In an early, unpolarized era it was normal for politicians to pick and choose positions without enforced consistency. They could be liberal on social issues yet conservative on economics, conservative on race, yet liberal on other aspects of domestic policy, and so forth. That is now rare. To be conservative in the polarized period is to be conservative, period. And the same for liberals. Where policy is polarized, there is little nuance, and the signal of a bundled public opinion, such as mood, should be all the stronger.

MACRO-ISSUES, MACRO-ANALYSIS VERSUS SINGLE-ISSUE ANALYSIS

As summarized in chapter 2, our analysis of the opinion-policy connection tests for the impact of global opinion, measured as a single dimension of liberalism-conservatism (mood) on policy activity and policy, measured again as one-dimensional liberalism-conservatism. Jacobs and Shapiro say that by aggregating so much we miss the nuances and subtleties of policymaking. Moreover, they note that the political world contains ideological inconsistencies—opinion does not always move the same way in one policy domain as in another, and Congress sometimes makes "liberal" decisions in one domain but "conservative" ones in another. Evidently, they think that each issue and policy decision should be examined separately, as if no common ideological context exists.

If one wishes to explain passage or failure of a specific congressional bill, one might consult opinion polls on that issue (if any) rather than global mood and be prepared to make causal judgments under conditions of few statistical degrees of freedom.[9] We prefer a macroscopic approach precisely because, by aggregating and averaging, "errors" cancel out. The electorate's global taste for liberalism or conservatism will predict the liberal or conservative tone of policy decisions, averaged over many issues. Indeed, this is what we find, and it is difficult to explain away as a statistical illusion.

General versus specific is a familiar argument. How is it to be resolved? If we asserted that the general was also universal, that every specific opinion manifested underlying mood, then finding a single exception would defeat the generalization. But we make no such assertion. We find a common domestic policy domain that does not include issues related to crime or to the abortion controversy. We claim only a high degree of commonality across issues. Then an occasional exception is nothing more than an error term. We can do better than simply argue the matter. We estimate how much variance in public opinion series is common; it is about half.[10]

How do Democrats and liberals manage to overcome the odds and line up on the "liberal" side of health care and the "contract?" How do conservatives managed to sort themselves into the "conservative" position on both? The odds of doing so by chance, taking exception and nuance at face value, are appallingly small. But no reasonable person, Jacobs and Shapiro included, actually believes that everything is independent. Exceptionalism is a useful argument as criticism, impossible to defend as theory.

Actually, when important proposals are both on the legislative agenda and in the public eye, the circumstantial evidence shows that public opinion plays a major role. We have examined available public opinion polls regarding major laws on the eve of their passage. Because the legislative path is fraught with obstacles, one should not expect all popular ideas to become law. But if public opinion is an important part of the policy mix, one should expect Congress to be wary of passing major legislation that polls show to be unpopular. That is the case. Policies that were controversial in our collective memory were popular at the time of passage,[11] including the major civil rights bills of the Johnson years and the major legislation of the early Reagan presidency. In more recent times, the polls showed that the George W. Bush tax cut of 2001 enjoyed a plurality in support. Moreover, we are struck by how roll call support for major legislation tends to be one-sided on final passage, with close votes the interesting exceptions. It is as if much major legislation obtains not only the support of the nation's median voter but also the support of the median voter in the vast majority of states and congressional districts.[12] Could it be that when the preponderant weight of public opinion is unambiguous, members of Congress run like antelopes to the popular position?

Jacobs and Shapiro critique our bundling of disparate issues into a composite measure of liberalism-conservatism for mood. They worry that preferences on different issues—for example, social policy issues and social welfare issues—can move differently over time. By forcing all issues into one aggregation, we compress the variance and "obscure critical patterns of the data" (p. 28). Of course, public opinion does not move in precise lockstep across all issues at the same time. The methodology of mood measurement takes into account that opinion on disparate issues tends to change *in part* due to common currents of shifting ideological change. The mood measurement extracts this commonality, discarding the differences. Specific opinion items are reflected in mood only if they show opinion following the common trend on the dominant dimension.

Assume that the public evaluates politicians in a piecemeal fashion (Fiske 1986), from the sum of their separate behaviors on separate issues rather than merely identifying their global ideological position. Assume also that this is how politicians perceive their reputations, as the sum of the evaluations of their behaviors rather than an evaluation of their global position. The complication (for us) is when a conservative policy might be popular in a liberal era or vice versa.[13] Even so, measuring opinion as the weighted average across many issues distills a common component of policy preference, just as aggregating policy activities or policies distills the common component. Even if voters are inclined to judge by summing microscopic evaluations, the evidence should be visible in an opinion-policy correspondence at the macroscopic level.

Jacobs and Shapiro misunderstand the consequences that would result if public opinion were more multidimensional than our portrayal. A worst case would be if responses to poll items on salient issues move independently of the common trends mood identified. Opinion on these items would be heavily discounted, ignored, or (if countercyclical) even given the wrong sign in the measurement of mood. Such a hypothetical distortion of the evidence would work against the representation hypothesis, not provide false support. If mood misses opinions on key issues salient to the public, these omissions make all the more remarkable the fact that a flawed measure still predicts policymaking and policy.

CONCLUSIONS

The title of this chapter sets up a false dichotomy. Politicians in the representation process do not choose pandering or shirking. These choices imply excessive reliance on opinion polls or constituency abandonment. Elected politicians deal with the complex trade of satisfying constituents (to stay elected) versus achieving "good" policy. Jacobs and Shapiro show one solution to this problem: convince the constituents of the "goodness" of one's preferred policies. But even through politicians try to persuade (and are sometimes successful) the public controls its policy destiny.

NOTES

1. This usage of "shirking" traces to certain economists who have ventured into the study of politics. Interestingly, economists view the representation process differently from political scientists. Whereas political scientists are conditioned to be skeptical of claims that democracy works the way it is supposed to, economists are conditioned to believe in

their theories, not the facts. For economists, the starting point for understanding democratic politics is that politicians must behave as the agent for the median voter (e.g., Downs 1957). The interesting questions to economists are why theory sometimes fails and why elected officials often shirk their duty by, among other things, following their own conception of the public interest.

2. We plead guilty as charged for the offense of portraying a causal "system." "System" is one of a handful of great unifying ideas in science. A political science that rejected it would itself need resuscitation.

3. In this example of cops and crime, the two simultaneous effects have opposite signs. The same logic can apply for two simultaneous effects with the same sign. A political science example is the relationship between a nation's electoral system and its number of political parties. A system of proportional representation encourages multiple parties. This only encourages the complementary effect—that nations with multiple parties tend to adopt proportional representation.

4. The logic of Downs's model of party competition would apply. Both candidates in a two-candidate race must represent the median voter because the opponent would successfully exploit any deviation.

5. We lay no claim to the originality of this idea. For an excellent explication, see Geer (1996).

6. Jacobs and Shapiro hint at a nonelectoral motivation for politicians influencing voter opinion. At several places, they write of politicians engaging in "simulated responsiveness," whereby politicians "influence public opinion in order to create the *appearance* of responsiveness to public opinion" (p. 30, their italics). They do not fully develop the reasons why politicians would wish to engage in this baroque maneuver.

7. A good example of elite manipulation of public opinion is provided by the Public Accommodations Bill of 1964. Before passage, polls show that opinion shifted from about an even split to about 2:1 in favor of the bill. This growth is generally attributed to the appeals of President Johnson and to the acquiescence of Republican congressional leaders, awakened to the need for legislative change (countering a rival Southern elite message). If we grant that elite propaganda molded this change in mass opinion, public opinion's degree of responsibility for the bill's enactment does not correspondingly diminish. It is doubtful that the Public Accommodations Act would have passed without a decisive majority of public opinion. Moreover, continuing the role of public opinion in shaping policy, Republican presidential nominee Barry Goldwater's opposition to the Public Accommodations Act contributed to the 1964 Democratic landslide for both president and Congress.

8. Or at least that is the commonly believed causal story. The attribution of reasons for election outcomes is not easily subject to validation.

9. Health care is an intriguing exception. In the 1990 to 1993 period leading to the health care debate of 1994, movement specific to the health care domain was notably more liberal—the trends stronger—than was the case for the full domestic agenda. (Notably also in this period of great public support for change, nonpanderers from both sides of the aisle were jumping on board the reform bandwagon.) One would have done better predicting the eventual defeat from global mood than from measures specific to health care. Eventually the specific converged on the global; the support for radical change did not exist.

10. More specifically, we estimate explained variance by an Eigenvalue analogue. Using the full set of all known repeated question series, a set that includes large numbers of series on crime and abortion controversies that we know do not belong to the mood domain, we estimate an overall first dimension explained variance of 42. Excluding the

nonloading items produces numbers in the 50–60 range. These numbers imply correlations between series and scale that average .80 or more.

11. We define major laws as those in Mayhew's (1991) "sweep one"—seen as important at the time. Our inspection is item-driven, limited to bills that were unambiguously in the public eye as they became law. In admirable studies, Monroe (1979, 1998) performs poll-driven searches for congruence between majority opinion in polls and subsequent policy decisions. His data also show that policy changes in the face of public opposition are rare events.

12. Although not actual legislation and therefore technically outside the bounds of this discussion, the majority votes for Clinton's impeachment and conviction could be cited as a prominent contrary example when a majority of Congress members willingly took high-profile positions contrary to majority opinion. We offer a simple explanation for this salient counterexample: like almost all Washington insiders, congressional Republicans believed that support for Clinton would plummet as the revelations grew, making momentary polls irrelevant. By the time the error of this assessment became obvious, it was too late for the majority Republicans to change. They could retreat at considerable political embarrassment or they could continue in their impeachment quest, hoping that public opinion would eventually catch up to their interpretation. This act of nonpandering carried a political cost, arguably being the major reason Republicans were denied gains in the 1998 congressional elections.

13. Both liberal and conservative policy ideas vary in their popularity quite independent of mood. For instance, expansion of the minimum wage (liberal) and reducing welfare (conservative) are generally popular but vary with the national mood.

5

Public Opinion and Congressional Action on Labor Market Opportunities, 1942–2000

PAUL BURSTEIN

Most of those who study the impact of public opinion on public policy believe that the more salient the issue, the greater the impact of public opinion (Jones 1994; Page and Shapiro 1983). If this is true, groups with public support would want to increase the salience of issues on which they want action, whereas their opponents would want the issues decided as quietly as possible (Schattschneider 1960). Because salience appears so important to the outcome of political conflict, those who study democratic politics (Hilgartner and Bosk 1988; Jones 1994) have devoted their attention to determining why some issues become the object of intense public concern yet others do not.

Much less attention has been devoted to the implications of several cold, hard facts about salience: few issues will be salient at a time, issues salient at one time will almost inevitably lose the public's attention eventually, and most issues will never be salient to much of the public. The public cannot deal with many issues at once, and, indeed, legislatures cannot give more than routine attention to most issues either (Krehbiel 1991). If governments respond to public opinion mainly on salient issues, and most issues are not salient, then overall responsiveness will not be great. This would be the result not of a failure of democratic institutions but of limitations intrinsic to individuals and organizations.

But is the relationship between public opinion and public policy strongly affected by issue salience? There is certainly some evidence that this is the case (Burstein 1998b; Jones 1994; Page and Shapiro 1983), but surprisingly few studies examine the impact of salience on responsiveness across a wide range of issues or over a substantial period of time. This chapter adds to our knowledge by examining the relationship between public opinion and policy on an issue sometimes of great concern to the public, but most often not, over a period of almost sixty years: labor market opportunities for minorities and women, as addressed by Congress since the early 1940s. Federal action against labor market discrimination was long a key demand of the civil rights movement; it became central to the women's movement; and in recent years Congress has been asked to enhance opportunities for new groups and in new ways.

Salience, it seems, does not matter as much as some think. Congressional action *is* consistent with public opinion when salience is high. But congressional action is also consistent with public opinion when salience is low, provided trends in public opinion are clear. When salience is low *and* public opinion divided or ambiguous, congressional action is affected by other factors, particularly party ideology.

SALIENCE, PUBLIC OPINION, AND PUBLIC POLICY

That salience affects democratic responsiveness has long been taken for granted. Elected officials must please their constituents to be reelected. However, responsiveness is especially important on issues that matter greatly to their constituents; those are the issues most likely to affect constituents' votes (Arnold 1990; Jones 1994; Kingdon 1984). Groups involved in political conflict know this and act accordingly. Those whose desires match the public's try to get the public involved; those whose policy goals counter public opinion try to limit conflict, hoping to keep the issues that matter to them off the public agenda altogether (Jacob 1988).

Many studies report how difficult it is to win the public's attention. Until relatively recently, though, the reasons why, and their implications, have received little systematic attention. Analyses of the cognitive capacities of individuals and the processing capacities of legislatures reach similar conclusions: neither individuals nor organizations can give sustained, focused attention to many things at once. In politics, no more than a few issues can be salient to the public at any one time (Hilgartner and Bosk 1988; Jones 1994; Krehbiel 1991; McCombs and Zhu 1995).

This conclusion has a striking implication for democratic responsiveness: if legislators are most responsive on issues salient to the public, but the vast majority of issues cannot possibly be salient, then responsiveness becomes problematic. Indeed, if most citizens care about only a few issues, then why should governments be responsive on others, even when all the institutions of democracy—the electoral system, freedom of speech, voluntary organizations, etc.—are working well?

Two related arguments suggest that responsiveness might be substantial anyway, at least over the long term; the first pertains to the variability of salience, the second to the possible importance of the public's general "policy mood." Legislators may be reluctant to depart too far from what they believe their constituents want, even on issues constituents care little about, because they worry that a challenger at the next election may *make* issues salient and portray the incumbent as out of touch with district opinion (Arnold 1990; cf. McCombs and Zhu 1995). Difficult as it may be to increase an issue's salience to the public, doing so may often be easier than altering substantive public opinion. Policy may drift away from public opinion when the public is indifferent, but, should an attempt to increase salience succeed, policy will likely follows public opinion (Jones 1994).

But how far can policy "drift away" from public opinion? If it can drift far away, for a long time, the concept of responsiveness to public opinion may become so attenuated that it is almost meaningless.

One conventional response to this question is to contend that even if public opinion does not force legislators to adopt specific policies, it limits their freedom of action; they fear that if they depart too far from public opinion, they risk electoral defeat. How are legislators' actions circumscribed? Some say that legislators must conform to the "national mood" or enact legislation manifesting "an idea whose time had come" (Kingdon 1984, pp. 153–57; Skocpol 1995, p. 728). Unfortunately, these vague terms offer little help in assessing the responsiveness of a legislature to public opinion.

Recently, though, Stimson (1999) has rigorously defined and measured what he calls the "domestic policy mood," the public's view toward the size of government. Changes in policy mood have a substantial effect on policy change; when public opinion moves in a liberal direction, so does public policy; when it moves in a conservative direction, policy follows. Purportedly, elected officials are effectively deciding that, although most issues are not salient to their constituents and not likely to become so, the safe thing is to support policies consistent with broad trends in public opinion. We still do not know how far public policy drifts from public opinion on most issues, but we think that legislators, aware of broad trends in public opinion hesitate to let it drift very far.

This still leaves us with the fact that the policy mood may be consistent with many policies. For example, there may be numerous ways of making welfare policy more conservative or liberal. When trying to choose among policies, elected officials often find that the public favors no particular policy more than the others, or that people are ambivalent about the proposals (Feldman and Zaller 1992). Often, too, public opinion data (if there are any) are ambiguous. In such circumstances, elected officials may make decisions based on factors other than public opinion. Political ideology often seems especially important (Aldrich 1995, chap. 6; Page, 1978, chap. 2). Clear public opinion (policy mood or opinion on a particular issue) pushes both major parties in the same direction. When it is not clear, ideology may dominate legislators' decision making.

In sum, recent work leads us to expect that (1) on issues salient to the public,

public opinion strongly affects policy; (2) few issues will be salient at a time, and many will never be salient; (3) on nonsalient issues, policy is likely to drift away from public opinion, constrained to some degree by the public's general policy mood; and (4) when the public is ambivalent about an issue, or data about preferences are ambiguous, then political ideology, among other factors, will likely influence what elected officials do. We now try to determine whether these expectations accord with congressional action on labor market opportunity since the 1940s.

CONGRESSIONAL ACTION ON LABOR MARKET OPPORTUNITIES, 1942–2000

Twentieth-century congressional action on minorities' labor market opportunities began in 1942, with the introduction of the first bill proposing to prohibit labor market discrimination on the basis of race, religion, and national origin. That first bill had only one sponsor, but support grew, slowly but fairly steadily, until, twenty-two years later, equal employment opportunity (EEO) legislation was enacted as Title VII of the Civil Rights Act of 1964. During this entire period, support for EEO almost always meant one thing: support for the "classic" bill, written during the mid-1940s and hardly changed subsequently (Burstein 1998, chap. 2).

One element of the classic bill was altered dramatically and unexpectedly during floor debate on Title VII in the House of Representatives. For reasons never entirely clear, one of the Southern opponents of the civil rights bill proposed that Title VII be amended to prohibit discrimination on the basis of sex (Burstein 1998b, pp. 22–23). Initially the amendment divided congressional supporters of civil rights (which was one of the sponsor's purposes), but in the end it was enacted. To the surprise of practically everyone, Title VII prohibited discrimination not only on the basis of race, religion, and national origin but on the basis of sex as well.[1]

The amendment had been adopted with little discussion or thought about the consequences. Gradually, however, its implications started to emerge. The amendment had not simply added to the classic bill one more basis on which discrimination was prohibited; it was the basis for two transformations in thinking about labor market opportunities and, soon enough, the stimulus of much congressional action.

The first transformation was a seemingly simple conceptual breakthrough. Almost all EEO bills introduced before 1964 had proposed to prohibit discrimination on the basis of race, religion, and national origin; this standard set of categories, repeated over and over (and included without alteration in most of the Civil Rights Act), had become a litany central to discourse about discrimination. After sex was added to the list, it occurred to people that groups defined in other ways could be protected from discrimination as well. Enactment of the

Americans with Disabilities Act of 1990 and ongoing efforts in Congress to prohibit labor market discrimination on the basis of sexual orientation were made possible by this breakthrough.[2]

The second transformation was more complex. Unlike prohibiting discrimination on the basis of race, religion, and national origin, banning sex discrimination raised questions not only about labor markets but also about the connection between work and home. Traditionally, according to conventional middle-class ideology, women quit work when they became pregnant, and then they stayed home to raise their children and care for their husbands (and possibly other family members, such as grandparents). Women who did not accede to this view voluntarily were often forced into it, as employers limited their opportunities and relatives and friends pushed them into conventional roles.

Once sex discrimination was prohibited, however, new questions arose. Employers could not legally treat women as a class differently than men, but could they single out women who were pregnant and treat *them* differently? If women increasingly remained in the labor force when pregnant and when they had small children, who would be at home to take care of family emergencies? These and related questions, stimulated in part by the implications of Title VII, led to the development of a new set of ideas about work and family and a new "package" of legislative proposals directed at work-family accommodation (Burstein, Bricher, and Einwohner 1995).

Thus far, issues raised by the prohibition of sex discrimination have prompted the enactment of three federal laws: the Pregnancy Discrimination Act of 1978, which declared differential treatment on the basis of pregnancy to be a form of sex discrimination; the Retirement Equity Act of 1984, which takes changes in gender roles into account in the regulation of pensions; and the Family and Medical Leave Act of 1993, which requires many employers to give employees time off (unpaid, but on a gender-neutral basis) to care for newborns, newly adopted children, and family members who are ill or injured.

Thus, congressional action on labor market opportunities after 1964 branched off in two new directions: toward banning discrimination against more groups and dealing with the consequences of gender equality. But that was not the full extent of congressional action; it continued along the same path it had been following since the 1940s as well. Its first major action after 1964 was to complete the agenda set down in the 1940s, enacting in 1972 the Equal Employment Opportunity Act enforcement provisions rejected in 1964 (see Burstein 1998). Later, prompted by a series of Supreme Court decisions that consistently read EEO laws narrowly and weakened their enforcement, Congress passed in 1991 an additional civil rights act to overturn those decisions and strengthen Title VII in other ways (Public Law 102–166, the Civil Rights Act of 1991).

No discussion of congressional action (or the action of any legislature) would be complete without a consideration of *in*action as well—that is, a consideration of actions Congress might have taken but did not. Analyses of public opinion and public policy that ignore inaction run the risk of underestimating respon-siveness, by failing to account for the many policies not changed because current policy is consistent with public opinion. A list of all possibilities for inaction would be virtually infinite, but three seem especially worth noting. First, Congress could have voted to significantly weaken, or even to repeal, Title VII. This may seem unlikely, but it is important to remember that, while running for president in 1968, George Wallace "demanded that national Democrats repeal the civil rights law, and foretold otherwise an 'uprising' on a par with the revolt against Recon-struction" (Branch 1998, p. 456). White Southern opposition to the civil rights laws was intense, and given the history of Reconstruction to which Wallace re-ferred, it is not at all unreasonable to expect a great deal of effort devoted to repeal, or at least to weakening it. Attempts to weaken or abrogate major pieces of social legislation have occurred; the Taft-Hartley amendments to the National Labor Relations Act and the recent abrogation of New Deal welfare legislation are examples.

Second, and somewhat more narrowly, Congress could have acted to end probably the most controversial aspect of EEO enforcement: affirmative action. Certainly there have been many calls for ending it, and President Reagan proposed ending that part of affirmative action based in presidential executive orders, but he did not act, and neither has Congress.

Finally, Congress might have responded to a Supreme Court decision limiting enforcement of Title VII's ban on religious discrimination. Title VII did not just require employers to treat adherents of all religions the same way; it went beyond that, requiring that when equal treatment had the effect of harming an employee because of his or her religious practices or beliefs, then the employer had to make a "reasonable accommodation" to those practices or beliefs. (For example, if a requirement that all employees work on Saturdays harmed observant Jews for-bidden to work on the sabbath, the employer might have to rearrange their work schedules.) In 1977, the Supreme Court ruled (*Hardison v. Trans World Airlines, Inc.* 432 U.S. 63) that significant accommodations amounted to preferential treat-ment, so employers could not be required to make more than minimal accom-modations. This decision was made on statutory, not constitutional, grounds and could have been overturned by Congress, just as Congress overturned Supreme Court decisions when it enacted the Pregnancy Discrimination Act and the Civil Rights Act of 1991 (Beckley and Burstein 1991). Considering how important re-ligion and religious observance have become in political discourse during the last several decades, one might have expected Congress to act on behalf of the reli-giously observant, whose practices seemingly led to their being denied employ-ment opportunities. But beyond the introduction of a few bills, there was no congressional action.

In sum, it has been sixty years since the question of labor market oppor-tunities for minorities and women entered the congressional agenda. The first thirty of those years were devoted to winning passage of the classic 1940s EEO bill, twenty-two to achieve enactment of much of the bill—without much of its provision for government enforcement—as Title VII of the Civil Rights Act of 1964, and another eight to win a strong provision for government enforcement. The years since 1972 have seen much more varied activity. The unanticipated addition of a prohibition of sex discrimination to Title VII in 1964 led to subsequent developments along two paths—attempts to protect additional groups from discrimination and to address the consequences of EEO for women—while disputes with the Supreme Court led to the clarification and strengthening of Title VII. Instances of congressional inaction (lack of attempts to weaken or repeal Title VII, to end affirmative action, or to strengthen requirements for the accommodation of minority religious practices, see table 5.1) have been just as important. How have congressional action and inaction been affected by public opinion and by the salience of labor market opportunity issues to the public?

Table 5.1 Congressional Action and Inaction on Employment Opportunities

Protect New Groups	*Strengthen Title VII*	*Gender and Family*
Action		
1942–64 Fight to prohibit employment on the basis of race, religion, national origin		
	1972 Enforcement by EEOC	
		1978 Pregnancy Discrimination Act
1979 Bills to prohibit discrimination on the basis of sexual orientation		
		1984 Retirement Equity Act
1990 Americans with Disabilities Act		
	1991 Civil Rights Act	
		1993 Family and Medical Leave Act
Inaction		
1964 No repeal or weakening Title VII		
1979–80 Peak support for more religious accommodation: 32 sponsors		
1981–82 Peak support for bills broadly attacking affirmative action: 5 sponsors		

PUBLIC OPINION, SALIENCE, AND
CONGRESSIONAL ACTION

Many of those who study democratic politics believe that (1) public opinion strongly affects public policy on issues salient to the public; (2) most issues, however, are not salient, and on those issues, policy is likely to drift away from public opinion, constrained, perhaps, by the public's general policy mood; and (3) when the public is ambivalent about an issue or its preferences are unclear, elected officials' political ideology will affect their actions. Are these expectations consistent with congressional action on labor market opportunity since the early 1940s?

When Issues Are Salient

Congressional action on EEO from 1942 to 1964 is a classic case of responsiveness to the public's opinions *and* intensity of concern. When the first EEO bill was introduced, a majority of whites favored racial discrimination in the workplace, and a very substantial proportion of Americans were prejudiced against Jews and other minorities; the bill got just one sponsor. As public support for equal treatment increased during the following decades, congressional support for EEO legislation—measured in terms of sponsorship—increased as well. But increased public support for equal treatment did not lead to legislation until the issue came to matter greatly to the public; only when a majority of the public saw civil rights as one of the most important issues facing the country was the Civil Rights Act of 1964 adopted. Neither civil rights demonstrations, lobbying, nor the party balance directly affected congressional action; Congress was responding to the opinions of an intensely concerned majority (Burstein 1998b, chaps. 3–5).

There are three interesting parallels between the enactment of Title VII and the welfare reform Weaver describes (chap. 6). Congress acted only when the salience of the issue rose dramatically; the public demanded congressional action, without being too concerned about what form the action would take; and control of the agenda mattered a great deal. The nature of agenda control differed, however. On welfare, the party balance mattered; Republican proposals for welfare reform differed from Democratic proposals, and the Republican victory in the 1994 congressional elections influenced which proposals would pass. On EEO, interest groups mattered. All the interest groups strongly concerned about the issue (meaning all major civil rights organizations) had been promoting the classic bill for over twenty years when Congress felt overwhelming pressure to act. With no alternatives on the agenda, and the public unconcerned about details, it was almost inevitable that any bill enacted would be favored by the proponents of the classic bill, that is, the civil rights organizations and their congressional allies (see also Burstein 1998).

Public concern about civil rights, at least as measured by Gallup's "most important problem" question, fell rapidly after the mid-1960s and has never approached its former peak; the same is true of newspaper coverage (Burstein 1998, p. 80; McCombs and Zhu 1995). None of the other labor market opportunity issues described has evoked widespread concern either. For example, while the bill that became the Civil Rights Act of 1991—a bill of great importance to civil rights and women's organizations, and to liberal organizations generally—was being considered by Congress, the *Los Angeles Times* conducted a national survey that virtually invited people to declare civil rights an important issue by asking: "If Congress and the president could do only one thing in the next few months, which would you prefer to see them do: would you prefer that they harden laws against criminals, or require people to wait seven days before buying a handgun, or strengthen civil rights laws, or allow workers more time off for family emergencies, or deal with this country's energy problems?" The percentage of respondents preferring action on civil rights? Nine. (For information about this and other surveys, including question wording when not here in the text, see the appendix, unless another source is specified.) Indeed, approximately three-fifths of the public had neither seen, read, nor heard anything about the bill, about the same proportion as those who had seen nothing about the family and medical leave bills first introduced in the mid-1980s. As expected, in other words, after the mid-1960s the public as a whole was not too concerned about the labor market opportunity issues Congress addressed. Was Congress responsive to the public nevertheless?

When Issues Are Not Salient

When the public cares relatively little about an issue, policy is likely to drift away from public opinion, influenced, perhaps, by the public's general policy mood. And when the public is ambivalent about an issue or its preferences are not clear, then political ideology is likely to influence elected officials. Was congressional action on labor market opportunity in line with these expectations?

For the most part, the answer is yes. Congressional action was very much in line with public opinion on the Equal Employment Opportunity Act of 1972, the Americans with Disabilities Act, the Family and Medical Leave Act, the Pregnancy Discrimination Act, and the Retirement Equity Act; and its disinclination to weaken or repeal Title VII was consistent with public opinion as well (table 5.2). Congress was seemingly unresponsive on just one issue: it did not address affirmative action, even though the public opposed it.

Of all the issues examined here, it was the EEO Act of 1972 on which public opinion was clearest, and Congress acted accordingly. Although public intensity of concern about civil rights declined rapidly after the mid-1960s, opinions about discrimination became ever more liberal. By 1972, almost everyone favored EEO for blacks in principle, prejudice against religious minorities was declining, and two-thirds of the public said they would be more likely to vote for a candidate who favored improving opportunities for blacks and women (Burstein 1998b, pp. 48, 67). These trends also explain why members of Congress never tried to

Table 5.2 Public Opinion and Congressional Action or Inaction,
Low-Salience Issues

Action or Inaction	*Action*	*Inaction*
Consistent with		
Public opinion on specific issue	Equal Employment Opportunity Act of 1972	Not repealing or weakening Title VII
	Americans with Disabilities Act of 1990?	
	Family and Medical Leave Act of 1993?	
General trends in public opinion, opinion on specific issue unknown	Pregnancy Discrimination Act of 1978	
	Retirement Equity Act of 1984	
Inconsistent with		
Public opinion on specific issue		Failure to end affirmative action
General trends in public opinion, opinion on specific issues unknown		
Public is ambivalent, or **data are ambiguous**	Increasing *sponsorship* of bills to prohibit discrimination on the basis of sexual orientation	*Enactment* of bill to prohibit discrimination on the basis of sexual orientation
	Civil Rights Act of 1991	
No data		Lack of action on religious accommodation

weaken or repeal Title VII. Although prejudice against minorities and women in the labor market remains a problem, the long, liberalizing trend that lasted from the 1940s through the 1970s has never been reversed (Schuman, Steeh, Bobo, and Krysan 1997); there has never been any reason to think that a majority of the public would want Title VII weakened or repealed.

Congress had fewer poll data on most of the other labor market issues, but on several the general trend in public sentiment would have been clear. There seem to be almost no data on discrimination against people with disabilities, but the one survey I found shows 95% of respondents supporting legislation banning employment discrimination against the disabled, with 83% still supporting a ban even if employers had to make reasonable accommodations to the needs of disabled employees, and 89% when told that the law might be expensive to implement. The relevance of this survey is problematic because it was conducted almost a year after the Americans with Disabilities Act became law, but the one-sided results suggest that, had the questions been asked a year earlier, support would have been comparable.

Public support for the Family and Medical Leave Act must, for the most part, be inferred from trends in responses to survey questions about men's and women's roles in the labor force and at home. Every trend shows increasing support for women's labor market participation and greater equality in the home. For example, the percentage of the public approving married women's labor force participation rose from 60 in 1970 to 81 in 1990; the percentage disagreeing with the claim that it is better for everyone if the husband works and the wife stays home rose from 34 in 1977 to 60 in 1990; and the percentage agreeing that working mothers can establish relationships with their children just as warm as those that mothers who do not work form rose from 49 in 1977 to 70 in 1994 (see Burstein and Wierzbicki 2000 for more details).

These trends would suggest to members of Congress that the public was increasingly favorable to a family and medical leave act, intended to help employees deal with family responsibilities without being penalized at work. The one survey item I found that focuses specifically on family and medical leave policy is consistent with this view. After President Bush vetoed a family and medical leave bill passed by Congress in 1992, 57% of the public to whom the situation was described said he should have signed the bill, while 36% said he had done the "right thing." Congressional reenactment of the leave bill the next year, and President Clinton's signing it, were consistent with the public's views.

Apparently no polls gauged public opinion on the Pregnancy Discrimination Act or the Retirement Equity Act. This means that members of Congress wanting poll data would have had to rely on broad opinion trends that, as already noted, showed ever more support for gender equality in the workplace. Congressional action was consistent with these trends.

Congress has not enacted any labor market opportunity legislation in the face of majority public opposition, but there is one issue on which its inaction seems to defy public opinion: affirmative action. During the 1960s and 1970s there was a great deal of public debate about what affirmative action meant, essentially a political and philosophical struggle over what could be done to overcome discrimination. Initial attempts to get the public to perceive affirmative action as remedial, as a way of "redressing the continuing effects of a history of racial discrimination" (Gamson and Modigliani 1987, p. 145) were eventually defeated by the "no preferential treatment" frame, in which affirmative action becomes preferential treatment and unfair advantage to some at the expense of others (Gamson and Modigliani 1987, pp. 145–46).

The vagueness of the term and the struggle over meaning have made interpreting the public's responses to questions about affirmative action difficult; even knowing what questions to ask is problematic (Steeh and Krysan 1996, p. 129). The suggestion that blacks or other minorities get preferences in jobs generally wins the support of no more than a quarter of the general population (Steeh and

Krysan 1996, p. 130). One analysis of data from many surveys conducted between 1970 and 1995 concludes that white adults do not favor preferences, quotas, or economic aid for blacks when these questions are generally phrased (Steeh and Krysan 1996, p. 140). The recent success of state referenda opposing affirmative action also suggests considerable public antagonism to it.

The pervasiveness of opposition to affirmative action leads Steeh and Krysan (1996, p. 140) to ask "why we still have affirmative action programs if public opposition has always been and continues to be so strong." This is a good question. They suggest that the public is actually ambivalent about affirmative action, favoring a bit of help for blacks, provided it does not turn into quotas or much preferential treatment (also see Burstein 1992, p. 917). In addition, it should be noted that "affirmative action" as a legal term employed in Title VII is one of the key indicators of how the law is to be enforced; when discrimination has been found, the courts may require the discriminators to take action to rectify what they have done—that is, they must take "affirmative action." Eliminating affirmative action in this sense would drastically weaken Title VII, something that the public does not want. Still, why have even the strongest congressional opponents of affirmative action made no serious legislative attempt to end it? Congressional action does seem to be inconsistent with public opinion in ways that are difficult to dismiss and to explain.[3]

What about issues on which the public is plainly ambivalent, or data are ambiguous or altogether lacking? The suggestion that Congress should prohibit employment discrimination on the basis of sexual orientation is relatively new, and it is easy to imagine members of Congress being very uncertain how to respond to public opinion on this issue. On the one hand, a majority of the public has favored "equal rights in terms of job opportunities" for homosexuals (to quote Gallup's question wording) ever since the late 1970s, when the first bills on the subject were introduced, and the percentage has increased substantially, from 56% in 1977 to 80% and more during the 1990s. On the other hand, over 40% of the public says that "homosexual relations between consenting adults" should not be legal, a percentage that changed little between the late 1970s and the late 1990s, and members of Congress would be very aware of the storm of protest that erupted when the newly inaugurated President Clinton proposed a prohibition of discrimination against gays in the military.

In this context, congressional sponsorship of bills to prohibit employment discrimination on the basis of sexual orientation has risen in recent years. After an initial burst of support in 1979–80, when such bills had 61 sponsors, support fell to almost zero during the Reagan and Bush presidencies, but rose immediately to 137 sponsors when Clinton took office and has risen in every congress since, to 207 in the current Congress; such a bill narrowly failed in the Senate in 1996, losing by 49–50. Public opinion may be read as increasingly favorable to EEO for homosexuals, and congressional support for such bills has increased. It may also be read as implying that the public is quite uncomfortable with homosexuals, so no such bill has been enacted.

Similarly, public opinion on the Civil Rights Act of 1991 did not clearly point in one direction or another. Bills whose content became the core of the act were first introduced during the 1989–90 Congress. Neither then nor later did most people know that such a bill was being considered. In a Gallup poll conducted just after Congress had passed a civil rights bill in fall 1990 and President Bush had vetoed it, 61% said they had never heard of it. In May 1991, after a similar bill had been introduced in the new congress, 77% had not heard of the bill and another 5% were not sure. When only those who had heard of the bill were asked their opinion of it, the answers were quite evenly split: 8% in favor and 5% opposed in May 1991, for example, and 12% in favor and 14% opposed in June. After President Bush vetoed the bill in 1990, 40% of the public, when told what he had done, agreed that he should have vetoed it, while 47% said he should have signed it. In May 1991, when the bill was again on the agenda and there were significant differences between the Republicans and Democrats in Congress, 49% of a half-sample approved of the way Republicans were handling civil rights, 47% approved of the Democrats, and 53% of the whole sample approved of the actions of Congress as a whole. It would be difficult to read into these data a strong endorsement either supporting or opposing the bill.

One issue remains: religious accommodation and congressional failure to act in response to the Supreme Court's 1977 decision severely limiting the extent to which employers might be expected to accommodate the needs of religious minorities. This decision was a significant matter to those concerned about religious discrimination (Beckley and Burstein 1991), but it provoked little congressional reaction and no public opinion polling at all. It would certainly be fair to say that congressional inaction was consistent with public inattention.

In summary, congressional action on labor market opportunities was strongly influenced by public opinion on the one issue highly salient to the public, namely, Title VII, as part of the Civil Rights Act of 1964. In addition, it was consistent with public opinion on all but one of the issues on which public opinion was fairly clear, even if the only opinion data available pertained to general trends in relevant attitudes, rather than opinions on specific legislative proposals. Congressional action on discrimination on the basis of sexual orientation—increasing sponsorship, but no passage—seems in line with public ambivalence about homosexuals, and its inaction on religious accommodation seems reasonable, given the complete lack of demand for action.

On two issues Congress does not appear to be responding to public opinion on a low-salience issue. By passing the Civil Rights Act of 1991 when the public was about evenly split, to the extent it had any opinions at all, Congress could not be said to have been responding to public opinion, but it was not going against public opinion either. The one issue on which congressional action (or, rather, inaction) seems opposed to public opinion is affirmative action; the public opposes it, but Congress has not acted to end it. Thus, of the ten issues in table 5.2 (counting bills to prohibit discrimination on the basis of sexual orientation only once), congressional action has been consistent with public opinion on eight, has acted when the public was split on one, and contradicted public opinion on one.

Congressional action is generally quite consistent with public opinion on labor market opportunity policies, not necessarily because Congress responds to public opinion. Public opinion was perhaps manipulated by political elites; perhaps the public was responding to policymakers rather than policymakers responding to the public. Party leaders have affected the political ramifications of some race and gender attitudes (Carmines and Stimson 1989). But the trends in attitudes on minorities and gender reported here are of long standing, and though some have suggested (Zaller 1992, pp. 8–13) that these trends were influenced by elite discourse, no one has shown that the trends are the product of manipulation. It seems far more likely that Congress responded to public opinion than the reverse.

Focusing on differences between the two major parties, we now consider how congressional action was influenced by political ideology when the public was ambivalent or information about its preferences has ambiguous.

PARTY, IDEOLOGY, AND CONGRESSIONAL ACTION

Ideological differences between the Democrats and Republicans influence their stances on labor market opportunities in two ways. The first is party differences on minorities and gender. Between 1942 and 1964, EEO was not a partisan issue. Both Republicans and northern Democrats sponsored EEO bills to win blacks' votes, and the parties did not differ overall in their support for such bills (Burstein 1998b, chap. 5; cf. Carmines and Stimson 1989).

Beginning during the 1950s, however, some Republicans began to think that they could split the New Deal coalition by appealing to white Southern Democrats antagonized by the increasing racial liberalism of their northern counterparts. The potential impact of such an appeal was manifested dramatically in 1964, when Barry Goldwater's victory in several Southern states was attributed directly to his opposition to the Civil Rights Act of 1964. Continuing huge Republican gains among white Southerners led blacks, split between Democrats and Republicans as recently as 1960, to swing practically unanimously into the Democratic Party. The resulting racial polarization of the parties has been one of the major developments in American politics since the mid-1960s.

Accompanying this polarization has been a growing gender gap, as women have become disproportionately Democratic and men Republican. As with race, the first hints of partisanship on gender issues appeared during the 1950s. The gap grew during the 1960s and 1970s and almost reached its current level during the 1980 presidential race, when Ronald Reagan repudiated long-standing Republican support for the Equal Rights Amendment (Manza and Brooks 1999, chap. 5). The Republicans have increasingly been identified with views favoring the "traditional" family, in which the mother stays home with the children, and as less sympathetic than the Democrats to the movement for gender equality and women's autonomy (Costain 1992). Republican Party support for what its leaders proclaim to be traditional values has been associated with antipathy toward homosexuals as well.

The second relevant difference between Democrats and Republicans is their position on the regulation of business. Labor market opportunity bills are, for the most part, a type of labor legislation, regulating how employers are to treat employees and applicants for employment. Before the racial polarization of the parties, much of Republican opposition to EEO legislation (and to some other types of civil rights legislation, such as legislation prohibiting discrimination in the sale and rental of housing) was based on opposition to its regulation of business. That has been a consistent Republican rationale for opposing other proposals affecting employer-employee relations. Democrats, in contrast, have been committed (relative to the Republicans) to legislation regulating labor relations ever since the New Deal.

Party stances on both minority and gender issues and on business push the parties in the same direction, the Democrats toward support of labor market opportunity legislation and the Republicans toward opposition. To what extent do these ideological differences affect what happens in Congress?

For the most part, when public opinion points in a particular direction, it seems to override ideology, even on issues not particularly salient to the public (table 5.3). The parties both supported the one piece of legislation enacted when the salience of the issue was high, namely, Title VII (with the exception of Southern Democrats, who were responding to their own restricted, predominantly white electorates). Since then, the parties have generally acted together, even on issues that were not very salient, when the direction of public opinion was apparent: nonrepeal of Title VII and enactment of the EEO Act of 1972, the Americans with Disabilities Act, the Pregnancy Discrimination Act, and the Retirement Equity Act.

There are two exceptions to this pattern. The first is the failure of either party to propose legislation that would end affirmative action in employment, even though the public arguably supports doing so. (This is all the more surprising in light of how Republicans have seemingly gained and Democrats lost from different attitudes toward affirmative action; Gilens, Sniderman, and Kuklinski 1998.) The second is the division between the parties on the Family and Medical Leave Act. Almost 90% of the Democratic representatives who voted favored the 1993 act, while over three-quarters of Republicans were opposed; almost all Democratic senators favored the bill, but only two-fifths of Republicans. (The division had been similar in 1992.) When a family and medical leave act passed in 1992, it was vetoed by Republican President Bush; when one was passed in 1993, it was signed by Democratic President Clinton. This contrast is not surprising, given the parties' differences on gender and business issues. More striking, only on this issue was public opinion reasonably clear, salience low, and the parties in conflict.

Table 5.3 Clarity of Public Opinion and Differences
in Congressional Party Positions

Public Opinion	Democrats	Republicans
Clear on specific issue		
Repeal or weaken Title VII	No support from either party	
EEO Act of 1972	Significant objections only from Southern Democrats	
End affirmative action	No support from either party[a]	
Americans with Disabilities Act	Virtually unanimous support from both parties	
Family and Medical Leave Act	House: 224–29	House: 40–134
	Senate: 55–2	Senate: 16–25
Clear with regard to general trend, no data on specific issue		
Pregnancy Discrimination Act	Support from large majorities of both parties	
Retirement Equity Act	Virtually unanimous support from both parties	
Divided or ambivalent, or **data are ambiguous**		
Prohibiting discrimination on	1996 Senate vote: 41–5	1996 Senate vote: 8–45
the basis of sexual orientation	1999–2000: 188 sponsors	1999–2000: 18 sponsors
Civil Rights Act of 1991	1990 House vote: 239–15	1990 House vote: 34–139
	Senate: 53–0	Senate: 9–34
	1991 House: 250–15	1991 House: 22–143
	Senate: 55–0	Senate: 38–5
No data		
Religious accommodation	Almost no support from either party	

[a] In contrast to other issues, parties agree but oppose public opinion.

When the public is divided or the data ambiguous, party differences appear most clearly, as expected. Over 80% of the senators voting to ban employment discrimination on the basis of sexual orientation in 1996 were Democrats, as were 90% of the sponsors of such bills in the 1999–2000 Congress. When Congress voted on a civil rights act in 1990, almost all the Democrats who voted were for it, and 80% of the Republicans against. That bill was vetoed by President Bush, but a very similar bill was enacted in 1991, due to a dramatic shift of Republican votes in the Senate (*Congressional Quarterly* 1992, p. 37B) and of President Bush as well.

CONCLUSION

Strong reasons lead one to expect overall congressional response to public opinion to be low. Congress is likely to be responsive on issues that are highly salient to the public, but most issues are neither salient nor likely to become so. Low levels of responsiveness would not be the result of failures of democratic institutions (due to the power of interest groups, campaign finance laws that favor the wealthy, etc.), but rather due to to inherent limitations in the capacities of individuals and organizations. Nevertheless, a lack of responsiveness would almost necessarily raise profound questions about the utility of democratic institutions and undermine the public commitment critical to their survival.

It has been suggested that substantial levels of responsiveness could be achieved despite limitations in individuals and organizations. If electoral competition leads incumbents to fear challengers raising the salience of many issues, then incumbents will be alert to public opinion even on nonsalient issues. Even when the public's preferences on specific issues are unknown, incumbents may try to respond to the public's policy mood.

Such seems to be the case for congressional action on labor market opportunity since the early 1940s. Congressional action has been consistent with shifts in public opinion on most policies, even on issues the public cared little about. On some issues Congress may not know how to be responsive, because the public is ambivalent or its preferences unknown; congressional action then is most likely to be influenced by party ideology.

It is somewhat surprising that Congress is generally responsive to public opinion even on issues not salient to the public. I have suggested that part of the explanation may be that when little information about public opinion is available, members of Congress may fall back on the general policy mood as a rough guide to what the public wants of them.

If this is the case, though, how does the analysis in this chapter differ from Erikson, MacKuen, and Stimson's (chap. 4)? Might trends in public opinion and congressional action on specific issues be nothing more than particular manifestations of the general trends in liberal and conservative directions that they discuss?

Although Erikson, MacKuen, and Stimson's approach and findings are extremely important, analyses like the one in this chapter, focusing on particular issues, cannot be subsumed under theirs. One key reason is that so much policy making cannot be described in liberal-conservative terms. Within policy domains, conflict is frequently about how issues will be defined—what the dimensions of conflict will be—rather than about the relative power of liberals and conservatives along a given dimension (Baumgartner and Jones 1993; Kingdon 1984; Weaver chap. 6). Often long-term conflicts within policy domains find organizations divided along dimensions other than liberal versus conservative (Heinz, Laumann, Nelson, and Salisbury 1993; Laumann and Knoke 1987). And many specific issues cannot be seen in liberal versus conservative terms either; Page and Shapiro (1983, p. 183) found that this was true for 40% of the policies they examined.

Over the last sixty years, the public has come to favor equal employment opportunity for religious, national origin, and racial minorities, and women; it has adopted more egalitarian views of gender roles and has accepted the notion of women participating almost continuously in the labor market, even when they have young children; it has come to believe that the disabled deserve equal opportunities as well. Congress has responded by enacting laws prohibiting employment discrimination, enhancing opportunities for pregnant women, guaranteeing a (very modest) family and medical leave policy for many workers, and protecting Americans with disabilities. Undoubtedly, on many issues Congress is not responsive to public opinion, and perhaps Congress is becoming less responsive over time. But on labor market opportunities for minorities and women, neither is the case.

APPENDIX SURVEY QUESTIONS AND DATA SOURCES

Surveys are national surveys of American adults unless otherwise noted.

Concern and Knowledge about Civil Rights and Family and Medical Leave

Concern about civil rights as compared to other issues, data from a poll conducted by the *Los Angeles Times*, April 1991, archived at the Roper Center of the University of Connecticut and available through the Lexis-Nexis Academic Universe.

Other questions:

"Have you seen, heard, or read anything about the civil rights bill before Congress?" Yes, 40%; no, 59%; no opinion, 1%. Gallup Organization, June 1991, Roper Center.

"Have you seen or heard anything about the new civil rights bill currently before Congress?" No, 77%. Hart and Teeter Research Companies, May 1991, Roper Center.

"How much, if anything, have you heard or read about legislation being considered by Congress called the Family and Medical Leave Act, which deals with parental leave for the birth, adoption, or serious health condition of a child?" Nothing, 59%. Opinion Research Corporation, April 1987, Roper Center.

Disabilities

All questions are from a poll of American adults conducted by Louis Harris and Associates, May–June 1991, archived at the Roper Center of the University of Connecticut and available through the Lexis-Nexis Academic Universe.

1. (Let me read you some key provisions of a new law called The Americans with Disabilities Act and let me know whether you support each one or not. . . .) "Employers may not discriminate against someone who is qualified to do a job just because they are disabled." Support, 95%; do not support/not sure, 5%. 2. Employers with more than 15 employees must make reasonable accommodations for employees with disabilities. Support, 83%; do not support/not sure,

17%. 3. "While this new law (the Americans with Disabilities Act) will open up new paths of participation for disabled people, it will also in some cases be expensive to implement. Do you feel the cost will be worth it, or not?" Yes, worth it, 89%; no, not worth it, 6%; not sure, 5%.

Family and Medical Leave Act

"Congress passed a family leave bill which would have required large companies to allow up to 12 weeks of unpaid leave for employees who are parents of a new child or anyone dealing with a seriously ill family member. George Bush refused to sign the bill, saying the federal government should not mandate employee benefits. Do you think George Bush should have signed the family leave bill, or did he do the right thing in refusing to sign the bill?" Should have signed it, 57%; did the right thing, 36%; don't know/no answer, 7%. CBS News, *New York Times*, October 1992, Roper Center.

Sexual Orientation

"As you may know, there has been considerable discussion in the news regarding the rights of homosexual men and women. In general, do you think homosexuals should or should not have equal rights in terms of job opportunities?" Yes: 1977, 56%; 1982, 59%; 1989, 71%; 1992, 74%; 1993, 80%; 1996, 84%; 1999, 83%. Gallup Organization.

"Do you think homosexual relations between consenting adults should or should not be legal?" Not be legal: 1977, 43%; 1982, 39%; 1985, 47%; 1986, 54%; 1987, 55%; 1989, 36%; 1992, 44%; 1996, 47%; 1999, 43%. Gallup Organization.

Civil Rights Act of 1991

"Have you heard or read anything about the new Civil Rights Act of 1990 which is now being discussed in Congress?" Yes, 38%; no, 61%; don't know/refused, 1%. Gallup Organization, October 1990.

"Have you seen or heard anything about the new civil rights bill currently before Congress?" Favor, 8%; oppose, 5%; have not heard of bill, 77%; not sure if heard of bill, 5%; not sure, 5%. Hart and Teeter Research Companies for NBC and the *Wall Street Journal* (survey of registered voters), May 1991, Roper Center.

"Have you seen or heard anything about the new civil rights bill currently before Congress?" (If "Yes," ask:) "Do you favor or oppose the civil rights bill?" heard of bill/favor, 12%; heard of bill/oppose, 14%; heard of bill/not sure, 10%; not heard of bill, 63%; not sure, 2%. Hart and Teeter Research Companies for NBC and the *Wall Street Journal* (survey of registered voters), June 1991, Roper Center.

"Congress recently passed a civil rights bill it said would increase job rights for minority groups and women. George Bush vetoed the bill saying it would have required quotas. Do you think George Bush should have vetoed that bill or should he have signed it into law?" Vetoed, 40%; signed, 47%; don't know/no answer, 13%. CBS News/*New York Times*, October 1990, Roper Center.

(Half sample asked) "Do you approve or disapprove of the way the Republicans in Congress are handling civil rights?" Approve, 49%; disapprove, 31%; don't know/no opinion, 20%.

(Half sample asked) "Do you approve or disapprove of the way the Democrats in Congress are handling civil rights?" Approve, 47%; disapprove, 30%; don't know/no opinion, 23%.

"Do you approve or disapprove of the way Congress is handling civil rights?" Approve, 53%; disapprove, 33%; don't know/no opinion, 13%. ABC News/*Washington Post*, May 1991, Roper Center.

NOTES

This research was partially supported by National Science Foundation grant SES-0001509.

1. A group of women members of Congress had planned to introduce such a provision anyway and were well prepared to push for its adoption, but their planning was not well known at the time.

2. Congressional thinking about discrimination policy has not always been entirely logical or predictable. Congress had been considering equal pay bills (prohibiting sex differences in pay for men and women doing the same job) since 1945, but it had not occurred to anyone to link the concerns about pay discrimination to concerns about sex discrimination more broadly, or to think of sex discrimination as analogous to discrimination on the basis of race, religion, and national origin. In addition, congressional action on age discrimination (including passage of the Age Discrimination in Employment Act in 1967) does not seem to have affected congressional action on the other issues discussed in this chapter; given its very separate history, that act will not be examined here.

3. It could be argued that there is no need to attack affirmative action in Congress, because it never had much economic impact and the courts have undermined what little force it had (Burstein and Edwards 1994). But such facts need not stop members of Congress who believe they have something to gain from such attacks.

6

Polls, Priming, and the Politics of Welfare Reform

R. KENT WEAVER

Welfare reform was one of the most contentious legislative issues in the early and mid-1990s. The Clinton administration in 1992 and the new Republican congressional majority in 1994 both came into office with ambitious policy agendas for low-income families generally and for reform of the Aid to Families with Dependent Children program (AFDC) in particular. The content of those policy agendas was quite different, however. Bill Clinton promised in his 1992 presidential campaign to "make work pay" through a dramatic expansion of the Earned Income Tax Credit (EITC) and an increase in and indexation of the minimum wage. He also pledged to "end welfare as we know it" through a package of reforms to the AFDC program that stressed work requirements, training and supportive services, and better child support enforcement. Of these three planks, only the EITC expansion was enacted before the Republicans won control of Congress in 1994. Clinton's welfare reform package was not released until the administration had been in office for 17 months, and it never got serious congressional attention before the Democrats lost control of Congress in the 1994 election.

The new Republican majority in the House of Representatives came into office with an even more ambitious family policy agenda than Clinton's. The House Republicans' "Contract with America" proposed a welfare reform plan quite different from the administration's proposal: it would have capped and reduced AFDC funding to the states, ended individual entitlement to AFDC benefits, restricted benefits for women who have children outside marriage, and placed time limits on receipt of AFDC benefits. However, the new Republican agenda initially encountered serious obstacles as well. The Republican welfare reform initiative was rolled into a huge December 1995 budget reconciliation package, along with unpopular cuts in Medicare and Medicaid that President Clinton vetoed. Seeking to embarrass the president, congressional Republicans passed their welfare reform bill separately in January 1996, and the president vetoed it again. But in summer 1996, when congressional Republicans brought forward a welfare reform bill that met some of the president's objections and omitted unpopular Medicaid cuts (Medicare cuts had been dropped earlier), he agreed to sign it. The new Personal Responsibility and Work Opportunity Reconciliation Act of 1996 (PRWORA) abolished the sixty-year-old Aid to Families with Dependent Children program and replaced it with a block grant program (Temporary Assistance for Needy Families, or TANF) for the states. The PRWORA also ended legal entitlement to benefits and contained stiff new work requirements and time limits for welfare recipients.

This chapter addresses questions about the relationship between public opinion and PRWORA legislation. Did public opinion contribute to the passage of welfare reform after the failure of many prior welfare reform initiatives, and if so, how? Did politicians "pander" to the public by adjusting their positions in response to poll results, and if so, under what conditions, and at which stages in the policy making process, did this occur?

Another question addressed in this chapter is how polling affects the decision making of politicians. Does it give them an accurate portrait of the political potential of specific reforms, or can it in fact mislead them? And do politicians simply follow public opinion like "antelopes in an open field" (Stimson, MacKuen, and Erikson 1995, p. 545), or do they use polls and focus groups to engage in "crafted talk" (Jacobs and Shapiro 2000), framing the debate in terms consistent with their own policy preferences? If so, how successful are they in shifting the terms of debate in their preferred direction?

The evidence presented in this chapter suggests that public opinion and polling played several distinctive roles in the process leading up to the 1996 welfare reform legislation. The extreme unpopularity and racialized perceptions of the AFDC program helped to put welfare reform on the agenda in the early 1990s by leading politicians to believe that proposing welfare reform could be politically rewarding. Public resentment of AFDC was reinforced by elite priming, especially after President Clinton's "end welfare as we know it" pledge, as politicians competed to establish their bona fides as critics of the welfare system. Strong public consensus also affected the content of the 1996 legislation in areas such as work requirements. But because the current welfare system was so unpopular, public opinion also gave the Republicans control of the policy agenda after 1994 to shape the legislation where there was no public consensus, because politicians (including President Clinton) thought that opposing Republican welfare reform legislation would leave them electorally vulnerable as "defenders" of the unpopular status quo.

PUBLIC OPINION AND POLICY CHANGE

Shifting public opinion is clearly a plausible explanation for why comprehensive welfare reform was enacted in 1996 when such initiatives had largely failed in the past. But public opinion can affect policymaking in several distinctive ways. One plausible hypothesis is that policy change reflects changes in public opinion on substantive issues. If the public increases its support for reforms associated with specific approaches to welfare reform—increased emphasis on work requirements or measures to prevent out-of-wedlock births, for example—parties and politicians may feel compelled to adapt these positions. If this "opinion change" hypothesis is correct, we would expect to see both a growing public consensus on the substance of welfare reform issues in the early 1990s and a convergence between public opinion and the policies enacted.

An alternative argument, the "elite adaptation" hypothesis, suggests that the public had long expressed fairly clear views about appropriate AFDC policy. In particular, the public had expressed preferences for a shift to more work-based policies. However, elite dissensus had prevented policy change. As the salience of the welfare issue increased in the early 1990s, elites moved closer to this public consensus. If this hypothesis is correct, salience for welfare issues would increase, but public views would not change, with a high degree of public consensus on approaches to welfare both prior to and during the Clinton administration.

However, public opinion may affect the prospects for welfare reform in two additional ways, even if there is no public consensus on a particular direction for reform. If the public has a high level of trust in a particular party or politician—President Clinton or the Republicans in control of the 104th Congress, for example—to address welfare reform issues and is willing to defer to that political leadership on the substantive details of reform, that popular leader or party may win over otherwise recalcitrant politicians to that leadership's own favored prescriptions. In this "public deference" scenario, welfare reform may result through public and legislative acquiescence to those leaders' policy preferences, even if the salience of welfare reform is relatively low and the fit between public views and those leaders' preferences on welfare issues is not close. In this model, agenda control is critical.

Finally, if public discontent with AFDC is so high that the public demands change, and is willing to accept virtually any change from the status quo as an improvement (or at least believe that it could not be any worse), political elites may feel compelled (or may want) to respond to public discontent. But as in the third scenario, those who have control of the legislative agenda are strongly empowered versus their policy rivals. If they can maneuver so that opposing elites, by seeking to block their proposals, are perceived as defenders of a hated status quo, they are in a strong position both to enact their own policy preferences and to benefit politically. In this "public anger" scenario, public disdain for the status quo rather than support of specific leaders and their policy preferences facilitates welfare reform.

ANALYZING OPINION ON "WELFARE"

A basic problem in analyzing public opinion about "welfare" and "welfare reform" is that what the public means by the terms when responding to questions may not be clear, as many surveys often do not identify specific programs. Does the public associate welfare just with AFDC or more broadly with other means-tested programs from Food Stamps to Head Start to Medicaid and Supplemental Security Income? A January 1995 survey for the Kaiser Family Foundation suggests that *when prompted by the names of specific programs*, the public identifies a broad array of means-tested programs as welfare and will exclude contributory social insurance programs (Social Security and Medicare) from that definition. People also overestimate the share of the federal budget spent on means-tested programs (Henry Kaiser Family Foundation 1995). It is less clear, however, whether the broad concept of welfare is triggered by general survey questions about welfare that do not include prompts about specific programs.

A second problem in analyzing public opinion on welfare stems from the long-noted phenomenon that public opinion on programs for low-income Americans differs significantly depending on the precise wording of questions—most notably between questions relating to "welfare" and those relating to "programs for poor children." "Welfare" is likely to stimulate responses focusing on parents, in particular on images of abuse and fraud by welfare recipients (Jaffe 1978; Smith 1987; Rasinski 1989). It is also likely to stimulate associations with racial minorities (Gilens 1999). The term "poor children," however, stimulates images of a sympathetic clientele not responsible for its own condition.[1] Thus, the same surveys that show overwhelming rejection of spending on "welfare" also show that strong majorities believe too little is being spent on "assistance to the poor" and "government spending on programs for poor children," although support for these positions eroded significantly in the early 1990s (Weaver 2000, p. 173; see also Kluegel 1987). Moreover, most spending programs targeted on the poor (e.g., Medicaid, retraining programs) remain popular, with the conspicuous exceptions of cash "welfare" and Food Stamps (Gilens 1999, p. 28).

Most Americans—almost two-thirds in 1995 polls—think that too much is being spent on welfare. That percentage increased from about 40% of those surveyed between 1991 and 1995, after a period of substantial stability through most of the 1980s and a decline after passage of the Family Support Act of 1988.[2] Part of that change is probably due to the increase in AFDC caseloads and expenditures in the late 1980s and early 1990s. But the unprecedented high levels of support for the position that too much was being spent on welfare by the end of 1994 may also reflect the combined effects of conservative arguments about bloated welfare programs and President Clinton's oft-repeated message we must "end welfare as we know it." Despite the president's intention to increase overall spending on poor families, the effect of this message was, not surprisingly, to increase discontent with the current welfare system among Democrats as well as Republicans.[3]

The view that the welfare system is a failure was clearly widespread in the American public by the early 1990s. Only one-sixth of Americans polled at the end of 1993 thought that the welfare system was working very well or fairly well, whereas 79% thought that it was not working very well or not well at all. This put the welfare system at the bottom of six policy sectors rated in the poll—even lower than the criminal justice system.[4]

The most basic judgment that the public can make about the efficacy of a program is whether it does more harm than good. Much of the public was concerned that welfare benefits may be too high, that the system encouraged long-term dependence, discouraged work, and caused women to have more children than they would if they did not go on welfare.[5] Welfare, in short, was perceived as contrary to the widely shared American belief in individualism and the work ethic. These attitudes, Martin Gilens has argued, are intertwined with racial stereotypes: "The American public thinks that most people who receive welfare are black, and . . . the public thinks that blacks are less committed to the work ethic than are other Americans" (Gilens 1999, p. 3). But although public support for cutting welfare expenditures to reduce the budget deficit increased greatly since the late 1980s, public willingness to spend more for job training and public service jobs remained high and stable.

The most plausible explanation of these results is that much of the public wanted a welfare system consistent with their own beliefs and values[6] (and less ridden with fraud and perverse incentives) more than deficit reduction. This interpretation is supported by polls that asked respondents what most important goals should be pursued in a welfare reform initiative. Moving welfare recipients into the workforce, ending dependence on welfare as a way of life, and giving recipients skills needed to make them self-sufficient consistently were top goals, whereas saving money for taxpayers rests near the bottom (Weaver 2000, p. 176).

CAUSES OF POVERTY AND WELFARE DEPENDENCE

Too often, poll questions trying to ascertain the public's beliefs about why people are poor and become dependent on welfare programs pose overly simplistic dichotomies: for example, does receiving welfare result more from poor motivations or from circumstances beyond people's control, or from poor values or bad policies? Given these choices, the public's responses were split fairly evenly through most of the 1980s. The percentage of the public emphasizing individual failings fell at the end of the 1980s and then rose dramatically in the period from 1992 to 1995, no doubt reflecting both economic recovery and "priming" by politicians stressing the evils of welfare dependence (Weaver 2000, p. 177). Americans also believe that a large number of welfare recipients should not be receiving benefits.[7] However, when surveys offer several possible reasons for receiving welfare, large percentages of the public appear to have fairly sophisticated and complex beliefs about why people are poor or receive welfare, emphasizing both socioeconomic problems such as a shortage of jobs, poor education, breakdown in families, and individual failings such as poor motivation (Weaver 2000, p. 178). Even many of those who believe that large segments of the poor are to blame for their condition also believe that government has a (limited duration) duty to care for those who cannot care for themselves.[8]

ATTITUDES TOWARD SPECIFIC REFORMS

Five distinctive approaches to policy toward low-income families can be found in the welfare debates of the early and mid-1990s, posing distinctive answers to questions such as how best to limit program entry or stimulate successful exits into the labor market (Weaver 2000, chap. 5). Liberals tended to support *incentives* and *prevention/rehabilitation* approaches to welfare reform. The former concentrates on reforming disincentives to work and maintenance of two-parent families in current policies, while trying to "make work pay" and weaken "poverty traps" that make it difficult to exit welfare. Affordable health care available to low-income working families so that they do not have to rely on Medicaid is perhaps the most prominent example of incentive-oriented approaches to welfare reform. Subsidizing low-income work through the EITC increasing the minimum wage, or disregarding some of the earned income of welfare recipients to ease their transition into the workforce are also consistent with this approach. Incentives for family breakup can be reduced by making both single-parent and two-parent families eligible for programs such as AFDC and public housing. The prevention/rehabilitation approach to problems of low-income families focuses on overcoming human capital deficiencies and structural barriers to labor market entry by potential earners through the provision of services—for example, basic education, job training, family planning, and child care.

A third approach, *new paternalism,* is associated with conservative writers like Lawrence Mead, but has increasingly been voiced by "New Democrats" like Bill Clinton as well. It begins with the argument that current policies demand too little of recipients; public policies must demand responsible behavior and punish irresponsible behavior. The centerpiece of new paternalist approaches is work requirements, with penalties for noncompliance, such as lowering welfare benefits for recipients who do not stay in school or do not get their children immunized. Many social conservatives like a fourth approach, *deterrence.* This premise suggests that it is not enough to provide obligations for people in low-income families—disincentives to prevent undesirable behaviors (notably, out-of-wedlock births and long-term dependency on AFDC) from occurring in the first place are also necessary. Prohibitions on payments to mothers for children conceived while the mother was receiving AFDC ("family caps") and bans on cash payments to teen mothers ("teen mother exclusions") are examples. Long-term receipt of benefits can be addressed by "hard time limits"—a set period after which recipients will not be eligible for cash benefits or a government-provided or subsidized job.

Finally, both New Democrats and Republicans have supported a fifth approach, *devolution.* Proponents suggest that uniform federal policies are unlikely to lead to adequate solutions to the problems of teen pregnancy, family breakup, and getting and keeping parents in low-income families in the labor force. A better mechanism would devolve most responsibility for such families to the states allowing a number of experiments that may yield new knowledge about which policies to pursue.

Growing public unity around any one of these approaches to welfare reform might provide an impetus for policy change. A major problem with tracking public opinion on proposals for welfare reform, however, is that the terms of the debate among policymakers shifted so dramatically in the early 1990s that a long time series on many policy options does not exist: polltakers tend to ask only about proposals under serious discussion. And, when confronted with a battery of proposals for policy change about which they may know little and a program they do not like, respondents may say that they favor the proposal when they do not have a well-defined opinion at all.

Public opinion survey data show that, while people detest the welfare status quo, they are also hesitant to embrace wholeheartedly some of the proffered alternatives. These data also suggest that, with a few exceptions, changes in attitudes toward specific reforms were relatively modest in the early 1990s.

Program Entry Issues

Most survey research on program entry issues has focused on deterrence approaches to reducing out-of-wedlock births. These proposals have enjoyed mixed support. Denying an increase in benefits to mothers who bear children while on welfare (known as "family caps") is the most popular of these deterrence measures. Family caps enjoyed a tremendous surge in public support between 1992 and 1993 that dropped somewhat in 1994, but most polls continued to show majority—although far from consensus—public support for the idea through 1995 (Weaver 2000, p. 179).

Support for a related set of deterrence provisions—an outright ban on cash benefits to some or all unwed mothers—was significantly lower than for family caps. Only a requirement that unmarried teen mothers live with a parent or other responsible adult rather than setting up their own households (a provision that had been a state option under the Family Support Act) has gathered clear majority support. Denial of benefits to unmarried teen mothers attracts significant support (in the 40% range), but that support drops substantially if the question includes a clause noting that the mother lacks any other means of support. Support for exclusion also declines if the age of exclusion is raised. Moreover, the public is uneasy, by margins of more than two to one, about proposals to ban benefits to teenage mothers if it means that some of these children might end up in orphanages or foster care. In general, wording of questions that "prime" concern for the welfare of children as well as awareness of the mother reduces support for exclusionary provisions.

Chap. 2

Exit to the Labor Market

Several prevention/rehabilitation approaches to moving AFDC recipients into the labor force enjoyed broad public support in the period leading up to the new welfare reform legislation enacted in 1996. Job training and subsidies for child care were extremely popular, receiving about 90% approval. Solid majorities of respondents also supported paying transportation costs and providing public sector jobs (Weaver 2000, p. 181; Gilens 1999, p. 187).

The clear public favorite among specific approaches to welfare reform is work requirements, consistent with the new paternalist approach to welfare reform. Indeed, a bipartisan consensus has, long favored work instead of cash welfare,[9] at least in the abstract. The public particularly supports work requirements for noncustodial parents who are not paying child support and is most willing to exempt the mothers of young children from such requirements. But support for applying work requirements even to mothers of young children also increased dramatically during the first Clinton administration.

Long-Term Self-Sufficiency

The public's ambivalent opinion about welfare is most evident on the matter of time limits for benefits. There is widespread and apparently stable support for the principle of limiting receipt of cash welfare benefits to a few years, with the broadest support for time-limited cash benefits followed by a community service or job requirement (Weaver 2000, p. 184). However, a poll taken at the end of 1993 suggested that most people would exempt large portions of the AFDC caseload from a time limit if that limit did not include a job guarantee. A three-to-one majority also believed that people should be able to receive benefits as long as they work for them rather than being subject to hard time limits after which no benefits would be received.[10] And when asked in a December 1994 poll what should happen to individuals who hit a time limit, only 10% of respondents said that benefits should simply end; more than 81% favored a community service requirement or job guarantee instead.[11] Again, the implication is that the public is more concerned with responsible behavior on the part of welfare recipients—in particular engaging in work effort—than with the principle of hard time limits.

A Fundamental Ambivalence

Examining expressions of public opinion on various welfare reform options suggests a number of conclusions about the structure of that opinion. First, single questions about welfare policy options likely provide a misleading reflection of patterns of public opinion. Because of the dual clientele of welfare—parents who are viewed with some suspicion, and children who are viewed sympathetically— the opinion registered on specific questions can vary widely depending on whether it primarily taps opinion toward poor children, or their parents. Moreover, because of the public's overwhelmingly strong dislike of the current system, there may be a positive bias in the public's response to questions that ask how the public feels about specific changes to current policy. But the data also suggest that the American public is much less concerned with getting people off welfare and reducing the costs of the system than they are with having recipients make an effort to help themselves.

WHOM DO YOU TRUST?

There has been far more volatility in the public's views of whom within the federal government they trust to carry out welfare reform than in their views on specific reforms. The Clinton administration came into office with a huge advantage: the public trusted the president far more than congressional Republicans to do the best job in carrying out welfare reform. By the beginning of 1994, however, the administration had squandered most of its advantage as it failed to come forward with a welfare reform plan. Meanwhile, House Republicans did introduce a plan. By the time the administration finally released its reform proposal in the middle of 1994, its advantage in public trust on welfare had turned into a deficit that became, after the 1994 election, immense. Congressional Republicans continued to enjoy a margin of between 10 and 20 points in public trust on handling of welfare matters from January through March 1995 (the period in which the House committee and full chamber debate on welfare reform took place). The gap closed to six points by mid-July 1995 as the administration increased its attacks on the Republican bill, and the GOP in the Senate became bogged down in disputes over conservative mandates and allocation of block grant funds among the states. By fall 1995, it had closed to a virtual tie, where it remained into 1996. Opinions on which political party voters trusted to reform welfare shows a similar overall pattern, although Republicans continued to hold a modest advantage into 1996, which may reflect voters' mistrust of the liberal wing of the Democratic Party in Congress. Perhaps the best evidence of the public's ambivalence about its political leaders on welfare issues can be found in responses to questions that did not ask *which* party or leader participants preferred, but simply whether whether they approved of the handling of the welfare issue by specific leaders. A majority of the public frequently expressed lack of confidence in the leaders of both parties (Weaver 2000, p. 192).

PRIMING AND POLLING IN THE POLICYMAKING PROCESS

Of course, politicians do not just sit idly by and listen passively to public opinion. As alternative welfare reform proposals were debated between 1993 and 1996, both the Clinton administration and Republicans in Congress invested heavily both in gathering information about public attitudes and in trying to influence how the public perceives the welfare issue—and, in particular, trying to associate the other party with unpopular positions (on Republican efforts, see, in particular, Charen 1995; Harwood 1995). Republicans like Representative Jan Meyers of Kansas charged that the AFDC system was full of perverse incentives for parents—most notably the incentive to have children out of wedlock at government expense— and argued that "what is really cruel is the current incentive that pulls young women into the system and holds them forever in this cruel trap" (quoted in Brownstein 1995). Congressional Democrats and children's advocacy groups argued that Republicans should not finance tax breaks to the wealthy by cutting benefits and services to poor children (Binder 1995). Both sides charged the other with being "weak on work." And both sides perceived the stakes to be very high: the side that was able to convince the public that its vision of welfare and proposed solutions were the most appropriate would have an advantage in winning enactment of its proposals, and perhaps also in future electoral contests.

The key change in this period was in the balance of messages that Americans heard about welfare reform. The debate over welfare changed dramatically when Bill Clinton pledged in his 1992 campaign to "end welfare as we know it" and to move people from income assistance to work. In addition to its policy appeals, this pledge clearly offered some potentially important political advantages in the Clinton campaign's efforts to promote, and benefit electorally from, a broader "New Democratic" political project. Clinton and other "New Democrats" argued that erosion in the party's political support could be stopped only by a new image and by new policies that would show the party to be more than an agglomeration of liberal interests (e.g., racial minorities, labor unions, feminists, and homosexuals). Bruce Reed, Clinton campaign issues director (and later co-chair of the administration's welfare reform task force), saw "a growing consensus among Democrats that we have an obligation to end dependency and reform welfare, to move beyond the rhetoric of the right and the mistakes of the left" (Toner, 1992). A public philosophy that emphasizes work and individual responsibility offered the Clinton campaign the opportunity to seize the moral high ground in the welfare debate, inoculate Democrats against charges that they coddle the (disproportionately minority) nonworking poor, and take away (and even turn to Democrats' advantage) one of the race-tinged "wedge" issues that had long alienated blue- and white-collar constituencies from the Democratic Party (Greenberg 1996, especially pp. 206–7). Moreover, pressing the ideals of "making work pay" and ensuring that people who "work hard and play by the rules should not be poor" resonated well with constituencies who had suffered declining or stagnant real income in recent years. In short, work-oriented welfare reform offered an opportunity not only to neutralize an issue on which Democratic candidates had traditionally tried to avoid blame but also to claim credit with centrist voters.

Although the Clinton administration avoided most of the harsh rhetoric of the conservative critics of welfare, packaging its proposal under the slogan "ending welfare as we know it" implicitly reinforced the wholesale condemnation of AFDC—and the notion that nothing could be worse for poor children than the status quo—in conservative critiques.[12] Criticizing AFDC was part of an overall administration strategy to win support for welfare reform on its terms by convincing the public that the Clinton administration's approach neither put children unduly at risk or coddled their parents. This approach created several problems, however. In the short term, the president's rhetorical "end welfare as we know it" flourish may have strengthened public opposition to spending more on welfare recipients—which the Clinton administration would have done by increasing spending on training, child care, and job provision. In public perceptions, "ending welfare as we know it" is likely to be interpreted as something more akin to "ending welfare" than "dramatically increased expenditures in the short term in order to reduce welfare dependence in the long term." Why, many policymakers and members of the public wondered, was it necessary to spend more money on welfare if we were supposed to be ending it (see, for example, Birnbaum 1996, p. 135)? And if we were spending a lot more money, did not that support Republican charges that the Clinton people were just the same old tax-and-spend Democrats rather than New Democrats who were going to transform how government worked?

In the longer term, the Clinton administration's attacks placed the administration at a severe bargaining disadvantage with a Republican-controlled Congress after 1994 (Besharov 1995). Having wholeheartedly condemned the status quo and focused public attention on the behavior of parents rather than on the welfare of children, President Clinton would be in the awkward position of implicitly defending the status quo if he vetoed Republican-inspired welfare reform legislation. This was not a concern when the pledge was made in 1992, of course: candidate Clinton was then understandably concentrating on the grand strategic game of realigning the image of the Democratic Party on welfare issues rather than on the serious legislative bargaining that might follow his election. Nor could he anticipate the Republican takeover in Congress that would seize control of the welfare reform agenda and force him into a defensive posture on welfare issues.

From both Republicans and the Clinton administration, the dominant messages "priming" attitude formation toward welfare reform concerned the evils of the welfare system rather than the welfare of children. Many congressional Democrats followed the administration's rhetorical and political lead, leaving AFDC almost devoid of powerful and vocal defenders within government. As a result, the most recent round of welfare reform focused on *how* to reform welfare, with Republicans pushing for reforms that would turn over increased responsibility to the states, increase disincentives for out-of-wedlock births, and reduce federal expenditures and the Clinton administration stressing the need to provide additional child care and job guarantees. A steady stream of critiques of AFDC from both Republican and Democratic politicians contributed both to a marked increase in the salience of welfare reform and to a heightened dissatisfaction with the current system. These factors, in turn, gave a tremendous advantage to the political forces controlling the welfare reform agenda and dramatically weakened the bargaining position of those who could be presented as opposed to fundamental change in the welfare system.

The importance of agenda control became evident when Republicans won control of Congress in the 1994 elections. House Republicans were committed to a radical, deterrence-focused set of reforms negotiated between social conservatives and Republican members of the House Ways and Means Committee in summer 1994, in a process overseen by Republican Dick Armey, then chair of the House Republican Conference. The provisions were clearly aimed primarily at the party's base among social conservatives rather than at median voters. Indeed, Armey had been determined that the welfare provisions of the bill would be tough ones, in part because Gingrich had insisted on leaving out of the Contract with America provisions on abortion and school prayer that energized the party's political base among religious conservatives but also divided Republican legislators and candidates. Armey later argued that those omissions "made the welfare provisions tougher and more imperative because we had a very, very important, significant part of our base already disappointed" (quoted in Balz and Brownstein 1996, p. 39).

Although Republicans in Congress sought to move public opinion through their rhetoric, they also were willing to adapt their views when that message did not sell. The original version of the welfare reform legislation included in the Contract with America provided grants that states could use "to establish and operate orphanages" and "to establish and operate closely supervised residential homes for unwed mothers." On the surface, the proposal—and particularly the orphanage provisions—appeared to be a political plus. It seemed to offer a solution to the problem of AFDC's dual clientele: if (politically popular) poor children were physically separated from (politically unpopular) welfare mothers, the latter could be cut off and the former helped. The orphanage appeal did not play well with the public, however, and Republicans quickly began to back away from a focus on orphanages, arguing that group homes where mothers and children would live together would be better. By late January 1995, Republicans were heeding the advice of pollster Frank Luntz to avoid mentioning orphanages (Devroy 1995).

Interest groups also engaged in the process of "framing and blaming," including the use of poll data to bolster support for their preferred policy positions among legislators. For example, the Family Research Council (FRC), a social conservative lobbying group (Stone 1995), sought to counter concerns among conservative Republicans that a vote for family caps would earn them the wrath of the National Right Life to Committee, which opposed family caps as likely to lead to an increase in abortions. The FRC commissioned a national poll on the

use this Quostin in Chap 2 as not a contrefactual

family cap in October 1995. Framing the question in a way most likely to draw support for a family cap, asking if those surveyed favored "increasing a welfare mother's monthly welfare check if she has another child out of wedlock," the poll indeed found overwhelming support for a family cap. In reporting the results, the FRC argued that they should "allay any doubts Congressional Republicans may have about whether the public supports their 'family cap' proposal" and argued that "support for the family cap among rank-and-file pro-lifers is at least as strong as support from other Americans" (Bauer 1995). In short, FRC information was designed to appeal to the blame-avoiding instincts of Republican legislators fearing flak from one of their key constituencies.

Perhaps the most important role of public opinion polling in bringing welfare reform legislation to closure, however, did not concern opinion on the substance of the legislation at all, but rather electoral forecasts. In spring 1996, welfare reform legislation appeared hopelessly deadlocked, with congressional Republicans linking welfare reform to politically unpopular Medicaid reform in a single legislative package, and President Clinton adamantly stating that he would not sign such legislation. But a changing mood among Republican members in the House eroded their commitment to the welfare/Medicaid linkage. Polls in early summer 1996 showed voters favoring Democratic candidates over Republicans by a substantial margin, indicating that the Republicans might lose control of Congress in the upcoming election.[13] These polls served as a dual wake-up call to Republicans. First, if members hoped to get reelected, they should enact welfare reform so that they would not be vulnerable to Democratic charges that their revolutionary fervor had resulted in little legislation (Hook 1996). Second, if they might lose control of Congress in the fall, they should act quickly to "end welfare as we know it" on Republican terms.

Once Republicans agreed to break the welfare/Medicaid linkage, the legislation moved forward quickly. Conferees sought to head off mobilization efforts of liberal advocacy groups and to force the president to declare before the Democratic convention whether he would sign a final welfare bill. As the Republicans moved to bring the conference report up for final passage in the House the day after reaching an agreement, Democrats sought a strong signal from the president about his intentions. Once again, electoral calculations were critical. In the words of Representative Robert Matsui (D-CA), "Most members would like to know what he is going to do. If the President supports it, they will support it. . . . A lot of members just don't want to be to the left of the President on welfare" (quoted in Shogren 1996). On the morning of the scheduled House vote, the president held a long meeting with his cabinet and top political advisors. Health and Human Services Secretary Donna Shalala, Treasury Secretary Robert Rubin, Chief of Staff Leon Panetta, and others urged a veto, but Bruce Reed, presidential political advisor Rahm Emmanuel, and Commerce Secretary Mickey Kantor urged that he sign it. Presidential pollster Dick Morris, although not present at the meeting, sent a warning that failure to veto the bill could turn a projected fifteen-point Clinton victory over Dole in the fall presidential election into a three-point loss.[14] After meeting privately with Panetta and Vice President Gore, the president simultaneously announced that he would sign the bill and work for revisions (mostly in non-AFDC provisions) in the next Congress. Both chambers quickly passed the welfare bill by margins of more than three to one, with Democrats strongly split.[15]

CONCLUSIONS AND IMPLICATIONS

This chapter began with questions about the role of public opinion in promoting welfare policy change in the 1990s. First, did trends in public opinion compel or create a permissive environment for the dramatic changes in assistance to low-income families that occurred in 1996? Did politicians adjust their positions in seeking the positions of median voters generally, or their median constituents? Further, how did politicians use information to lead public opinion, and were they successful in doing so? This section draws on the evidence presented in the chapter to present some answers to those questions.

Public Opinion and Policy Change

The evidence presented in this chapter suggests that public opinion on welfare in the early and mid-1990s did not compel welfare policy change; that is, changes in public opinion were insufficient by themselves to force a change. But the public opinion environment was a fertile one for politicians to bring forward and move welfare reform initiatives.

I suggested four alternative arguments at the beginning of this chapter about how public opinion may create fertile conditions for welfare reform: increasing public consensus around a particular set of reforms, an increase in the salience of the welfare issue that forced elites to bow to a preexisting public consensus, an increase in public deference to a specific political leader or elite group to implement reforms of the elite's choice, and a growing antipathy for the status quo that makes the public willing to accept any change. The evidence presented in this chapter suggests that the first, second, and fourth of these factors—especially the last—helped to make welfare reform more likely in 1996. Overwhelming public rejection of the current system led politicians to believe that there was political credit to be gained by ending it. Thus, changing public opinion supported, if it did not drive, the push to reform welfare reform *in some direction*.

But if public opinion has played a major role in pushing welfare reform onto the policy agenda, it has played a more mixed role in terms of promoting specific solutions to the "welfare problem." There was some change in attitudes over the course of the first Clinton administration, notably, an increase in the number of people who thought that too much was being spent on welfare, that the poor are primarily responsible for their own condition, and that work should be required for mothers of young children. Public support was widespread for the core concerns of work and training requirements for welfare mothers. Strong support emerged for time limits after which work would be required, but there was less agreement on time limits without a work guarantee. The popularity of a strong work requirement could act as a powerful force propelling a welfare reform package that contained other, more controversial, provisions. The final welfare legislation enacted in 1996 contained many provisions on which there was a strong consensus (e.g., tightened work requirements, a requirement that unmarried teen mothers live at home, increased funding for child care), but also provisions, including a five-year "hard" time limit on federally subsidized cash benefits, on which there was no consensus.

Little evidence supports the third argument, that the public simply trusted one political leader or another (e.g., President Clinton or congressional Republicans) to solve the welfare problem. On the contrary, the survey evidence shows that public views on this question were quite volatile. Both President Clinton in 1993 and congressional Republicans in the 104th Congress began with strong public confidence, but this confidence rapidly dissipated. Rather than a firm advantage for a single party on the welfare issue in this period, poll data suggest a public that had high hopes and demands for reform but was also quick to lose faith when politicians failed to deliver on welfare reform.

Strong evidence supports the final argument—that public support for almost any policy change as an improvement over the status quo increases the policy leeway to those who control the legislative agenda. Certainly, dislike of the status quo had reached unprecedented levels. Public opinion gave politicians the sense that they could score political gains by promising a dramatic change. The strong negative attitude of the public to the pre-1996 welfare system, and the resulting "positivity bias" of the public toward any reform proposals, led politicians to believe that they could sell the public on welfare reform packages close to their own policy preferences. Indeed, polls showed that the public preferred almost any possible package of reforms to AFDC (Weaver 2000, p. 193). Surveys suggest that most Americans did not completely abandon their concern for poor children or complex views about the roots of poverty in the 1990s; this concern continued (albeit uncomfortably) alongside Americans' dislike for welfare programs and their perception that the behavior of many adult welfare recipients was irresponsible and unacceptable. When conflicting beliefs co-exist, dominance depends heavily on whether they are "primed" by opinion leaders and the media (see, for example, Iyengar 1987; Jacobs and Shapiro 2000). Republican initiatives were aided substantially by the fact that powerful opinion leaders, Democratic as well as Republican, repeatedly "primed" concerns about welfare dependence. If concerns about the potential negative effects of welfare reform on children had been primed by messages delivered by political leaders with wide credibility, the public might have expressed stronger reservations about some welfare reform proposals, as they become more aware of their potential negative consequences. But the Clinton administration raised these concerns only intermittently, since they wanted to enact, and claim political credit for, welfare reform themselves.

Given the public's intense dislike of AFDC, the critical issue for policy makers was not finding a welfare reform package that would command the support of the maximum number of voters but rather maintaining control of the welfare reform agenda. Indeed, the Clinton administration's 1994 welfare reform proposal was probably closer to the views of the mythical "median voter" than the welfare provisions of the Contract with America or the 1996 PRWORA legislation. But that would be of little aid to Clinton and the Democrats after they failed to move a welfare bill before the 1994 election. Because the public demanded policy change and preferred almost *any* possible package of reforms over the status quo, whoever could control the agenda in Congress would have an important advantage in getting reform enacted on their terms, for public pressure on the president to accept whatever Congress passed would be intense. In short, public opinion ultimately worked to the benefit of the Republican welfare reform package in 1996 less because of public identification with Republican positions or deference to Republican leadership than because congressional Republicans' control of the agenda meant that President Clinton would have to choose between approving a bill written largely on Republican terms and appearing to prefer the "default position"—the universally maligned status quo.

Polls, Political Signaling, and Pandering Politicians

Politicians and interest groups clearly used polls and focus groups during the welfare reform debate of the mid-1990s for multiple purposes: testing alternative policies, testing alternative ways of framing policies to find those that best appeal to the public, and changing course when the alternatives they were backing failed to persuade the public. However, the welfare reform debate also suggests important limitations on these processes. Politicians may be misled by polling data to overestimate the political prospects for a proposal if those data suggest that a reform proposal is popular when it is framed in a particular way. Political opponents may succeed in reframing that proposal in another way that makes it much less popular (the Health Insurance Association of America's "Harry and Louise" ads on health care reform are a classic example), or they may devise another proposal that is equally popular or even more popular.

Do politicians "pander"—that is, adjust their positions to follow perceived popular preferences? The evidence here is mixed. It suggests that politicians may, as Jacobs and Shapiro suggest, largely follow their own preferences when formulating policy alternatives *so long as they believe that they can control the policy agenda* or that voters do not care about the issue. They most certainly do pander, however, when they are compelled to respond to proposals made by others, at least in situations when (1) the issue is highly salient to voters, (2) the status quo is highly unpopular, (3) the politician's own ideal point is far from that of most voters, and (4) the issue choice is framed as one of an alternative versus the unpopular status quo.

Overall, the welfare reform case is a good illustration of the argument made by the editors of this volume that the responsiveness of politicians to public opinion is contingent. In the mid-1990s, most American politicians in the United States did coalesce around those elements of policy reform on which there was broad public agreement, notably, on the nature of work. But because the status quo was highly unpopular and there was no elite consensus on other elements of welfare reform, politicians engaged in much "crafted talk" to win support for their own proposed changes. Ultimately, however, outcomes were driven less by the success of one side or another in developing convincing rhetoric than by the fact that Republicans rather than President Clinton controlled the legislative agenda and were therefore in a position to frame choices facing legislators and the president in terms of their proposal versus the status quo.

NOTES

This chapter draws heavily on the author's collaborative work with Robert Y. Shapiro and Lawrence R. Jacobs on public opinion about welfare reform, which was part of a larger collaborative project on the Clinton administration and social policy supported by the Russell Sage Foundation and a project on welfare reform funded by the Annie E. Casey Foundation. See Weaver, Shapiro, and Jacobs (1995a) and (1995b), Weaver (2000, chap. 7). Jim Abrams provided valuable research assistance in preparing this chapter.

1. On distinctions made by the public among recipients of income transfer programs, see Cook (1979) and Cook and Barrett (1992).

2. As Teles (1996) notes, the biggest drop in support for increased welfare spending was between 1961 and 1973, with a drop from 60% to 20% in the percentage of the population believing that too little was being spent on welfare. At least some of this change probably resulted from "a shift in the public's impression of how much the government was actually spending rather than underlying support for any given level of welfare spending" (p. 44).

3. In the Kaiser-Harvard welfare reform survey in December 1994, 57% of Democrats as well as 78% of Republicans said that too much was being spent on welfare. Kaiser-Harvard study, table 5. Teles (1996, pp. 46–47) notes that the substantial increase in hostility to welfare spending between 1991 and 1993 was not accompanied by similar increases in opposition in aid to blacks or aid to big cities, suggesting that opposition to welfare in particular rather than increases in racial hostility was at work.

4. Two percent of respondents thought that the welfare system worked very well, 14% fairly well. Comparable figures were 1% and 19% for the criminal justice system; 4% and 32% for the health care system; 5% and 34% for the education system; 3% and 36% for the tax system; and 9% and 49% for the Social Security system. Telephone poll of 1,020 respondents conducted between November 12 and 15, 1993, by Peter D. Hart Research Associates.

5. See Weaver, Shapiro, and Jacobs (1995a) for a detailed presentation of poll data.

6. See Feldman (1998) for an examination of the role of beliefs and values in public opinion.

7. When asked, "Of the people currently on welfare in the United States, how many would you say deserve to be receiving welfare benefits—nearly all, most but not all, about half, less than half, or almost none at all?," 4% of respondents said "nearly all"; 14% said "most, but not all"; 42% said "about half"; 32% said "less than half"; 5% said "almost

none at all"; and 3% were not sure. Telephone poll of 1,020 respondents conducted between November 12 and 15, 1993, by Peter D. Hart Research Associates.

8. See Heclo (1994). When asked in December 1994 whether "it is the responsibility of government to take care of people who can't take care of themselves," 65% agreed, 29% disagreed, and 65% didn't know. See Dowd (1994). In another survey the same month, only 14% of respondents thought that government should have the primary responsibility for ensuring that nonworking low-income people have a minimum standard of living, with 26% believing that people themselves, their friends, and voluntary agencies should be responsible and 57% saying that responsibility should be shared. Most (71%) of those who believe that responsibility should be shared believed that government's obligation should be limited in duration, however.

9. See Heclo (1994). For an argument emphasizing Americans' support for a work-based approach to supporting poor families, see, in particular, Teles (1996).

10. When asked the question, "Which is closer to your view: welfare recipients should continue to get benefits as long as they work for them or after a year or two welfare recipients should stop receiving all benefits," in a December 1994, CBS/*New York Times* survey, 71% chose getting benefits, 24% chose ending benefits, and 5% did not know (Dowd 1994).

11. When asked, "If government is going to cut off AFDC . . . or welfare benefits after a specific period of time and after it provides education, training, health benefits and child care to those families, should it. . . . ," 10% of respondents chose "simply end the families' benefits, including Aid to Families with Dependent Children"; 56% chose "make the parent or parents do community service work in exchange for welfare benefits"; 25% favored "guarantee jobs to the parent or parents after they are cut off welfare"; 4% did not know; and 5% refused to answer. Kaiser-Harvard, *Survey on Welfare Reform*, table 18. These results are similar to those of a 1993 Hart/Teeter poll, which asked, "Which one of these two approaches to welfare reform would you say is better: 1) after two years, benefits would be ended for all able-bodied recipients, and the government would not provide any job; or 2) after two years, welfare recipients who have not found other employment would be required to work at a public service job?" Twelve percent of respondents chose cutting off benefits, 83% preferred requiring recipients to work at a public service job, and 2% each said both the same, neither, and not sure.

12. For a critique of the Clinton administration's rhetoric by one of its own officials, see Ellwood (1996, pp. 20–22).

13. *New York Times*/CBS and *Washington Post*/ABC polls published in June showed Democratic candidates favored over Republicans by margins of 45% to 38% and 50% to 38%, respectively, in "generic" (i.e., without candidates being named) preferences for the House of Representatives (Berke 1996; Morin and Brossard 1996).

14. For accounts of the meeting, see Broder (1996) and Purdum (1996). Firsthand accounts of the meeting appear in Reich (1997, pp. 319–22) and Stephanopoulos (1999, pp. 419–22).

15. The House passed the bill by a margin of 328 to 101, with Democrats split 98 to 98. The Senate passed the bill 78–21, with Democrats split 25–21 in favor of passage. Only one of seven Democratic Senators up for reelection, Paul Wellstone (D-MN), voted against the conference report.

7

The Power Elite, Public Policy, and Public Opinion

G. WILLIAM DOMHOFF

Most theories concerning the structure and distribution of power in the United States accord public opinion at least a moderate degree of influence on policy outcomes, and some theories claim its impact is large. Many of the chapters in this volume are based primarily on correlational studies suggesting that changes in public opinion precede alterations in public policy. The presumed influence is said to occur through both direct lobbying by voluntary associations and, even more important, through the normal competitive pressures of the electoral process. However, these theories do not consider the possibility that public opinion on economic and foreign policy issues generally fluctuates within the narrow parameters shaped by wealthy and well-organized interests and thus matters only within these circumscribed limits.

This chapter presents a different perspective. I suggest that public opinion has little or no independent influence on foreign, defense, or economic policymaking. Instead, these policies are the province of a power elite, the leadership group for a dominant social class consisting of the owners and managers of large income-producing properties. These owners and managers come together as a corporate community on the basis of common ownership, shared law firms, and interlocking directorships, among many connections. Their predominant power is demonstrated by their large—and growing—share of the wealth and income distributions, their disproportionate share of high-level appointments in Washington, and the fact that they win far more often than they lose on the policy issues of concern to them. They enter the policy arena with a leg up on their liberal and labor opponents due to the large structural advantages conferred upon them through their control of the investment function and job creation in a market economy (Lindblom 1977). The power elite prevails more often than not through four specific processes that connect it to the political parties and government: special interest, policy planning, opinion shaping, and candidate selection.

However, in one general policy arena public opinion does matter in the way mainstream theories say it should: the hot-button religious, racial, and gun issues usually brought together under the rubric "social issues." In terms of maintaining their class dominance, these issues are of no relevance to the corporate leaders, except as wedge issues in the electoral arena, so they make no effort to shape opinion on them. These issues are therefore a battleground between the conservative political operatives centered in the Republican Party and the liberal and labor groups that generally coalesce behind moderate and liberal candidates of the Democratic Party. These issues are of deep concern to many Americans.

Polling results suggest that most people do not believe that their opinions matter much on most policy issues (Bernstein 2000; Jacobs, Hinckley, and Shapiro 1999; Kull 1999). However, this perceived lack of citizen influence has no negative consequences for the power elite, as long as people have stable social roles to fulfill and can see no low-cost method to redress their grievances. Put another way, routine involvement in a compelling daily round of activities, the most important of which are a job and a family, combined with the unresponsiveness of the American party system to liberal and labor concerns, explains why most people accept policies they do not like (Flacks 1988).

Still, an energy that could be called public opinion can have an impact when people are forced out of their routines by depressions, wars, and strategic nonviolent forms of social disruption (Piven and Cloward 1977). In those rare cases, public sentiment can lead to a strong social movement that threatens some aspect of the established order, which, in turn, leads members of the power elite to seek solutions to restore social stability. Public opinion that congeals into a social movement also can set limits on corporate actions in specific locales or industrial sectors when there is a serious accident, such as an oil spill, mining explosion, or nuclear plant breakdown (Molotch 1970).

The remainder of this chapter presents the major evidence and arguments for the claims I have made. It shows how the findings on public opinion can be accounted for within a class-dominance framework. A more complete presentation of the full model, along with a detailed discussion of public opinion, is provided in Domhoff (2002).

HOW THE POWER ELITE DOMINATE PUBLIC POLICY

The Special-Interest Process

The most visible and best-known means by which the power elite dominates public policy is through special interest groups. Specific corporations and economic sectors lobby to realize their narrow and short-run interests relating to taxes, subsidies, and regulatory issues. This process is carried out by lawyers, former government officials, and public relations figures, now known collectively as "K Street." The rate of success for the corporate community in this process is very high, but there are also some "defeats" for two reasons. First, the special-interest process often pits one corporation or corporate sector against another, so some corporations are bound to lose. These in-group battles are not of theoretical importance in terms of a class-dominance model. Second, a coalition of liberal and labor groups is sometimes able to block new initiatives by corporations, or at least pare them back. These liberal-labor victories show that class domination is not absolute (Domhoff 2002, pp. 144–45 and 158–61).

As often pointed out, this process usually operates outside the public limelight because of its narrow and sometimes highly technical nature. Indeed, it is generally thought that corporations seeking special favors are most successful when public opinion is not part of the equation. When those who work within the special-interest process decide it is necessary to bring "grassroots" public opinion into their efforts, the polling results that follow their targeted efforts are intended to show fence-sitters that voters in their district or state would not be alienated by a pro-corporate vote on the issue (Goldstein 1999).

In terms of the more general policy issues of concern in this chapter, the primary role of the operatives within the special interest process is to help create the voting coalition that will provide the majority for the particular issue at hand. These operatives have the information necessary to judge which legislators have the most leeway on the issue with their home constituencies. They also know which legislators owe them favors or want to raise money for taking the next step in their political careers (Clawson, Neustadtl, and Weller 1998). These are not trivial matters, but they are not the heart of the problem in the relationship between major policy issues and public opinion.

The Policy-Planning Process

For purposes of this chapter, then, the policy-planning process is the critical starting point for providing an alternative to the mainstream models of public opinion and policymaking. This corporate-financed network of foundations, think tanks, and policy discussion groups, which developed gradually over the twentieth century, often in response to specific policy crises, has been the subject of several historical and sociological studies (Domhoff 1970; Kahn 1997, chap. 7;

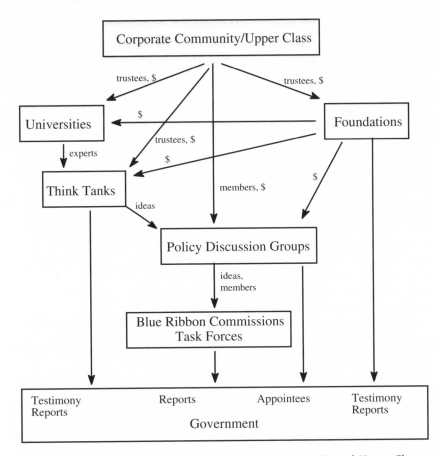

Figure 7.1   The Flow of Policy from the Corporate Community and Upper Class to Government through the Policy Formation Network

Peschek 1987; Weinstein 1968). Its close relationship with the corporate community through money flows and director interlocks has been pinpointed through network analysis (Burris 1992; Colwell 1993; Salzman and Domhoff 1983). Its role in creating the Agricultural Adjustment Act and Social Security Act during the New Deal has been documented through archival studies (Domhoff 1996, chaps. 3 and 5), as has its role in building the framework during World War II for a new postwar international economy (Domhoff 1990; Shoup 1975, 1977). An overview of the policy-planning network and its connections to government is presented in figure 7.1.

There is no one central point in this network; different organizations take the lead on different issues. However, the policy network is not totally homogeneous. Reflecting differences of opinion within the corporate community on a range of issues, moderate and ultraconservative subgroups have long-standing disagreements, although some of those differences have been muted since the 1970s. The ultraconservative organizations are most often identified with "big business" in the eyes of social scientists and the general public. The fact that these ultraconservative groups often lose to the moderate conservatives, especially in times of social turmoil, is why some social scientists doubt that the corporate community is the dominant influence in shaping government policy. They do not see that moderate conservatives have supported what are advertised as liberal or labor victories, except in a few instances relating to labor unions (Domhoff 1970, chaps. 5 and 6, 1990, 2002).

The existence of a policy-planning network also explains how seemingly independent experts, who often provide new policy ideas, fit into the power equation. They do their work as employees and consultants of key organizations in the network. These organizations, and in particular think tanks like the Brookings Institution, the Rand Corporation, and the American Enterprise Institute, give them financial support, confer legitimacy on their efforts, and provide the occasions for them to present their ideas to decision makers. Such experts often come to the attention of corporate leaders through their involvement in the study groups sponsored by the policy discussion groups.

From a research point of view, an understanding of the policy-planning network is an ingredient missing from models that simply correlate public opinion with later policy changes. By studying the "output" of this network—policy statements, written attempts at persuasion, testimony to congressional committees, and speeches—it becomes possible to determine empirically which policy issues are of concern to the corporate community and its power elite. In fact, just such an examination led to the claim in the introduction that the power elite is not focused on social issues. In addition, careful studies of policy output make it feasible to trace if and how corporate policy preferences come to the attention of elected officials and to assess the degree to which these preferences are enacted.

The Opinion-Shaping Process

By starting with the output of the policy-planning network, one can track power elite attempts to shape public opinion before policy proposals become visible in the political arena. Such a search is another ingredient missing from the mainstream studies that focus exclusively on the correlation between public opinion and public policy. This network research has led to the mapping of an elaborate opinion-shaping process that centers around many of the same foundations, think tanks, and policy discussion groups that operate in the policy-planning network. In this process, however, these organizations are supplemented by public relations firms and the public affairs departments of major corporations (Domhoff 2002, chap. 5).

These core organizations are connected to a large dissemination network that includes local advertising agencies, corporate-financed advertising councils, and

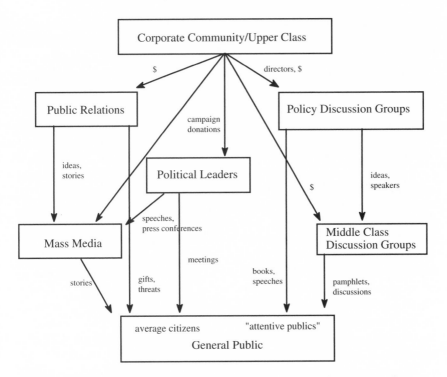

Figure 7.2   The General Network through Which the Power Elite Tries to Shape Public Opinion

special committees to influence single issues. Many polling organizations are also part of this process; their role is to monitor the success of corporations and policy discussion groups in shaping public opinion. In addition, as Herbst (1993, p. 166) argues, "the rigid, structured nature of polling may narrow the range of public discourse by defining the boundaries for public debate, and by influencing the ways that journalists report on politics." In contrast to the policy-planning process, where a relatively small number of organizations do most of the work, hundreds of organizations within the opinion-shaping process specialize in public relations and education on virtually every issue. Thus, at its point of direct contact with the general public, the opinion-molding process is extremely diverse and diffuse. The opinion-shaping process also relies on the mass media to disseminate its messages, where experts from the policy-planning network can have a direct effect on the general public (Page and Shapiro 1992, pp. 343–48; Zaller 1992, p. 319). A general overview of the opinion-shaping network is provided in figure 7.2.

The policy discussion groups do not enter into the opinion-shaping process directly, except through releasing their reports to newspapers and magazines. Instead, their leaders set up special committees to work for changes in public opinion on specific issues. Sometimes it is not possible to illustrate this close connection between the policy groups and the new public committees until historical archives are available. For example, leaders of the Council on Foreign Relations routinely denied that they had any guiding role in several different committees set up to shape opinion on foreign policy between 1939 and 1952, but papers and correspondence related to the organization later revealed otherwise (Wala 1994). It seems likely that the Committee on the Marshall Plan created in 1948 had the greatest influence by countering isolationist opinion in the Midwest and Congress, using a range of approaches as complete as any public relations firm can offer today.

According to Shapiro and Jacobs (chap. 10), changes in public opinion mattered "notably" in Nixon's overtures to China, but the source they cite does not explain how the changes in either opinion or policy occurred (Kusnitz 1984). This dual-level process likely began in 1958 and 1959 with statements by leaders in the Foreign Policy Association and Council on Foreign Relations calling for a new look. They were soon followed in 1959 and 1962 by two Council on Foreign Relations study groups funded by the Ford Foundation. These study groups included a mixture of the top business leaders and scholars of the day, many of whom also had served in government. They led to articles in the council's prestigious journal, *Foreign Affairs*, along with several books widely reviewed in elite media outlets, along with statements by corporate leaders and appointed government officials on television news shows.

The United Nations Association, yet another discussion and opinion-shaping group involved in foreign policy, published reports in 1966 and 1967 that advocated policy changes and received wide media coverage. Then a new National Committee on U.S.-China Relations, composed of leaders and experts from all three of the aforementioned organizations, launched a highly visible effort in March 1969 to influence public opinion by hosting a large convention of 2,000 people in Washington, followed by forums in other cities, frequent press releases, and appearances by its leaders and spokespersons on television. Throughout this whole period, leaders in the corporate community and policy-planning network were in close contact with political leaders, including Nixon, who advocated new directions in China policy in an article for *Foreign Affairs* in 1967. This process, which awaits more detailed study, prepared attentive public opinion for the negotiations with China that became public in 1971 (Page and Shapiro 1992, pp. 248–49; Shoup and Minter 1977, pp. 207–12).

To create an atmosphere in which the general public more readily accepts policy changes, these committees often attempt to picture the situation as a great crisis. For example, the Committee on the Present Danger did this in the mid-1970s to gain public support for increased defense spending, claiming that government estimates of Soviet defense spending and military capability were far too low (Sanders 1983). These efforts were followed by growing public support for greater defense spending from 1975 to 1979. However, the biggest jump in support came after the Iranian hostage crisis and Soviet invasion of Afghanistan in late 1979, both events used by the power elite and politicians to confirm their views and to smooth the way to the arms buildup in the 1980s (Page and Shapiro 1992, pp. 264–65).

Crisis-mongering is also the modus operandi of the opinion-shaping organizations that advocate cutbacks on Social Security benefits and the privatization of at least part of the system. They are guided by a handful of corporate CEOs, university presidents, former elected officials, and former cabinet officers who serve as the directors and financial backers of the Concord Coalition, Empower America, and the Cato Institute. (Pollster Daniel Yankelovich is on the board of the Concord Coalition.) With help from conservative foundations and wealthy individuals, several young anti–Social Security activists in an advocacy group called the Third Millennium have supplemented these organizations by working hard since 1993 to convince young adults that Social Security is unlikely to be around when they retire (Farley 1993; Shin 1997). Third Millennium claims, on the basis of polling results generated by a right-wing Republican pollster, that most young adults already agree that Social Security is as good as gone, a "fact" used by a wide array of politicians in their speeches (Cook, Barabas, and Page, chap. 8).

Public relations firms usually do not run campaigns aimed to shape overall public opinion. Instead, they are hired to work on specific issues and are asked to focus on relatively narrow target audiences. They often run all-out attacks on the organizations that express a growing public sentiment, leaving public opinion on the issue without a legitimate lobbying capability. Public affairs, on the other hand, is a more benign form of public relations, practiced by departments within the large corporations themselves. Here, the emphasis is on polishing the image of corporations rather than criticizing opposition groups and any journalists who may support them. The efforts of the public affairs departments are in good measure based on the large financial gifts they are able to provide to middle-class charitable and civic organizations through the corporation's foundation. These donations topped $6.1 billion in 1994, 33% of which went to education, 25% to health and charitable services, 12% to civic and community affairs, and 11% to culture and the arts (Himmelstein 1997). These efforts, in effect, attempt to buy goodwill and mute any future criticisms or lobbying efforts by a wide range of ongoing voluntary associations.

The opinion-shaping network achieves its clearest expression and greatest success in foreign policy, because most people have little information or interest in it and are predisposed to agree with top leaders out of patriotism and a fear of the strange or foreign. "Especially in the realm of foreign policy," according to Page and Shapiro (1992, p. 205), "where information can be centrally controlled, it seems especially likely that public opinion is often led." They add that this leading is done by "public officials and other influential groups and individuals." This "leadership" tendency seems to have increased in recent years (Shapiro and Jacobs, chap. 10). Because so few people take a serious interest in foreign policy issues, the opinion-shaping efforts by the Foreign Policy Association, World Affairs Councils, and the United Nations Association are aimed toward a small stratum of highly interested and concerned college-educated citizens. Their activities are financed by both private and corporate foundations (Domhoff 2002, pp. 109–10). This focus on attentive publics is consistent with evidence Kull and Ramsey (chap. 11) provide that policymakers do not think highly of public opinion on foreign policy and have no incentive to learn what voters think on these issues. Indeed, Kull and Ramsey's emphasis on the "self-serving" bias in people's tendency to misperceive what other people are thinking can be seen in this instance as a strong class bias.

Despite the efforts of the opinion-shaping groups, and public deference to popular presidents on foreign policy, there are limits to the shaping of public opinion on foreign policy when social stability is threatened and there is potential for social protest. For example, troop withdrawal from Vietnam increased in apparent reaction to growing protests and disapproval of the war (Shapiro and Jacobs, chap. 10).

Attempts to influence public opinion on domestic economic issues are many and varied. They even include a three-step process that tries to shape how economics is taught in middle schools and high schools. Interestingly enough, the organization at the heart of this process was founded by the moderate Committee for Economic Development with the help of Ford Foundation money to counter the overly simplistic materials circulated by the more conservative National Association of Manufacturers (Fones-Wolf 1994). But these efforts are often unsuccessful because people feel directly involved in domestic economic matters and have their own experiences to rely on. They generally favor more liberal policy options than members of the power elite prefer, which organizations in the opinion-shaping network attribute to "economic illiteracy." Spokespersons in the opinion-shaping network try to discredit the liberal options.

The success of the power elite in containing liberal policy preferences is revealed on the complex and highly emotional issue of welfare. As polls show, most people have a sensible view of why people may be unemployed for long periods, such as failures in the socioeconomic system, a lack of the proper job skills, or family problems. Therefore strong majorities support public-sector jobs, job training, child care subsidies, and subsidies for transportation to work. But government jobs have been anathema to business owners since the dawn of capitalism because they tighten labor markets and might contradict the claim that governments are incompetent (Piven and Cloward 1993; Rose 1994). Welfare therefore has to be understood as the power elite's fallback solution in the face of large-scale unemployment or potential social disruption by stigmatized minorities. However, spokespersons in the opinion-shaping nonetheless constantly criticize welfare recipients as lazy and undeserving, perhaps as a way of reinforcing the work ethic and minimizing the number of people who resort to welfare for subsistence.

Faced with the power elite's rejection of the liberal, job-oriented alternative to welfare, and in part buying into the anti-government and anti-dependency ideologies constantly stressed by the organizations in the opinion-shaping network, the majority of poll respondents resolve their policy dilemma by concluding that any reform is better than the current system, which ends up "increasing the policy leeway to those who control the policy agenda" (Weaver, chap. 6). Because the public's preferred policy preferences are stymied by conservative politicians, and its overall judgment of the welfare system is "primed" by opinion leaders and politicians, public opinion cannot be accorded a large role in the policy process on this issue. For the most part, it is another example of the closed loop between the opinion-shaping network, elected officials, and the media, with polls playing a legitimating role by showing, through a mixture of leading questions and brief presentations of complex policy options, that many people are "fed up" with one or another situation and want "something done."

Although the power elite usually is not able to alter Americans' liberal views on many other economic issues, this does not necessarily mean that their liberal opinions have much influence. To the contrary, a large body of evidence suggests that the majority's opinion is often ignored. This point is made most clearly by the "right turn" taken by the Carter and Reagan administrations from 1978 to 1983, despite strong evidence that the public remained liberal on the issues under consideration: "Throughout that period the public consistently favored more spending on the environment, education, medical care, the cities, and other matters, and it never accepted the full Reagan agenda of 'deregulation' " (Page and Shapiro 1992, p. 117). Another detailed analysis of survey data relating to the alleged rightward shift during this period found little support for the claim except on issues about crime, which have drawn lengthy noise from the opinion-shaping network and right-wing Republicans since the urban disturbances of the 1960s made crime a potential wedge issue. This analysis concludes that Democratic and Republican leaders embraced conservatism in the 1970s but that the American electorate did not follow their lead (Gold 1992).

The Candidate-Selection Process

The frequency with which public opinion is ignored on domestic economic issues presents a problem for theories that emphasize politicians' responsiveness to public opinion, but it is consistent with a class-dominance model. This model stresses two intertwined historical factors in explaining why the American electoral system functions primarily as a candidate-selection process and seldom as a way to provide citizen input into the policy process. First, the single-member district plurality system that evolved out of American colonial history makes it all but impossible to develop new third parties of the Left or Right, and at the same time puts a premium on attracting the median voter who gives one of the two major parties a winning plurality; both tendencies are enhanced by the presidential rather than parliamentary nature of the system (Lipset and Marks 2000; Rosenstone, Behr, and Lazarus 1996).

Because such a system does not foster parties and elections that articulate clear policy preferences, candidates emphasize their personal qualities rather than policy differences. The two parties may even collude to avoid some issues or to avoid competition in some districts. Thus, a two-party system leads to the possibility of little relationship between politics and policy. Candidates can say one thing to be elected and then do another once in office, which gives the well-organized groups that fund political campaigns an opening to shape legislation. (Hamilton [1972, chap. 1] argues against the assumption that the two-party system is of necessity responsive to voter preferences.)

In the United States, moreover, other well-known historical reasons led to a situation where bankers and industrialists from the North dominated one party and Southern merchants and plantation owners dominated the other until very recently (Domhoff 1990, chap. 9; Webber 2000; Woodward 1966). This control of both political parties by members of the power elite reinforces the worst tendencies of a two-party system. It also creates a context within which large campaign donations can influence which candidates enter and win primaries, so that the primaries of both parties become a "choke point," eliminating candidates unacceptable to the power elite (Alexander 1992; Heard 1960, p. 34). This control also magnifies the importance of the lucrative speaking engagements, consulting contracts, and jobs that members of the power elite can offer to politicians during and after their careers (Domhoff 2002, pp. 140–41).

Still, the liberal-labor coalition did begin to elect about a hundred Democrats to the House starting in the mid-1930s, where they joined roughly a hundred Southern Democrats and fifty machine Democrats from Northern urban areas to form a strong Democratic majority in all but a few sessions of Congress before 1994. By 1938, however, the Southern Democrats and Northern Republicans had formed a conservative voting bloc that stopped the liberal Democrats from passing legislation concerning union rights, civil rights, and the regulation of business (Alston and Ferrie 1999; Patterson 1981; Potter 1972). These issues define class conflict. This generalization included "civil rights" in the era of plantation capitalism because that was a code phrase for issues concerning the coercive control of the low-wage African American workforce in the South.

For the most part, the liberal-labor coalition, despite its majority support in public opinion polls on most economic issues, had to settle for occasional small victories when it could attract the support of some Southern Democrats. More generally, the Democratic Party became a pro-spending alliance in which Northern Democrats supported agricultural subsidies and price supports that greatly benefited Southern plantation owners (Clausen 1973; Domhoff 1990, chap. 9). In exchange, the Southerners were willing to support government spending programs for housing, hospital construction, highway construction, school lunches, and even public assistance, but with three provisos. The spending programs would contain no attack on segregation, they would be locally controlled, and they would differentially benefit Southern states. This arrangement hinged on a tacit agreement that the liberal-labor coalition would not vigorously oppose continuing segregation in the South (Brown 1999).

Thus, formal control of Congress by a supposedly liberal and pro-labor

Democratic Party for most of the years between 1932 and 1994 did not translate into economic policies a majority of Americans favored. Put another way, many politicians in urbanized Northern states may have responded to public opinion in the way assumed by standard models, but Congress as a whole did not. Instead, a conservative congressional majority—many from states where a large number of citizens could not vote and the party had a regional monopoly status—could ignore citizen preferences on many issues. Conservatives therefore could vote together on the issues that relate to economic liberalism and employee power, giving control of the policy agenda to the power elite and its policy-planning network. There are two crucial exceptions to this generalization, the mid-1930s and the mid-1960s, times of great social turmoil, when the pressures from social movements led to divisions between Northern Republicans and Southern Democrats.

The activism of workers in the 1930s, in conjunction with the exclusion of the Southern workforce to placate Southern plantation owners, led to passage of the pro-union National Labor Relations Act in 1935, despite the nearly unanimous opposition of Northern corporate leaders, showing how vulnerable they were without the help of their Southern allies (Domhoff 1990, chap. 4). Similarly, the pressures generated by the civil rights movement of the 1960s made possible the Civil Rights Act of 1964 when Northern Republicans, under pressure from many corporate executives as well as religious leaders and civil libertarians, finally voted to end the longest filibuster in Senate history (Whalen and Whalen 1985).

Contrary to Burstein's analysis (1998b and chap. 5), the conservative voting bloc likely would not have permitted a strong version of the Equal Employment Opportunity Commission as part of the Civil Rights Act if there had not been a powerful social movement capable of further strategic nonviolent social disruption to back up the supportive changes in public opinion. Nor is Burstein's emphasis on the 1972 amendments persuasive as a way of arguing that strong public support is sufficient to enact liberal legislation (1998b, pp. 82–87). The Southern political economy had been transformed since the 1930s (Alston and Ferrie 1999; Bloom 1987), so once the logjam was finally broken in 1964, there were few or no members of the power elite in any part of the country who opposed these amendments. Even the conservative U.S. Chamber of Commerce, which had opposed equal pay for women in 1963, favored the amendments.

The conservative voting bloc was pronounced dead at various points in the 1960s, 1970s, and 1980s, but it seldom lost when it materialized, playing an important role in modifying or blocking liberal-environmental-labor initiatives and in passing the Reagan administration's tax cuts (Domhoff 1990, chap. 10; Ferguson and Rogers 1986; Manley 1973; Shelley 1983). This voting bloc also gave Clinton his victories on NAFTA and permanent trade status for China in the face of vigorous liberal-environmental-labor opposition (Dreiling 2001; MacArthur 2000). The conservative voting bloc gradually disappeared in the late 1990s with the replacement of conservative Southern Democrats by even more conservative

Southern Republicans in the House and Senate, and by sixteen liberal African American Democrats in the House. It is now possible that a nationwide liberal-labor coalition could transform the Democratic Party and cause the electoral system to function in the way most theories of public opinion suggest it already does (Domhoff 2002, pp. 131–33, 194–96).

Within the structural and historical context created by a market economy, the American electoral rules, and the four networks that connect the power elite and government, there is room for what Jacobs and Shapiro (chap. 3) call a "political and institutional theory of policymaking." Such a theory would encompass the extensive political science literature, summarized and augmented by Jacobs and Shapiro (2000), on how elected officials from both parties vote their policy preferences, even when most voters oppose those preferences. This literature shows the complexity of politics and electioneering at the intersection between the power elite and ordinary citizens.

CONCLUSION

As Page and Shapiro (1992) show, average Americans hold sensible opinions within the demands of their everyday lives, their time constraints, and the information available to them, and they are generally liberal on economic issues. Their opinions show adaptation to new circumstances, such as the increasing participation of women in the workforce at all levels and the greater opportunities for African Americans. However, it is unlikely that any focused public opinion exists on most of the complicated legislative issues of concern to the corporate community. If there is such public opinion, it is divided by race, religion, class, and gender, and it is blocked in terms of legislation by conservative dominance in Congress. The power elite and politicians therefore enjoy leeway on most policy questions.

At the same time, politicians are highly responsive to the power elite's agenda because of how it can help and hinder them in their careers. Moderate and conservative politicians therefore use every means possible, including opinion polls, to craft a message that allows them to vote the policy preferences of business while trying to minimize any negative impacts of these votes on their electoral success (Jacobs and Shapiro 2000). This delicate and difficult enterprise is often balanced by taking strong stances on social issues of concern to key constituencies. When defeat comes, or an interest in holding office declines, moderate and conservative politicians are richly rewarded with positions as corporate directors, business association lobbyists, and advisors to organizations in the policy-planning and opinion-shaping networks.

The openness of the American political system to a wide range of opinions, along with the eagerness of rival politicians to win office, means there is always the possibility of changes that owners and managers of large corporations would not like. If most Americans had their way, there would be a much higher minimum wage, a much lower level of unemployment, a better safety net, less opportunity for American corporations to employ low-wage labor outside the nation's borders, and much else. None of these changes is likely to occur, despite the democratic nature of the country, because of the power of the wealthy few to shape foreign, defense, and economic policies to their liking.

Part II

HOW POLITICAL ELITES USE
PUBLIC OPINION

8

Policy Elites Invoke
Public Opinion

Polls, Policy Debates, and
the Future of Social Security

FAY LOMAX COOK, JASON BARABAS,
AND BENJAMIN I. PAGE

A central tenet of democratic theory and practice holds that policy elites are responsive to citizens' preferences. The increasing number of opinion surveys since the 1930s suggests that at least the *potential* for public opinion to play a major role in political processes has increased dramatically. Thus, one might expect that political leaders, policy experts, and others would draw on data from these polls to learn about public opinion—perhaps to respond faithfully to the public or at least to buttress the claim that their own positions affirm the popular will. And one might expect that their claims about the public's preferences would be accurate, backed by evidence.

Are these expectations actually met? To provide the answer, we report the results of an investigation into two research questions. First, how do policy elites invoke public opinion about Social Security? Second, are the claims accurate, based on evidence available to us through public opinion surveys? The complexities of elite behavior should reveal some of the inner mechanics and actual degree of democratic responsiveness in the United States.

For the purposes of our research questions, Social Security is a good issue to study. First, it is clearly an important program. It represents the largest single component of the U.S. federal government budget, with spending estimated at $455 billion, or about 23% of the budget, in fiscal year 2002 (U.S. Office of Management and Budget 2001). More than 44 million Americans receive benefits. In addition, Social Security has long been a major area of interest in U.S. politics, including the 2000 presidential race (Dao and Bruni 2000). As we shall see later, beginning in 1997, attention to Social Security increased dramatically. That year, the Advisory Council on Social Security, appointed by the Secretary of Health and Human Services, Donna Shalala, delivered a report that fueled an ongoing debate in Washington about what should be done to help finance the impending retirement of the baby boom generation. President Clinton highlighted Social Security in his 1998 and 1999 State of the Union addresses, and Congress held a series of hearings on the program. For these reasons and others, policy elites have talked about it often in the last decade and, as we will see, opinion pollsters have asked the public about it often during the same period.

PUBLIC OPINION AND PUBLIC POLICY CONNECTIONS

A fundamental goal in most democratic societies is a close connection between citizens' preferences and public policies. Thus, not surprisingly, scholars have tried to understand the relationship between public opinion and policy and have studied it in different ways. Some focus on how close the link is. They have demonstrated a relationship at the congressional district level (Miller and Stokes 1966; Erikson 1978; Hill and Hinton-Anderson 1995; Page et al. 1984), within the states (Erikson, Wright, and McIver 1993; Ringquist, Hill, Leighley, and Hinton-Anderson 1997), nationally (Page and Shapiro 1983; Monroe 1979, 1998; Jacobs 1992a; Wlezien 1995; also see Page 1994), and in specific policy areas such as defense (Bartels 1991; Hartley and Russett 1992) or across all three branches of national government (Stimson, MacKuen, and Erikson 1995).

Others use intensive case studies to help define the role of mass public opinion in policy making. For example, Paul Quirk and Joseph Hinchliffe (1998) study the influence of public pressure in six issue areas. They argue that the public has become an increasingly important force, a change resulting from the way that citizens connect with the political world. By the late 1960s, the public was becoming more aware of issues and more oriented to policy debate. As voters have become more likely to judge politicians on the basis of policies, politicians have expended more effort in figuring out what policies they want. Similar themes of elite responsiveness to public opinion emerge in John Geer's case studies of Abraham Lincoln's Emancipation Proclamation and George Bush's health care changes. Geer (1996) claims that, although Lincoln and Bush both wanted to pursue publicly supported policies, the difference is that "Lincoln adopted his particular course of action with questionable information about what the public wanted. Bush, on the other hand, possessed much better information, allowing him to react to the electorate's opinions" (p. 80).

Still others try to understand how policy elites think about and use public opinion (Herbst 1998; Jacobs 1992). As part of an ongoing project, Jacobs and Shapiro (1995) examined how Presidents Kennedy, Johnson, and Nixon connected presidential activity with public opinion by developing a "public opinion apparatus" in the White House to assemble public opinion data and conduct public relations activities. They find that all three presidents used the public opinion apparatus for symbolic and instrumental purposes. Symbolically, the knowledge of public opinion helped these presidents sell, legitimize, or justify presidential actions. Instrumentally, it helped them connect public opinion to strategic policy decisions. Our work resembles this type of research as we probe how policy elites invoke public opinion.

Not everyone considers the influence of public opinion in American politics to be a positive development. Some, like Benjamin Ginsberg (1986), see the rise of public opinion as something that expands the power of the state over the public. Ginsberg argues that polls and public opinion have become synonymous in American politics and that other forms of public expression (e.g., opinions of interest groups, parties, or grassroots organizations) are no longer considered "public opinion," because they have been displaced by the sample survey. Others, like Quirk and Hinchliffe (1998), see dangers as polls invade policymaking. They report that on four of the six issues they examined, public opinion "drove policymakers to overlook serious concerns, advanced by credible experts, about the workability of their proposals. The defeat was for careful thinking about public policy" (pp. 26–27).

Often the debate turns on the question of citizen competence and whether members of the public can be trusted to form meaningful preferences. On the one hand, evidence on citizen competence might make us think twice about entrusting so much to the public because of low levels of information (Delli Carpini and Keeter 1996), their adherence to misinformation (Kuklinski, Quirk, Jerit, Schwieder, and Rich 2000), or the inability to make policy trade-offs (Quirk and Hinchliffe 1998). However, other evidence suggests that the public as a whole forms rational beliefs (Page and Shapiro 1992) and can do so with surprisingly little information by using cues or heuristics (Ferejohn and Kuklinski 1990; Popkin 1994 [1991]; Sniderman, Brody, and Tetlock 1991; Lupia 1994; Lupia and McCubbins 1998).

Despite reservations about the influence of public opinion in American politics, a close correspondence between mass opinion and public policy remains an important goal in democratic theory. For John Geer (1996), following the public is the essence of leadership in many circumstances:

> Polls allow politicians to conduct a kind of democratic triage. For the highly salient issues, the rational politician acts in a manner consistent with the public's will. For those issues that are highly unlikely to capture the public's attention, politicians can follow the classic trustee strategy. Then for those issues that might become important, politicians can tackle the subset that will yield them the most public support. (p. 191)

Geer argues that making policy decisions based on public opinion is the only sensible response from the perspective of a rational politician seeking popular appeal and reelection. To do what Geer suggests, politicians must make rhetorical arguments in favor of their proposals. In this chapter, we examine how policy elites invoke public opinion in their arguments, specifically, in one particular policy arena: Social Security.

RESEARCH DESIGN

We used presidential statements on Social Security and witnesses' statements in congressional hearings on Social Security to learn about the claims policy elites make about public opinion on Social Security. To find presidential statements on Social Security, we used Presidential Papers CD-ROM (for the comparison period 1969–1992) and the *Weekly Compilation of Presidential Documents* database (for the study period 1993–99), archived by the National Archives and Records Administration of the Government Printing Office and available via the Internet at www.gpo.gov/nara/nara003.html. Presidential documents include all statements, speeches, remarks, and press conferences released by the White House. Using the key word "Social Security," we downloaded and printed every document that mentioned Social Security. For January 1993 to December 1999, we found 705 such documents. To find references to public opinion, we read each document and listed all statements invoking public opinion. A single document could contain more than one reference to public opinion, though in fact only a few did.

To find references to public opinion in congressional hearings, we conducted a document search using the Lexis-Nexis Congressional Universe database (http://web.lexis-nexis.com/congcomp) to locate all hearings on Social Security. Between 1993 and 1999, there were 108 hearings. We either found the published hearings in the government documents room at the Northwestern University Library or downloaded and printed the hearings from the Internet. Of the 108 hearings, 40 dealt with long-term issues of Social Security reform, in particular those that mention privatization or partial privatization of Social Security. We restrict our attention to these hearings for two reasons. Substantively, they provide a window through which to view the current Social Security debate and how public opinion is invoked in discussions related to changes in the program. Logistically, they offer a good way for us to narrow our examination of the statements of hundreds of individuals to a manageable number. To locate references to public opinion, we read the forty hearings and listed all statements invoking public opinion. As with the presidential documents, a single testimony could contain more than one reference to public opinion, and in the congressional testimonies they often did.

We coded each elite claim about public opinion—the unit of analysis in our research—on three dimensions. First, we coded whether the claim was "specific" or "general." Specific references include those in which the speaker cited percentages or used words such as "majority, "minority," "most," "few," "two-thirds," etc. General references use no quantitative reference to the distribution of public opinion—that is, not even reference to "a majority" or "most"—but rather phrases such as "Americans support" or "the public favors" or "young people believe," and so on. Second, as we read the invocations of public opinion,

ELITE CLAIMS

EVIDENCE	General (G)	Specific (S)
Clear-cut (1)	G-1	S-1
Mixed (2)	G-2	S-2
Little to None (3)	G-3	S-3

CODING CRITERIA
Evidence
Clear-cut: The public clearly supports or opposes the proposal or idea.
Mixed: Slim majorities in support or opposition or methodological issues
   (e.g., question order, wording, etc.).
Little to None: No way to evaluate the validity of the claim because no data
   existed or because we failed to locate data (e.g., no publicly available
   data).[1]

Elite Claims
Specific: Specific words that appear to refer to a quantitative distribution of
   public opinion. Use of percentages or words like "majority," "minority,"
   or "most," "few," "two-thirds," etc.
General: No specific reference to a quantitative aggregate distribution of
   public opinion. Use of terms like "Americans support," "young people
   are worried," "the public favors," "many," or "a lot."

[1] Many organizations conduct surveys but do not release their results to the public. The only way we can substantiate the elite claims is through publicly available data.

Figure 8.1 Framework for Assessing Elite Claims about Public Opinion and
Evidence for the Claims

we categorized the issue to which the claim referred into five topical categories:
the popularity of Social Security, confidence or concerns about the future of Social
Security, changes or reforms of Social Security, specific presidential positions or
initiatives and others. Third, we categorized the type of person who made the
claim: the president, a member of Congress, an interest group leader, an expert
(defined as researchers from think tanks, academics from universities and colleges, consultants, and subject-area specialists).

   Our next task was to determine whether evidence from public opinion surveys supports the claims. We coded the available evidence as clear-cut support
for the claims, mixed support (either majorities were slim, or methodological
issues such as question order, wording, etc., obscured the interpretation), or little
or no support (no way to evaluate the validity of the claim either because no
data existed or because we failed to locate data due to lack of publicly available
data).[1] To locate public opinion data, we conducted a Lexis-Nexis search of the
archives of the Roper Center for Public Opinion Research. Using "Social Security"
as a key word, we found that 2,352 questions had been asked in polls between
1990 and 1999. Our framework is schematized in figure 8.1.

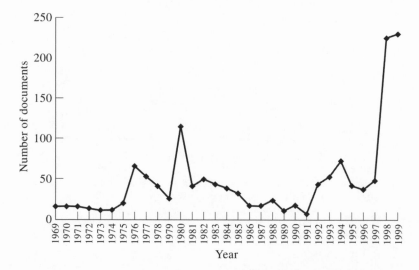

Figure 8.2   Presidential Addresses in Which Social Security Is Mentioned, 1969–1999. *Source:* Developed by the authors using Presidential Papers CD-ROM for 1969–1992 and Weekly Compilation of Presidential Documents for 1993–1999. *Note:* Addresses are defined as speeches, weekly radio addresses, press conference, etc. We coded only addresses where a president mentioned "Social Security" at least once during his remarks.

Quite simply, as illustrated in figure 8.1, we assessed each claim as general or specific. Then, we attempted to "fit" the claim to the evidence and to assess whether the evidence was clear-cut, mixed, or little or none. In the section that follows, we first examine the claims about Social Security and then present the evidence concerning the accuracy of each claim.

FINDINGS

President Clinton Invokes Public Opinion

From the time President Clinton took office in early 1993 until December 1999, he discussed Social Security in 705 public speeches, weekly radio addresses, press conferences, and so forth.[2] As figure 8.2 shows, the number of such addresses increased sharply over time. For example, in 1998, he discussed Social Security in various formats four and a half times more than he did in 1997—a total of 225 times as compared to 48 in 1997. This high level of attention continued in 1999, when he had something to say about Social Security in 230 separate public addresses.

Figure 8.2 illustrates the trends over time in these Social Security addresses for all presidents since 1969 to make another important point. Clinton paid far more attention to Social Security in his public addresses than his predecessors. Previous presidents said something about Social Security in their public addresses on a level near that of Clinton during the mid-1970s and again in the early 1980s. In 1976, President Ford mentioned Social Security in 65 public addresses. In 1980, President Carter raised the issue of Social Security in 115 addresses. By contrast, Clinton's sustained high interest was unique. Only two other presidents approached this level and then only in isolated years.

If President Clinton devoted more attention to Social Security than other recent presidents and most of the increase is recent, to what can we attribute such an intense interest? We think it grew out of the convergence of three largely separate streams of development (Kingdon 1984). From the "problem stream" came the concern that when the baby boom adults retired, fewer workers would be supporting more elderly persons, thus putting a financial strain on Social Security. In some circles, this was classified as a "crisis," and there was talk of "bankruptcy."

The second stream, which can be labeled "political," had many currents, but a major one was that in 1994 Clinton saw his party lose control of both the House and the Senate, the most disastrous first-term loss for a president since Herbert Hoover in the Great Depression in 1930 (specifically, eight seats for Clinton in 1994 in the Senate and fifty-two in the House; Barone and Ujifusa 1995). In his first term, his health care plan, economic package, and crime package were liabilities, and he needed a hardcore Democratic Party issue around which to unify the party and the public. Social Security has long been seen as a Democratic issue that wins with the public, and Clinton capitalized on it.

The third stream—policy proposals—contained two currents. One was a growing level of attention to privatization of Social Security as a way to "solve" Social Security's financial problem. Spearheaded by such groups as the Cato Institute, the Concord Coalition, and a young adults group called the Third Millennium, the privatization bandwagon had gained considerable momentum by 1997. A second important factor was the new policy possibilities due to the economy and the budget surplus. Rather than facing a budget deficit as he did when he came into office, President Clinton had a budget surplus. The Republicans wanted to use the surplus to cut taxes, a popular move. Clinton needed to find a way to co-opt this Republican proposal with a proposal that would garner even more public approval than tax cuts.

The three streams of problems, politics, and policy proposals converged in the second half of the 1990s and caused Clinton to decide that concentrating on Social Security would accomplish a number of goals: co-opt the Republicans on their tax cut plans, act as a counteroffensive against the privatizers, pull the country together around a major Democratic program, and ally him with Franklin D. Roosevelt, who launched Social Security and remains a president with bipartisan appeal.

The heightened attention to Social Security during the last few years of Clinton's presidency can be seen in the promises he made early in his State of the Union Address in 1998:

Table 8.1   Claims Made about Public Opinion by President Clinton (%)

Claims	President Clinton (N = 50)ᵃ
I. Confidence or concerns about the future of Social Security	44
II. Support for specific presidential positions or particular initiatives	20
III. Support for changes, reforms, or the privatization of Social Security	16
IV. Social Security is a popular program	10
V. Other statements	10
Total %	100

ᵃ The N refers to number of claims about public opinion. These claims were made in 44 addresses in which public opinion on Social Security was mentioned.

> Now, if we balance the budget for next year, it is projected that we'll then have a sizable surplus in the years that immediately follow. What should we do with this projected surplus? I have a simple four-word answer: Save Social Security first. [Applause] Thank you. Tonight I propose that we reserve 100 percent of the surplus—that's every penny of any surplus—until we have taken all the necessary measures to strengthen the Social Security system for the 21st century. Let us say to all Americans watching tonight—whether you're 70 or 50, or whether you just started paying into the system—Social Security will be there when you need it. Let us make this commitment: Social Security first.

With those words, President Clinton embarked on a public mission to make Social Security reform a lasting legacy for his administration. Interestingly, at the same time he increased his emphasis on Social Security after that State of the Union speech, he also began to invoke public opinion on this issue more than in the past. Until 1998, President Clinton rarely referred to public opinion while discussing Social Security—he made only two references to public opinion in 1995, one in 1996, and none in 1993, 1994, or 1997. Then, in 1998, he invoked public opinion in 31 addresses. These references fell into the five categories listed in table 8.1.

Overall, we identified fifty separate instances in forty-four addresses where President Clinton invoked public opinion across these five categories. As table 8.1 depicts, President Clinton commonly invoked public opinion to underscore confidence or concern about the future of Social Security. About two-thirds of his references to the public's concern expressed a worry that the costs of paying for the retirement of his fellow "baby boom" generation would intolerably burden younger workers. For example, at an elementary school in 1979, President Clinton referred to himself as "the oldest of the baby boomers" and said, "One of our biggest worries, my whole generation, is that because we are so big, and bigger than our children's generation, that we will retire and impose such a burden on our children that they won't be able to do it right by our grandchildren. We can avoid that now if we save Social Security and Medicare" (Clinton 1999b).

In seven of the twenty-two statements related to confidence, President Clinton alluded to a finding from a 1994 poll from the Third Millennium organization that claimed more young people believed in unidentified flying objects (UFOs) than in the long-term survival of Social Security. In one speech at the University of Illinois, President Clinton said, "There are polls that say that young people in their twenties think it's more likely that they will see UFOs than that they will ever collect Social Security" (Clinton 1998b). Later we address the accuracy of the claim, but for now the important point is that the president often commented on the public's perceived lack of confidence in the future of Social Security. His aim, it appears, was to emphasize the urgency of acting (presumably by adopting his own proposed solutions), and to do so in a way that identified with his audience's worries (in this case, college students).

From table 8.1, we see that the second most common way that President Clinton invoked public opinion was to talk about public support for his own specific proposals or initiatives. For example, the president said, "I am heartened by the strong support this approach [saving the budget surplus until Social Security is saved] has gained from the American people, including the young people to whom I spoke yesterday at Georgetown University" (Clinton 1998c).

Sixteen percent of his invocations of public opinion were about public support for changes or reforms in Social Security in general. In one speech, President Clinton remarked, "But let me just say this—there is a huge amount of discussion about this out there now, and I think most Americans know we've got to make some changes. And I think most Americans will support us making some substantial changes, because there is no point in being dishonest about it, we can't sustain the present system as the baby boomers retire at the present rates of return" (Clinton 1998d). Statements like these seemed to show that Americans were ready for change.

President Clinton invoked public opinion to point out that Social Security is widely popular in only 10% of his addresses. To demonstrate the historic and continuing popularity of Social Security, he pointed to support for former President Franklin D. Roosevelt's path-breaking establishment of the program. For example, during his 1999 State of the Union address, Clinton notes, "When President Roosevelt created Social Security, thousands wrote to thank him for eliminating what one woman called 'the stark terror of penniless, helpless old age' " (Clinton 1999a). Invoking the president with perhaps the greatest amount of bipartisan support in the twentieth century was a rhetorical device to promote Clinton as the savior of Roosevelt's legacy.

Most of President Clinton's public opinion claims (35 out of 50 or 70%) were general rather than specific. When invoking public opinion, he used terms like "the American people support," "young people," "everybody I know," "people in the baby boom generation I've talked to," or "the people I know in my generation." In one particular attempt to be inclusive, he draw out a string of referents to invoke public opinion: "my people, the people I grew up with, middle-class people, people without a lot of money." In the third subsection here, we will revisit the generality of his claims and ask whether data support his assertions.

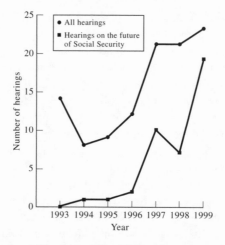

Figure 8.3 Congressional Hearings on Social Security, 1993–1999. *Note:* The overall number of hearings denotes hearings in which the focus was either on Social Security directly or on issues related to Social Security. The hearings on the future of Social Security are those in which privatization of Social Security is discussed (of these three were solely devoted to privatization—one in 1995, one in 1996, and one in 1998).

What have we learned from these presidential claims regarding public opinion. In particular, why might we see such patterns of attention to the public's confidence in the future of Social Security, especially given the prevalence of general claims without much specificity? The most straightforward explanation seems to be that President Clinton clearly wanted to reassure his audiences and identify with them. By acknowledging their concerns, he tried to persuade them that his proposals should be adopted. By portraying himself as a person who listens to "the American people," he could then convincingly imply that since "the American people" support his proposal, so too should his audience members.

Congressional Witnesses Invoke Public Opinion

From January 1993 to December 1999, Congress held 108 hearings on Social Security. Figure 8.3 shows that the number of hearings increased sharply beginning in 1997, rising from twelve in 1996 to twenty-one in 1997. This increase appears to coincide with actions of the president—first, the release of the report of the Advisory Council on Social Security, a council appointed by Donna Shalala, his Secretary of Department of Health and Human Services, and second, the statements he made about Social Security in his 1998 and 1999 State of the Union addresses.

In this chapter, we examine the forty hearings that dealt with long-term issues of Social Security reform, using the mention of privatization or partial privatization of Social Security as a filtering mechanism. In our examination of all statements by members of Congress and the representatives of interest groups and experts who were invited to testify, we focus on their invocations of public opinion. As with presidential statements, we classified each public opinion reference into one of five topical categories (confidence, support for changes, popularity, support for presidential initiatives, other).

DECLINING CONFIDENCE/RISING CONCERNS   As table 8.2 shows, the largest proportion of those who invoked public opinion did so to point out that confidence has declined. Members of Congress, interest group representatives, and experts said that Americans had grave doubts about the Social Security system's long-term financial viability. Some provided clear-cut evidence using actual survey results (for example, "A survey released by the Employee Benefit Research Institute reports that . . ."); others made very general claims (for example, "there is an alarming erosion of public confidence in the Social Security system").

Many of the claims about public opinion cited a poll allegedly showing that young people were more likely to believe in unidentified flying objects than to think that Social Security would be there for them when they retire. The following representative comments from an interest group spokesman, a member of Congress, and an expert illustrate how well known the supposed UFO finding seemed to be:

Table 8.2   Claims Made in Congressional Hearings about Public Opinion: Congress Members, Interest Groups, and Experts (%)

Claims	Total % (N = 264)[a]	Congress Members (N = 105)	Interest Group (N = 96)	Experts[b] (N = 60)	Other (N = 3)
I. Confidence or concerns about the future of Social Security	38	39	32	41	0
II. Support for specific presidential positions or particular initiatives	7	10	2	6	33
III. Support for changes, reforms, or the privatization of Social Security	19	13	18	27	0
IV. Social Security is a popular program	13	12	15	13	33
V. Other statements	23	25	33	14	33
Total %	100	100	100	100	100

[a] The Ns refer to number of claims, not to number of persons in each group.
[b] We define experts as researchers from think tanks such as Brookings Institution, academics from universities and colleges, consultants, and subject-area specialists.

Almost twice as many young people believe in unidentified flying objects or UFOs as believe in the long-term existence of the Social Security system. (Robert Lukefahr, Third Millenium 1994)

I have heard it said that young people think that they are more likely to see a UFO in their lifetime than be able to retire on Social Security. (Congressman Charles Grassley 1997)

You have seen the same polls that we have, these *USA Today* polls that have young people trusting more that they will see a UFO than that will get their Social Security benefits. (Edward M. Gramlich, Ph.D., Chair, Advisory Council on Social Security, and at the time a professor at the University of Michigan School of Public Policy 1997)

Later, the UFO story was told with even more dramatic flair. For example, Senator Ron Wyden (D-OR) energetically declared, "We all know we have a demographic tsunami coming, 75 million baby boomers. At home, I can tell you, more of the young people think they are going to have a date with an extraterrestrial than to get a Social Security check. I mean, that is essentially the landscape I find at home" (Wyden 1998).

Whereas from 1994 to 1997, most of the claims had to do with the views of young people 18–35 years old, later some members of Congress generalized the UFO finding to baby boomers. According to Senator John Breaux (D-LA), "There are 77 million baby boomers waiting to become retirees, beginning in the year 2010. Many of those baby boomers believe more in UFOs than they believe in the fact that Social Security will be there when they are ready to retire" (Breaux 1998).

No speakers who testified disputed the claim that the public's confidence in Social Security has undergone a dramatic decline, even though, as we shall see in the next section, there are reasons to dispute it. However, some argued that the public, regardless of age, should *not* have little confidence. For example, Yale professor Theodore Marmor (1977) said, "Too many Americans already believe that they will not receive their public pensions because (a) those pensions will be unaffordable or (b) there will no longer be public support for acting on earlier commitments. Neither of these arguments can be realistically defended—but that has not prevented their distribution and effect."

Why are there such a disproportionate number of claims about falling public confidence? In order for an issue to be given a high priority on the national agenda, a case must be made that it deserves attention. With regard to Social Security, policy elites—concerned about projected problems or simply eager to attack the existing system—seem to believe that it is not enough to cite dates and statistics about projected pressure on the trust funds. They want to show that the public is worried about a risky future and feels insecure. By invoking public fears, they make a stronger case for the need for action.

SUPPORT FOR CHANGES/REFORMS/PRIVATIZATION   Nineteen percent of all citations of public opinion in Congress focused on claims about the public's support for some type of change to Social Security. In particular, a frequent claim was that the public supports privatization or partial privatization. Cato commissioned Public Opinion Strategies to conduct a survey, and Cato's Michael Tanner (1996) quoted extensively from the results to show that the public wants privatization:

> More than two-thirds believe that Social Security will require "major" or "radical" change within the next 20 years. The support for change cuts across ideological and party lines. . . . More than two-thirds of all voters, 69 percent, would support transforming the program into a privatized mandatory savings program. More than three-quarters of younger voters support privatization. As this public support emerges into the political process, Social Security will no longer be the third rail of American politics. Indeed, if politicians refuse to deal with Social Security's problems, they may soon face a new third rail in their search for support among younger voters.

Although in the 1980s the Cato Institute alone called for privatization of Social Security, this is no longer true. Several members of Congress spoke out for privatization in the hearings. For example, Senator Chuck Hagel (R-NE) was forceful in invoking public opinion to support his preference for privatization: "Personal retirement accounts would harness the power of private markets and compound interest, giving individuals ownership of their retirement savings. Americans want more power, more choice, more responsibility in deciding their own future and economic well-being. It's their money" (1998).

But was the public really "ready" for privatization? Several members of Congress asked this question in hearings. One think tank expert, appearing to draw on a vast reservoir of knowledge about public opinion, answered with no caveats, "Absolutely! There's not the slightest doubt in my mind that they are" (Glassman 1998).

Curiously, although some who testified were against privatization, they cited no public opinion data to argue against it. It is not clear why not. We will see below that public opinion data were considerably more ambiguous than the hearing testimony of privatization advocates indicated.

POPULARITY OF SOCIAL SECURITY   Only 13% of all claims about public opinion focused on its popularity among the public. No speaker disagreed that the public supports Social Security. Even a spokesman for the Cato Institute, which is highly critical of the program, acknowledged, "No one should doubt the continued popularity of Social Security. Our poll results clearly showed that Social Security remains one of the most popular of all government programs, with two-thirds of those polled holding a favorable view of the program" (Tanner 1996).

Robert Ball, a former commissioner of Social Security, linked the popularity of Social Security to the history of congressional attempts to find bipartisan solutions: "Whenever Social Security's long-term stability has been threatened by circumstances warranting a legislative response, strong public support for the program has encouraged political leaders to seek bipartisan solutions that build on Social Security's inherent strengths" (1997).

When Senator Robert Kerrey thought that Senator Grassley was attacking Social Security by citing poll data that young people are more likely to believe in UFOs than in the future of Social Security, he defended the popularity of Social Security among the young: "I have seen the same poll that Senator Grassley referred to. . . . That does not say much about our educational system, but I will leave that for another hearing. Social Security is a program that has strong intergenerational support. Polls show that people under the age of 35 support Social Security as much as people over the age of 65" (1997).

Given the consensus on the popularity of Social Security from one side of the political spectrum to the other, why were there so relatively few mentions of the program's popularity? Presumably, many speakers simply assumed that Social Security is an important program, well accepted by the public, and thus felt no need to make a point that they considered basic. In addition, some advocates of privatization may have preferred to de-emphasize the great popularity of the existing program.

GENERALITY VS. SPECIFICITY OF THE CLAIMS   Similar to the presidential statements about public opinion about Social Security, the majority of claims about opinion in the congressional hearings were general also—73% (70% of President Clinton's references to public opinion were general).

Why? One possibility is that specific data about public opinion are simply hard to find or remember, and therefore policy elites use cognitive shortcuts and shorthand phrases rather than concrete percentages. But survey data were abundant. Presidents and congressional witnesses generally write out their words in advance and have access to research assistance; surely they could have handled a few marginal frequencies. Another possibility is that policy elites consider their audiences uninterested in or incapable of understanding concrete data. That explanation would seem more applicable to presidents' speeches to broad public audiences rather than congressional witnesses' testimony to highly elite audiences. A third possibility is that many policy elites simply do not believe the results of surveys and prefer other ways of judging public sentiment (see Herbst 1998). But we are inclined also to give some weight to a fourth possibility: that policy elites who cannot find solid evidence of public agreement with their own positions sometimes choose to make vague (even factually insupportable) assertions that "the people" stand with them.

Evidence on Claims about Public Opinion

How accurate are policy elites' claims about public opinion? To address this question, we used the Roper Center archives to find relevant questions asked of respondents in national surveys from 1990 to 1999. During this time, opinion polling organizations asked approximately 2,352 questions about Social Security.[3] As Figure 8.4 depicts, the number of questions increased dramatically over the 1990s. Fewer than 100 questions were asked in each year between 1990 and 1993. These

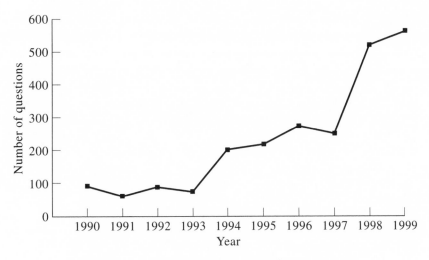

Figure 8.4 Social Security Survey Questions, 1990–1999

numbers more than doubled from 1994 to 1997, ranging between 201 and 275 questions each year. In 1998, again the number of questions asked in polls more than doubled—to 521, and this number increased slightly in 1999. What do these polls tell us about public opinion about Social Security and about whether the policy elites' claims were accurate?

PUBLIC CONFIDENCE IN SOCIAL SECURITY   In the two earlier sections, we read the claims that public confidence in the future of Social Security has declined. Again and again, President Clinton and those testifying in congressional hearings reported that young people are more likely to believe in UFOs than in the future of Social Security.

In opinion polls over the years, the public has answered many questions about confidence in Social Security that can help us evaluate these claims. Beginning in 1975, the public was asked, "How confident are you, yourself, in the future of the Social Security system? Would you say you are very confident, somewhat confident, not too confident, or not at all confident?" The trend in responses appears in figure 8.5. The decline in confidence from 1975 to the 1990s is indeed dramatic if you compare only 1975 (when almost two-thirds of the public were very or somewhat confident) to 1996 (when it was just the opposite—almost two-thirds were not too or not at all confident). However, the story in figure 8.5 is more complex than a simple comparison of two time points. The proportion of Americans who were "very confident" or "somewhat confident" about the future of Social Security has fluctuated over the years, and the largest decline in confidence occurred between 1975 and 1982. There was nothing sharp or recent about this decline. Noting the timing of the decline, Jacobs and Shapiro (1998a; see also

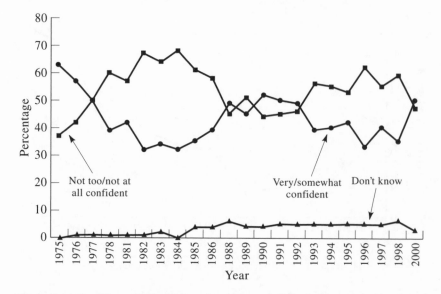

Figure 8.5 Confidence in Social Security. *Sources:* A "Monitoring Attitudes of the Public" survey sponsored by the American Council of Life Insurance and conducted by Yankelovich, Skelly, and White (1975–1982) and the Roper Organization/Roper Starch Worldwide (1983–2000). More than 1,000 respondents participated in each survey. The question was: "How confident are you, yourself, in the future of the Social Security system? Would you say you are very confident, somewhat confident, not too confident, or not at all confident?" *Note:* The question was not asked in 1979, 1980, 1987, and 1999.

1998b) point out, "that trust began to fall in the '70s suggests that the real cause is the public's general loss of faith in government after Watergate and Vietnam, not any focused critique of Social Security" (p. 13).

Still, the low level of expressed confidence was real. Why? One possibility is that it may have been based on misinformation. Another is that it may have been fueled by alarmist rhetoric about "crisis" and "bankruptcy" from elites them-selves—rhetoric that may have been misleading (Skidmore 1999). Survey evidence supporting both these possibilities comes from the finding by the Princeton Survey Research Associates (PSRA) in four 1998 and 1999 surveys. Table 8.3 shows that more than half the public say they think Social Security is headed for financial trouble in the future. The same proportion think that "big changes" are needed. When the public is asked about reasons for the changes, it becomes clear that their views of "major trouble" and the need for big changes may be based on misinformation. Most appear not to know that Social Security is headed for financial trouble because of the changing ratio between workers and retirees.

Further, many respondents had a very bleak view—not shared by program actuaries or other experts—of what would happen if "no changes are made" in the program for twenty years. Large majorities (69%, 66%, 66%, and 68%) said

Table 8.3 Perceptions of Problems with Social Security

Perceptions of SS Problems	% in Survey			
	March 1998	July 1998	Feb. 1999	May 1999
Degree of trouble with system[a]				
Major trouble	55	52	53	57
Minor trouble	29	29	31	30
Secure and solid (no trouble)	10	10	10	9
Don't know / refused	6	9	6	5
Size of changes needed[b]				
No changes	7	4	3	4
Small changes	30	29	30	33
Big changes	57	60	61	58
Don't know / refused	6	7	6	5
If no changes, what happens[c]				
Run out of money	32	34	34	32
Pay less than half benefits	37	32	32	36
Pay three-quarters benefits	12	11	10	12
Pay full benefits	9	13	13	10
Don't know / refused	10	10	11	10
Reason for upcoming troubles[d]				
Gov't spent SS reserves	45	47	41	42
More retirees than workers	26	26	32	27
Cost-of-living too high	12	10	10	12
Wealthy get benefits	6	6	7	8
Retirees get too much	5	5	6	6
Don't know / refused	6	6	4	6

Source: Princeton Survey Research Associates. N = 1.200 for 3/98 and 7/98. N = 1,000 for 2/99. N = 1,001 for 5/99.

Note: Percentages do not always sum to 100% due to rounding.

[a] "Some people now think the Social Security program is heading for financial trouble in the future, while other people think the program is basically secure and solid. What is your view? Do you think Social Security is headed for major trouble, minor trouble, or do you think the program is secure and solid?"

[b] "Which of the following comes closest to describing what you think is needed to keep the Social Security program out of trouble in the future? Do you think this program needs no changes, small changes, or big changes?"

[c] "If no changes are made to the Social Security program over the next twenty years, what do you think will happen? Will Social Security. . . ." The N for this question was 628 in 7/98, 502 in 2/99, and 508 in 5/99.

[d] "And, which of these do you think is the main reason the Social Security program might be headed for financial trouble? [The choice categories were as follows:] The government has spent the Social Security reserves for other programs; the number of older people is growing faster than the number of workers; the cost-of-living increases are too high; even people who could afford to live comfortably on their own get benefits; most older people get more money than they paid in; none of these [volunteered]; don't know/refused."

that Social Security would "pay less than half of the benefits" or even "run out of money" altogether. Experts, on the other hand, all agreed that even after the alleged "bankruptcy" point when the trust fund might be depleted and promised benefits exceed revenues, about 75% of benefits would continue to be paid (Social Security and Medicare Boards of Trustees 1999; Baker and Weisbrot 1999).

The most dramatic claim that policy elites made about the public's lack of confidence in Social Security was that young people are more likely to believe in UFOs than to believe that they would receive Social Security. Do poll data really substantiate this claim? The answer is "mixed," in the language of our framework in figure 8.1. In 1994, the Luntz Research Company conducted a survey of 500 18–34-year-olds to get the "Generation X" perspective on Social Security. The question for Social Security was "Do you think Social Security will still exist by the time you retire?" Sixty-three percent said no. Eight questions later, interviewers asked, "And one final question, and I ask you to take this seriously—Do think UFOs exist?" Forty-six percent said yes. Thus, technically it is true that, according to this survey, a larger percentage of young adults 18 to 34 thought UFOs exist than think Social Security will exist when they retire. However, the way the results were reported made it appear that respondents were asked to compare their belief in UFOs to their belief in Social Security in the context of one question. Clearly, they weren't.

Following up on the "UFO finding," a survey was conducted in 1997 for the Employee Benefit Research Institute in which it was possible to compare beliefs about Social Security and UFOs in the same question. Interviewers asked young adults ages 18 to 34: "Which do you have greater confidence in—receiving Social Security benefits after retirement or that alien life from outer space exists?" Asked this way, as table 8.4 shows, 63% have greater confidence in Social Security, while 33% have greater confidence in the existence of alien life. As Jacobs and Shapiro (1998a) note, "the true state of public opinion on Social Security turns out to be more complicated than this popular sound bite suggests—a lot more complicated. ... It has as much to do with leading (or misleading) poll questions as it does with the merits of the actual plan." In the statements in congressional hearings we read, *none* offered information to correct and update the UFO story. Why? Did the members truly not know about the new data, or was it simply more in line with their positions to continue to use the UFO finding? We do not know. But it appears that once the dramatic research finding was quoted and repeated by policy elites, it took on a life of its own as conventional wisdom and was then difficult to dislodge.

In summary, the poll data show that although evidence existed to justify the claim that the public lacked confidence in the future of Social Security, that confidence did not decline only recently. Rather, it was low since the late 1970s. Further, the finding on UFOs was overstated and overgeneralized. Nowhere in the presidential statements and in the congressional testimonies were the findings questioned or corrected with the later data in which respondents were given a choice in the same question. Moreover, some of the lack of confidence appears to be based on misinformation.

Table 8.4   UFOs and Social Security Confidence

	% in Survey	
	All Respondents	18–34-Year-Olds
1994 Luntz/Siegel & Third Millennium[a] **Social Security will exist in retirement?**		
Yes	—	28
No	—	63
Don't know/refused	—	9
Do UFOs exist?	—	
Yes	—	46
No	—	43
Don't know/refused	—	11
1997 Greenwald & Employee Benefit Research Institute[b] **Greater confidence?**		
Receive Social Security	71	63
Alien life exists	26	33
Don't know/refused	3	4
1999 Hart & 2030 Center[c] **Expectations about Social Security benefits**		
Same as today's level	—	15
Less	—	45
No benefits at all	—	31

[a] The Third Millennium survey was conducted September 8–10, 1994, by Luntz Research Companies and Mark A. Siegel and Associates. A total of 500 18–34-year-olds were interviewed to get the "Generation X" perspective on Social Security. The Social Security question was the sixth item and the UFO was asked as the fourteenth item. The question for the Social Security was, "Do you think Social Security will still exist by the time you retire?" The question for the UFO item was, "And one final question, and I ask you to take this seriously—Do you think UFOs exist?"

[b] In July 1997, Matthew Greenwald and Associates conducted the Retirement Confidence Survey for the Employee Benefit Research Institute and American Savings Education to compare beliefs about the existence of Social Security and UFOs in the same question. In their survey of 18-to 34-year-olds (N unavailable), the question asked, "Which do you have greater confidence in . . . receiving Social Security benefits after retirement or that alien life from outer space exists?"

[c] Peter Hart Research Associates poll conducted for the 2030 Center. A total of 403 18–34-year-olds participated in the survey conducted May 17–24, 1999. The question was, "When you reach retirement age, do you think that Social Security will be paying the same level of benefits as it pays now, paying less than now, or will it not be paying benefits at all?"

POPULARITY OF SOCIAL SECURITY   Both Social Security critics and supporters pointed out that Social Security is a highly popular program. In the words of one expert who testified before Congress, Social Security has "the overwhelming support of the American public," and further, "the voting public wants the benefits and is perfectly willing to pay for them" (Schultz 1995). Does the evidence support the claims?

Beginning in 1984 and continuing in most years in annual General Social

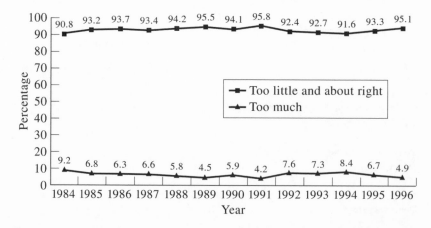

Figure 8.6 Support for Social Security Spending, 1984–2000. By "support for So-cial Security spending" we mean the percentage of people responding that we spend "too little" or "about the right amount," rather than "too much money," on Social Security. *Source:* The data are from NORC General Social Surveys. The question was: "We are faced with many problems in this country, none of which can be solved easily or inexpensively. I'm going to name some of these problems, and for each one I'd like you to tell me whether you think we're spending too much money on it, too little money, or about the right amount. Are we spending too much money, too little money, or about the right amount on Social Security?" *Note:* This question was not asked in 1992, 1995, 1997, and 1999. These percentages do not include "Don't know" and other volunteered responses.

Surveys, the National Opinion Research Center (NORC) asked a large nationally representative sample of respondents, "Are we spending too much, too little, or about the right amount on Social Security?" We defined support as saying we are spending too little or about the right amount. As figure 8.6 shows, by this defi-nition, in every one of thirteen surveys through 2000, 90% or more of the general public supported Social Security.

The University of Michigan's National Election Studies (NES) asked a similar question in each election year between 1984 and 1996: "If you had a say in making up the federal budget this year, for which of the following programs would you like to see spending increased and for which would you like to see spending decreased. Should federal spending on Social Security be increased, decreased, or kept about the same?" Defining support as saying spending should be increased or kept the same, the findings from the NES surveys tell the same story as the NORC data in figure 8.6: more than 90% favored maintaining or increasing spending in every one of the surveys. As Schultz noted, the public is over-whelmingly supportive.

Clearly, the data on support match the claims. When policy elites invoke public opinion to make the point that Social Security is popular, they stand on firm ground. Again, however, the strange fact is that the program's popularity was seldom invoked.

SUPPORT FOR CHANGES/REFORMS/PRIVATIZATION   Policy elites frequently invoked public opinion to make claims about the public's readiness for changes or reforms in the program and about their support for partial or full privatization. In table 8.3, we saw that roughly 60% of the public in surveys in both 1998 and 1999 said that big changes were needed in Social Security to keep it out of trouble in the future. What kinds of changes?

Moderate changes that have been recommended by experts (which in various combinations would solve the projected financial problems: see Social Security Advisory Board 1998, pp. 25–26; Baker and Weisbrot 1999; Page and Simmons 2000, chap. 3) include lowering the cost of living adjustments (COLAs), reducing benefits for the wealthy elderly (e.g., wealthy defined as those with incomes of over $60,000); increasing the payroll tax; raising the earnings ceiling or cap that exempts all income above a certain level from payroll taxation; raising the age of eligibility for full Social Security retirement benefits to 70; and raising the minimum age of receiving reduced Social Security benefits from 62 to 65. The results of a survey conducted by Princeton Survey Research Associates appear in table 8.5. A majority of the public is not in favor of four of the six proposals. Only two proposals—reducing benefits for the wealthy and raising the earnings ceiling—received support from more than half the respondents (54% and 60%, respectively).

Most of the claims about public opinion have focused on attitudes toward partial or full privatization. In four PSRA and NPR/Kaiser/JFK School polls, interviewers asked respondents their opinion about privatization proposals. As table 8.6 shows, in three out of four polls, a majority of the public opposed having the government invest a portion of Social Security reserve funds. But majorities ranging from 52% to 65% said they favored having individuals invest "some" or "a portion" of their payroll tax contributions themselves. Clearly, however, the public does not want to abandon Social Security completely. The one poll we found on full privatization in March 1999 shows a majority opposed "allowing workers to take all of their Social Security taxes out of the Social Security system and invest them on their own."

Since March 1996, at least nineteen survey questions with various wordings have asked about partial privatization. As table 8.7 shows, majorities were in favor. This would seem to support policy elites' claims. But some important qualifications are in order. Several of these survey questions alluded to benefits of privatization (for example, the early surveys sponsored by the Cato Institute mentioned "no reduction in benefits for current Social Security recipients," and "choice of staying in the current system"). Others alluded to a need for action ("if nothing is changed, the system will go broke"). But none of them mentioned any possible costs or risks of privatization. Given that the idea of privatizing

Table 8.5 Social Security Policy Option
Preferences (%)

Policy Option	August 1998
Cut benefits by lowering cost of living adjustment	
Strongly or moderately favor	34
Strongly or moderately oppose	61
Neither/don't know	5
Reduce benefits for the wealthy (over $60,000)	
Strongly or moderately favor	54
Strongly or moderately oppose	40
Neither/don't know	6
Increase payroll tax from 6.2% to 6.7%	
Strongly or moderately favor	40
Strongly or moderately oppose	54
Neither/don't know	6
Raise earnings ceiling from $68,000 to $100,000	
Strongly or moderately favor	60
Strongly or moderately oppose	29
Neither/don't know	11
Raise the retirement age to 70 years old	
Strongly or moderately favor	23
Strongly or moderately oppose	74
Neither/don't know	3
Gradually increase early retirement age from 62 to 65	
Strongly or moderately favor	47
Strongly or moderately oppose	47
Neither/don't know	6

Source: Princeton Survey Research Associates. $N = 2,008$.

Social Security was at that time new to most Americans, and that few had much information about it, one could argue for the use of balanced questions listing both advantages and disadvantages. One-sided, pro-privatization questions like Cato's were likely to overestimate support for privatization. Even neutral questions that just brought up the idea of free choice of retirement investments (inherently attractive to individualistic Americans), without mentioning pros and cons, might well overestimate the degree to which the public would support privatization as people learned more about the idea.

What happens when respondents have a chance to consider the risks of privatization? Table 8.8 presents six sets of results from surveys by Yankelovich

Table 8.6 Support for Social Security Privatization Options

Social Security Policy Reform	% in Survey			
	8/98[a]	2/99[b]	3/99[c]	5/99[d]
Partial privatization				
Gov't invests SS[e]				
Favor	40	36	38	40
Oppose	48	53	61	52
Neither / don't know / refused	12	11	2	8
Individuals invest SS[f]				
Favor	52	55	65	58
Oppose	38	37	33	33
Neither / don't know / refused	10	8	3	9
Full privatization				
Full privatization option[g]				
Favor	—	—	42	—
Oppose	—	—	57	—
Neither / don't know / refused	—	—	1	—

Note: Figures do not always sum to 100% due to rounding.

[a] Princeton Survey Research Associates (PSRA) data, 8/6/98–8/27/98, N = 2,008.

[b] Princeton Survey Research Associates (PSRA) data, 2/2/99–2/14/99, N = 1,000.

[c] NPR/Kaiser/Kennedy School Poll (NPR/Kaiser/JFK) data, 3/4/99–3/24/99, N = 1,203.

[d] Princeton Survey Research Associates (PSRA) data, 5/3/99–5/17/99, N = 1,001.

Question Wording: All PSRA questions began with the following statement: "Now I'd like to get your opinion on some specific proposals for how Social Security might be changed in the future. If I ask you anything you feel you can't answer, just tell me. Do you favor or oppose the following proposals. . . . (INSERT—READ AND ROTATE). Do you strongly (favor/oppose) this proposal, or moderately (favor/oppose) it. The NPR/Kaiser/JFK questions began with the statement: "I am going to read you a list of some ways that have been suggested to deal with the future financial problems of Social Security. For each one, please tell me if you would favor or oppose such a proposal. How about (READ ITEMS)? Do you (favor/oppose) this proposal strongly, or not strongly?" See specific wording below.

[e] PSRA: "Changing Social Security from a system where the money in the trust fund is invested in government bonds to a system where some of the money is invested in the stock market." NPR/Kaiser/JFK: "As a way of dealing with the future financial problems of Social Security, do you favor or oppose having the government invest in the private stock market a portion of Social Security reserve funds, which are currently invested in government bonds? (GET ANSWER, THEN ASK) Do you (favor/oppose) this proposal strongly, or not strongly."

[f] PSRA: "Changing Social Security from a system where the government collects the taxes that workers and their employers contribute to a system where individuals invest some of their payroll tax contributions themselves." NPR/Kaiser/JFK: "People having individual accounts and making their own investments with a portion of their Social Security payments."

[g] NPR/Kaiser/JFK: "Allowing workers to take all of their Social Security taxes out of the Social Security system and invest them on their own."

Table 8.7 Support for Social Security Partial Privatization When No Risks Are Considered

	% in Survey		
	Favor	*Oppose*	*No Opinion/Don't Know*
March 1996[a]	72	13	15
June 1996[b]	69	15	16
June 1996[c]	74	13	13
April 1998[d]	80	16	4
April 1998[e]	66	20	13
April 1998[f]	76	20	4
May 1998[g]	64	32	4
June 1998[h]	69	20	11
December 1998[i]	74	22	5
July–Sept. 1999[j]	70	22	8
January 2000[k]	62	33	5
May 2000[l]	64	31	5
May 2000[m]	53	38	9
June 2000[n]	65	30	5
June 2000[o]	51	36	13
September 2000[p]	59	37	4
September 2000[q]	53	39	8
October 2000[r]	66	30	4
October 2000[s]	58	35	8

[a] Public opinion strategies for the Cato Institute, 3/27–3/31/96, $N = 800$. National registered voters likely to vote only. The question was, "Now that you have heard all six parts of the new proposal to change the Social Security system, do you favor, oppose, or have no opinion of the entire plan, or would you like me to read the key points of the plan to you again before you make a decision? (Read plan only if respondent asks.) People would be allowed to keep and invest the amount they now pay in Social Security taxes to save for their own retirement. You would decide how to invest the money, with some restrictions to limit very risky investments. Money could not be drawn until retirement and any money left in your account when you die becomes part of your inheritance. There will be no reduction in benefits for current Social Security recipients. People under age 65 years old but over age 18 would have the choice of staying in the current Social Security system or moving to the new privatized system. Those choosing the new system will receive some partial benefits under the old system. (If favor/oppose, ask:) Would that be strongly (favor/oppose) or just somewhat (favor/oppose)? (If no opinion, ask:) Which way do you lean? Do you lean to favor the proposal or do you lean to oppose the proposal?"

[b] Public opinion strategies for the Cato Institute, 6/12–6/16/96, $N = 800$. National registered voters likely to vote only. The question was, "Now that you have had an opportunity to hear more about Proposal B (to change the Social Security system), the proposal that would allow you to invest your Social Security taxes into your own personal retirement account like an IRA (Individual Retirement Account) or 401K, do you favor, oppose, or have no opinion of the proposal? (If favor/oppose, ask:) Would that be strongly (favor/oppose) or just somewhat (favor/oppose)? (If no opinion, ask:) Which way do you lean? Do you lean to favor the proposal or do you lean to oppose the proposal?"

[c] Public opinion strategies for the Cato Institute, 6/12–6/16/96, $N = 800$. National registered voters likely to vote only. The question was, "Now that you have heard all seven parts (people would be allowed to keep and invest the amount they now pay in Social Security taxes to save for their own personal retirement, you would decide how to invest the money with some restrictions to limit very risky investments, money could not bedrawn until retirement, any money left in your account when you die becomes part of your inheritance, there will be no reduction in benefits for current Social Security recipients, people under age 65 years old but over age 18 would have the choice of staying in the current Social Security system or moving to the new privatized system, those choosing the new system will receive some partial benefits under the old system) of the Proposal B (to change the Social Security system), do you favor or oppose, or have no opinion of the entire plan, or would you like / me to read the key points of the plan to you again before you make a decision? (If favor/oppose, ask:) Would that be strongly (favor/oppose) or just somewhat (favor/oppose)? (If no opinion, ask:) Which way do you lean? Do you lean to favor the proposal or do you lean to oppose the proposal?"

Table 8.7 (continued)

[d] I.C.R. Survey Research Group for Associated Press, 4/27–4/31/98, N = 1,012. The question was, "I'm going to read some proposals that have been made for changes in the Social Security system. For each proposal, tell me whether you favor or oppose it ... Letting workers shift some of their Social Security tax payments into personal retirement accounts that they would invest on their own."

[e] American Viewpoint National Monitor Survey, 4/98, N = 1,000. The question was, "As you may know, each year there are more and more retirees collecting Social Security benefits and fewer workers whose payroll taxes fund the system. In fact, by the year 2012, the government will be paying out more Social Security benefits than it is collecting in payroll taxes and if nothing is changed, the system will go broke by the year 2029. As you may know, workers are now required to contribute 12.5% of their income to Social Security. Would you favor or oppose changing the formula so that they would continue to pay the same amount toward their retirement but just 10.5% would go to Social Security and the other 2% would be used by workers to invest in their own private retirement accounts? (If favor or oppose, ask:) Is that strongly favor/oppose or somewhat?"

[f] Yankelovich Partners Inc. survey for Time/CNN, 4/8–4/9/98, N = 1,011. The question was, "Do you favor or oppose allowing Americans to put a portion of their Social Security taxes into a personal savings account to be used for retirement?"

[g] Chilton Research Services/Harvard University, 5/6–5/10/98, N = 1,014. The question was, "I am going to read you a list of some ways that have been suggested to deal with the future financial problems of Social Security. For each one, please tell me if you would favor or oppose such a proposal. How about ... people having individual accounts and making their own investments with a portion of their Social Security payments?"

[h] Princeton Survey Research Associates, 6/4–6/8/98, N = 1,012. The question was, "Generally, do you favor or oppose this proposal (which would allow Americans to put a portion of their Social Security taxes into a personal savings account to be used for retirement)?"

[i] Associated Press, 12/2–12/6/98, N = 1,006. The question was, "I'm going to read some proposals that have been made for changes in the Social Security system. For each proposal, please tell me whether you favor it or oppose it. ... Letting workers shift some of their Social Security tax payments into personal retirement accounts that they would invest on their own."

[j] Princeton Survey Research Associates, 7/14–9/9/99, N = 3,973. The question was, "Generally, do you favor or oppose this proposal (which would allow Americans to put a portion of their Social Security taxes into a personal savings account to be used for retirement)?"

[k] Gallup Organization, 1/13–1/16/00, N = 1,027. The question was, "A proposal has been made that would allow or require people to put a portion of their Social Security payroll taxes into personal retirement accounts that would be invested in private stocks and bonds. Do you favor or oppose this proposal?"

[l] ABC News, Washington Post, 5/7–5/10/00, N = 1,068. The question was, "Would you support or oppose a plan in which people who chose to do so could invest some of their Social Security contributions in the stock market?"

[m] Opinion Dynamics, 5/10–5/11/00, N = 900. The question was, "With regard to Social Security, do you believe it should continue working as it currently does, or do you think people should have the option to invest part of their Social Security contributions themselves?" (Choices were Continue, Option to invest privately, and Don't know).

[n] Gallup Organization, 6/6–6/7/00, N = 1,059. The question was, "A proposal has been made that would allow people to put a portion of their Social Security payroll taxes into personal retirement accounts that would be invested in private stocks and bonds. Do you favor or oppose this proposal?"

[o] Princeton Survey Research Associates, 6/22–6/23/00, N = 750. The question was, "As you may know, the (2000) presidential candidates have made some proposals to change or supplement Social Security to help Americans save more money for their retirement. One of these proposals would change Social Security to allow workers to invest some of their Social Security payroll taxes in the stock market. In general, do you favor or oppose this proposal?"

[p] ABC News, Washington Post, 9/4–9/6/00, N = 1,065. The question was, "Would you support or oppose a plan in which people who chose to could invest some of their Social Security contributions in the stock market?" (Choices were support, oppose, and no opinion.)

[q] Yankelovich Partners Inc., 9/6–9/7/00, N = 1,278. The question was, "Do you favor or oppose allowing individuals to invest a portion of their Social Security taxes in the US (United States) stock market?"

[r] Gallup Organization, 10/25–10/28/00, N = 1,004. The question was, "Suppose that on election day this year [2000] you could vote on key issues as well as candidates. Please tell me whether you would vote for or against each one of the following propositions. Would you vote ... for or against a law that would allow people to put a portion of their Social Security payroll taxes into personal retirement accounts that would be invested in private stocks or bonds?"

[s] ABC News, 10/28–10/30/00, N = 1,020. The question was the same as in note p.

Table 8.8 Support for Social Security Partial Privatization
When Risks Are Considered

	% in Survey		
	Favor	Oppose	No Opinion/Don't Know
December 1996[a]	36	56	8
January 1997[b]	22	61	17
March 1997[c]	35	63	2
April 1998[d]	52	41	7
October 1998[e]	43	52	5
March 1999[f]	44	51	5

[a] Yankelovich Partners, 12/11–12/12/1996, $N = 818$. The question was, "Some people favor investing a portion of Social Security tax funds in the stock market because this might lead to higher investment returns. Other people oppose this because this is too risky. What is your opinion? Do you favor or oppose investing a portion of the tax money collected for Social Security in the stock market?"

[b] Hart and Teeter Research Companies, 1/25–1/27/97, $N = 1,002$. The question was, "This proposal to allow people to invest Social Security contributions in the stock market also includes an increase in the payroll tax for current employees, as well as an increase in the federal deficit, so that benefits to current retirees also can be maintained. Do you think the benefits of allowing people to invest Social Security contributions in the stock market outweigh these costs of higher payroll taxes and deficits, or do you think the costs outweigh the benefits?"

[c] Washington Post, 3/13–3/23/1997, $N = 1,309$. The question was, "Some people favor investing a portion of Social Security tax funds in the stock market because this might lead to higher investment returns. Other people oppose this idea because they say the stock market is too unpredictable. What is your opinion? Do you favor or oppose investing a portion of the tax money collected for Social Security in the stock market?"

[d] Hart and Teeter Research Companies, 4/18–4/20/98, $N = 1,004$. The question was, "One proposal has been made that would allow or require people to put a portion of their Social Security payroll taxes into personal retirement accounts that would be invested in private stocks and bonds. Some people think that individuals would have more money for retirement if they were allowed to invest and manage some of their Social Security payroll taxes themselves. Others think that it is too risky and could leave some people without adequate money for retirement if the stock market were to decline in value significantly. Do you favor or oppose this proposal?"

[e] Hart and Teeter Research Companies, 10/24–10/28/98, $N = 1,025$. National registered voters only. The question was, "A proposal has been made that would allow or require people to put a portion of their Social Security payroll taxes into personal retirement accounts that would be invested in private stocks and bonds. Some people think that individuals would have more money for retirement if they were allowed to invest and manage some of their Social Security payroll taxes themselves. Others think that it is too risky and could leave some people without adequate money for retirement if the stock market were to decline in value significantly. Do you favor or oppose this proposal?"

[f] Hart and Teeter Research Companies, 3/4–3/7/99, $N = 2,012$. The question was the same as in note e.

Partners, Hart and Teeter, and the *Washington Post* that mention possible risks and costs of privatization ("the stock market is too unpredictable," "could leave some people without adequate money for retirement," "higher payroll taxes and deficits") along with possible benefits ("higher investment returns," "more money for retirement"). The results present the most direct challenge to the claim of public support for partial privatization: in five of the six surveys Americans opposed privatization when offered a balanced choice. Other data not shown here indicate that the mention of other possible costs of privatization—high administrative costs or severely restricted investment choices for private accounts, for example, or cuts in guaranteed benefits or high transition costs—severely erodes support for privatization (Cook and Jacobs 2002; see Page 2000, p. 199).

The importance of question wording is made clear by the results of a May 1999 Princeton Survey Research Associates survey that reported that 58% of Americans favored a system that would include private accounts, whereas only 33% opposed it. The results were almost exactly reversed when the same survey asked respondents to choose between a program that guaranteed a monthly benefit based on lifetime earnings, as under the current system, and a program that would allow individual investment in the stock market with no guarantee. When they had the latter choice, 59% favored the guaranteed payment, and only 33% supported private investment. As Evans Witt, the president of Princeton Survey Research Associates, said, "The American people seem to favor the idea of individual retirement accounts in theory. The question is, how do you do it, and what does it cost, and does it put my benefits at risk?" (Stevenson 2000, p. 1).

Issues of question wording in the privatization survey findings should have been apparent to anyone a carefully looking at the data. Yet, although policy elites frequently invoked public opinion to claim the public was ready for partial or full privatization of Social Security, we found very little questioning of the proposition that the American public supported partial privatization.

Evidence for General and Specific Claims

Both the president and congressional witnesses appeared to invoke public opinion mainly to underscore the points they wanted to make. Earlier, we reported that the majority of their claims—roughly 70%—were general, using words like "Americans support," "the public favors," and "many" or "a lot." Only a minority of their claims included specific references to a representative aggregate distribution of public opinion. In addition to coding the level of generality of each claim about public opinion, we coded the extent to which each was supported by evidence: clear-cut, mixed, or little or none. The data appear in table 8.9.

The *specific* claims about public opinion made by both the president and congressional witnesses were more likely to be backed by at least some evidence (mixed or clear-cut) than were their general claims. That is, when policy elites used specific percentages or words like "majority" and "minority," there was likely to be poll data in the public domain to back them up.[4] As shown in table 8.9, we found poll data substantiating 69% of the specific claims made in congressional hearings by policy elites. But President Clinton's specific claims, despite his access to an elaborate White House public opinion apparatus, were much less often (only 27% of the time) supported by clear-cut evidence.

On the more frequent occasions, when the president and congressional witnesses made general claims about public opinion, little to no evidence usually existed to support their claims. This was true of 52% of the general claims by congressional witnesses and 80% of the general claims by President Clinton. Why

Table 8.9 Claims about Public Opinion by Policy Elites:
Level of Generality and Evidence

Evidence	Percentage of Presidential Claims (Column %)			Percentage of Congressional Claims (Column %)		
	General[a] (N = 35)	Specific (N = 15)	Total % (N = 50)	General[a] (N = 193)	Specific (N = 71)	Total % (N = 264)
Clear-cut	6	27	12	32	69	42
Mixed	14	47	24	17	17	17
Little to none	80	27	64	52	14	42
Total %	100	100	100	100	100	100

[a] The Ns refer to number of claims about public opinion.

was there such a low level of evidence for the general claims? In some cases—we cannot know how many—the speakers may have misrepresented the public as agreeing with their own preferences. Other speakers may have guessed or cited generalizations they had heard or read. Still others may have used nonsurvey evidence of views from constituents, interest groups, newspaper editorials, town meetings, or party activists with their ears to the ground (Kingdon 1984). Herbst (1998) demonstrates that legislative staffers, at least in Illinois, use few polls to gauge public opinion. Instead, she found that, to gauge public opinion, they relied on the activity of pressure groups and the content of mass media. This may be the source of our policy elites' invocations of public opinion. In the president's and congressional witnesses' general comments about public opinion, we found they often referred to "all the people I've talked to," "everyone I know," "people in my district," "people who care," and the "seniors I visited." Obviously, we were not able to find public opinion data to substantiate claims about these groups and therefore coded the evidence for these references as "little to none." Even if such data existed, however, most scholars would find them less compelling than systematic surveys of representative samples of the general public.

CONCLUSION

Over the last decade, both the president and Congress have devoted considerable attention to Social Security. In fact, no president in the last three decades discussed Social Security in public speeches, press conferences, and weekly radio addresses more than President Clinton. This chapter has explored how the president and policy elites who testified in congressional hearings invoked public opinion about Social Security, the types of claims that they made, and the extent to which the claims were accurate based on evidence available to us through public opinion polls.

In brief, we found most claims about public opinion concerned confidence in the future of Social Security, the public's desire for reform of Social Security, the popularity of Social Security, and support for presidential initiatives and positions. The preponderance of all claims concerned confidence about the future of Social Security. Of all the times President Clinton invoked public opinion, 44% were to make the point that the public was not confident about the future of the program. Among witnesses in congressional hearings, 38% invoked public opinion about the public's lack of confidence. Why did this point seem so important to policy elites? Whether the speaker was a spokesman from the Cato Institute, who wanted to dismantle Social Security as we know it, or President Clinton, who wanted to "save" Social Security, policy elites seemed to believe that they needed to establish the problems that Social Security was experiencing in order to push their own proposals. Declining public confidence in Social Security was the "problem" that helped pave the way for them to attempt to gain acceptance for their vision of the solution.

The high proportion of references to declining public confidence is troubling when we study actual public opinion surveys. Confidence was low, but it has been low since the late 1970s, and the dramatic decline emerged only in comparing two points in the time trend. Further, it is not clear whether the real cause of low confidence was a legitimate critique of Social Security or simply lack of knowledge—possibly abetted by exaggerated attacks on the system—about the workings of Social Security and what would happen if and when the program could no longer pay full benefits.

Policy elites invoked public opinion about confidence by frequently citing the story that young adults were more likely to believe in UFOs than to believe Social Security would exist when they retire. As we reported, this oft-quoted reference to public opinion was based, not on a survey in which young people were asked to compare their belief in Social Security with their belief in UFOs, but rather on two questions asked at different points in the survey using different wording. Moreover, later surveys in which respondents could choose directly between the two response categories revealed that young people have more faith in Social Security than in the existence of alien life. Yet no statements that we were able to find by the president or in congressional hearings ever offered a corrective to the UFO story. Once a dramatic finding about public opinion works its way into the "conventional wisdom" about public opinion, it is hard to dislodge.

Among congressional witnesses, the second most frequent reference to public opinion concerned the public's readiness for changes in Social Security, especially partial privatization. Yet we have seen that when respondents had a chance to consider the risk of privatization, they became less certain that they preferred this direction.

Ironically, one of the least frequent references to public opinion—about the popularity of Social Security—had the most consistent data to support it. Only 10% of President Clinton's references to public opinion about Social Security alluded to its popularity. Similarly, only 13% of all the claims made in congressional hearings alluded to its popularity. Why? Some policy elites may simply take it for granted. Others, however, especially opponents of the program, had an incentive to underplay this fact.

Democracy, we noted earlier, is supposed to involve policymakers paying attention to the public. We have explored one way they do this—by explicitly acknowledging, mentioning, and discussing public opinion. Certainly, policymakers have a huge array of systematic polls and surveys of public opinion to draw on. From 1990 to 1999, opinion polling organizations asked approximately 2,352 questions about Social Security. We have learned that policy elites drew on responses to these questions. The issue for us is how well and how accurately they used the data. The results are mixed at best. Perhaps on topics of concern to the American public such as Social Security, we need an objective body—a "court" of sorts—to make sense of public opinion data, to discern what it is and is not telling policymakers, and to make recommendations for the questions that might be asked to better elicit what people think. This suggestion is in line with the 1997 presidential address to the American Association for Public Opinion Research (AAPOR) by Diane Colasanto, who noted that the use of public opinion research in debates about policy is not well examined. She called for a new effort to "monitor systematically the use of public opinion research in public debate" (p. 527) by probing media, legislative, and polling archives as we did in this study (see also Lippmann 1922; Traugott 2000). Of course, there are risks to the kind of objective body we propose, but perhaps there are greater risks to propagating misunderstandings and misinterpretations of public opinion.

NOTES

The authors are grateful to the Institute for Policy Research at Northwestern University for supporting the research on which this article is based. They also express a special thanks to Ina Ganguli for her research assistance. The data presented in this chapter were previously published in an article in the Summer 2002 issue of *Public Opinion Quarterly*, titled "Invoking Public Opinion: Policy Elites and Social Security" (vol. 66, no.2).

1. Some organizations conduct surveys but do not release their results to the public. Similarly, the Executive Office conducts polls that are not released to the public. We can substantiate elite claims only through publicly available data.

2. For simplicity of terminology, we use the term "addresses" to refer inclusively to all public speeches, weekly radio addresses, press conferences, and so on that are transcribed and archived in the *Weekly Compilation of Presidential Documents*.

3. This number may increase because Roper continues to add questions to its archives when they are submitted by polling organizations.

4. The number of claims backed by evidence may be even higher than we were able to code using the poll data available to us. That is, presidents historically have conducted their own opinion surveys, as have interest groups like the AARP. Thus, sometimes when they invoke public opinion they may know something that publicly available polls do not reveal.

9

How State-Level Policy Managers "Read" Public Opinion

SUSAN HERBST

Although all engaged American citizens have an interest in the nature of public opinion on policy matters, our leaders think about public opinion constantly, as an environmental factor that guides all of their work. While this volume focuses primarily on national public opinion and decision making among national leaders, this chapter turns to state policymaking. The relationship between public opinion and the activity of state legislatures is vitally important, yet it has received little attention in the political science literature (cf. Erikson, Wright, and McIver 1993).[1] I argue here that legislative assistants in at least one important statehouse (Illinois) have far more nuanced and complicated views on assessing public opinion than we might expect from the conventional literature in our field. My findings corroborate others in this volume, in particular, chapter 11 by Stephen Kull and Clay Ramsay. Kull and Ramsay find that, in the realm of foreign policy at least, there is a quite significant *gap* between how the public may feel about U.S. intervention abroad (as measured by opinion polls) and the views policymakers hold about public opinion. Here I dig deeper into the micro-politics of this phenomena: how and why do policymakers commit these errors? I confirm the disjuncture that Kull and Ramsay find but also point to the sources of misinterpretation that should give us pause in our confident assessments about the nature of public opinion. A variety of social scientific experiments and interventions might narrow the gap between public opinion and policymakers' perceptions of it (see chap. 14 in this volume), but opinion-gathering processes in the typical statehouse and in Congress is far from sophisticated at this point. And policy-makers, journalists, and others who work in the chaotic and high-pressure world of legislative politics typically do not have the luxury to think in sustained ways about public opinion: they use their usual tools and rules of thumb to figure out—as quickly as possible—what initiatives are possible and how to serve narrow constituencies, interest groups, and the general public.

We build our causal models about the political world incrementally, weaving together our direct perceptions of local events, media reports of distant occurrences, the opinions of fellow citizens, and our past experience. Though the definitions and "theories" we hold about political life are important, since these notions likely determine the nature of our political activity (and inactivity), those who are directly involved in policymaking must rely on their own theories for guidance in their day-to-day work. When the Illinois legislature is in session, staffers laboring in Springfield—as in most state capitals—are far too busy to develop new philosophies or approaches to policy work: they must fall back on the frameworks and tendencies in their repertoires. We should think of these staffers, who are vital to the design, revision, and success of legislative initiatives, as policy *managers*, for they help orchestrate what political scientists call the "dance of legislation."

In a state with a large, diverse population, a set of highly bureaucratized state agencies, and myriad complex regulations in all arenas, legislative committee work would be impossible without a highly skilled and sensitive staff. Members of the legislature wear many hats: they are ideological leaders, servants to their constituencies, and lawmakers. With these demands tugging members in multiple directions, their staff become technical experts who drive the legislative process along on its bumpy path. In addition, they are often thought to be—along with journalists—the repository of collective memory about policy matters, a function served by staffers that is crucial to understanding their role at the capitol. They add a certain stability to a system constantly experiencing the departure of members and shifting ideological currents. I report on the theories or models twenty committee staffers in Springfield use as they go about their work. These informants tend not to believe that they *have* theories or abstract notions about public opinion. Yet when I asked them about democratic concepts and ideas, they were both forthcoming and engaged. At times, they seemed surprised by their own statements, but they were pleased to articulate the connections between their "theories" and their work.[2]

WHAT PUBLIC OPINION IS NOT

A way to begin is to discern what public opinion is not. Public opinion is not, for the large majority of staffers, the result of opinion polls or sample surveys. In fact, only four mentioned polls, and those informants viewed polls as useful only occasionally. I was most interested in issue polls, not preelection polls; upon close questioning, those informants who mentioned polls as useful normally were referring to the typical horse-race surveys during campaign season. One staffer told me that the House Democrats and Republicans "do polling virtually constantly." I asked for more explanation, for I had learned from previous interviewing that issue polls were rare, given the sheer number of issues and bills each session. It became clear that he was speaking about preelection polls conducted during primary season and before the general elections. Are issue polls used strategically in the policy process? Scholars find that presidents have long used polls for strategic planning (see Eisinger 1996; Jacobs and Shapiro 2000), but we still have few empirical studies that demonstrate this instrumental use of polling in legislative settings. In Springfield, it seemed that issue polls—concerning pending legislation—are suspect because they are used so selectively by the parties for rhetorical purposes. Issue polls were not mentioned as central to planning legislative maneuvers. One of the few extended comments about polling I heard was about the strategic and rhetorical use of surveys:

> Polls, they're used by us when it's to our advantage and kind of discounted when they're not. For example, this spring we had a bill that went through the [other house] with a lot of fanfare. It got over here and our members weren't that crazy about it. . . . And they [party members in the originating body] had polling data that showed that the public according to their numbers, overwhelmingly supported a number of the concepts in the bill. And we were like, "No, that doesn't make any sense. We don't buy it." We fought them on that. . . . [Polling data can be used to] bolster your case. And I don't think we have a problem with discounting it. If it's not going in the trash, we feel it should, at least as far as policy matters.

This staffer, and most with whom I talked, is able to critique polling quite easily—speaking to a range of problems, from the difficulty of wording a question to the time-bound nature of poll results. In fact, participants in the depth interview study across all three informant categories—policy managers, journalists, and political activists—could readily articulate their skepticism of polls. Their critiques of surveys are like those we generate in our own methodological literature, minus the social science jargon. Those involved in politics know firsthand that survey design, implementation, and data analysis are a tricky business. For example, one of the staff members noted that the public polled is not necessarily the informed public: "The questions [on Illinois statewide polls] are not particularly specific. They don't ask specific hard line [questions]—'yes, no, do you know about this? Do you know how much?' I guess they're more [about] what you think, what you feel. So it's kind of fairly squishy."

Why are so few polls used in a large state legislature? First, survey research is expensive, as many staffers pointed out to me. One quite powerful staffer noted that, although the governor has many resources, legislators do not, so polls are rare: "A poll has got to be done with political money. So, right there you're cutting into your actual campaign spending when you take a poll. It's the governmental funds against the political [funds]. And polls are expensive: A poll might be $25,000. . . . Polls are expensive, very expensive."

Newspapers in the state, particularly the larger ones, occasionally publish issue polls, but staffers seemed rather uninterested in the statewide polls, as they tend not to break the data down by district or region. Yet even if there were more monies available for polling, I intuited that the data would not be particularly useful to those who help to initiate bills and work for their passage or defeat. Trying to integrate poll findings into legislative work is problematic because details of bills are simply too complex to be collapsed into a few survey questions, and citizens are not informed enough to answer questions intelligently. One staffer pointed out how difficult it is to use polls for one of the most common and most controversial issues in state politics: the balance between property taxes and income taxes. This difficult problem requires the self-interested citizen to analyze his own financial situation, and few have time to engage in such mathematical work, especially as multiple proposals and counterproposals swirl around:

> One of the things that's interesting that I've noticed in my phone polling experience is that you'll ask people if they would like to see a reduction in property taxes, and everyone will say "yes." And the interest groups will all say that their members will support a property tax reduction. However, you ask them if they want property tax reduction with an offsetting income tax increase, then they don't want property tax reduction anymore. . . . [W]hat I'm saying is that many times public opinion doesn't really [help us]. . . . The poll's going to ask the general voter [about this issue] when what we're trying to find out is different.

A few of the informants who mentioned polls thought that perhaps the state polls, and certainly the more abundant national polls we find in the mass media, give us a general sense of public feeling. For instance, one staffer noted that the public is very "anti-criminal" right now and that much legislation, from sentencing guidelines to prison reform, is driven by this sentiment. He claimed that his vague public feeling against criminals, which he finds unjustifiable and counterproductive to good anti-crime policymaking, can be found in opinion poll data. Yet this staffer also argued that direct lobbying from victims and their families is far more persuasive and compelling to members and to their staffs than are poll data.

Staffers in Springfield find a chronic mismatch between the legislative process and the data available through opinion polling. Internal party or media issue polling could never "keep up" with the dynamic and complex debates on bills before the legislature. A timing problem makes it difficult to envision how polling might become a part of legislative activity at the capitol. During House and Senate sessions from January to May, work on legislation is so intense that members and staffers rarely have time to attend to what they believe are vague or dubious indicators of public opinion. This is not to say that they do not attend to public

opinion while in session, because they are quite sensitive to the needs of constituents and interest groups. However, in their search for public feeling that will
enable them to make policy under the pressures imposed by a strict legislative
cycle, staffers find polling of little value. On the whole, staffers read the occasional
issue poll and, more often, preelection poll but do not find them particularly
useful. One staffer noted, for example, "I don't ever deal with poll data. I see it.
I remember an article in the *State Journal Register* a couple of months ago. There
was a statewide [preelection] poll that determined that voting citizens were lean-
ing toward Democrats more so than Republicans. So that article was of course
copied and distributed throughout our offices and it was kind of like a rallying
cry for Democrats. That's the kind of [use] those kind of public opinion polls
have."

Occasionally, interest group leaders present members and staff with poll data
regarding the attitudes of their membership or the public at large on a particular
issue. One staffer gave the example of a poll of the general public conducted by
a state police organization and presented to legislators as part of a lobbying
strategy. The use of this poll did not have the intended persuasive impact and,
in fact, angered many of the members and staffers working on the issue. The staff
member explained that the use of polls by public servants—like police officers—
seemed particularly inappropriate. I asked if it was unusual for the police to use
a poll in a lobbying effort, and he explained:

> Yes, very unusual. [The poll] was not liked by a lot of legislators. . . . [The members
> didn't like the use of poll data] because they're [the lobby group] manipulating the
> process. Money is for arresting people, putting people in jail, not trying to manipulate
> the system so much where you can put in your two cents' worth regarding it [and]
> trying to generate your own news, I guess.

In this case, the poll was regarded as "dirty politics," as somehow lowly and
manipulative. When talking to this staffer and others, I observed that members
and staffers can often take offense when presented with issue poll data: these
policy professionals think they have a complex and broad understanding of the
public mood—what people want and the kinds of trade-offs they are and are not
willing to make for legislative maneuvers. In members' and staffers' eyes, poll
data are simplistic and disconnected from the particulars of policy debate, so they
have a rather elementary quality. Preelection polls are a different story, of course,
because they are, in most cases, fairly accurate predictors of real election outcomes. The content of specific policy outcomes, in contrast, is not discrete and
certainly not always predictable via the use of surveys. Polls may demonstrate
that citizens in a state share general ideological tendencies with their elected
officials, but this vague matching is a far cry from predicting actual legislative
activity.

Staffers' views of polling show that the content of public opinion is quite
directly shaped by our means of assessing it, and here—among the staffers—we

see resistance to polling as technology. Staffers focus not on the people or institutions that conduct polls but on the methodology itself. From their perspective,
polling comes out of the blue: it is a standard method, not fitted to the idiosyn-
crasies of Illinois legislative politics. This is an advantage of survey research for
social scientists, because surveying can provide data comparable across political
settings. But many staffers believe it is a disadvantage of polling as technology.

PUBLIC OPINION AS GROUP SENTIMENT

Legislative staffers were quick to speak of interest group opinion as either synonymous with "public opinion" or one of the more reliable indicators of popular
sentiment available to staff and legislators. This view was popular among legislative staffers, eight of whom mentioned interest and lobby groups when I asked
them a simple open-ended question about the meaning of public opinion. Other
staffers eventually spoke about special interests in the context of discussing public
opinion and were quite comfortable talking about interest groups as a "stand-in"
for public opinion. Elections matter, as do letters and calls from constituents,
though the latter are always looked on with skepticism because one cannot truly
gauge a constituent's level of knowledge about the issue or the intensity of his or
her opinions. However, staffers seem to think that the nuances and intensity of
public opinion are best captured in the communications of interest groups. This
argument—that interest group opinion is public opinion—took several forms in
the statements of my informants. Staffers who made this argument mentioned
four interrelated characteristics of interest groups that make them reliable indicators of public opinion: their communicative efficiency, their ability to crystallize
nebulous public sentiment, their perceived honesty, and their capacity to communicate the intensity of opinion. Staffers tend to treat their interactions with
lobbyists carefully, understanding full well that interest group leaders are intent
on persuasion.

Lobbyists are efficient in their role as purveyors of public opinion because
they are so well informed about their issues: they can get right to the point, keenly
understanding their opponents. And the better interest group representatives are
well attuned to the needs of legislators and the constituencies they must be ac-
countable to. Because staffers find that the public and public opinion are fairly
amorphous entities, some exhibit a fair degree of impatience with knowledge
levels among the general public, so lobbyists seem to them a reasonable and
appropriate stand-in for the public. In response to my open-ended question about
the meaning of public opinion, one staffer said:

> I immediately think of interest groups. That's how we gauge our public opinion. . . .
> I very rarely am clueless about where that constituency is because of the interest
> groups keeping me informed. . . . [V]ery rarely does personal public opinion matter
> to the General Assembly. . . . [Interest group communication is] just more indicative

of what's really going on out there. Rarely will a group of people unorganized be able to, just normal constituents, be able to call up and change the way a vote is taken. I can only think of one issue in the General Assembly in the last year in my area where that actually mattered. I would have to say that from a public opinion standpoint, we don't really care what the average Joe thinks. I don't say that as if we're not representing them, but we're representing the people who represent them. It's one step removed from the general public.

Interest groups are more than simple surrogates for public opinion, according to this informant. They translate opinion, but during this translation process they also help solidy public opinion. Lobbyists are perceived to crystallize or clarify the content and intensity of vague public moods. On only a handful of the hundreds of bills before the legislature is the intensity of mass opinion apparent. One such case is the debate and legislative maneuvering over legalized gambling across the state, particularly land-based casinos in Chicago. The religious right, business leaders, and casino operators have all been extraordinarily vocal in this debate, and many citizens do have strong feelings about this issue. But on most issues, mass opinion is unformed or difficult to discern, so lobbyists help staffers and members with this task. One staffer spoke directly to the issue of opinion intensity and how interest groups enable staff to measure intensity (or lack thereof) on particular issues. In answer to an open-ended question about the meaning of public opinion, she immediately mentioned interest groups and said:

> If I only have one complaint about something [a bill], I'm not going to be too exercised over that. [This is a contrast to situations where] I have hundreds of complaints and I see hundreds of interest groups coming forward on a particular issue. . . . We're trying to [pass particular legislation but] we can't do it because the [name of interest group] is very aggressive in their opposition to promoting this. Now, *that's* public opinion, but that's also one particular group that is in opposition.

I asked this staffer if she would distinguish at all between interest group opinion and public opinion, and she said that she did not. She cares what the "average person" has to say but relies so often on interest group opinion as a public opinion measurement that she has internalized the positions and arguments of such lobbyists: "I take it all in [interest group opinion and opinions of the average person] and, obviously, I've become sensitized to what each interest group will be touting in their position on particular issue. I can tell you which ones will be supportive of any issue." Some staffers think that if a segment of the public really cares about an issue, they will form a lobby around that issue:

> Obviously I think that the lobbyists and organized groups are much more effective [than average citizens] because they have an organized message. They have money and they're here. Whereas a lot of people, I think there's a lot of people in the state that just really don't care what goes on in Springfield. And that's one thing, you have

a lot of people are always griping about [issues but] only people with money and . . . organizations have influence. Well, don't gripe about it, get involved, get a message, get organized, and raise money, and get in the game.

Staffers listen to lobbyists they perceive as honest, and most interest group leaders tend to be quite straightforward in their discussions with staff members. Several staffers underscored a point well known by scholars—that a lobbyist's reputation is ruined if he or she lies (either point-blank or through omission of facts), so interest group representatives tend to be forthright about the facts while they try to persuade. One staffer, when asked about the meaning of public opinion, said that public opinion was both media content and the statements of interest groups, although she prefers the latter for their honesty:

> Listening to, especially the interest groups, as they come to us and talk to us about how maybe a particular constituency feels about a certain issue: that's probably the quickest, easiest way that we have to gauge public opinion. . . . I've had people [lobbyists] who have blatantly either misrepresented the truth or just lied to me. And I have a hard time dealing with them from that point on because I can't trust the information they're giving. And if I can't trust the information, then they really don't serve me that much of a purpose.

PUBLIC OPINION AS MEDIA CONTENT

Perhaps more surprising than the readiness of staffers to think of public opinion and interest group opinion as nearly interchangeable is the belief held by many of these informants (twelve mentioned it directly) that *mass media content is public opinion.* Media scholars from a variety of empirical traditions have argued that exposure to the news and public opinion formation are linked: some researchers posit that media "set agendas" for citizens and policymakers; other researchers argue that media content can change the basic nature of our beliefs and values (McCombs and Shaw 1993). These arguments propose that public opinion and media content are two distinct and measurable entities, a dichotomy with which social scientists have long been comfortable. Few of us are willing to take seriously Walter Lippmann's (1925) more extreme position, that public opinion is in fact journalistic opinion. For all the citation of Lippmann on issues of stereotyping and elite behavior, little of his theorizing about the conflation of media and public opinion has been acknowledged or explored. What explains our lack of attention to Lippmann's notions about the conflation of media and public opinion? One reason is the decidedly undemocratic nature of this conception: if public opinion is simply a "phantom" protected by an elite corps of journalists and policymakers, what does this mean for democratic theory? Where is the *vox populi* if we have only media representation of it? Second, Lippmann's views on the conflation of media and public opinion present a plethora of measurement problems. Media content is most often found in narrative news stories, investigative reporting, cartoons, dramas, and so on, and it is a challenge to think of political cognition or public attitudes as structured in narrative fashion. Media content is, in other words, creative and imaginative, whereas we have long thought of public opinion as expressed in linear or (on occasion) in simple dialogic formats: academics or pollsters design queries—experimental or survey-based—and citizens answer (or fail to answer). In rare instances researchers probe respondents beyond a simple categorical query, but they typically accept answers quickly and move on to new questions. In any event, respondents or experimental subjects are not generally asked to put their ideas in narrative form.

Upon hearing my open-ended question about the meaning of public opinion, twelve of the staffers answered "the media." Some of these men and women mentioned interest groups as well, but all believed that newspaper, television, or radio content was not simply a *conduit* for public opinion expression: in their view, it is the very essence of public opinion and can support or destroy legislative initiatives. One staffer said that, when he thinks of public opinion, he conjures up "the major newspapers putting the spin of the moment on different issues." Another said that he thinks of public opinion as

> the editorial page and certain commentary-type people, people like Thomas Hardy [of the *Chicago Tribune*]. Things like the "Inc." column [also in the *Tribune*] where you get little snippets. That's what I think of when I think of public opinion. We don't do a lot of polling. At least if we do I don't know anything about it. I know they do some [polling] in the campaign side of things, but I don't deal with that [as legislative staffer]. And we only do that [have poll data] once every year or so. Mostly it's listening to people and the senators themselves have a pretty good instinct for what's important to them and what their constituents want. We follow people like Thomas Hardy and Kup's column [in the *Chicago Sun-Times*], and people like Bill O'Connell [a longtime journalist, recently retired, who was based] in Peoria.

Again, an experienced staffer implies that quantitative opinion data in the form of survey research is rare in the legislature. Polls are used frequently in campaign season, of course, but policy workers must do without such indicators. And, as noted, policy polling not trusted because it does not measure intensity of feeling (e.g., what polled respondents would or would not be willing to do or pay to achieve particular policies). This staffer cites the influential *Tribune*, the *Chicago Sun-Times*, the Springfield newspaper, and the few others that cover legislative events carefully as places to find evidence of public opinion. Why is the content of both news and editorial media useful to legislative staffers interested in public opinion? For one thing, newspapers are efficient venues for public opinion. Staffers note that journalists can create public opinion themselves but also are conduits publishing the opinions of "regular folks." Media content indicating the nature of public opinion is available regularly for the more important issues like education and crime. The staffers consider an often mind-boggling number of bills while the assembly is in session, so they use any information efficiencies available.

Media representations of public opinion are helpful to staffers and members in the assembly who use evidence about public opinion. One staffer talked about a report he wrote on an amendment to a bill, in which he cited media accounts to represent public sentiment. Another said that, in one case, media were used in conjunction with other forms of opinion data:

> We were arguing against the position of the House and a lot of the media coverage seemed to focus on concerns about the legislation. We would use newspaper articles. We would use radio stories and that type of thing in our negotiations with the House and say, "Look. This doesn't have a lot of support statewide. We need to change this. . . ." We used the media articles. We used letters from people. We used phone calls. Some of the groups that we're concerned about generated a lot of phone calls on this issue. So, we used all of those things.

Note how this staffer easily arrays media alongside other more traditional legislative means of knowing public opinion (constituent mail and phone calls): media are thought to occupy a place in the category of opinion measurement techniques. Were media used strategically, as ammunition in the specific case this staffer described? Yes, they were: "We were kind of inclined not to favor [the bill] anyway. And so when the articles came out that had the coverage of negative comments about it, it just served to bolster what our members' initial thoughts were anyway." Another staffer explained, in answer to my open-ended query about evaluating public opinion:

> I read about five or six articles over a week period, and then I'll sit back and think about it, and we'll have discussions on staff, informal discussions, just talking about the issue or politics, and we try to get one step beyond it and try to think, "What did the voters, how did the voters, see this. Did the voters care about this? . . ." Just reading, it's amazing. Reading newspapers in the morning is most important because that's how the editorials in the newspapers will give us some insights on how people out there are thinking about government. You really have to be careful because most of those editorials in the newspapers are from the policy staffs here in Springfield. Or how they want you to spin it. We have so many spinmasters.

In this comment and others, informants do not simply use using media as conduits of public opinion. If they were simply treating media content as one indicator of mass sentiment, this would be worth noting, but indications from this small study are that media portrayals of issues and narrative descriptions of policy debates in the news are themselves public opinion data to legislative staffers. If media were only conduits for public opinion data, staffers would have named specific bits of media content—published polls or letters to the editor. But such specific items within media are rarely mentioned. Instead, it is the *totality* of media attention, the general slant or tendency of coverage that is synonymous with public opinion for them. This is unsatisfying to the public opinion analyst, of course, who is looking for cues about the specific media content of most interest to legislative policy workers. Perhaps even more problematic is the reminder from reception theorists of media: people view and use media content selectively and treat the text with seemingly boundless creativity. If so, and examples abound in the mass communication literature at present, it is difficult for the analyst of media as public opinion to speculate on professionals' uses of media content without talking to those users: perceptions of content by readers (in this case, legislative staffers) are vital, as they try to glean meaning about public opinion on specific bills from newspapers, radio, and television. Finally, if policy manager conflate media and public opinion, we scholars might reassess our own models for understanding the relationship between these two phenomena.

Even more interesting, as we try to discern the "lay theories" or arguments staffers make about the public sphere, is that *many who see media as synonymous with public opinion also believe that media are biased* (for details, see Herbst 1998). Because they are so knowledgeable about state issues, these staffers believe they can "see through" media bias and still glean some useful data about public opinion. They are, in fact, reading the papers (among the media, newspapers cover the legislature most thoroughly) much the way nineteenth- and early twentieth-century political leaders read the partisan papers of their eras—with great interest and great skepticism. Staffers are stuck, in a way: they rely on media and on interest group communication because polls are rare and not particularly useful to them. And other indicators of the public sentiment, such as letters or calls from constituents or small demonstrations at the capitol, are also quite infrequent and difficult to interpret. When a citizen writes or sends a postcard to his legislator, it is rarely clear whether that person holds the expressed opinion with great intensity. What might the citizen do if the legislator does not act in the way this citizen would like him to act? Demonstrate? Vote against the member in the next election? The consequences of "going against one's mail" are hardly predictable, and with the ability of interest groups—on all sides of an issue—to instigate mass mailings, letters from constituents are far less useful than they were during previous periods in American politics (see Sussmann 1963). In the end, then, many staffers believe that interest groups and media can communicate *intensity* of feeling about an issue quite well, despite the recognized problematics associated with both indicators. Both reporters and lobbyists can write, talk, and argue with a focused and sustained attention one does not find in the citizenry. After all, attention to the legislature is what both journalists and lobbyists are paid for, so their interest in doggedly pursuing issues is great. Interest group communication and media reports are excellent sources for information on public opinion: their communications are perpetual, articulate, and readily available.

ON DEFINING PUBLIC OPINION

These results are provocative, and although one cannot make more general claims about legislative staff or policymakers beyond these data, they do help us to build theory about public opinion and leadership. Illinois is an excellent milieu for legislative study, for the legislature serves a large, diverse state that is, in many ways, a microcosm of the nation. Illinois is also a "bellwether state" in national elections, with a lively and competitive two-party system. Though states are still relatively understudied in political science, more and more scholars have turned to state legislatures as sites for research, given how vital lawmaking in this venue is for the daily lives of most Americans. A next step in this research might be to dig deeper into the issues raised, to press informants on the rift between elite and more popular views of public opinion, or to replicate the research protocol on the national level with congressional staffers.

Scholars have their preferences for measuring public opinion, of course, depending on theoretical conceptions and methodologies. Yet the legislative managers interviewed here have their own notions of what constitutes public opinion and how it might be discerned in the context of policy scenarios. These definitions and theories are, perhaps, less complex and well articulated than we would like, but they are theories nonetheless: they specify variables and the causal relations among them. Staffers resist aggregation-oriented views of public opinion that surveys or even elections provide, as neither gives the precise information about public opinion one needs when engaged in research and strategic planning on particular bills. This resistance to aggregation is not simply a rationalization because opinion polling is expensive: even when legislative managers have poll data, they are skeptical of it.

Some may find the definitions and theories about public opinion held by people in key state policy positions somewhat disturbing. To think about interest groups and the content of mass media as synonymous with, or useful indicators of, public opinion ignores the many issues of sampling and representation that scholars in political science have struggled with since midcentury. Recent scholarship on interest groups demonstrates that they are somewhat less worrisome than more popular conceptions of their role would have us believe, but this is no evidence that lobbies entirely represent mass opinion. And such representativeness is rather difficult to measure, as we know, because the raison d'être of interest groups is to crystallize and communicate nebulous public moods.

Mass media serve much the same role. Journalists conduct constant informal and formal surveillance of public moods, trying to crystallize issue debates, creat stories, educate us, and entertain us. Unlike interest group communication, which is directed and strategic, news reports about policy issues and debates are written for readers and audiences, so many of the staffers I interviewed thought the two sources (news and interest group communication) quite valuable. Strategic communication from interest group representatives displays clear issue positions and usually clarifies where constituencies within the mass public might fall. In some cases, it is easy for staffers and the members they advise to discern just how many citizens are represented by particular interest group communications, but for most legislative initiatives, this quantitative work is nearly impossible. Much the same problem exists with media, but despite this problem and the biases staffers recognize in media content, news reports are still enormously valuable as public opinion artifacts. Journalists can create compelling narratives about a policy debate, weaving together quotations from members, from interest group representatives, and—most important—from "regular folks." These stories, made even more vivid with photography, have their own inherent persuasive power.

We should remember what technological theorists of mass communication tell us about the impact of media: much of its power lies in the sheer fact that we know thousands of readers are reading the same material (e.g., Meyrowitz, 1985). So whether staffers are themselves affected by content or not is important, but their perceptions that this content does affect the mass audience are also vital. This is sometimes called the "third person effect": regardless of whether a staffer, a member, or an average reader of a newspaper finds an article or editorial persuasive, he or she may believe that thousands *are* in fact persuaded by that article. This belief ("I'm not persuaded, but I know everyone else will be") does affect individuals' behavior, as several researchers have demonstrated.[3]

It is always difficult to make direct connections between generalized political cognitions of policymakers (or in this case, policy managers) and their actual behavior in legislative strategizing and debate. This linkage is particularly problematic for lay theories about the public sphere, which tend to be somewhat vague and highly contextualized. In my interviews with staffers, however, I observed as that, public opinion for them is, typically defined, media content or interest group communication, *uninformed* or passive citizen opinions are not part of their universe. This is not to say that staffers do not think of the common citizen and what he or she might think about important policy issues debated in Springfield. In fact, several staffers mentioned particularly compelling citizen testimony at hearings or demonstrations. Yet, often, in their world, democracy runs quite smoothly without attention to surveys, direct constituent contact, or other forms of conventional public opinion measurement. In an interesting way, the legislative enclave studied here is very much—to borrow words from Robert Entman—a "democracy without citizens." Citizens are certainly the ultimate *object* of policy, but they are conceptualized as peripheral to the policymaking process.[4]

NOTES

Parts of this chapter appeared in *Reading Public Opinion* (Chicago: University of Chicago Press, 1998) and are reprinted with permission.

1. An exception is, of course, Erikson, Wright, and McIver (1993). This study matches general ideological tendencies in public opinion to state policymaking but does not address the nuts and bolts of policymakers' behavior since it has a somewhat different agenda.

2. Staffers were interviewed for 30 to 90 minutes during July, August, and September 1996. Details from these open-ended interviews, as well as the interview protocol, can be found in Herbst (1998).

3. See, e.g., Mutz (1989).

4. See Entman (1989).

10

Public Opinion, Foreign Policy, and Democracy

How Presidents Use Public Opinion

ROBERT Y. SHAPIRO AND LAWRENCE R. JACOBS

The relationship between public opinion and government policymaking is fundamental to understanding how democracy works in the United States and in liberal democracies generally. Some theorists argue that the existence of free and periodic elections of leaders in government is all that (procedural) "democracy" requires to assure citizens' control of public policy (from the American founders to Schumpeter [1950] and Zaller [1992]), others maintain that there should also be identifiable influences of public opinion on some important portion of government policies (e.g., the "substantive democracy" of Key 1961; Page and Shapiro 1983, 1992; Stimson, MacKuen, and Erikson 1995; Jacobs and Shapiro 1994d, 2000), not only on a country's domestic policies but also on a nation's foreign and defense policies. Foreign policy issues, it should be noted, do not contribute to the American liberal-conservative policy mood that government policy making broadly responds to as Erikson, MacKuen, and Stimson describe in chapter 2. For foreign and defense policy in the United States, as the government's response to the September 11 terrorist attack again made clear, the president is the central institutional figure, both as chief executive and commander-in-chief with constitutionally defined or justified prerogative powers and other advantages that potentially give presidents greater discretion than in domestic policy making (e.g., see Pious 1979; Page and Petracca 1983). So any examination of how presidents have used polling and public opinion information, might ultimately downplay presidents' responsiveness to public opinion. Indeed, we reach this conclusion

about contemporary foreign policy making—but for reasons that go beyond the
constitutional bases of presidential power.

Foreign policy and national defense issues do not claim a privileged place in
public opinion—requiring that we think about them differently from domestic
matters—despite the claims and longings of presidents themselves, other government officials, foreign policy experts, international relations scholars, and others
(see Russett 1990; Russett and Graham 1989; Shapiro and Page 1988, 1994; Kull
and Destler 1999). *The Rational Public* (Page and Shapiro 1992) examined fifty
years of trends in Americans' policy preferences and found no profound differences between foreign and defense and domestic issues in the overall nature and
capabilities of public opinion. Foreign policy issues do tend to be less salient, in
part due to their complexity, but also because of the lower level of visibility of
these issues in the mass media—*unless* dangerous crises occur (such as the war
in Serbia and Kosovo and, at this writing, the war in Afghanistan and against
terrorism) or an issue like the America versus Elian Gonzalez controversy arises
that fits into the news media's preoccupation with stories involving domestic
conflict and human interest (and in the custody battle involving Gonzalez's Cuban
father and Cuban-American relatives, an issue arising *during* a presidential campaign). Events in foreign affairs also usually spring on the public through the
media more quickly than domestic issues, so that we find more *abrupt* shifts in
public opinion in response to foreign than domestic issues (on domestic issues,
cf. Page and Shapiro 1992, chap. 2; on some of the influences of events, the mass
media, and the president's own behavior on public support for presidents' foreign
policies, see Meernik and Ault 2001).

But what, then, can be said in contemporary history about the impact of
public opinion on American foreign policy in general and presidential policymaking in particular? In the research literature, there is considerable evidence
that government policies in the United States, since the 1930s (when national
survey data first became available), have reflected what the public has wanted (see
the data reported in chap. 3 in this volume). We cannot infer that this overall
pattern represents a steady-state relationship in American politics. Moreover,
while the correspondence between public opinion and policy is apparent, the
evidence that claims *causal* relationships is far from conclusive (see Page 1994).
Alternative explanations need to be ruled out or controlled for. An important
one posed in chap. 3 is that politicians and policymakers have come to use public
opinion research in foreign and defense policy as part of a strategy of "crafted
talk" to determine the rhetoric, arguments, and symbols (based on poll results,
focus groups, and the like) that will enable them to move public opinion.

Specifically, despite decades of research and growing data on public attitudes
and public policy in the United States, we have only recently begun to understand
how the public affects the policymaking process on salient domestic issues. We
know less about the effect of public opinion on foreign policy, because such issues
have tended to be less salient. Though we know much about the volatility and
stability of public opinion concerning foreign and defense issues, we have limited

systematic knowledge about the causal links that connect public opinion and foreign policy.

In this chapter, we briefly review the existing evidence for the effects of public opinion on foreign and defense policy and consider the causal connections that link public opinion and presidential policymaking. Some evidence suggests that presidents have paid increasing attention to public opinion and polling, indicating perhaps that policymaking processes have become more responsive to public opinion. Yet the end of the Cold War, as well as developments in American politics and changes in the mass media's coverage of foreign affairs, has still allowed presidents and government ample opportunity to direct or manipulate public opinion.

This chapter elaborates on how presidents, as political elites, have used information about public opinion in the area of foreign policy, and it reviews some of the new evidence. The end of the Cold War raised questions about the distinctiveness of foreign policy, suggesting further the need, as we emphasized in chapter 3, to examine how the relationship between public opinion and foreign policymaking might change over time.

THE EFFECT OF PUBLIC OPINION ON FOREIGN POLICY

Procedural democracy—the control that voters exert through reward and punishment in elections—provides the public with the means to constrain minimally what governments do. Clearly, electoral motivations that lead policymakers to anticipate what voters will do at election time are an important reason to expect government policies not to deviate greatly from what citizens want. But government can be, and has been, more responsive than this passive constraint from elections suggests. How much correspondence or "congruence" do we find between foreign policy and public opinion? Such correspondence can be defined in many ways: matching of policy changes with majority opinion supporting or opposing change ("majoritarian congruence"; see Monroe 1979; Weissberg 1976); matching of legislative representatives' policy votes with the preferences of their constituents (see Miller and Stokes 1963; Weissberg 1976, 1978); matching changes in public opinion with changes in policy, to see if both move in the same direction ("covariational congruence"; see Weissberg 1976; Page and Shapiro 1983); and comparing trends in public opinion and policy over time (e.g., Hartley and Russett 1992; Ostrom and Marra 1986; Stimson, MacKuen, and Erikson 1995).

Evidence has accumulated to show that foreign and defense policymaking has been, in a circumstantial correlational sense, responsive to majority opinion (Monroe 1979). In addition, as defense issues become salient, legislators' votes in the U.S. Congress have shown responsiveness to constituency preferences (contrast Bartels's [1991] with Miller and Stokes's [1963] results for congressional voting on foreign policy).

Page and Shapiro (1983; Shapiro 1982) analyzed "covariational congruence" between changes in public opinion and subsequent changes in policy; that is, in a congruent case, opinion changes significantly in a particular direction, and *subsequent* policy in the following year shows movement in the same direction. Though we find more frequent congruence for domestic than foreign policy issues (72% to 62%), there is noticeable variation among foreign policy issues, with congruence occurring most often for clearly salient wartime issues (World War II, Korea, Vietnam). Moreover, the American public ultimately did not constrain the United States from entering World War II or going to war in Vietnam; clearly the public can push and pull in different directions. The same might be said about the Gulf War in 1991 (cf. Mueller 1994) and perhaps the war in Kosovo. In foreign policymaking generally, any congruence between public opinion and policy might be due to the flexibility—to lead or manipulate—that the public allows policymakers. In opinion-policy agreement, the public may be permissively going along with government policies. Indeed, many of Page and Shapiro's (1983) findings and others already cited may manifest the reverse effect of policy on opinion. Nonetheless, the striking frequency of opinion-policy congruence from 1935 to 1979—significantly greater that 50%—challenges arguments that policymakers have ignored public opinion yet also suggests that policymakers' incorporation of public preferences into decision making has changed over time.

Further, some of the fuller time series data and the time-series analyses of them provide even stronger evidence for a causal influence of public opinion up to the mid-1980s. In the example of public opinion and U.S. troop withdrawal from Vietnam, the rate of troop withdrawal was sensitive to public attitudes toward the war in general and toward the rate of troop withdrawal in particular (see Page and Shapiro 1992; Shapiro and Page 1994). There was an even more impressive correlation between the level of U.S. defense spending and public support for increasing spending (see Shapiro and Page 1994; Hartley and Russett 1992; Ostrom and Marra 1986; Bartels 1991; Wlezien 1995, 1996). The public gave defense spending a big boost in the early 1980s, peaking after the Iran hostage crisis and the Soviet invasion of Afghanistan. Both the opinion and policy trends subsequently reversed course sharply, with far fewer people thinking we were spending too little on defense and more responding that we were spending too much. Defense spending subsequently was cut after the nation entered into a deep recession and as the Reagan administration's fiery rhetoric toward the Soviet Union subsided. Public opinion hardly appeared to play a passive role with regard to the behavior of elites and consequent government policies.

This evidence for effects of public opinion on policy in the United States, covering the period into the early 1980s, is compelling. But it is also limited in two respects. First, it rests on circumstantial correlational evidence; it does not pinpoint causal direction—is opinion driving policy or the reverse? Persuasive support for a causal effect requires evidence concerning intervening variables and processes that link public opinion to subsequent policy decisions. Second, it does not cover the period near the end of and after the Cold War.

We need additional evidence about the status and nature of the causal connection between public opinion and policy. As we reported in chapter 3 (see tables 3.1 and 3.2), some data show that this relationship has varied over time and that since 1980, government policymaking has been less responsive to public opinion than in the prior period beginning in 1960. Page and Shapiro's (1983) analysis, combined with Alan Monroe's later (1998) work comparing majority public opinion with changes (or lack of change) in government policy, suggests that the period from 1969 to 1979 was a high point in congruence between changes in public opinion and policies. During this time the Johnson and Nixon administrations began institutionalizing the analysis of public opinion in the White House. When Monroe (1998) updated his earlier analysis (1979) of the congruence between majority public support for (or opposition to) proposed changes in government policy and subsequent policy, he found that the consistency between public opinion and policy declined from 1980 to 1993. As we said in chapter 3, Monroe (1998) found an overall decline from 84% to 67% in the frequency with which foreign policies corresponded with majority public opinion. In contrast, defense policy moved a bit in the opposite direction. (The overall drop for all foreign and domestic policies was 8%, from 63% to 55%.) This change in responsiveness to public opinion, particularly in foreign policymaking, requires examination of additional evidence and, especially, the causal processes that directly connect public opinion to presidential policymaking.

STUDYING THE CAUSAL CONNECTION

A detailed review of the different processes by which public opinion can influence policymaking requires more space than allowed here. These include the role of political parties (Monroe 1983; Jacobs 1993; Shapiro and Jacobs 2000; Erikson, Wright, and McIver 1993; Dalton 1996) and other institutional bodies and mechanisms (e.g. Risse-Kappen 1991, 1994). Now we need historical and in-depth case study research (the discussion that follows draws heavily on Shapiro and Jacobs 2001). Although this analysis of specific cases may lack the generalizability of research encompassing a large number of cases, it can best provide the essential evidence needed to disentangle causal processes and mechanisms and to unpack the "blackbox" of policymaking. This type of research requires archival searches, interviews, secondary analyses, and other ways of gathering evidence to track how policymakers learn about and respond to public opinion. Case studies have helped complement and supplement the research that has already been described. These include, for example, Lawrence Jacobs's (1993) study of health care policy in Britain and the United States that uncovered a "recoil effect" in which political leaders' efforts to manipulate public opinion led them to track and *respond* to mass opinion to more effectively influence it. Studies of specific foreign policy issues and processes have confirmed that public opinion has mattered notably (subject to different interpretations concerning the speed or degree of responsiveness) in U.S.-Chinese relations (Kusnitz 1984), in U.S. policymaking toward the Contras in Nicaragua (Sobel 1996), and in foreign policymaking during the Carter (Katz 1998), Reagan, and Bush years (Hinckley 1992).

A more expansive strategy, however, beyond case studies of individual issues and particular time periods, attempts to synthesize in-depth research to unravel *historical* and *current trends* in the causal relationship between public opinion and policy. This strategy requires finding trends over time in the extent to which policymakers seek out or otherwise get information on public opinion and respond to, or are otherwise affected by, this information. Jacobs (1993) did this for health care policy, and Thomas Graham (1989, 1994), more relevant to this chapter, did the same for nuclear arms control from the beginning of the Cold War to the 1980s. Powlick (1991, 1995a), in particular, found an increase in serious and responsive attention to public opinion in the State Department, representing a change in what Bernard Cohen (1973) had found earlier; but the most recent trend was for the Reagan and Clinton administrations to emphasize *leading* foreign policymaking rather than following public opinion.

In a major treatment of this subject, Douglas Foyle (1999) also emphasizes that presidents from Truman to Clinton have, in general, tended to behave as "realist" (in contrast to Wilsonian "liberal") theorists in international relations have posited they should: they have tended to choose to lead or direct, not respond to public opinion in foreign policymaking. However, this tendency has varied from president to president. Foyle emphasizes that whether presidents choose to lead or follow public opinion depends on their beliefs about the appropriate role of public opinion in foreign policymaking and the context in which a foreign policy choice has to be made (Foyle 1999, preface). His research focused on the Eisenhower administration, but he included case studies involving later presidents. Though realist decision making occurred in a number of cases, some presidents at certain times, most notably President Clinton in the withdrawal of American troops from Somalia, were clearly more receptive to the public's input.

Overall, the historically oriented research that has focused on finding out how presidents and others *directly* used information about public opinion suggests a *reciprocal* relationship between public opinion and policymaking, with evidence showing government efforts to respond to, as well as lead, public opinion (see also Heith 1998a, 1998b, 2000). One must track these processes over time to discern whether particular trends or tendencies have emerged, or if, as Foyle argues, the influences at work hinge on the beliefs and decision-making contexts of individual presidents.

With this as our objective, we have been examining, through primary source research, the increasing institutionalization of public opinion analysis by American presidents. Our focus has been somewhat different from that of others who have focused on different presidents or different aspects of presidential politics or decision making (see especially Heith 1998a, 1998b, 2000; Katz 1998). We started our research with the Kennedy administration and have completed substantial work on the Nixon, Reagan, and Clinton presidencies. We have found that presidents have increasingly assembled and analyzed their own information on public opinion. Specifically, only since Kennedy has the entire process been routinized into the institutional functioning of the presidency. The driving force for this is electoral, as presidents, once in office, strive to be reelected and to use the electoral goals of other politicians as leverage to pressure them to accept policy proposals. Presidents started to use their own pollsters and public opinion consultants or staff during their campaigns, with private polls paid for by the political parties or other nongovernmental sources. The history of this process is described in Jacobs (1993), Jacobs and Shapiro (1995a) and Heith (1998a, 1998b, 2000). In these histories, the most important data are the numbers of polls that Johnson, Nixon, and later presidents conducted, and, most notably in our judgment (though we have not yet examined all the available data), the figures for Reagan and Clinton during their two terms in office (especially during the *governing* period, not just during election campaigns), which show that the level of this polling has become substantial indeed. The attention to public opinion during Clinton's 1996 election campaign, and perhaps continuing through his second term, may well put him at the top. Recent research on Reagan, however, suggests that he, along with Clinton, made greater use than other recent presidents of public opinion data for purposes of governing (see Murray 1999; Murray and Howard 2000).

Beyond the clear electoral objectives of presidents, the other important aspect of the process is that, since the Carter administration, the scope of the sharing and deliberation over public opinion information within the administration has expanded (Heith 1998a, 2000). The White House has become better positioned than in the past to respond to, or to attempt to lead—or manipulate—public opinion.

What patterns, then, have emerged? To date, we have found striking evidence for government responsiveness to public opinion, opinion leadership, and presidents working against the public's wishes for particular reasons. Responsiveness occurred on salient issues, especially those that clearly had immediate or potential electoral consequences. For example, as Kennedy ran for the presidency in 1959 and 1960, his pollster and consultant, Louis Harris, provided public opinion data that enabled Kennedy's campaign to use issues to heighten Kennedy's image as the candidate who could "get America on the move at home and abroad" (Jacobs and Shapiro 1994a, p. 531; Jacobs 1993, chap. 4). His emphasis on keeping national defense strong and being vigilant abroad resonated with the American public, but Kennedy did knowingly take an unpopular position supporting foreign aid. He was motivated by his need to establish credibility in elite circles and to attempt to educate the public about policies that advanced the nation's interests (p. 534).

Though Harris did not follow Kennedy into the White House, he continued to provide the president with poll data. Although this was not a formal relationship, it revealed an increased presidential demand for this kind of information in a routinized manner in modern politics. Responding to public opinion based on polls early in his administration, Kennedy emphasized his support for the Peace Corps, better relations with allies, strengthening the United Nations, and ameliorating the country's balance of payments (Jacobs and Shapiro 1992).

After the Kennedy years, White House polling and analysis of public opinion became a regular part of the Johnson and Nixon administrations, with Johnson obtaining information from pollster Oliver Quayle, and Nixon (privately and through the Republican party) commissioning full polls regarding his public image, support, and policy proposals. During the Johnson administration, the 1964 election provided an important juncture in how the president used information on public opinion. Concerned about being reelected, Johnson at first tended to respond to the public's wishes, emphasizing the popular desire to pursue world disarmament and peace in sharp contrast to the widely perceived positions of his Republican opponent, Barry Goldwater. Based on his polling reports, Johnson made sure to distinguish himself regarding the use of U.S. military force, including the use of nuclear weapons in Vietnam. But Johnson, like Kennedy, attempted to lead rather than respond to the public on the issue of foreign aid. Johnson's apparent strategy of responding to public opinion was particularly pronounced on domestic issues as well (see Jacobs and Shapiro 1993). Johnson continued this responsive behavior even after it became clear that he would easily defeat Goldwater. He wanted to solidify his public support for purposes of leading the public on his racial and social policy agenda *after* the election (Jacobs and Shapiro 1993).

Our analysis of the relationship between Johnson's policy positions and objectives and his proprietary polling information reveals that, beginning after the election, in 1965, Johnson did indeed choose to *lead*, not follow the public. His forceful leadership on domestic proposals, especially the War on Poverty, had not been demanded by the public, but the public came to support this effort. In foreign policy, the Vietnam war became an issue of extreme contention, and here Johnson had no intention of letting the public influence his actions. There was a clear break in this opinion-policy relationship between 1964 and 1966, with responsiveness declining and direction of opinion increasing from the first to the second period, with Vietnam the dominant issue in foreign policy (Jacobs and Shapiro 1993). In the end, however, after 1966, the failure to respond to what Johnson knew to be public opinion on particular aspects of the Vietnam war had increasingly adverse effects on his presidency, which raised normative questions for realist arguments about public opinion and foreign policymaking (Jacobs and Shapiro 1999). Polling could provide important information about the need to respond to public opinion, yet polling might also provide insights about the best means to move the public in directions presidents might want.

The Nixon administration strikingly expanded the institutional organization and sophistication of White House–directed polling and public opinion analysis. Despite his claims that political leaders should not be influenced by polls, Nixon and his advisors used polling data to avoid taking unpopular positions and to enhance their ability to lead the public on policies that they wanted to pursue. Nixon clearly wanted to leave his historical mark on foreign policy. The archival evidence shows that Nixon ultimately responded to public opinion in a manner consistent with the trends in public opinion and the withdrawal of troops from Vietnam that we described earlier (see Katz 1997). Clearly, the Vietnam war was a crucial election issue in 1972, and Nixon became more responsive as the election approached (Jacobs, Druckman, and Ostermeier 2001a, 2001b).

Although our research on Nixon is not complete (see Jacobs and Shapiro 1995a, 1995b, 1996a, 1996b), we have found that the Nixon administration was persistent in tracking public opinion on a wide range of policy and political concerns (especially approval of the president). Thus, it is not surprising that the opinion-policy correlation described earlier was higher during the Nixon administration than in previous periods (see Monroe 1979; Shapiro 1982; Page and Shapiro 1983). Indeed, the White House itself not only had a veritable warehouse of its own private polls but it also possessed the same publicly available opinion data on which such academic analyses were based (see Shapiro 1982; Page and Shapiro 1983), as well as more and better defined data for political purposes (see Jacobs and Shapiro 1999). Analysis of the relative influence of Nixon's private polling on policy preferences and the president's personal image found stronger and more consistent evidence of responsiveness to policy preferences (especially as the election approached; Jacobs, Druckman, and Ostermeier 2001a, 2001b).

An especially impressive case of both opinion responsiveness and leadership in foreign policy concerned the admission of China to the United Nations, paving the way for formal recognition of China. Archival evidence shows that Nixon and his advisors had seen the softening of the public's hostility toward China, making people more receptive to efforts to lead them further in a less belligerent direction. The result was Nixon's trip to China and China's admission to the U.N., which Nixon and his administration did not finalize until they found further public support for it in their own polling data (based on our archival work in progress; Kusnitz 1984). Nixon increased the salience of this issue for the public in a way that enhanced his and his party's electoral appeal.

Overall, during this period through the Nixon administration, there is evidence for presidential responsiveness to public opinion in foreign policy. This responsiveness occurred in ways associated with actual or anticipated electoral advantages, during a period in U.S. history in which Cold War foreign policies could become major election-year issues. As the Cold War ended, however, we might have expected this trend to change: foreign policy issues might no longer arise as critical election issues, as the Korean war, Vietnam, and the 1979–1980 Iran and Afghanistan crises had been before. Further, while polling, public opinion analysis, and the institutionalization of public relations activities within the presidency might provide the means for responding to public opinion and gaining the public's favor, these tools and institutions also offered the means to direct, not respond to, public opinion by pursuing the strategy of crafted talk.

Though we have emphasized the reciprocal relationship between public opinion and presidential policymaking and have cited examples of responsiveness to public opinion, we have reason to believe that the dominant contemporary trend is toward less presidential responsiveness and greater efforts at leading or manipulating public opinion. We suspect that the war in Afghanistan and against terrorism fits this pattern, though this requires careful study. We do not think that this trend solely reflects the personal characteristics of presidents whom Americans choose to elect. Rather, changes in the political system, the institutionalization of the means to track and follow public opinion, and, especially, the process of learning how to use these means as political resources to lead and manipulate, public opinion have contributed to this.

Responsiveness varies across the election cycle. As election day approaches, the motivation to be reelected creates compelling incentives to respond to public opinion, to avoid falling too far out of line with the voters (see Downs 1957, and, especially, Geer 1996). But election campaign periods aside, as we emphasized in chapter 3, there is a fairly long period during which presidents have the freedom and opportunity to act without worrying immediately about electoral repercussions. Come the next election, voters' memories may fade about government actions that they did not support, especially as other issues eclipse policymakers' past behavior. A president may have time to explain and even claim credit for actions that the public had not supported, as, for example, Bill Clinton did in the U.S. invasion of Haiti and intervention in Bosnia (in which there was ultimately probably supportive but divided public opinion; see Sobel 1996). Further, the electoral incentives for presidents are likely to wane for them, though not for their parties, during their second terms in office.

To exemplify trends toward or away from presidential responsiveness to public opinion, the Carter administration provides a critical test. Carter was the first president to have a publicly visible pollster, Patrick Caddell, who was brought in from Carter's successful presidential campaign. Caddell was the institutional successor to the relatively effective polling analysis operation of the Nixon administration. President Ford continued to use Nixon's polling and public opinion arrangements through the Republican party involving pollster and consultant Robert Teeter. He did not benefit, however, as Nixon and later presidents did, from continuing relationships that began during election campaigns and that were maintained and evolved for presidents while in office.

To what extent did the Carter presidency try to be responsive to public opinion? Our answer is: not as much as we would have anticipated. This is particularly surprising for a president who believed that public opinion should have some influence on foreign policy (but cf. Jones 1988). As Foyle (1999) observed, Carter thought public involvement in open decision making would benefit foreign policymaking by preventing the mistakes that might mar a policy formed in secret. That said, it is not obvious that Carter would use polling and public opinion analysis to facilitate this end, and the Carter White House clearly did not continuously poll as later administrations would. The most widely prevalent conclusion about Carter was that he was a "trustee" president more concerned with acting effectively on behalf of the people but not taking direct "delegate" style guidance from them (see Jones 1988; Hargrove 1988; Shapiro and Jacobs 1999).

As Diane Heith (1998b) and we (Jacobs and Shapiro 1993b, 1994a) have noted elsewhere, polling may determine which issues presidents push to the top of their political agenda, but actual policymaking is a different story. And presidents can independently raise issues that the public will then take up (see Jacobs and Shapiro 1993b). Carter was influenced by the actual issues the nation faced and by his own personal assessments of them, and he acted accordingly (cf. Katz 1998; Heith 2000; Foyle 1999; Graham 1989, 1994). In practice, then, Carter was not especially responsive to public opinion. Further, when it came to using information about public opinion to gain public support in foreign policy, he was ineffective. Later presidents, beginning with Ronald Reagan, in effect picked up where the Nixon administration left off and got better at it. What is striking is that Carter, a president who was not personally inclined to track and analyze public opinion, paid it much attention. Presidential attention to public opinion may reflect institutional rather than simply personal influences or needs.

The Reagan administration is the most informative reference point for future research on public opinion and presidential policy making. During his presidency the ideological polarization and other changes in politics that we emphasized in chapter 3 began to pick up steam. This changed the incentives and political calculations and strategic behavior of political leaders. These politicians had more incentives to attempt to lead or manipulate public opinion rather than to respond to it during the governing periods between elections. Our preliminary research, based on archival evidence from the Reagan Library, confirms this and suggests that the main purpose of public opinion analysis was to enhance the White House's ability to shape and persuade public opinion. In this context, the behavior of the Clinton administration represents a later point in an evolutionary process. Our extensive research on domestic policymaking during Clinton's first term in office, described in chapter 3 (based on Jacobs and Shapiro 2000), revealed that his administration used polling and public opinion analysis to attempt to direct public opinion to support health care reform and related policy efforts from 1993 to 1994; the administration became especially responsive in the lead-up period to the 1996 presidential election (Jacobs and Shapiro 2000). If domestic issues were largely treated this way, reflecting politicians' policy goals, we do not expect to find foreign policy treated differently (but cf. Foyle 1999). In the cases of U.S. intervention in Somalia and Bosnia, there was noticeable public opposition early on regarding Bosnia, and public opinion began moving against further intervention *before* American soldiers were killed, wounded, and humiliated in Somalia in the unsuccessful effort to capture the enemy clan leader there (see Jacobs and Shapiro 1995b, p. 203–6). Clinton made decisions that lacked public support and used polling and other information about public opinion to identify the effective means to "win" the public's support. This type of behavior was informed by apparently well-orchestrated polling and public opinion analysis in the White House, which certainly did not begin with the Clinton administration.

In short, the start of this use of polling to move and not follow public opinion during the Reagan years was propitious: public opinion was regularly monitored in the Reagan White House, and Richard Wirthlin and his firm, Decision Making Information (DMI), conducted most of Reagan's public opinion analysis. (We have identified at least 184 privately commissioned surveys in the Reagan archival papers; we believe that more remain buried in papers not yet publicly released.)

The president's polls were considered a major political resource and were usually controlled by the chief of staff, who would select sections to distribute to the appropriate administration officials. Reagan's team carefully tracked polls in published materials; they were quite concerned with monitoring how the public and elites were *perceiving* the state of public opinion. The White House carefully evaluated the public's reaction to the president's speeches to pinpoint the most effective language or presentations: small groups of fifty adults were regularly assembled to view Reagan speeches and to use hand-held devices to record on a 5-point scale (from very positive to very negative) their reaction to the president's message, style, and delivery. This "pulseline" analysis was conducted, for instance, on the president's foreign policy speeches related to peace and national security in 1986 and the Venice Summit in June 1987. This analysis provided a detailed evaluation of what the audience found appealing or distressing in each section of the president's address. For instance, DMI's analysis of Reagan's nationally televised 1986 address on peace and national security issues reported "negative reaction" to early sections of the speech because of "anticipation that Reagan is going to ask for more money for defense" and suspicion that the military purchases of new fighters is characterized by "waste and fraud." But the report found that Reagan's claim in his speech that a sustained military buildup would allow the United States to bargain from strength and produce a "secure peace" was favorably received because it offered "hope of real progress."[1] These analyses were apparently incorporated into future presidential addresses.

One main part of the White House's analysis of public opinion used Wirthlin's "big monthly surveys" on a variety of topics. These were labeled "Flash Results" and typically used identically worded questions to compile trends of attitudes and detect changes or stability in public opinion. Major new issues also received attention and, if they persisted, were added to the pool of questions consistently asked. The regular foreign policy topics in Wirthlin's monthly surveys included international trade, the strategic defense initiative, terrorism, and Central America (aid to the Nicaraguan rebels and policies regarding El Salvador and Mexico). Wirthlin used his analysis to identify a potential weaknesses in public support for the president's arms control policy among different subgroups (e.g., 18–24-year-olds who were unusually critical and consistently listed foreign policy as their top national concern).[2] In addition to probing public preferences on specific issues, DMI tracked the public's approval or disapproval of Reagan's performance on a range of foreign policy issues, including the Persian Gulf, arms control, Central America, relations with the Soviet Union, terrorism, and international trade. Two foreign policy issues that received particular attention were aid for the Nicaraguan rebels and the Iran-Contra scandal. The White House carefully monitored the public's reaction to the administration's support for Nicaraguan aid. In this case, the public largely opposed the administration's policy, and the administration was monitoring the public to see how—and ultimately, as it turned out, how long—it could maintain a policy at odds with public opinion (for further discussion of this important case, see Sobel 1993; Shapiro and Jacobs 2000). The White House also conducted extensive daily tracking surveys during the Iran-Contra scandal. The data showed the White House that the public would not be sympathetic to blaming the media; majorities believed the press had been both accurate and responsible.[3]

In brief, the reason the White House devoted the time and money to commissioning and analyzing public opinion research was that, according to Wirthlin, the public's evaluations and support represented the president's "most valuable of all political resources."[4] In recognizing the political significance of public support, the Reagan White House did not accept public opinion as a given. Rather, it attempted to shape it to support the positions the administration already favored. Although further archival research is required, it appears that the White House's extensive public opinion analysis was often used as part of a strategy of crafted talk—to design the presentation of already decided policies. We have found little evidence thus far that the Reagan White House's public opinion research systematically led to decisions directly responsive to public opinion on major issues (as opposed to how previously decided policies were presented publicly). For instance, Wirthlin repeatedly reported to the White House that aiding the Nicaraguans was consistently unpopular. The pollster's best hope was simply to distance Reagan from a major public campaign that reminded Americans of the president's distance from their views.

INCREASING OPPORTUNITY TO LEAD OR MANIPULATE PUBLIC OPINION

Our discussion of how presidents have used polling and public opinion information downplays presidents' responsiveness to public opinion. We think the pattern of behavior that we have described will continue as long as the incentive structure in the current political system continues. Presidents will continue to use polling and public opinion analysis to attempt to lead or manipulate public opinion, though the approach of imminent presidential elections will provide at least some mechanism for restraint.

Other recent developments have pointed further in this direction. If certain current trends continue, we could find an increasing difference in the observable role of public opinion in domestic versus foreign policy. How the September 11 terrorist attack will change this over the long term is not certain. First, foreign policy issues, historically much less salient than domestic issues, became increasingly less salient with the end of the Cold War. The end result may be that presidents will have increasing opportunity to lead rather than respond to public opinion in foreign affairs. This leadership may be facilitated by the fact that since World War II the public has fundamentally had an activist, not isolationist, orientation toward foreign policy and has been favorably disposed toward multilateralism (e.g., given the public's long support for the U.N. and NATO; Page and Shapiro 1992, chaps. 5 and 6; see Wittkopf 1996; Destler 1996; Kelleher 1994; Sobel 1996; Kull and Destler 1999).

The end of the Cold War has decreased the visibility of foreign policy in three ways. First, the East-West threat driven by the Soviet Union has disappeared. This has made national security a far less urgent and persistent issue than it had been since the end of World War II. Crises can arise, but they get resolved and disappear, unlike the steady Soviet military and nuclear threat during the Cold War. Second, the end of the bipolar world of the Cold War has made foreign affairs more complex to follow and interpret, which is yet an additional barrier to increasing the public's attention to foreign policy (we will say more about this later). Third, domestic policies have easily filled the gap in the public's attention space.

This potentially diminishing public attention to foreign policy but support for a strong U.S. presence in world affairs may give presidents and other policymakers greater opportunity than during the Cold War to lead, manipulate, or otherwise control public opinion. This low level of salience, interrupted only by occasional major world events and crises, provides a barrier to public engagement in foreign policy, which, in turn, makes democratic control of foreign policy more difficult. If, however, crises like the war in Kosovo become frequent or, more stunningly, the war against terrorism define the nature of international affairs in the twenty-first century, then this could substantially increase the public's attentiveness to foreign policy and possibly alter the nature of the opinion-policy relationship. Whatever happens, however, will have not only short-term consequences but also long-term ones bearing on what young adults learn about foreign affairs and how new generations perceive the relationship between the public and foreign policymaking. Because of the low salience and high complexity of foreign policy with the end of the Cold War, young adults may come to know less about world affairs than previous generations—and, to be sure, the latter's level of knowledge has not been very great (see Delli Carpini and Keeter 1996; Jennings 1996). The public's level of engagement in foreign policymaking in the future is an important open question.

New issues intersect directly with domestic concerns but have strong foreign policy implications (cf. Yankelovich and Immerwahr 1994): the global economy, the global environment, energy, and immigration. NAFTA (North American Free Trade Agreement; cf. Jacobs and Shapiro 1995b) in 1994, which the public belatedly came to support, may be an example of the future. At this writing we look to the domestic effects of terrorism and the war against terrorism on the economy, civil liberties, and immigration. Beyond this, for example, domestic protests against the actions and policies of the World Trade Organization and the International Monetary Fund, and the United States's role in them, may arouse the American public. Such issues could break down the distinctions between purely domestic and purely foreign policy concerns, as a wider range of issues becomes important in electoral politics in the United States.

But up until September 11, with neither the Cold War nor foreign policy crises at issue in American elections, foreign policy was less visible to the American public. Evidence for this is quite apparent and persuasive. For example, even during the period when the press could cite (in January 1997) a "Crowded, Ambitious Foreign Policy Agenda Awaits President in New Term," (Erlanger 1997), it had also just reported, "Foreign Coverage Less Prominent in News Magazines" (Pogrebin 1996). Pippa Norris's (1995) study of the effect of the end of the Cold War on American news coverage of foreign affairs reveals the striking change in television news coverage: international news coverage in general fell off; coverage of the Soviet Union/Russia sharply fell off; after rising during the transition period, lead stories or headline international news fell off as we entered the post–Cold War world; and while crises such as war and other unrest continued to make the headlines, international news on politics, human interest, disasters, and economics failed to do so. Although this might genuinely reflect the urgency and salience of these issues, it is apparent that because the press could no longer *frame* foreign affairs news in terms of Cold War, East-West, or communist-anticommunist terms for evaluating and understanding foreign policy issues, news organizations opted to cover such issues less than they had previously. This, in the long run, could give presidents and policymakers even more of a monopoly over such information; thus, they will have a further advantage in their efforts to direct rather than respond to public opinion.

Furthermore, and perhaps more important, the "Cold War frame" had given the public a heuristic or cognitive short-cut for understanding foreign affairs and thereby some vantage point from which they might constrain, if not attempt to influence, the direction of government policy. Without this frame in the post–Cold War world, presidents and other policymakers and political leaders may have greater opportunity to *reframe* issues for the public and thereby gain greater opportunity to direct public opinion. This reframing has been occurring at present in the United States' war against terrorism. Thus, in addition to improved capacities for presidents to obtain and use information about public opinion to lead or manipulate the public, real-world changes in foreign affairs themselves have made presidents less concerned with responding to rather than directing public opinion by framing or reframing issues.

PRESIDENTIAL AND GOVERNMENT HEGEMONY?

If there is a dominant new frame that presidents and other political elites come to use in foreign policy, the mass media may tend to amplify it and thus increase the likely influence of these leaders on public opinion (see Zaller and Chiu 1996). This would appear to describe what occurred with the September 11th attack. The public will be more dependent than it has ever been on vigorous competition of positions and ideas *among elites* (Zaller 1992), because it will have both less information and fewer predispositions based on relevant frames of reference that it already has.

However, perhaps the end of the Cold War and the resolution of the current war against terrorism can provide the opportunity for this competition of ideas and policy positions and also (presumably for the better not worse) give the mass media more autonomy, so that they will exert separate influences on public opinion and offset government's advantage in gaining and maintaining public support for its actions.

The setting of the Cold War may have given presidents and government a particular advantage in efforts to direct public opinion in foreign policy. One of the best analyses was offered by W. Lance Bennett (1990), who went beyond emphasizing that the press (i.e., journalists) are heavily dependent on their sources in general and on government sources for policy issues; he argues and shows that the media's coverage paralleled or "indexed" the positions of major and visible government officials and political institutions. While Bennett studied U.S. policy toward Nicaragua, subsequent researchers found similar patterns of news coverage on other American interventions and crises in foreign affairs (and on domestic affairs; see Jacobs and Shapiro 2000, chaps. 5 and 6). One of the main conclusions from this research was that while there might be broad debate about the effective implementation of U.S. policies, there would be no broad debate about the formulation of the policies themselves unless there were intense and critical debate in Washington and among prominent officials (Mermin 1999).

With the end of the Cold War, however, does this "indexing" by the press represent a persistent form of behavior or does it reflect the press's behavior toward or relations with government during a period of persistent threat to the nation? Whereas Zaller and Chiu's (1996) first study showed how the press not only indexed authoritative officials' opinions and amplified them in ways advantageous to Washington, their follow-up of study of foreign policy crises after the end of the Cold War revealed a less clear pattern of media behavior and news coverage (Zaller and Chiu 2000). This pattern supports Robert Entman's (2000) contention that the end of the Cold War foreign policy consensus has given the news media the leeway to frame issues in ways less constrained than in the past by the stated positions of political elites. The post–Cold War cases suggested that the press was less tied to congressional and executive officialdom and in certain ways more balanced when issues did not involve communist foes; more coverage appeared on other experts, including non-American sources (Zaller and Chiu 2000).

Whether the press's behavior has in fact changed in a way that has and will affect the power of presidents and authoritative figures in Washington to direct public opinion is an important question for further research and political analysis. The war on terrorism and its aftermath deserve top priority. Recent developments—the end of the Cold War and the corresponding decline in salience and increase in complexity of foreign policy issues—allowed presidents and government increasing opportunity to lead or manipulate public opinion, but it is not clear whether the changing nature of foreign policy issues and the way the mass media cover foreign policy can alter this trend.

For proponents of popular control of American foreign policy (Russett 1990; Shapiro and Page 1988, 1994), there is little reason to be sanguine. Beyond the changes that have occurred in the world of foreign affairs, other signs also point in the wrong direction—toward less responsiveness and more manipulation of public opinion. As described in chapter 3 and noted in our discussion of the Reagan administration, changes in partisan and other aspects of American politics have substantially increased the incentives for presidents, as well as other political leaders, to seize the opportunity to lead or manipulate the public. In addition, foreign policy issues are *not* part of the liberal-conservative policy mood that presidential and other government policymaking responds to in ways that involve ideological and partisan linkage processes, as Erikson, MacKuen, and Stimson show in chapter 2 and elsewhere (Erikson, MacKuen, and Stimson 2002). All of this has contributed to a political and policymaking environment in which political leaders and policymakers are (compared to previous historical periods) relatively free to ignore or misperceive public opinion on foreign affairs. Kull and Ramsey, in the next chapter, explain why this occurs in contemporary American politics.

NOTES

We thank the Pew Charitable Trusts for research support and the organizers of the Conference on Polls, Policy, and the Future of American Democracy (Institute for Policy Research, Northwestern University, Evanston, Illinois, May 13, 2000). The editors and reviewers of this volume provided excellent advice and comments. The responsibility for all analysis and interpretations is our own.

1. Reagan Library, PR15, "Analysis of the President's Peace and National Security Address," DMI, March 1986, attached to cover note from David Chew to president, 3/4/86.
2. Reagan Library, PR15, "Flash Results, #3084–01," DMI, 4/9–11/85.
3. PR15, "American Attitudes toward the Iranian Situation," DMI, 1/14/87 (#459046).
4. Reagan Library, PR15, Letter to president from Wirthlin, 4/10/85.

11

How Policymakers Misperceive U.S. Public Opinion on Foreign Policy

STEVEN KULL AND CLAY RAMSAY

A substantial amount of polling data has shown a widespread feeling among the American public that the U.S. government has a poor understanding of majority preferences and that its decisions are out of step with the wishes of the majority. In this chapter, we examine evidence that in the realm of U.S. foreign policy in the post–Cold War era, members of the foreign policy elite have misperceived public attitudes—which may indeed be a key factor in creating a disjunction between U.S. foreign policy and majority preferences.

The evidence that the Americans public feels that the majority's preferences are poorly understood and frequently not followed is manifold. For example, in an October 1994 Gallup poll, 75% said Congress is "generally out of touch with average Americans." In a January 1999 study by the Center on Policy Attitudes (COPA), 63% said they thought that "people in government understand what most Americans think" either "not that well" or "not well at all." Asked to estimate how much of the time the decisions the U.S. government makes are the same as the decisions the majority of Americans would make, the median response was a shockingly low 40%.[1] In May 2000, CBS/*New York Times* asked: "How much say do you think people like yourself have about what the government does?" Sixty-four percent replied "not much" ("some," 25%; "a good deal," 10%).

There is a widespread feeling that special interests run government decisions, not majority wishes. For some years, in response to a trend line question, strong majorities have said that the government is "pretty much run for the benefit of a few big interests," not "for the benefit of all the people" (70% in a Gallup July 2000 poll; 75% in the COPA January 1999 poll). This is in marked contrast to the 1960s, when this was a minority point of view—only 29% in 1964 (National Election Studies). In a February 1997 Louis Harris poll, an overwhelming 83% agreed that "special interest groups have more influence than voters," while 76% agreed that "Congress is largely owned by special interest groups."

The public also thinks that it should have more influence. In the COPA poll, respondents were asked "how much influence the views of the majority of Americans" have on "the decisions of elected officials in Washington," and told to answer on a scale of 0 to 10, with 0 meaning not at all influential and 10 meaning extremely influential. The average answer was 4.6. Respondents were then asked how much influence they thought the views of the majority of Americans *should* have on the decisions of elected officials in Washington. The average response was 8.4.

Interestingly, there is evidence that the public's perceptions of a gap between majority preferences and government decisions may have some validity and that this gap may be growing—in conjunction with the growing public perception that the government is not being run for the benefit of all the people. As Lawrence Jacobs and Robert Shapiro discuss in depth in chapter 3, studies have found a significant decline over the last few decades in the correspondence between public opinion and public policy decisions; the most recent study found only 55% correspondence (Monroe 1979, pp. 3–19; 1998, pp. 6–28). Although it is not possible to conclude a causal relationship, this decline has occurred in conjunction with the increasing perception of nonresponsiveness.

The public may gravitate to the view that this lack of correspondence is due simply to the influence of special interests. However, policymakers may have genuine misperceptions of public attitudes that prompt them to act or that make it easier for them to be influenced by special interests whose goals are in line with the public's assumed preferences.

A major study that we conducted, together with I. M. Destler, suggests strong reasons to believe that policymakers can in fact misperceive majority public opinion. This study focused on an assumption, widely expressed in the policymaking elite, that in the wake of the Cold War the American public has been wanting to disengage from the world. In particular, many members of the policy community believed that cooperative forms of engagement were unpopular. Thus, they have assumed that the public dislikes the United Nations, opposes contributing troops to international peacekeeping operations, and intrinsically opposes foreign aid. (Defense spending, on the other hand, was assumed to be popular, though it is a form of international activity, because it is seen as directly protecting U.S. interests and asserting U.S. leadership.)

This assumption about public attitudes apparently had a significant influence on U.S. foreign policy. Throughout the 1990s, there was a trend away from international engagement—typified by reductions in the international affairs budget, closing of embassies, cutting foreign aid, failure to pay UN dues, and a resistance to committing U.S. troops to UN peacekeeping operations.[2] A major exception to this trend, though, was in defense spending, which, while reduced from its high point in the 1980s, was maintained at levels close to those during the Cold War. Within the policy discourse, there were frequent references to these trends as not only consistent with public opinion but prompted by it.[3]

Our research project sought to answer several key questions. First, how widespread was this view that the American public was going through a phase of wanting the United States to disengage? Second, and most important, was there evidence to support this view of the public? Third, if policymakers were given some control over the polling process, would they be able to elicit the presumed public desire for disengagement? To answer these questions, we undertook a multipart research project.

The first stage of the project was a series of interviews with 83 members of the policy community, including members of Congress, congressional staffers, executive branch officials dealing with foreign policy, foreign policy journalists, and members of nongovernmental organizations that dealt with foreign policy. We asked these policy practitioners about their perceptions of public attitudes on the question of America's role in the world, U.S. relations with the United Nations, the U.S. role in UN peacekeeping, foreign aid policy, and defense spending. We also asked about their perception of the impact of these public opinions on U.S. foreign policy.

The second stage of the project was a comprehensive review of the existing polling data. Analyzing data from all publicly available sources, we sought to determine whether policymakers were perceiving the public correctly and—to the extent that there was a gap between elite perception and public attitudes— whether any dynamics in public attitudes could account for the elite perception.

In the final stage, policy practitioners were given an opportunity to propose poll questions that might elicit the attitudes they assumed to exist in the public. These ideas were then incorporated into a nationwide poll designed to test these assumptions.

THE GAP BETWEEN ELITE PERCEPTIONS
AND PUBLIC OPINION

The net result of the elite interviews and the analysis of public attitudes did indeed reveal a substantial gap in all areas. What follows is a brief synopsis of this gap. (A complete analysis can be found in the report and book that issued from the study [Kull, Destler, and Ramsay 1997, Kull and Destler 1999].)

America's Role in the World

When asked what they thought the majority of Americans felt about the U.S. role in the world in the wake of the Cold War, approximately three out of four respondents interviewed said that most Americans want the United States to disengage from the world. The recurring theme was that this was a result of a resurgence of isolationism in the wake of the Cold War and a renewed parochialism in American thinking. This view was especially strong among members of Congress and their staffs. It was less strong among executive branch officials, but was still a majority opinion.

Polling data, however, indicate clearly that the majority of Americans do not want to disengage—nor has the proportion who do increased significantly since the end of the Cold War. Trend line data asked for decades show no significant change since the fall of the Berlin Wall. About two out of three Americans still say the United States should take an active part in world affairs, and in response to some questions, the majority supporting this view rises to 90%.[4]

Some features of American public opinion may contribute to the perception that the public wants to disengage from the world. Americans do want their nation to move away from the role of dominant world leader—or "world policeman." But on further questioning, it becomes clear that these sentiments do not reflect a fundamental desire to disengage. To move away from the role of dominant world leader, most Americans want the United States not to withdraw, but to emphasize working together with other countries, especially through the UN.

Another factor that can contribute to the impression that the public wishes to disengage is that many Americans complain that the United States does more than its fair share in international efforts. However, on further examination, it

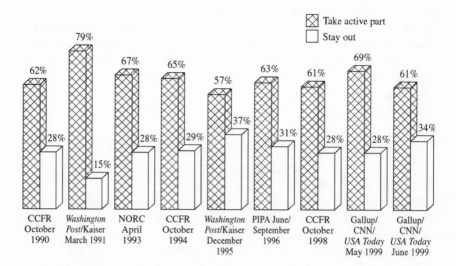

Figure 11.1 Attitudes toward U.S. Involvement in World Affairs, 1990–1999. The question posed was: "Do you think it will be best for the future of this country if we take an active part in world affairs or if we stay out of world affairs?"

As the sole remaining superpower, the US should continue to be the preeminent world leader in solving international problems.

 11%

The US should withdraw from most efforts to solve international problems.

15%

The US should do its share in efforts to solve international problems together with other countries.

72%

Figure 11.2   Public Prefers Shared Role in Solving International Problems. The question posed was: "Which statement comes closest to your position: As the sole remaining superpower, the U.S. should continue to be the preeminent world leader in solving international problems; The U.S. should withdraw from most efforts to solve international problems; The U.S. should do its share in efforts to solve international problems together with other countries." *Source:* PIPA, July 2000.

becomes clear that this view is founded on extreme overestimations of how much the United States actually does. Asked to specify how much the United States should do, most Americans specify an amount greater than the actual amount. When told how much the United States does, most do not find it objectionable.

The United Nations

A substantial majority of practitioners believed that the American public is either negative or ambivalent about the United Nations. Less than a quarter of those interviewed said that the majority of Americans has positive feelings toward the UN. Less than a fifth believed that Americans would like to see a stronger UN. Only one in ten thought that the majority of Americans wants the United States to pay its UN dues in full. An overwhelming majority of practitioners thought that, in a situation requiring the use of military force, Americans would prefer acting together with NATO over acting together with the UN. The view of public attitudes as negative toward the UN was distinctly stronger among congressional members and staff.

Public attitudes diverge sharply from these perceptions. A strong majority reports positive feelings about the UN,[5] while an overwhelming majority supports U.S. participation in the UN as an active member. An overwhelming majority would like to see the UN strengthened. Only a small minority worries that this could threaten U.S. sovereignty. A majority supports full payment of U.S. dues to the UN. Majorities even support some forms of international taxation to bring revenue to the UN and the creation of a standing UN peacekeeping force made up of volunteers.

Support for the UN is especially strong for the use of military force. When offered a choice of using U.S. military force unilaterally, or as part of a UN operation, the public opts overwhelmingly for the latter. When also offered the option of acting through NATO, the plurality still prefers the UN. Concurrent with this strong support for the UN, however, at times there has been significant public criticism of UN performance, especially the passivity shown by some UN peacekeeping operations. However, this frustration tends to evoke majority support for strengthening these operations, rather than discontinuing them.

UN Peacekeeping

Only about one in ten of the practitioners interviewed thought that a majority had positive feelings about UN peacekeeping. Half thought that most Americans take a negative view of UN peacekeeping in general. Another quarter thought that Americans could support a specific UN operation only if certain conditions were met—such as high potential for success, no use of American personnel, or a direct connection to U.S. national interests.

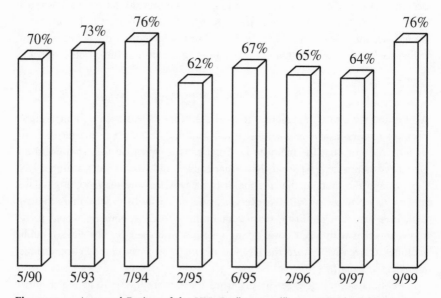

Figure 11.3   Approval Rating of the UN. By "approval" we mean the percentage calling their opinion of the UN "mostly favorable" or "very favorable." *Source:* Pew and *Times Mirror*.

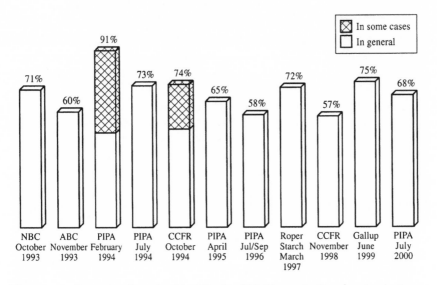

Figure 11.4   Percentage Favoring Contributing U.S. Troops to Peacekeeping in Some Cases or in General

On the question of contributing U.S. troops to UN peacekeeping, the majority of practitioners thought most Americans were opposed: members and staff on Capitol Hill were nearly unanimous on this point. Almost three-quarters also thought that the majority of the public was opposed to placing U.S. troops under a non-American commander in a UN operation. Finally, a plurality of policy practitioners thought that any American casualties would generate strong public pressure for immediate withdrawal from a UN peacekeeping operation. Almost three-quarters, including all media interviewees, said a majority of the public had favored immediate withdrawal from Somalia after the death of 18 U.S. Rangers in October 1993.

In fact, UN peacekeeping in principle garners strong majority support from the public, while counterarguments (based on cost or lack of connection to U.S. national security) do poorly in polls. Support derives both from peacekeeping's potential for burden sharing and from humanitarian and moral concerns, especially in cases in which genocide is a factor. At the same time, very large majorities have had reservations about UN peacekeeping performance, most notably in Bosnia, where the operation was perceived as too passive.

The majority has consistently favored contributing U.S. troops to peacekeeping operations in principle. Support for contributing to specific operations varies, however, according to a number of variables, including whether the operation is clearly perceived as multilateral, whether the United States is perceived as contributing its fair share, whether the operation is perceived as likely to succeed, whether the U.S. leadership is acting coherently and decisively, and whether the operation could mitigate widespread civilian suffering.

On the question of putting U.S. troops under a foreign UN commander, in some polls the public is divided, whereas in others a clear majority finds it acceptable. In polls in which the public is divided, follow-on questions have revealed that a very strong majority finds a foreign commander acceptable if the United States is contributing only a minority of the troops.

Finally, there is little evidence that most Americans would respond to U.S. troop fatalities in the course of a peacekeeping operation by wanting to withdraw. In response to the actual fatalities in Somalia in October 1993, numerous polls showed that only about four in ten favored immediate withdrawal. Indeed, in the short run, a majority of Americans favored *more* involvement to reinforce U.S. troops. A majority did want to withdraw eventually, but this was true before the fatalities. In retrospect, strong majorities have continued to approve of the United States having undertaken the humanitarian operation in Somalia.

Further, a poll conducted in spring 1998 revealed that nearly two out of three Americans mistakenly believed that the United States had suffered substantial fatalities as part of the NATO operation in Bosnia over the previous year, but this did not lead to calls for withdrawal. Finally, in response to a variety of hypothetical scenarios, only a small minority would favor withdrawing U.S. troops in response to a significant number of U.S. fatalities.[6]

Foreign Aid

A very strong majority of practitioners believed that Americans have a negative attitude toward foreign aid in principle, thinking the money should be spent on domestic priorities. A substantial minority—and a large majority of those members of Congress interviewed—said that most Americans would like to eliminate foreign aid completely. Nearly every interviewee said that the public overestimates the amount spent on foreign aid, but less than a tenth cited this misperception as a primary source of opposition. Only a small minority cited dissatisfaction with the performance of U.S. foreign aid programs as a major reason for the public's negative attitude.

In fact, polling data show that an overwhelming majority of Americans embraces the broad principle of giving foreign aid to the needy. Only a tiny minority wants foreign aid eliminated. When asked to prioritize, Americans rank domestic needs higher; but when asked to distribute resources, most Americans assign more to foreign aid than is currently allocated. Support derives from both altruism and self-interest. Majorities embrace the ideas that giving foreign aid helps the United States to develop trading partners, preserve the environment, limit population growth, and promote democracy. But overwhelming majorities reject the idea that the United States should give aid only when it serves the national interest.

A strong majority feels that the United States gives too much foreign aid (though this majority fell between 1995 and 2000).[7] But—contrary to practitioners' perceptions that this is because Americans prefer to spend the money at

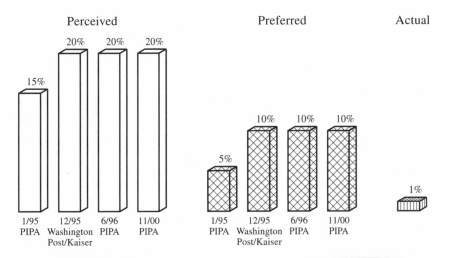

Figure 11.5   Beliefs about Foreign Aid as a Percentage of the Federal Budget (Medians): Perceived, Preferred, and Actual

home—polls suggest that this feeling is largely due to extreme overestimations of the amount of foreign aid given by the United States, both as a percentage of the federal budget and relative to other countries. When Americans are asked what percentage of the federal budget would be appropriate, they set an amount far higher than the actual level. Only a small minority finds objectionable the actual amount—1%. A strong majority said that the United States should give the same amount as other countries as a percentage of GNP—considerably more than the United States gives in reality.

Defense Spending

A majority of policy practitioners believed that Americans support current levels of defense spending. Only about a fifth thought that most Americans want to see cuts in defense spending. Likewise, only a fifth said that the public would be supportive if the president and Congress were to decide on a 10–20% cut in defense spending, whereas a plurality said that the public would not support such cuts. Most significant, practitioners interviewed thought that support for the current level of spending was derived from concerns that cuts would impair homeland defense, a desire to preserve jobs, and a desire to maintain the dominant U.S. role in the world. A desire for burden sharing through greater multilateralism was rarely mentioned.

   In this case, the gap between the public and policy practitioners is more subtle. Most Americans support a strong defense, and polls that simply ask for feelings about the current level of defense spending show majority comfort.

However, polls that probe more deeply show support for substantial cuts, including polls that ask respondents to (1) specify their preferred spending level; (2) consider defense spending in a budgetary context when respondents are informed about the actual amount of defense spending; (3) propose defense spending levels relative to potential enemies; (4) make tradeoffs between defense spending and nonmilitary international spending; and (5) evaluate the requirement for the United States to be prepared to fight two major regional wars. If the president and Congress were to agree to cut defense spending 10–20%, strong majorities say they would be supportive. If these funds were to be explicitly redirected into popular domestic programs, overwhelming majorities say they would approve.

But the gap is most apparent in policy practitioners' perceptions of why the public supports defense spending. Contrary to policy practitioners' perceptions, the majority does not express fears that defense cuts will make the United States vulnerable and does not favor maintaining defense spending to preserve jobs. Most centrally, the majority of Americans strongly rejects a level of U.S. defense spending perceived as being consistent with the role of the United States as dominant world leader. Rather, the public calls for a much greater emphasis on burden sharing through multilateral approaches to security.

LETTING THE POLICY PRACTITIONERS
ASK THE QUESTIONS

Although the evidence for a gap between elite perceptions and public attitudes was derived from a comprehensive review of polling data, there was still the possibility that policy practitioners have a unique insight into the public not yet revealed in the polls. The third stage of the project was to give policy practitioners the opportunity to propose poll questions and to predict what they thought the outcome would be.

In a series of workshops, policy practitioners were presented the findings from the interviews of policy practitioners and the contrasting polling data. We then asked them to challenge the notion that policy makers are misreading the American public by proposing ideas for poll questions that might reveal underlying trends toward disengagement and to predict the outcomes. These proposals were then developed into a questionnaire that was reviewed by workshop participants, as well by as a Democrat and a Republican pollster. The questionnaire was then used in a poll with a random sample of approximately 2,400 Americans. The poll was conducted in two waves, so the group was also reconvened and presented the preliminary findings to see if they prompted any new ideas for poll questions.

Overall, the most striking feature was that the policy practitioners were not good at predicting public responses. Essentially, all of the predictions they made in proposing questions that would show an underlying desire to disengage were not sustained by the polling data. The challenges, and the subsequent tests, can be divided into four broad areas.

Challenges Based on Dynamics of the Electoral Process

One challenge, frequently repeated, was that even if most Americans say in a poll that they support engagement, they actually prefer candidates who support disengagement. To test this notion, different samples were asked about their own opinion and about their feelings toward a hypothetical candidate's position. In fact, there was little difference in results between the two samples. Even on a question with a complex design that sought to factor out social desirability effects in favor of pro-engagement candidates, the pro-engagement candidate did better.

Another frequent challenge was that an incumbent who voted in favor of pro-engagement policies would be highly vulnerable to attacks from an electoral challenger, especially if the policies involve spending taxpayer money. With the help of political consultants, we created political ads in which hypothetical challengers attacked hypothetical incumbents for supporting foreign aid and paying UN dues, as well as rebuttal ads from the incumbents. Responding specifically to these ads, the majority of respondents preferred the pro-engagement incumbents over the challengers by robust margins.

Among other challenges, one held that even if the majority says it favors engagement, it does not like to see elected officials spending a significant portion of their time on foreign policy. However, when asked in a poll how much time was appropriate for the president or a member of Congress to spend on foreign affairs, the median respondent allotted a substantial portion—30% for the president and 25% for a member of Congress.

Challenges Based on Assumptions about the Effective Public

Numerous workshop participants declared that support for engagement is weak and fragile, while opposition is intense and resilient; thus, opposition is more relevant politically. But responses to survey questions indicated that, in general, supporters of engagement held their views as strongly as opponents. And when presented with strong counterarguments, pro-engagement respondents proved slightly less likely to change their positions than anti-engagement respondents.

Some argued in the workshops that the public that matters on foreign policy is an attentive, active minority, and that this group wants to reduce U.S. involvement in the world. But among those who declared themselves attentive and those who said they are active, support for international engagement was, if anything, a bit higher than in the general population. These groups were somewhat less enthusiastic toward the UN, however, and more critical of government performance.

Challenge Based on How the Public Makes Trade-Offs with Domestic Programs

Practitioners supposed that even if the majority of Americans embrace an internationally engaged U.S. foreign policy *in principle,* in practice they are not ready to spend the necessary money when faced with making trade-offs against domestic priorities. Thus, when members of Congress cut international spending in favor of domestic items, they are doing what members of the public *would do* if they were voting on the federal budget. The prevailing view was that members of Congress were also reflecting their constituents' wishes by maintaining the current level of defense spending.

To test this assumption, a budget exercise was developed in which respondents were asked to allocate money among major items in the discretionary federal budget. This included four international spending categories (the State Department, the UN and UN peacekeeping, military aid, and humanitarian and economic aid), seven purely domestic items, and defense spending. Contrary to the predictions, the majority chose to maintain or increase every category of international spending. However, defense was cut severely. On average, international spending was dramatically increased and fared better than many domestic items. Thus, the view, expressed in the workshops, that respondents would cut international spending in favor of domestic items while also sparing defense turned out to be the exact reverse of the majority's actual choices.[8]

Challenge Based on Confidence Congress Reflects Public

Frequently stated in the workshops (and in interviews) was the belief that individual members of Congress are good mirrors of attitudes in their districts, and thus the aggregate legislative behavior of Congress forms a good mirror of national attitudes, more reliable than national polls. The fact that Congress has taken legislative steps limiting U.S. international engagement was seen as clear evidence that the public must support these steps.

To test this challenge, we set out to determine if the constituents of strongly anti-engagement members of Congress were indeed also opposed to engagement. We began with the fifteen cosponsors of the 1995 legislation calling for the United States to withdraw from the UN (H.R. 2535), examined their voting records for consistent opposition to international engagement, and interviewed their aides over the telephone about how calls and letters were running on international issues and how they perceived majority views on these issues in the district. Through this process, we selected four geographically dispersed districts, in each of which the congressional aide had taken the unequivocal position that the majority of constituents would favor *withdrawing from the UN* and *eliminating foreign aid.*

We polled 500 randomly selected adults in each district (total 2,000). In all districts, only one in five respondents favored withdrawing from the UN and only

one in twelve favored eliminating foreign aid. Strong majorities favored strengthening the UN. Overall, these four districts were not only supportive of U.S. international engagement but on most questions indistinguishable from the national sample.

WHY DO POLICY PRACTITIONERS
MISPERCEIVE THE PUBLIC?

Why have policy practitioners come to believe Americans want to withdraw from
the world? Why have they persisted in believing this despite substantial survey
evidence to the contrary? Focusing on the interviews with policy practitioners
themselves, we have isolated four possible explanations: (1) the failure of policy
practitioners to seek out information about public attitudes, (2) policy practitioners' tendency to respond to the vocal public as if it were the majority, (3)
their assumption that Congress and the media reflect the public, and (4) their
tendency to underestimate the public.

Failure to Seek Out Information about Public Attitudes

In virtually every case, members of Congress said they did not poll on international issues. Nor did they show much interest in it. A congressional staffer,
speaking of his boss, said, "I'm trying to think, the last time—I can't remember
the last time he's asked for a poll, and I can't remember the last time I've actually
seen one." Explaining this low level of interest, another member said, "Foreign
affairs just doesn't win elections or lose elections."

This pattern of giving little attention to polls was also reflected in a recent
Pew study that interviewed 81 members of Congress, 98 presidential appointees,
and 151 senior civil servants, titled "Washington Leaders Wary of Public Opinion."
Asked, "What is your principal source of information about the way the public
feels about issues?" only 24% of the members of Congress, 21% of presidential
appointees, and 6% of senior civil servants mentioned public opinion polls (Kohut 1998).

Responding to the Vocal Public as If It Were the Majority

Consistent with their widespread negative attitudes toward polls, most policy
practitioners, especially in Congress, explained that their primary means of getting information about public attitudes is through informal contacts with self-
selected and outspoken citizens—the vocal public. A high-level congressional
staffer explained how he got his understanding of public opinion:

> You get it from constituencies. You get it from public interest groups. You get it from
> tons of junk that comes in your in-box every day from half the interest groups in

the country. You get it from talking to people . . . [who] come in here all the time [and say] they need this, they need that, do this for me, do that for me. So you get a constant feel for this stuff.

This orientation was also reflected in the Pew study: when members of Congress were asked about their "principal source of information about how the public feels," by far the most frequently mentioned (by 59%) was "personal contacts," while the second most common (cited by 36%) was "telephone or mail from citizens."

Whereas some respondents described an active constituency that initiates contacts specifically to denounce international engagement efforts, others implied, quite plausibly, that more contacts were initiated by concern about some other domestic program that the constituent was concerned would be underfunded. Attacking spending on international efforts was a way to rationalize increasing spending on the domestic program. For example, a congressional staffer said, "Usually people are saying . . . 'Medicare is going bankrupt. Why don't we just cut foreign aid and give all the money to Medicare?' "

When we probed about whether some contacts supported engagement, these were sometimes recognized but often brushed off as unrepresentative of the general population with comments like, "Those are just your World-Affairs-Council types."

Viewing Congress and the Media as Mirrors of the Public

Numerous comments from policy practitioners suggested that they base much of their thinking about the public on the assumption that Congress and the media are reliable mirrors of public opinion. In particular, journalists and Congress appear to each take cues from each other and build a shared image of the public that others in the policy elite tend to accept. Taken far enough, this tendency can generate a closed information system immune to disconfirming input from the public itself.

A key element of this system is the belief that the behavior of Congress is a reliable reflection of public attitudes. A reporter and columnist explained why he relied on Congress rather than polls to get his understanding of public attitudes, saying: "Congress is the best reflection of the American public's views. There is a good chemistry of mixing up ideas that goes on." A longtime congressional staffer said, "I think the Congress perfectly reflects public attitudes. . . . I do think they're good bellwethers."

At the same time, members of Congress and their staffs, as well as other members of the policy community, say that they get their cues about the public from the media.[9]

Most commonly, policy practitioners seemed to feel that they could get a sense of public attitudes by reading standard news reporting. A prominent policy analyst described how he gets his ideas about the public:

Chap 3

Mostly, I think, by talking to the press who are soaking in the public, they are re-flecting public attitudes.... I can't readily explain how it works, but daily press coverage does reflect what people are interested in, and does reflect their attitudes.... There is an underlying understanding of what people are thinking, and what people are willing to hear, and the press coverage is reflecting that.

In this regard, the findings of our study were practically identical to those of Susan Herbst in chapter 9, who found in the Illinois statehouse "the belief held by many of [her] informants . . . that *mass media content is public opinion*" (italics in original). There is, apparently, nothing strictly Washingtonian about the prevalence of this notion among political professionals.

Underestimating the Public

A fourth possible source of policymakers' misperception of the public is a tendency to view the public in a more negative light than is warranted. In the interviews, when policy practitioners characterized the public, they did so frequently with a disparaging, if not exasperated, tone. In a content analysis of the interviews, negative characterizations of the public (e.g., "uneducated," "self-contradictory") outweighed positive ones (e.g., "sensible," "responsive to argument") by more than four to one. Implicitly, and in many cases explicitly, policy practitioners were suggesting that the public was inadequate to the task of addressing significant foreign policy issues.

Apparently this view is not uncommon among the American elite. In a 1996 survey of 2,141 American opinion leaders, 71% agreed that "public opinion is too short-sighted and emotional to provide sound guidance on foreign policy."[10] On a more general note, in the Pew study, when asked "Do you think the American public knows enough about the issues you face to form wise opinions about what should be done about these issues, or not?" only 31% of the members of Congress, 13% of the presidential appointees, and 14% of the senior civil servants endorsed the public's ability.

The image of the public as lacking depth and sophistication in many cases was part and parcel of the image of the public as resisting international engagement. The public was widely viewed as narrow, parochial, and emotional, thus unable to think about foreign policy issues in a long-term framework.

This tendency to misperceive the public has been studied in the social sciences for some decades now. Floyd Allport is generally credited with coining the term "pluralistic ignorance" in the 1920s to describe a situation in which individuals make mistaken judgments about themselves relative to the majority (Gorman 1986, pp. 333–47). For example, studies have found that people tend to perceive others as more racist, more conservative, more sexist, and less willing to engage in socially desirable behaviors such as donating blood (Fields and Schuman 1976, pp. 427–48; Shami and Shamir 1997, pp. 227–60; Goethals 1986, pp. 137–57).

CONCLUSION

We started this chapter by reviewing evidence that the American public views policymakers as failing to understand, and to act consistently with, the preferences of the public. We noted that there is evidence of significant inconsistencies between public opinion and public policy (elaborated by Jacobs and Shapiro in chapter 3 of this volume) and that this inconsistency has increased over the same historical period that the public's perception of nonresponsiveness has increased. We then proposed the possibility that one factor in this growing inconsistency may be a misperception of public attitudes on the part of policy practitioners. A review of an extensive multifaceted study revealed strong evidence that in the area of foreign policy in the mid- to late-1990s, there was indeed a widespread misperception of public opinion among the foreign policy elite. While this evidence does not prove that policymakers misperceive public opinion in all policy areas at all times, it does arguably demonstrate that the political system is an imperfect market and that, despite their incentives to understand the public, policymakers may indeed err.

Several questions persist, though. First, how is it possible that the executive branch can misperceive the public on foreign policy when it has in place an extensive apparatus, described in the previous chapter, for determining public opinion? In our study, we did find that members of the executive branch were far more accurate in their perceptions of public opinion than were congressional members and staffers, journalists, or members of non-governmental organizations. Congressional members and staffers, on the other hand, were the least accurate. In interviews with executive branch officials, some did say that they understood that some of their policies were out of step with the public. However, they explained, they were constrained by Congress, which was necessarily treated as a kind of "stand-in" for the public, even though they recognized that, in fact, Congress was not a correct reflection of the public on many issues. After dealing with Congress on a day-to-day basis, for some, it seemed the distinction between Congress and the public became relatively fuzzy, and it was only when they were asked a direct question did the discrepancies between Congress and the public reemerge in the minds of these officials.

Another question flows from the previous chapter, which shows that policymakers do make efforts to understand public opinion and that, while far from perfect, substantial correspondence has existed between U.S. foreign policy and public opinion. According to Alan Monroe's study, U.S. foreign policy was consistent with public opinion 67% of the time between 1980 and 1993 (Monroe 1998, pp. 6–28). Does this suggest that the public's perception of an inconsistency may be exaggerated?

Four points are worth making in reply. First, the period of our study postdated the period that Monroe studied. Monroe had already found that in the 1980–93 period, correspondence between public opinion and public policy and foreign policy specifically had declined as compared to earlier periods. Thus, it is possible that in the period of our study (1996–97), the correspondence may have been even lower.

Second, even a 67% correspondence does not demonstrate a responsiveness as strong as the number initially suggests. Given that the methodology involves the comparisons of binary options, approximately half the time there would be correspondence just by chance. A 50% correspondence would provide no evidence of responsiveness; thus, the 67% level should be viewed in this light.

Third, even correspondence above 50% does not necessarily demonstrate responsiveness. Correspondence between public opinion and public policy does not necessarily mean that public opinion was causal.

Finally, it is difficult to quantify the portion of the time that policymakers are behaving consistently with public preferences because the public may favor ideas that are never seriously considered by policymakers (and thus are never included in the denominator). There is indeed evidence that the public may at times support ideas that are outside the dominant policy discourse. Perhaps the clearest case lies in how far the public is ready to go in giving power to the United Nations. For example, in 1995 while doing focus groups, we heard respondents propose that the United Nations should have its own military force to perform peacekeeping operations. When we subsequently tested this idea in a national poll, we found approximately two out of three supported it. Other polls have also found majority support for giving the UN the power to impose certain types of taxes (for instance, on international arms sales). American policy makers did consider rather strong steps for empowering the UN in the period shortly after World War II; however, they were ultimately abandoned and attempts to revive them have virtually no effect on policy processes today. The public, however, continues to show strong interest and support. Structural factors may contribute to this discrepancy. The policy community is essentially part of a national institution and thus is highly wary of yielding power to an international institution. The public, however, relatively less identified with national institutions, is more apt to see international institutions as simply another means for serving its interests and values.

For all these reasons, correspondences between public opinion and policy decisions do not contradict the public's perceptions. The public's perception that policymakers do not understand the public is supported by the findings of the study reviewed in this chapter; the perception that policymakers make little effort to respond to public preferences is supported by the research of Jacobs and Shapiro. Their recent book shows in extraordinary depth that although policymakers do sometimes pay attention to polls, they do so primarily as a means of learning how to manipulate public opinion, not to respond to it (Jacobs and Shapiro 2000). And, in fact, there are enough significant variations between public opinion and actual policy that the public's perception of unresponsiveness should be considered to have some degree of validity.

NOTES

1. For a report on this study, including a comprehensive review of polling from other sources, see Kull and Destler (1999).

2. It may be argued that, on balance, these changes did not really represent a meaningful trend toward disengagement. However, within the foreign policy discourse, as reflected in the interviews of the policy practitioners, it was widely interpreted this way by those who supported the trend, as well as those who bewailed it.

3. See Kull and Destler (1999, chap. 1) for a more detailed account of these assertions.

4. Gallup/CNN/*USA Today* found a recent high of 69% in favor of taking "an active part in world affairs" with 28% opposed (May 1999). In October 1999, Pew Research Center found 88% agreement with the proposition, "It's best for the future of our country to be active in world affairs."

5. One example: in September 1999 Pew found 76% with a very (19%) or mostly (57%) favorable opinion of the UN.

6. A comparable pattern was also evident in polling at the close of the Kosovo war in June 1999. *Newsweek* asked respondents to estimate the number of "casualties . . . you think U.S. peacekeeping forces in Kosovo will suffer" over the year to come. The median response was 50 casualties. Even so, in the same poll, 59% supported the "use of U.S. ground troops as part of the international peacekeeping force in Kosovo."

7. There have been significant changes in the percentage saying the United States spends too much on foreign aid—and, more important, there has been a marked decrease in the desire to cut foreign aid. In the Program on International Policy Attitudes' January 1995 poll, 75% said they felt "the amount the United States spends on foreign aid" is "too much." In a July 2000 PIPA poll this dropped to 55%, but rebounded a bit in its November 2000 poll to 61%. In November 2000, only 40% wanted to cut foreign aid—down from 64% in PIPA's 1995 study. For a full analysis of data from all sources, see Kull (2001).

8. When this poll was repeated in 2000, the results were largely the same. See Steven Kull (2000).

9. Based on his interviews with State Department and National Security Council (NSC) officials, Powlick (1995) also found news media and elected representatives to be the primary sources of the policymakers' information on public opinion. .

10. Reported in Holsti (1996a).

Part III

MEASURING PUBLIC OPINION

12

The Authority and Limitations of Polls

PETER V. MILLER

The first two parts of this book have examined how public opinion relates to public policy. The measurement of public opinion through polls or other means is crucial to understanding the relationship. This section explores a variety of issues in measuring public opinion, focusing mainly on aspects of polling methodology. The warrant for relying on public opinion polls in policymaking and evaluation rests largely on the claim that polling methods produce more accurate representations of public sentiment than do other sources of information. Scientific opinion polls (unlike other forms of expression that give voice to the most opinionated, the best organized, or the most readily accessible members of the public) involve statistical designs to represent the views of all segments of society. And, unlike other methods of understanding public opinion, scientific polls gather information in ways that permit replication and error measurement. Probability sampling methods, along with standardized opinion measurement procedures, are the foundation for polls' special claim on knowledge of the public will.

Chapters in this part by Gilens, Manski, and Witte and Howard follow a rich tradition of methodological debate that has contributed to polls' authority. Lee's chapter calls for less exclusive reliance on polls for understanding public opinion and a more "pluralistic" approach that takes advantage of other sources of information. Gilens and Manski focus on aspects of nonsampling error in polls—questionnaire design, interviewer behavior, and mode of respondent contact—while Witte and Howard's work treats both sampling and nonsampling issues in

Web surveys, an increasingly important mode of data collection. This introductory chapter offers a context for discussions of factors central to the claim that polls can provide useful knowledge about public opinion, and the limits on polls' contribution.

ARTIFACTS ARE IN THE MIND OF THE OBSERVER

In chapter 13 Gilens points to one of the key advantages of polls: the ability to embed experiments in order to measure the effect of optional measurement tactics, such as alternative questionnaire design features (question wording and order), interviewer behavior, mode of contact, and respondent recruitment methods. The authority of polls is bolstered by their ability to measure errors resulting from various aspects of their operation. The aim of these investigations can be to identify better measurement methods or to demonstrate how different frameworks for assessing public opinion affect the distribution of responses.

The Uses of Experimentation

The work of Cannell and colleagues exemplifies the use of experimentation in surveys to test different methods of interviewing (Cannell, Miller, and Oksenberg 1983; Miller and Cannell 1987). A series of experiments examined the effect of "commitment," "instructions," and "feedback" techniques interviewers used in some treatment groups, compared to routine interviewer practice as a control. These investigations pointed to some benefits of clearer communication with respondents about survey measurement objectives. An objective of such research is to *control* survey errors by standardizing interviewer behavior using the techniques that produced improved reporting.

Although controlling survey errors is one important outcome of experimentation, Gilens notes that the implication of the findings of survey experiments is not necessarily just "methodological." "Errors" discovered in many survey experiments are not simply miscues to be eliminated; rather, they are substantively significant findings for public opinion researchers. When we find, for example, that respondents give different answers to certain survey questions depending on whether they are questioned by an interviewer of the same or a different race, we learn something not only about the conduct of surveys but about the state of race relations. When alternative forms of a survey question produce different response distributions, we might infer that one form of the question is "better" than the other (see, e.g., Manski, chap. 14; Miller 1984) but in many cases we can regard alternative question forms as substantively different, but equally plausible frames within which to consider social issues. Following Schuman's (1982) dictum that "artifacts are in the mind of the observer," Gilens reviews examples of how alternative question frames can illuminate the range of perspectives on racial issues and how these perspectives interact with other respondent characteristics. Extending this line of reasoning one step further, studies that manipulate different appeals to increase survey participation give practical lessons for survey practitioners but also can teach us about the state of altruism in society or about evolving norms of privacy. As Witte and Howard point out in chapter 15, the Web offers a potentially fertile ground for survey-based experiments, as the range of stimuli that can be presented to respondents (audio, video, interactive) is far broader than typically possible in telephone or face-to-face interview settings.

THE "HORSE RACE" REDUX

One would be hard pressed to find in a volume of academic essays on public opinion in recent decades a discussion of how pollsters might improve the precision of their pre-election "horse race" estimates. What one would find instead are many heated objections to the number of preelection polls, the extent to which "horse race" figures dominate news coverage of campaigns and "dumb down" campaign discourse, and the likely (perverse) effect of poll reports on election turnout and voting. Not just academics and press critics, but members of the working press would be quoted in postelection conference summaries belittling the mindless use of "horse race" numbers in campaign stories. For example, here is a quotation concerning the *New York Times* election polls following the 1988 presidential contest (Kagay [1991] quoting an internal *Times* memorandum by Adam Clymer):

> These polls were not used to produce flashing maps to declare either a Dukakis victory in the spring or a Bush victory in the fall.... Such falsely predictive poll stories were the antithesis of *The Times*'s approach, which mined the data and found continual warning signs of fluidity and uncertainty.... We could usually find something more interesting than the horse race for a lead.

Morin (1995), writing about the *Washington Post*'s use of polls in 1992 election coverage, says that, in reaction to what was perceived as "poll driven" coverage in 1988, "we deliberately decided to de-emphasize the horse race by saturating the 'market' within the *Post* newsroom with horse race results.... [This strategy] appeared to have the desired effect ... more horse race numbers had indeed produced less horse race-driven copy." Elite news media practitioners are apologetic about horse race polls and argue that their polling information goes far beyond the simple tracking of candidate support as the campaign unfolds. They are also careful to state that horse race estimates are not forecasts of the election outcome (except for the final poll conducted just prior to the election), but "snapshots" of prospective voter sentiment at different points in the campaign.

The antipathy for horse race estimates extends to the public policy arena. Outside the United States, where the First Amendment to the Constitution stands in the way of legislation, national governments (e.g., Canada, the United King-

dom, Australia, Brazil, France, Germany, South Korea) forbid the publication of
these poll numbers for varying periods prior to and including election day. The
concern embodied in these restrictions is that poll estimates of candidate electoral
support can unduely influence whether and how people vote. The bandwagon
hypothesis, given credence by many in the United States, is taken seriously in
legislation in other parts of the world. This has dual implications for the authority
of polls: on the one hand, poll results are judged to be credible and therefore
effective in altering vote intentions. On the other hand, poll results are considered
a pernicious influence in the democratic process and therefore should be subject
to control. (Meyer [1990] and Taylor [chap. 17] are noteworthy exceptions to this
general view.)

Manski's chapter in this volume is, therefore, quite unusual. He argues simply
that, if queried with "probabilistic" questions, preelection poll respondents can
express their vote intentions more precisely than they are permitted to do when
answering typical horse race items. By allowing respondents to more fully express
uncertainty about their vote intentions, Manski asserts, the volatility in preelection
poll estimates, such as that observed in the 2000 presidential campaign, could be
reduced and better election predictions could be made. He offers evidence from
a pilot study in support of the argument and notes in an appendix some earlier
studies that employed a similar approach. Bypassing entirely the normative considerations about their use, Manski seeks to make horse race polls more accurate.

Those who see some value in estimates of voter sentiment during election
campaigns may find his recommendations useful (and there may be more such
observers after the considerable flaws in balloting and vote counting in the 2000
elections were publicized). But, regardless of one's attitude toward horse race
polls, it is instructive to examine how a decision about question wording fits in
the broader framework of survey design elements and objectives.

The judgment to adopt a new procedure for one aspect of a survey must
take into account the other aspects of survey design on which one could lavish
time, attention, and money. Though we commonly teach and write about components of surveys—sampling, questionnaire design, interviewing, length of field
period—as if they were independent, surveys are really a complex tapestry in
which these components are interwoven. The length of the field period, for example, affects the possibility of contacting potential respondents and also what
they may have in mind when responding to questions. Many survey organizations
had to decide whether to continue trying to contact respondents after the terrorist
attacks on the World Trade Center and the Pentagon because of how those events
might have affected people's willingness to participate and even their views of
unrelated issues. In the case of preelection polls of 2000, the volatility in vote
intention estimates in the latter part of the campaign noted by Manski may be
more the result of the small samples typically employed in tracking and postdebate polls than the wording of the vote intention questions. One prominent
organization, Gallup, showed large shifts in the partisan makeup of successive
waves of its tracking poll. As Traugott (2001) notes, the Gallup trend line was

substantially more volatile than those of other polling organizations. Gallup did not attempt to weight to party identification, believing, in contrast to a number of its competitors, that party identification naturally varies in the short term rather than being a relatively stable characteristic (Morin 2000). The decision to do nightly tracking polls or "quick reaction" postdebate surveys constrains the opportunity for recruiting respondents, heightens the potential for nonresponse bias, and makes it more likely that one will have to confront the choice of weighting to "correct" the composition of the achieved sample. Question wording is a key factor in analyzing why a poll produces a particular estimate, yet other aspects of polls can interact with it.[1]

MODES OF CONTACTING THE PUBLIC

"Scientific" polls use probability sampling. The now-familiar addendum to news reports of poll findings—that the survey has a "margin of error" of a few percentage points—gives an impressive aura of precision to the descriptions of public opinion. The fact that the impression of exactitude is probably exaggerated for many poll consumers (because the "margin of error" calculation is based on an assumption of simple random sampling rather than the more complex designs that most surveys employ and because it does not include an estimate of the effect of many sources of nonsampling error) does not diminish the extraordinary value of the mathematics of sampling to the conduct of public opinion research. The ability to make general statements about a large population, within a specified range of accuracy, based on contact with a relatively small, appropriately constructed sample of its members is remarkable.

Witte and Howard's chapter on Web surveys argues for a different conceptualization of "generalizability" in keeping with the limitations of such surveys—at least currently—to achieve probability samples of the population. Their argument gives us an opportunity to take a historical look at the relationship between modes of respondent contact employed in surveys and their relationship to sampling practice.

Sampling Frames

For the probability sampling process to work properly, we need a reasonable and clear definition of the population, an inclusive sampling frame from which to choose invited participants, and a selection method that gives each member a known chance of being invited. Satisfaction of these requirements depends in large measure on the channels of communication through which data are collected: face-to-face household interviews, telephone calls, mail solicitations, Web surveys. Over time, these channels of communication—because of changes in societal norms and uses of technology—have evolved in their utility for public opinion research.

For example, Gallup's storied contest with the *Literary Digest* poll to measure voter intentions in the 1936 presidential election pitted a survey that collected data through household interviews with one that relied on self-administered questionnaire responses solicited from people whose names appeared on automobile registration lists and in telephone books. As Witte and Howard note, the operational definitions of "the public" in these alternative contact approaches were clearly different, as the responses from the more "upscale" *Literary Digest* sample, coupled with probable nonresponse bias, produced an estimate of Republican victory in that election, whereas the household sample, derived from a more inclusive frame, captured the intentions of more of the Democratic-leaning voters who foretold Roosevelt's eventual landslide (Squire 1988).

In recent times, responses volunteered to various Web site "polls" during the Clinton impeachment imbroglio were consistently more negative toward the president than polls that invited people to express their views in telephone interviews (Wilt 1998). Those with access to the Internet and familiar enough with it to register their views on-line were a special subset of the larger population, just as telephone subscribers had been in the 1930s. Moreover, the Web poll opinions were expressed not by particular individuals specifically invited to participate in the polls, but by self-selected volunteers. (In the case of many Web site polls, like their television "call-in" counterparts, there is nothing to prevent people from responding multiple times). Probability sampling insists on a comprehensive list or frame from which to sample prospective survey participants and a careful designation of each sample member, guided by the operation of chance.

Evolution of the Telephone Survey

As household telephone penetration became nearly universal (around 95%) and as efficient methods for sampling both listed and unlisted numbers were developed (the Mitofsky-Waksburg multistage approach; see Waksberg 1978), the telephone became the established communication medium of choice for public opinion polls. Though in-person household interviewing still offers better coverage of the population and higher response rates, the cost and time involved in this method often outweigh its benefits for many researchers. The amount of time needed to field a telephone survey is a small fraction of that required to launch an in-person survey, and the cost per interview is markedly less. The development of computer-assisted interviewing systems in centralized calling sites allows for more complex questionnaire options and better interviewer monitoring than is possible in face-to-face household surveys. In short, the telephone, once eschewed by public opinion researchers because of coverage and other sampling problems, is now the standard method against which others are gauged. In such a comparison, Web surveys of the general public today offer the advantages of telephone surveys and more, but also suffer from the sampling difficulties that the telephone mode once had.

But, as Witte and Howards note, there are threats to the telephone's dominant status. For a variety of reasons, people's willingness to accept the invitation to do telephone interviews is declining. A common belief with some face validity is that the "clutter" of telemarketing and other unsolicited phone calls has made it difficult for researchers to make an effective appeal for survey participation. Survey "refusals" are often hang-ups in the first few seconds of interview attempts (Oksenberg, Coleman, and Cannell 1986). Because of increasingly lower response rates, the *achieved* sample in a telephone survey, though based on a probability selection of telephone numbers and of prospective respondents within households, may not provide an unbiased estimate of the population parameter of interest. To the degree that people refuse or, because of answering machines and other call-screening devices, never receive the proffered invitation to participate in a telephone poll, nonresponse bias may distort the view of public opinion that the survey produces.

The response rate problem is not unique to telephone polls; in-person household survey efforts, for example, have also seen a decline in cooperation (Groves and Couper 1998). But because the telephone mode is now the most prominent communication channel for surveys, the response rate issue for these polls receives more attention. The American Association for Public Opinion Research (2000) has published *Standard Definitions*, as Witte and Howard note, for accounting for the results of interview attempts in telephone, in-person and certain mail surveys. This extensive publication, coming long after the association adopted standards for disclosure that mandated reporting of response rates, is evidence of the increasing concern with which the profession views the potential effects of nonresponse. The number of paper sessions at the AAPOR annual meeting devoted to aspects of the nonresponse issue in recent years and the various book-length treatments of it (Groves and Couper 1998; Brehm 1993; Goyder 1987) are additional measures of the prominence of the issue.

Still, the connection between the level of response rate for a survey and the extent of nonresponse bias in its estimates is not well understood. Whereas it seems natural to assume that as the response rate declines the nonresponse bias will rise, it appears that this relationship is far from perfect (see, e.g., Keeter, Miller, Kohut, Groves, and Presser 2000; Curtin, Presser, and Singer 2000). A survey's response rate matters if the people who do not respond are different from those who do on matters of importance to the study. For example, the claims of some conservative commentators notwithstanding (e.g., Ladd 1996), there appears to be little evidence that conservative citizens are more likely to refuse to express their views in polls sponsored by the "liberal media." As Traugott (2001) notes, the vast majority of media preelection polls estimated that George Bush would win the popular vote in the 2000 election, throwing water on the claim that such efforts suffer from a conservative nonresponse bias. Considerably more research is needed to get a handle on the relationship between response rates and nonresponse bias. Witte and Howard are correct to highlight the potential impact of nonresponse in probability sample surveys, though it is important to maintain the conceptual distinction between surveys in which respondents designated by the sampling process refuse to be interviewed and surveys in which respondents with no sampling designation just "show up." Because the two cases are not the same sort of "self-selection," their effects are likely to be different. Further, the fact that nonresponse may affect the quality of estimates from probability samples does not imply that we should abandon the principle of probability sampling.

Web Surveys

For readers old enough to have witnessed the transition from in-person interviewing to telephone contacts as the norm in survey research, the current discussion of Web surveys may elicit a feeling of modified déjà vu. Some of the apparently major advantages of the Web—speed, reduced cost, number of respondents—were foci of the discussion on the merits of the telephone. But there was concern about communication constraints imposed by the telephone then: lack of visual cues, impersonal conversation quality, increased speed of interaction. Current discussions of the Web, such as Witte and Howard's, emphasize the expansion of interview communication opportunities, such as the ability to use video stimuli in questionnaires. Thus, whereas (after the development of random digit dialing [RDD]) cautions on the use of the telephone in the old days concerned nonsampling matters, now the nonsampling possibilities are cited as Web advantages and sampling is the major hurdle.

For example, returning to the nonresponse issue for a moment, the ability simply to calculate a response rate depends on probability sampling that produces a list of eligible sampled individuals who can be sorted after the study into the group who responded and the group who didn't. In many Web surveys, including Witte and Howard's Survey2000, the denominator of the response rate is not known because the respondents are garnered not through sampling but through an open invitation to anyone to participate. Some of these invitations result in large numbers of responses, but the size of the responding pool, as Witte and Howard acknowledge, does not speak to its ability to represent either the population of Web users or any other population. Such Web survey efforts are akin to SLOPs—self-selected listener opinion polls—an acronym Norman Bradburn coined to characterize media call-in polls (see Bradburn and Sudman 1988). As Couper (2000) notes in his extensive review, this is probably the most prevalent form of Web survey.

The strong Web cultural prohibition against unsolicited contacts ("spam") and the fact that—anti-spam rules aside—there is no way currently to construct a comprehensive frame of e-mail addresses means that probability samples of Web users need to be assembled through other modes of communication: telephone, in-person, or mail contacts, for example. To use the Web for surveying a sample of respondents representative of the broader population, the substantial coverage problem posed by the fact that Web access and use are still skewed toward the more affluent, educated, young, urban, and white segments of the population must be overcome (Couper 2000). Knowledge Networks (formerly Intersurvey) has attacked the coverage problem by recruiting a national panel of respondents through telephone interviews and installing Web TV devices with Internet access in households. Whereas the RDD recruitment approach offers the theoretical potential for a representative national probability Web-enabled sample, nonresponse in the recruiting process, to the extent that it produces nonresponse bias, tempers the optimism. Rivers (2000) reported that installed panel households constituted about 40% of those initially solicited to participate. Nie and Erbring's (2000) unpublished paper based on the Knowledge Networks panel is the foil for Witte and Howard's analytic comparison with their Survey2000 volunteer sample data.

If Internet household penetration reaches the level achieved by the telephone, the need for expensive efforts such as the Knowledge Networks panel may diminish. In the meanwhile, use of the Web for scientific polls will have to be restricted to probability samples of Web users to represent that population and samples drawn from the likes of the Knowledge Networks panel for inferences to the broader U.S. population. Another option, currently in use, is the volunteer Web survey panel. Harris Interactive and other firms interview subsamples of such panels and weight the results in an attempt to match the characteristics of the total Web and non-Web population. The weighting procedures, ironically, require information on population parameters from probability sample telephone surveys, complete with the low response rates and other limitations that some Web survey advocates highlight. In addition, the weighting procedures must correct the *relevant* biases in the Web sample, not just demographic imbalances.

And indications are that, in either case, the low response rates in other modes of survey communication—the telephone, for example—are apt to be a concern in Web surveys as well (Couper, Blair, and Triplett 1999). The lure of cheap and fast surveys with new methodological opportunities that are not available or are more expensive in telephone interviews—such as video stimuli in questionnaires—will compel investigators to work on ways to encourage survey participation in this new medium.

If the authority of polls rests largely on the pillar of probability sampling, shifts in societal norms and communication technologies that hamper the ability of researchers to create such samples threaten polls' special claim on knowledge of public opinion. Legislation aimed at limiting unsolicited telephone calls, the anti-spam norm in on-line communication, and call screening devices that deflect survey invitations are current examples of social and technological factors undermining the foundation of scientific polling. The fact that the functions of communication technologies in society and their norms of use are not static over time has tested the ingenuity of public opinion researchers in developing probability samples. More ingenuity will be required to face the current operational challenges to the principle of giving every member of defined survey populations a known chance of being invited to participate in public opinion measurement projects.

METHODOLOGICAL COSTS AND BENEFITS

Unlike the other chapters in this part, Lee's has a historical focus. He argues for the analysis of constituency mail to understand the opinions of an "active" public during the civil rights era. He notes that public opinion scholars' reliance on survey evidence may lead to erroneous conclusions about the roles of elites and nonelites in public policy formation. Routine survey practice may not capture the views of interested citizens whose attempts to influence government actions in a particular sphere do not coincide with survey efforts to measure public opinion in that topic area. During the civil rights movement, Lee argues, survey measurement of opinion lagged behind the efforts of letter-writing non-elites to influence government policy. As a consequence of this disjuncture in timing, Lee notes that analyses of the civil rights movement that rely on survey data overemphasize the role of elites in the effort. He urges a more "pluralistic" view of public opinion that does not rely exclusively on survey data.

In making his case, Lee cites several critiques of survey research that will be familiar to students of public opinion. What distinguishes Lee's work from that of others who have made this point is his more careful documentation of the substance and timing of polling efforts on civil rights and his laborious efforts to assemble and analyze an alternative public opinion data source—letters to the president concerning the civil rights issue for several administrations. Rather than simply recite the claim that survey data can give an erroneous perception of public opinion, Lee offers empirical tests. Readers will have to consult his forthcoming book judge the persuasiveness of his analysis of constituency mail, as the chapter presented here provides only a brief foreshadowing of that case. Here, he focuses on why it is important to go beyond survey data to consider other representations of public opinion.

Lee's argument shares with Witte and Howard's the notion that examining the views of a self-selected group of people is valuable in studying public opinion. But, unlike Witte and Howard, he does not argue for attempting to generalize from such a collection of individuals to the larger society. Rather, he argues that the views of active citizens—who may have more influence on public policy than others—may be understated in the data derived from typical survey practice. This point is as old as Blumer's (1948) argument so often cited by critics of polls. Unlike many of them, Lee does not say that polls are inherently wrongheaded, but that complementary data from other sources are needed to get a fuller picture of public opinion.

In theory, of course, capturing the views of the active citizens Lee wishes to study is possible in the course of public opinion research using surveys. Like others, such individuals are sampled through probability methods, and their level of interest and commitment and action concerning the topic can be measured. Their views can be compared to those of their less involved counterparts. They can be asked to express themselves in responses to open questions, and those "verbatims" can be subjected to content analysis just as letters can be examined.

In short, nothing intrinsic to the survey method precludes gathering data like those that Lee advocates, and surveys would provide the added benefit of offering uniform information for both involved and uninvolved individuals so that their differences can be examined.

The assembly and analysis of data from constituency mail, though not treated extensively in Lee's chapter, confront the investigator with challenges equal to or greater than designing a survey that would adequately capture the views of active citizens like those Lee is interested in. One must rely on the diligence of White House personnel and archivists to preserve, classify, and locate relevant correspondence. Requests to presidential libraries and archives must be framed in such a way that they elicit all germane material for analysis. Archivists must be trusted to provide relevant documents, regardless of their implication for the reputation of the government official to whom they were addressed. Once letters are obtained, the analyst confronts a highly complex content analysis exercise to glean useful information from the mass of material. There are necessarily major challenges for the validity and reliability of the coding procedures undertaken to summarize the data in the documents. Although, as Lee notes, the views expressed in constituency mail can be expressions of opinion, one needs to assess how this mode of communication might affect the sincerity and articulation of viewpoints, just as one is concerned about these issues in surveys that promise confidentiality. Understanding public opinion through study of constituency mail presents, in summary, daunting questions.

The effort needed to find answers to these queries may be justified, however, because, though survey research could be used to look at public opinion from the angle of interest to Lee, it usually is not so employed. The number of involved citizens sampled for a given study may be too few, depending on how involvement is defined, for adequate statistical analysis. Larger samples than are often employed would be required, with the attendant increase in cost for survey projects. Surveys also would need to be designed to capture more prospectively opinions on topics not currently in the news. There is precedent for ongoing surveys (see Neuman 1989) that attempt to capture in open-ended fashion issues of concern to the public; however, such investigations should envision a broader range of topics than "the most important problems facing the country" and would confront the difficult content analysis problems faced by analysis of correspondence. It seems useful, in the face of these issues, to take seriously Lee's recommendation for a plurality of methods for understanding public opinion. It is also useful to have a sophisticated understanding of the costs and benefits of each method so they can be used in concert.

NOTE

1. Readers may wish to consult the *Standards for Minimal Disclosure* of the American Association for Public Opinion Research for a useful list of survey components that should be considered when evaluating any poll.

13

An Anatomy of Survey-Based Experiments

MARTIN GILENS

Randomized experiments embedded in surveys are almost as old as surveys themselves. But over the past few decades, the use of survey experiments has expanded dramatically. Once limited to simple "split-ballot" designs, the survey-based experiment has become an enormously flexible and increasingly sophisticated tool for social scientists. Spurred by the development of advanced computer-assisted interviewing software, researchers have devised an impressive array of techniques that combine the causal power of the randomized experiment with the representativeness of the general population survey. In this chapter, I describe a range of survey experiments that address concerns from abortion to racial attitudes to voting preferences. I identify the dimensions of a survey interview that can be randomly varied, the characteristics that these dimensions can take on, and the kinds of analyses that can be used to extract meaning from randomized survey experiments.

SURVEY EXPERIMENTS

Surveys are typically designed to reveal respondents' attitudes or beliefs about some issue of interest. But this seemingly straightforward task is complicated by our inability to observe the objects of our interest. The data we collect when we conduct a survey are not observations of respondents' attitudes or beliefs but records of their verbal behavior in response to our questions; we must infer attitudes or beliefs from the behaviors we observe. Sometimes survey respondents' behavior bears a direct and unproblematic relationship to an underlying attitude or belief of interest. But not always.

If our interest, for example, is in Americans' attitudes toward legal immigration from Canada and Mexico, we might ask survey respondents whether the laws governing U.S. citizenship for immigrants from these two countries should be the same. We could then observe respondents' behavior in reacting to this question. The problem, however, is that the same behavior might reflect different underlying attitudes. Consequently, our interpretation of respondents' behavior— the assignment of meaning to their verbal responses—would be uncertain.

In this example, three survey respondents might behave identically in expressing support for equal treatment. For the first respondent, this expression of support might stem from the similar attitudes he holds toward immigrants from Canada and Mexico. For the second respondent, the expression of support for equal treatment might reflect a commitment to the principle of equality under the law, despite her different attitudes toward Canadian and Mexican immigrants. For the third respondent, the expression of support for equal treatment might arise neither from his equivalent attitudes toward the two groups nor from his genuine commitment to equal treatment, but from his reluctance to acknowledge a preference for disparate treatment in the face of egalitarian social norms.

As many strands of hermeneutics and communication theory stress, meaning is assigned to a statement by a receiver, not something that inheres in some determinate fashion in the statement itself. When the subject of our inquiry is human attitudes (rather than physical characteristics of the natural world), we unavoidably face a degree of uncertainty in assigning meaning. But by attending to the multiple meanings that can inhere in a given survey response, we can reduce that uncertainty and illuminate the alternative attitudes that respondents might hold.

In the pages that follow, I discuss one tool that the survey researcher can use to illuminate the meaning of the survey response: the randomized experiment. When attitudes on a given topic are complex or when survey respondents are reluctant to reveal their true thoughts, the randomized experiment can tease out the nuances of public opinion or uncover aspects of the public's thinking that may otherwise remain hidden.

To continue with the previous example, rather than asking respondents whether they think Canadian and Mexican immigrants should be treated equally, or asking each respondent about policy toward immigrants from the two countries, we might conduct a randomized experiment. One randomly selected half of the respondents could be asked a series of questions about legal immigrants from Canada: how long should they remain in the United States before becoming eligible for citizenship? Should they be deported if convicted of a crime? Should the citizenship status of family members bear on their own eligibility for citizenship? The other random half of the sample could be asked identical questions about legal immigrants from Mexico. By comparing the answers of these two subgroups of respondents, we might hope to gain a clearer picture of the true feelings of Americans toward immigrants from Canada and Mexico, without asking any respondent to make explicit comparisons

Over the past few decades, randomized survey-based experiments have evolved from a focus on the technical aspects of survey design to the substantive interpretation of respondents' attitudes and beliefs. Survey experiments have become a tool to dig below the surface of the traditional survey response to better understand the alternative meanings that a respondent's behavior might reflect. In this chapter, I offer an anatomy of survey experiments, identifying four dimensions that can be randomly varied, the characteristics that these dimensions can take on, and the kinds of analyses that can be used to extract meaning from randomized survey experiments. (For other discussions of survey-based experiments, see Piazza and Sniderman [1998], Sniderman [1992], Sniderman and Grob [1996].)

An ordinary survey question can be transformed into an experiment by randomly exposing different subgroups of respondents to (1) alternative wordings of the survey question, such as the reference to Mexican or Canadian immigrants in the hypothetical example; (2) alternative contexts in which the same survey question is asked, such as randomizing the order in which questions are presented; (3) alternative characteristics of the survey interviewer, such as race or sex; and (4) alternative survey modes including mail, telephone, in-person, and, more recently, Web-based surveys. In addition to these four dimensions of experimental manipulation, I describe a specialized form of question wording experiment, the "list experiment," particularly useful in assessing attitudes toward socially sensitive issues.

AN EVOLVING TECHNIQUE

Randomized experiments embedded in surveys are an old technique. In the early 1940s, Elmo Roper conducted a series of question wording experiments using a split-ballot design in which randomly chosen half-samples were asked different question versions. He found, for example, that in March 1940, only 13% of Americans said, "the U.S. should do more than it is now doing to help England and France." But when asked whether "the U.S. should do more than it is now doing to help England and France in their fight against Hitler," 22% of the public said yes (Cantril and Wilks 1940).

Survey experiments during the next few decades tended to share Roper's concerns with methodological issues, especially question wording and response options. During the 1970s and 1980s, this line of inquiry was raised to a new level of sophistication by the systematic research of Howard Schuman and Stanley Presser (Presser and Schuman 1980; Schuman, Presser and Ludwig 1981; Schuman and Presser, 1981). Schuman and Presser, for example, report the results of over

200 experiments from thirty different surveys the authors conducted. In this research program, Schuman and Presser replicated, extended, and systematized previous experimental studies of question form, wording, and context. They explored issues of question and response order, open versus closed questions, the assessment of "no opinion," and the number and nature of response categories, among other topics.

More recently, survey-based experiments have been employed to address substantive rather than methodological concerns. Of course, "substantive" and "methodological" concerns are not always easily distinguished. Experiments comparing different numbers of response categories are clearly methodologically motivated and those that compare reactions to different news stories are clearly substantive in orientation. But experiments like Roper's "fight against Hitler" example lie somewhere in between and might be analyzed with an eye toward either substantive or methodological concerns. In addition, methodologically motivated efforts to understand question wording or response option effects often reflect the cognitive processes that underlie substantive political phenomena like perceptions of fairness or reciprocity.

Although survey experiments have a long history, the recent growth of substantively oriented work in this area owes much to the vision and leadership of Paul Sniderman. In collaboration with colleagues from a wide range of institutions, Sniderman has conducted a series of telephone surveys over a period of two decades that have employed randomized experiments in innovative ways. The advent of computer-assisted telephone interview (CATI) software has greatly expanded the possible range and complexity of survey-based experiments. Rather than having to rely on the limited number of ballot versions feasible in a split-ballot design, CATI software allows for an almost unlimited number of independently randomized experiments on a single survey.

QUESTION WORDING EXPERIMENTS

The simplest and most common form of survey experiment involves random assignment to alternative question versions as the independent variable and responses to those questions as the dependent variable. A familiar example of this kind of experiment is the testing of alternative campaign messages by political candidates. To test message content on tax cuts, for example, a congressional campaign might tell a random subsample of survey respondents: "Last year, Congressman Smith helped President Bush pass a 1.3 trillion dollar tax cut to let Americans keep more of the money they earn." Another subsample might be told, "Last year, Congressman Smith helped President Bush pass the largest tax cut in twenty years, cutting taxes for Americans of all income levels." Both sets of respondents might then be asked: "Does Congressman Smith's support for President Bush's tax cut make you more or less likely to vote for Smith for Congress?" Using variations on this technique, campaign consultants can assess the impact of alternative messages about their own candidate or the opposing candidate and identify the subsets of voters for whom different campaign messages are most effective.

Similar experimental variations in question wording have been used regularly on academic surveys for the past few decades. Starting in the mid-1980s, for example, the General Social Survey (GSS) began asking split-samples different versions of anti-poverty spending questions. One randomly selected subgroup of respondents was asked whether spending for welfare should be increased, decreased, or kept about the same. (This version of the question had been on the annual GSS surveys since the early 1970s.) Another subgroup was asked whether spending on assistance to the poor should be increased, decreased, or kept about the same. Over the years, responses to these two formulations have been dramatically different. In 1996, for example, 58% of Americans said welfare should be cut, but only 18% wanted to cut spending on assistance to the poor (see Gilens [1999] for an exploration of this difference.)

The "welfare/assistance to the poor" comparison from the GSS involves respondents' judgments about two different attitude objects. A similar experimental design underlies the "welfare mother experiment" on the 1991 Race and Politics Survey conducted by the University of California, Berkeley.[1] In this case, a random half of the respondents were asked about a hypothetical welfare mother described as a black woman, in her early thirties, with one ten-year-old child, who had been on welfare for the past year. The other half of the respondents were given the identical description, but the welfare recipient was described as white instead of black. All respondents were then asked how likely they thought it was that the welfare mother described would try hard to find a job, and how likely it was that she would have more children in order to get a larger welfare check.

Like the GSS experiment already described, the welfare mother experiment can be analyzed by treating the random assignment as the independent variable and the responses to the job and children questions as the dependent variables. In this case, white respondents' perceptions of the two welfare mothers look quite similar. Fifty-three percent of white respondents thought the black welfare mother would try hard to find a job versus 54% of those asked about the white welfare mother (fig. 13.1). Similarly, 70% thought the black welfare mother would have more children in order to get a larger welfare check versus 66% in the white welfare mother condition.

Although the aggregate responses to the two versions of the welfare mother experiment look similar, their relationships with other attitudes are quite different. Rather than treating respondents' perceptions of the welfare mothers as dependent variables, we can use them as independent variables to predict respondents' policy preferences or other judgments about welfare. Whether we consider white respondents' preferences for welfare spending, their scores on a multi-item welfare attitudes index, or their views on whether poor people are lazy, we find that perceptions of black welfare mothers are far stronger predictors than perceptions of white welfare mothers (figure 13.2). African Americans

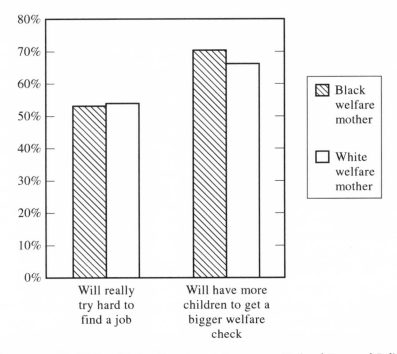

Figure 13.1   The Welfare Mother Experiment. *Source:* 1991 National Race and Politics Study; white respondents only. $N = 1{,}801$.

make up only 26% of the country's poor and about 38% of welfare recipients.[2] But these relationships suggest that white Americans' thinking about welfare and poverty is related far more strongly to their perceptions of poor blacks than poor whites.

A third kind of analysis of the welfare mother experiment sheds some light on *why* perceptions of black welfare mothers more strongly predict whites' welfare and poverty attitudes. Figure 13.3 shows whites' scores on the welfare attitudes index separately for white respondents expressing positive, neutral, and negative perceptions of either the black or white welfare mother.[3] The greater impact of perceptions of the black welfare mother are accounted for entirely by the difference in welfare attitudes associated with negative views of black and white welfare moms. Positive and neutral perceptions of these welfare mothers are associated with similar overall attitudes toward welfare, but negative perceptions of the black welfare mother are associated with substantially more negative welfare attitudes than are negative perceptions of the white welfare mother. In other words, negative images of black welfare mothers have a unique salience in shaping white Americans' overall views of welfare.

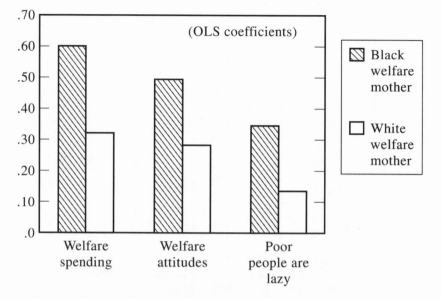

Figure 13.2   The Impact of Beliefs about Welfare Mothers on Three Measures of Welfare/Poverty Attitudes. *Source:* 1991 National Race and Politics Study; white respondents only. $N = $ 1,913, 1,107, and 1,100 for the three dependent variables. See Gilens (1996) for details.

QUESTION CONTEXT EXPERIMENTS

In the two experiments described, different respondents are offered different attitude objects to evaluate. A second form of randomized experiment elicits responses to the same attitude object but alters the environment within which that evaluation is made. Question order experiments fall into this category. For example, in *Reaching Beyond Race*, Paul Sniderman and Edward Carmines (1997) report the "mere mention" experiment in which respondents are asked to rate blacks as a group on a series of traits or stereotypes such as "lazy" and "irresponsible." For a random half of the sample, however, a question about affirmative action precedes the stereotype battery, whereas for the other half, the affirmative action question follows it. Sniderman and Carmines find that 20% of white respondents rate blacks as lazy when the stereotype questions come first (fig. 13.4). But when they are preceded by the affirmative action question, 31% of whites rate blacks as lazy. Similarly, 26% rate blacks as irresponsible when the stereotype questions come first, compared with 43% when the trait questions are preceded by the question on affirmative action. The mere mention of affirmative action, the authors conclude, is enough to "prime" particular aspects of racial perceptions, in this case, particularly negative aspects of whites' views of African Americans.

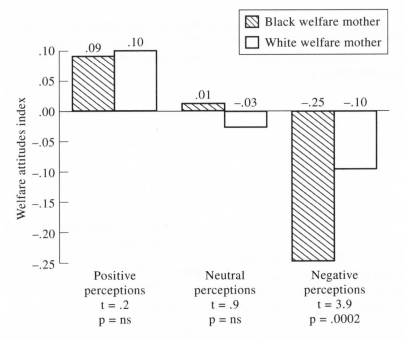

Figure 13.3 Whites' Welfare Attitudes by Perceptions of Black and White Welfare Mothers. *Source:* 1991 National Race and Politics Study; white respondents only. See Gilens (1996) for details.

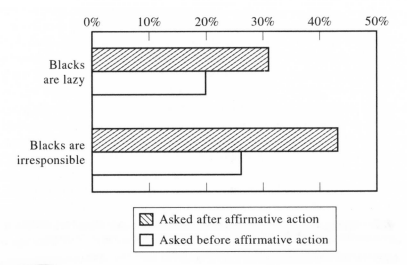

Figure 13.4 The Mere Mention Experiment. *Source:* 1989 Lexington, Ky., Survey; white respondents only. $N = 236$. See Sniderman and Carmines (1997) for details.

Another way in which survey respondents' decision-making environment can be altered is by providing different information to different respondents. Surveys show that Americans are woefully misinformed about a range of social and political conditions. For example, despite almost a decade of consistent declines in the crime rate, most Americans think crime has been rising. The 1998 Multi-Investigator Study found that 72% of respondents thought crime had increased over the previous decade; only 12% thought crime had declined.[4] The same survey asked respondents how much of every dollar spent by the government in Washington goes for foreign aid to help other countries. The median guess was 26 cents, when in reality less than 1 cent of each federal dollar goes to foreign aid.

It would be surprising if such misinformation did not influence Americans' preferences about anti-crime policy or foreign aid spending, and associational analyses do show the expected relationship: respondents who know that crime has been declining are less likely to support spending for prisons, whereas those who know that foreign aid constitutes a tiny percentage of the federal budget are less likely to favor cutbacks in foreign aid. But people who know these facts differ from those who do not in a variety of ways, so drawing causal inferences from these cross-sectional differences is risky (Achen 1986).

This problem can be addressed by using the power of the randomized experiment to establish causal influence. Rather than comparing people who happen to know particular facts about crime or foreign policy, information can be *provided* to a random subset of survey respondents (Gilens 2001). In the guise of asking respondents whether they have heard about a story that has been in the news, correct information is provided to some respondents but not others. In the treatment condition, respondents are asked:

> Our first questions are about two stories that have been in the news lately. The first story is about a new report that was just released about American foreign aid to help other countries. It said that the amount of money we spend for foreign aid has been going down and now makes up less than one cent of every dollar that the federal government spends. Have you heard about this story?

Respondents randomly assigned to the control condition are asked: "Our first questions are about two stories that have been in the news lately. The first story is about a new report that was just released about American foreign aid to help other countries. Have you heard about this story?" After hearing one of these two introductory questions, respondents are asked whether they think spending for foreign aid should be increased, decreased, or kept about the same. (Analogous story questions and policy preferences are asked about crime.)

By providing new information to randomly selected respondents, we can not only assess the overall impact of information on respondents' policy preferences but also identify the subgroups of respondents most and least likely to respond to new information. We might expect that respondents with the highest levels of political knowledge and engagement would be least affected by new information

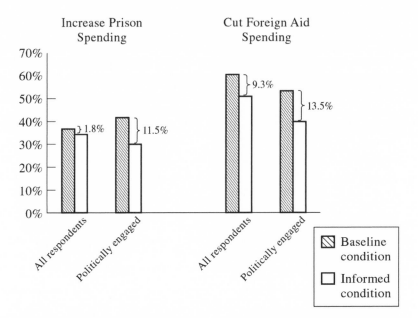

Figure 13.5 Information Experiments. *Source:* 1998 Multi-Investigator Study. *Ns* = 368 and 123 for prison spending and 1,058 and 345 for foreign aid spending.

because these respondents already have a larger stock of relevant information and a firmer basis for their existing preferences. On the other hand, we might expect more knowledgeable and engaged respondents to be more sensitive to new information because they have the interest and ability to process new facts and adjust their policy preferences accordingly.

The results of the information experiments described show that the impact of new information is, in fact, largest for the most politically knowledgeable and engaged respondents (fig. 13.5). High levels of political knowledge and engagement appear to facilitate the incorporation of new information into policy preferences rather than serving as a resource for resisting the impact of such information (see Gilens 2001).

THE LIST EXPERIMENT

The typical experiment, like the information experiments described, observes how people respond to being treated in different ways. People are provoked with different stimuli and then observed to determine the effects of those stimuli on the attitudes they express. But experiments can be put to a different use: to elicit already existing attitudes that respondents might otherwise be reluctant to reveal.

Baseline Condition	Affirmative Action Condition
1. Government increasing the tax on gasoline	1. Government increasing the tax on gasoline
2. Professional athletes earning large salaries	2. Professional athletes earning large salaries
3. Requiring seatbelts be used when driving	3. Requiring seatbelts be used when driving
4. Corporations polluting the environment	4. Corporations polluting the environment
	5. Awarding college scholarships on the basis of race

Figure 13.6   The List Experiment

Respondents' reluctance to reveal their true feelings has long been an issue in the measurement of racial attitudes. Many believe that Americans with conservative racial views have become reluctant to acknowledge those views to survey interviewers. The "list experiment" was designed by James Kuklinski to permit the measurement of racial attitudes by creating a situation in which individual respondents need not acknowledge those attitudes to the interviewer (Kuklinski, Cobb and Gilens 1997; Kuklinski et al. 1997; Gilens, Sniderman, and Kuklinski 1998).

In the list experiment, respondents hear a list of items that they are told "might make people angry or upset." Respondents are then asked to indicate how many of the items *but not which ones* make them angry or upset. In one version of this experiment, a random half of the respondents hear a list of four nonracial items, such as "government increasing the tax on gasoline" or "professional athletes earning large salaries" (fig. 13.6). The other half of the respondents hear the same list with the addition of a racial attitude item, such as "awarding college scholarships on the basis of race."

The responses to these questions are simply the number of items that each respondent finds upsetting. Unless a respondent answers "all" of the items, the survey interviewer (and the survey analyst) have no way of knowing *which* items make any given respondent upset. Consequently, the analyst has no way of knowing which respondents are upset by affirmative action. However, by comparing the mean number of upsetting items in the two conditions, the analyst can determine the *percentage* of respondents who find the additional item upsetting.

If *none* of the respondents is upset by affirmative action, the mean number of upsetting items will be identical for the two groups (within the bounds of sampling error). If *all* of the respondents are upset by affirmative action, the mean number of upsetting items will be exactly one higher among the group receiving the longer list. And if some intermediate proportion of respondents is upset by affirmative action, then the mean number of upsetting items will differ between zero and one. For example, if the mean response in the baseline condition is 2.3 and the mean response in the affirmative action condition is 2.9, then we can conclude that 60% of the respondents found the affirmative action item upsetting.

There is an additional twist to the list experiment: Later in the interview, only those respondents who were randomly assigned to the baseline condition are asked an identical question about affirmative action, but in a traditional format. These respondents are asked: "Now I'm going to ask you about another thing that sometimes makes people angry or upset. Do you get angry or upset about awarding college scholarships on the basis or race?" By comparing the percentage of respondents who answer "yes" to this traditional affirmative action question with the percentage of respondents expressing anger over affirmative action as measured by the list experiment, we can gauge the extent of reluctance to acknowledge anger over affirmative action and identify the population subgroups most and least likely to dissemble when asked about affirmative action in a traditional manner.

Figure 13.7 shows the basic list experiment result for self-identified conservatives. In the baseline condition, the mean number of upsetting items for these respondents was 2.7; in the affirmative action condition, it was 3.29. The difference of .59 indicates that 59% of conservatives found the affirmative action item up-

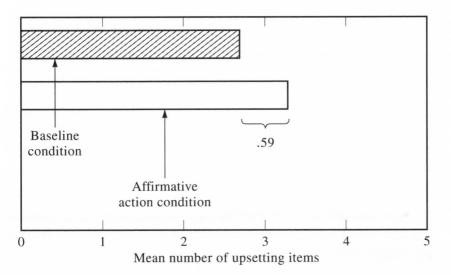

Figure 13.7   List Experiment: Conservative Respondents Only. *Source:* 1994 Multi-Investigator Study; white respondents only. *N* = 176. See Gilens, Sniderman, and Kuklinski (1998) for details.

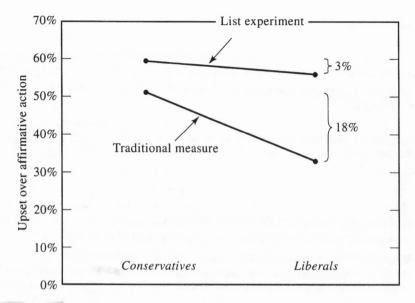

Figure 13.8 List Experiment vs. Traditional Measure. *Source:* 1994 Multi-Investigator Study; white respondents only. *Ns* = 246 for the list experiment and 147 for the traditional measure. See Gilens, Sniderman, and Kuklinski (1998) for details.

setting. This same 59% finding is shown in the top left of figure 13.8, which also shows the percentage of liberals indicating anger over affirmative action in the list experiment, as well as the results for liberals and conservatives using the traditional question format. The bottom line of figure 13.8 shows the relationship between ideology and opposition to affirmative action when measured with a traditional question: 18% fewer liberals than conservatives express anger over affirmative action when asked directly. But the top line in figure 13.8 shows that, when offered an opportunity to express their unhappiness with affirmative action in an "unobtrusive" way, liberals and conservatives are hardly distinguishable. When respondents need not reveal their opposition to affirmative action to the survey interviewer, liberals are only 3% less likely to express anger than are conservatives (see Gilens, Sniderman, and Kuklinski 1998 for details).

In the past, many have assumed that the tendency to distort one's true racial attitudes in a survey interview would be greatest among the most racially conservative members of the public. As the racial attitude climate has become more liberal and egalitarian (Schuman et al. 1997), those who think that blacks are inferior or that whites should be able to maintain racially homogeneous neighborhoods now find themselves holding widely condemned views. But the list experiment reveals a different dynamic, in which liberals are most likely to hide their true feelings. Moreover, the reason is clearly not concern over violating a broad consensus favoring affirmative action. On the contrary, a strong majority of whites (and the interviewers in this study were all white) oppose affirmative action, at least in the fairly strong form used in the list experiment.

Rather than a concern with offending the interviewer or violating a broad social norm, liberals' reluctance to acknowledge opposition to affirmative action may stem from a fear of *appearing* unconcerned with racial equality. If this interpretation is correct, then we should be able to identify more directly those respondents who would likely to hide their true opposition to affirmative action: those who place the highest value on racial harmony and equality. Figure 13.9 shows the difference between anger over affirmative action, as measured by the traditional question and the list experiment, for white respondents who give lower or higher priority to "racial harmony and equality between blacks and whites" in comparison with other values. Those who are least concerned with racial harmony show no tendency to hide their opposition to affirmative action, whereas those who are most concerned show a dramatic 26-point gap between the level of opposition expressed in the traditional and list experiment formats.

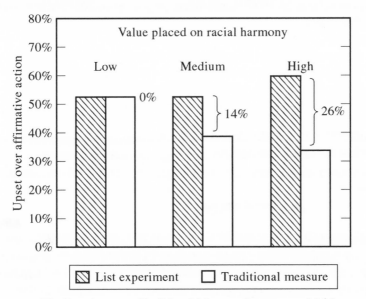

Figure 13.9 List Experiment vs. Traditional Measure. *Source:* 1994 Multi-Investigator Study; white respondents only. *N*s = 727 for the list experiment and 436 for the traditional measure. See Gilens, Sniderman, and Kuklinski (1998) for details.

EXPERIMENTAL MANIPULATION OF
THE INTERVIEW RELATIONSHIP

All of these examples of survey experiments manipulate the content of the survey as a way to gain insight into respondents' attitudes or beliefs. But the relationship between the respondent and the survey interviewer can be manipulated as well. The most familiar form of this kind of experiment takes advantage of naturally occurring differences between interviewers, such as their race or sex. Because the process that matches particular interviewers with particular respondents is typically random, the interviewer-respondent relationship is a naturally occurring experiment. Taking advantage of this natural experiment, researchers have found, for example, that both men and women give more egalitarian responses to questions about gender equality when responding to female interviewers than to male interviewers (Kane and Macaulay 1993) and that blacks and whites express more liberal racial attitudes to black than to white interviewers (Cotter, Cohen, and Coulter 1982).

In a recent study in the Netherlands, Sniderman, Hagendoorn, and Prior (2000) went beyond the typical examination of naturally occurring interviewer characteristics and purposefully manipulated the relationship between interviewer and interviewee. At the end of the interview, the interviewer tells a random half of the respondents: "We are at the end of the interview. I just want to say that I've really enjoyed speaking with you, and that your answers are very useful for us." All respondents are then asked either "Wouldn't you agree that ethnic minorities are, actually, responsible for many *more* social problems than is usually thought?" or "Wouldn't you agree that ethnic minorities are, actually, responsible for *less* social problems than is usually thought?"

The question that Sniderman and his colleagues are addressing is the extent to which an "empty compliment" from a survey interviewer can induce respondents to express pro- or anti-immigrant views that they otherwise would not express. The authors find that agreement with the pro-immigrant statement increases by about 14 percentage points when preceded by the empty compliment, whereas agreement with the anti-immigrant position increases by about six percentage points. That this extraordinarily minimal effort at persuasion—the inclusion of an empty compliment—can change respondents' willingness to agree with rather strong statements about a vital social issue suggests that such sentiments expressed in the "real world" may often represent very superficial commitments to their respective positions.

Another clever experimental manipulation of the interview environment is described in Bischoping and Schuman's (1992) account of the Nicaraguan "pen experiment." The 1990 Nicaraguan national election pitted the incumbent Sandinista Party, led by Daniel Ortega, against Violeta Chamorro, the candidate of the Union Nacional Opositora (UNO) coalition. Pre-election surveys, including apparently high-quality polls by reputable organizations, produced widely varying predictions of the election outcome. The pen experiment, initiated by Howard

Schuman, was designed to test the hypothesis that the voting intentions that respondents expressed were influenced by the perceived sponsorship of the survey or political leanings of the survey interviewer.

As a clue to the political orientation of the interviewer, responses to the in-person survey were recorded with one of three randomly chosen pens: a red and black pen with "DANIEL PRESIDENTE" written on it, a white and blue pen with the letters UNO prominently displayed, or a "neutral" red and white pen with no lettering. The impact of this seemingly subtle cue was enormous. In the "Sandinista pen" condition, 60% of respondents expressing an opinion preferred Ortega and 35% Chamorro. But in the "UNO pen" condition, only 40% expressed a preference for Ortega compared with 51% for Chamorro. Interestingly, the actual election results for the Managua region in which the experiment was conducted closely matched the survey results in the "UNO pen" condition. After a decade of Sandinista rule, it appears that many Nicaraguans were uncomfortable expressing support for the opposition party, unless they had the reassurance that the interviewer was not connected with the Sandinistas. Consistent with this interpretation, the "neutral pen" condition produced similar results to the "Sandinista pen" condition. In the absence of any contrary indications, respondents apparently assumed the survey to be connected with the Sandinista Party.

SURVEY MODE EXPERIMENTS

As the examples indicate, question wording, question context, and interviewer relationships can all be experimentally manipulated. A final dimension of the survey that can serve as the basis of a randomized experiment is the mode of data collection. Comparisons of responses to in-person, mail, and telephone surveys often find significant differences in response to "sensitive" questions. For example, in a study conducted in a Boston suburb in the early 1970s, 62% of those interviewed by telephone expressed support for legalizing abortion (Wiseman 1972). When asked the same question in person, 70% expressed support for legalization, and when responding to a mail survey fully 89% said they favored legalizing abortion. In a similarly conceived study of racial attitudes, Maria Krysan (1997) found more negative views expressed by white respondents to a mail survey than to an in-person survey (see also Krysan, Schuman, Scott, and Beatty 1994). These differences, however, were limited to racial policy questions (like affirmative action) and—perhaps surprisingly—did not extend to measures of "traditional prejudice," such as whether blacks have less inborn ability than whites.

A less common mode of survey data collection occasionally used in experimental studies compares responses to an in-person survey in which the respondent verbally reports his or her answers to an interviewer with a "secret ballot" design in which the respondent writes his or her answers down, seals them in an envelope, and (typically) deposits the envelope in a box. Using this technique, George Bishop and Bonnie Fisher (1995) found that a somewhat higher percentage of respondents said they had voted against a new county tax to provide home care services for the elderly in the secret ballot condition (38% versus 32%).

DISCUSSION

What can be said about survey experiments as an approach to social science inquiry? First, and most obviously, survey experiments enjoy the great advantage of all randomized experiments: they establish causal influence. Because respondents are randomly assigned to treatment groups, we know that—within the bounds of sampling error—the subgroups are identical in every way. Consequently, any differences we observe across subgroups must have been caused by the difference in the experimental treatments each received (again, within a confidence interval determined by sampling error). Thus, the problems of spurious associations and ambiguous causal relationships that plague cross-sectional survey analysis are avoided.

Less obviously, perhaps, but just as important, experiments all but force their designers to do their theorizing ex ante, rather than post hoc. Using traditional associational techniques, researchers can engage in "fishing expeditions" in an effort to identify the correlates of the characteristic of interest. But experiments oblige their authors to identify in advance the hypothesized factors that influence the characteristic under study. Moreover, to maintain sufficient size subgroups, they must limit the number of independent dimensions of experimental manipulation.

This is not to say that surveys using traditional techniques do not require careful ex ante theorizing in the selection and design of questions and response options. Nor does the analysis of survey experiments preclude post hoc theorizing (for example, in the identification of population subgroups among which the experimental effects are largest or smallest). But experiments impose a greater degree of theoretical discipline on the researcher than more traditional survey methods do.

It is often observed that experimental methods offer high internal validity but are more problematic in external validity. Internal validity refers to our confidence that observed differences across experimental subgroups reflect the impact of the experimental treatments; external validity refers to the generalizability of the experimental conditions to the environment outside the experiment. Survey experiments that focus on substantive concerns often raise issues of external validity. Many survey experiments attempt to mimic some experience from everyday life, such as the acquisition of information from the media or a social encounter with a more or less friendly stranger. But these efforts are often crude simulacra of the real-life experiences of interest.

Still, attending to issues of external validity can help to illuminate the proper dimensions of our experimental studies. For example, one common use of experiments is to test the effects of alternative ways of "framing" an issue (Kinder and Sanders 1990; Nelson, Clawson, and Oxley 1997; Nelson and Kinder 1996). The same tax reform proposal, for example, might be presented to some respondents framed as tax simplification and to other respondents framed in terms of its redistributive effects. But in the real world, frames are typically contested and people are exposed more or less simultaneously to competing frames (Sniderman and Theriault 1999). "Alternate frame" experiments can reveal much about the potential responsiveness of the public to alternative perspectives. But the lack of fit between this model and real-world framing processes points to the need for more complicated designs that attempt to assess the impact of competing frames under more complex and realistic conditions.

Another point about the design and analysis of survey experiments is that the interpretation of their effects often hinges on how those effects differ across population subgroups. For example, the interpretation of the list experiment already described rested on the different effects among liberals and conservatives, and among respondents with different levels of commitment to racial harmony. Subgroup differences in experimental effects are just one crude example of the broader category of interactions between individual characteristics and experimental treatments. We are just beginning to see more sophisticated use of multivariate techniques to examine interaction effects in survey experiments (e.g., Gilens 2001), and this appears to be a promising avenue for future development.

The "success" of a survey experiment depends on the quality of its design and implementation, not on the emergence of a statistically significant difference between the treatment groups. Finding no difference between treatment groups can be just as revealing as finding large differences, depending on the nature of the experiment. In a study of prejudice in Italy, for example, Sniderman et al. (2000) found that Italians do not evaluate immigrants from Central Africa more negatively than immigrants from Eastern Europe. Given the authors' expectation that racial distinctions would have a significant influence on attitudes toward immigrant groups, this "nonfinding" was critical in reshaping their thinking about the nature of prejudice in Italy.

Survey experiments help us understand the meaning behind respondents' behavior and thus provide a deeper and more complex picture of respondents' attitudes and beliefs. But for all its power, the survey experiment is not a "window" into the "truth" in any simple sense. Any given survey experiment provides a single lens through which to observe the object of our interest. If our experiments are well designed, that lens may reveal otherwise hidden aspects of our respondents' thinking. But most of the time the complexities of human attitudes are too elusive to be captured with a single tool, experimental or otherwise.

To return to the hypothetical example from the beginning of the chapter, we might find that respondents express substantially different attitudes toward immigration policy when asked about Mexican versus Canadian immigrants. But we also might find substantial support for equal treatment when respondents are asked (in a traditional, nonexperimental format) whether policy toward immigrants from these two countries should be the same. In this case, we might be tempted to consider the former (experimental) results to reveal Americans' "true" attitudes and their direct expression of support for equal treatment to represent a disingenuous or, at best, superficial commitment to a "socially desirable" position.

It would be a mistake, however, to identify only one of these results as revealing "true" attitudes. For, in fact, the public expression of support for equality—even if it is not "backed up" by equivalent responses to immigrants from these two countries—might nevertheless reflect a genuine reluctance to condone disparate treatment, and this reluctance might have important implications for the nature of public debate over immigration policy. In this example, both the traditional survey question about equal treatment and the randomized experiment would each reveal something about the public's attitudes. In combination, we would get a fuller range of Americans' thinking about immigration than we would get from either technique alone.

The survey experiments described here detail only a handful of the hundreds of survey experiments conducted. The development of CATI software for telephone (and, more recently, Web-based) surveys has opened up a host of new possibilities. By combining the power of randomized experiments with the large size and representative nature of the sample survey, we can investigate the social world in new ways.

NOTES

1. The 1991 Race and Politics Survey was directed by Paul M. Sniderman, Philip E. Tetlock, and Thomas Piazza with support from the National Science Foundation (SES-8508937).

2. These figures are from the U.S. Department of Health and Human Services for calendar year and fiscal year 1999, respectively (http://www.census.gov/hhes/poverty/poverty99/pv99est1.html and http://www.acf.dhhs.gov/programs/opre/characteristics/fy99/tab06_99.htm).

3. Respondents who say the hypothetical welfare mother will try hard to find a job and will not have more children are coded as expressing positive perceptions, those saying she will not try hard to find a job and will have more children are coded as expressing negative perceptions, and respondents giving mixed answers are coded as expressing neutral perceptions.

4. The 1998 Multi-Investigator Study was directed by Paul M. Sniderman, Henry Brady, and others with support from the National Science Foundation (SBR-9818742).

14

Probabilistic Polling

CHARLES F. MANSKI

Polling results fluctuated greatly throughout the year 2000 American presidential campaign. George W. Bush seemed well ahead during the summer, but Al Gore surged ahead after the Democratic convention. As the election drew near, major polling organizations reported a bewildering array of findings from week to week. The race turned out to be excruciatingly close, as the world finally learned on November 7 and thereafter.

Some of the volatility of the presidential polls may have resulted from the questions posed. Pollsters ask Americans to specify the candidate that they "lean toward," are "more likely to vote for," or "would vote for if the election were held today." These standard forms of questions do not enable respondents to express uncertainty about their future voting behavior. Small shifts in perceptions of the candidates can yield large swings in responses to standard polling questions. A simple example shows how.

Suppose that 40% of the voters in the 2000 election were committed Democrats certain to vote for Gore, 48% were committed Republicans certain to vote for Bush, and the remaining 12% were disenchanted Democrats who were not certain if they would vote for Gore or Nader. Suppose that, at the beginning of October, each disenchanted Democrat perceived a 70% chance of voting for Gore and a 30% chance of voting for Nader. Suppose that a week later, reacting to the efforts of the major parties to prevent Nader from participating in the debates, the disenchanted Democrats leaned slightly toward Nader; each one now perceiving a 45% chance of voting for Gore and a 55% chance for Nader. In this scenario, the fraction of voters who "lean toward" Gore falls sharply in the first week of October, from .52 to .40. Yet the expected vote share for Gore falls only modestly during this period, from 0.484 to 0.454.[1]

There is good reason to think that *probabilistic polling* would improve on standard polling practices by permitting Americans to express uncertainty about how they will vote (see also Manski 2000). Pollsters could ask respondents to state, in percentage terms, how likely it is that they will vote in an upcoming election. They could then go on to ask respondents how likely it is that they would vote for each candidate on the ballot. For example, pollsters could have asked these probabilistic questions during the 2000 presidential campaign:

P1. What do you think is the PERCENT CHANCE that you will cast a vote for President?

P2. Suppose now that you will vote for president. I will read five voting possibilities, and then ask you the PERCENT CHANCE that you would vote for each one. Please listen to the choices, allocating 100 percentage points total among all five: Al Gore, the Democrat; George W. Bush, the Republican; Ralph Nader, the Green Party candidate; Pat Buchanan, the Reform Party candidate; another candidate.

Adoption of probabilistic polling should eliminate the artificial swings in polling findings that result because standard questions do not enable Americans to express uncertainty. Moreover, probabilistic polling would eliminate the need for pollsters to stratify the electorate into such coarse categories as *likely voters, undecided voters*, and so on. Instead, citizens would themselves report how likely they are to vote and how certain they are of their preference.

Many pollsters appear to subscribe to a conventional wisdom that respondents would be unable or unwilling to respond to probabilistic questions such as P1 and P2. In the last ten years, however, economists and psychologists have accumulated substantial positive experience with similar questions in other settings, using them to learn how Americans perceive many aspects of their future. The nationwide Health and Retirement Study (HRS) elicits probabilistic expectations of retirement, bequests, and mortality from older Americans. The National Longitudinal Survey of Youth 1997 (NLSY97) queries American teenagers about the chance that they will become a parent or be arrested in the year ahead. My own annual nationwide Survey of Economic Expectations (SEE) elicits answers from a cross section of Americans about their perception of the percentage chance that they will lose their jobs, have health insurance coverage, or be victims of crime in the year ahead. We have learned from the HRS, NLSY97, SEE, and other surveys that most people have little difficulty, once the concept is introduced to them, using subjective probabilities to express the likelihood they place on future events relevant to their lives. There is good reason to think that probabilistic polling would similarly be practical and informative.

This chapter develops the rationale for probabilistic polling in three stages. The first section discusses general respects in which probabilistic elicitation of expectations may be preferable to traditional verbal modes of questioning and then summarizes the empirical experience to date. The second section considers the specific appeal of probabilistic polling. And the third section reports the findings of a small pilot study performed in the weeks before the 2000 presidential election. Appendix A describes related research on probabilistic polling. Appendix B gives the script of the pilot survey.

VERBAL AND PROBABILISTIC ELICITATION OF EXPECTATIONS

Surveys, including election polls, are used to elicit from individuals a broad array of subjective information. Social scientists have long sought to understand what surveys reveal about people's thinking and to make them more informative. In practical terms, what kinds of questions should be asked and how should the responses be interpreted?

These practical questions arise notably in the design of questions that seek to elicit expectations of future events. The traditional verbal approach of survey research is illustrated by this General Social Survey (GSS) question eliciting expectations of job loss (Davis and Smith 1994): "Thinking about the next twelve months, how likely do you think it is that you will lose your job or be laid off: very likely, fairly likely, not too likely, or not at all likely?" In contrast, a growing body of research in economics and cognitive psychology elicits subjective probabilities of future events, such as this SEE question on job loss (Dominitz and Manski 1997a): "What do you think is the PERCENT CHANCE that you will lose your job during the next twelve months?" Whereas the GSS question asks respondents to express their expectations in terms of four phrases expressing different degrees of likelihood of job loss, the SEE questions asks for a numerical response from 0 to 100%.

I first set out concerns about verbal questioning that have generated interest in probabilistic elicitation of expectations and then describe arguments for and against probabilistic elicitation. Then I summarize the history of research on probabilistic elicitation and describe recent empirical experience particularly relevant to election polling. (See Dominitz and Manski [1997a, 1999] and Manski [2001] for more detailed discussions.)

Some Basic Concerns about Verbal Questioning

The GSS question on job loss expectations illustrates well a basic problem that researchers face in interpreting verbal expectations data: assessment of the interpersonal comparability of responses. Respondents are often asked to report whether a specified event is "expected," "likely," or "probable." Do different respondents interpret these phrases in the same way? Cognitive research does not give us reason to think that responses should be or are comparable. Indeed, the available empirical evidence indicates that interpretations of verbal expectations questions vary substantially between persons (Wallsten, Budescu, Rapoport, Zwick, and Forsyth 1986).[2]

Concern about interpersonal comparability deepens when one considers the events about which respondents are asked. Attitudinal researchers often ask respondents about vaguely defined future outcomes, as in this University of Michigan Survey Research Center question (Curtin 1982): "Now looking ahead—do you think that a year from now you (and your family living there) will be better off financially, or worse off, or just about the same as now?" How should a respondent interpret the phrase "better off financially"? Do different respondents interpret it the same way? The data provide no way of knowing.

Even if the events about which respondents are queried are well defined and responses are interpersonally comparable, the coarseness of the response options limits the information contained in the responses. Consider, for example, the fertility question posed to female respondents in the annual June Supplement to the Current Population Survey of the U.S. Bureau of the Census: "Looking ahead, do you expect to have any (more) children? (Yes, No, Uncertain). The three response options can express little of the richness of the uncertainty that women may perceive about their future childbearing. Savage (1971, p. 795) called attention to this problem when he observed that "Yes, No, or Maybe is Not Enough."

Arguments for and against Probabilistic Elicitation

A consensus has yet to emerge on the relative merits in practice of verbal and probabilistic elicitation of expectations. However, there is reasonably widespread agreement that probabilistic questioning has several a priori desirable features.

Perhaps the most basic attraction is that probability provides a well-defined absolute numerical scale for expressing uncertainty about the future. Hence, there is some reason to think that responses may be interpersonally and intrapersonally comparable.

A second attraction is that empirical assessment of the internal consistency and external accuracy of respondents' expectations is possible. A researcher can use the algebra of probability (Bayes' theorem, the law of total probability, etc.) to examine the internal consistency of a respondent's elicited expectations about different events. In cases where probability has a frequentist interpretation, a researcher can compare elicited subjective probabilities with known event frequencies, as is done in calibration studies, and reach conclusions about the correspondence between subjective beliefs and frequentist realities.

A third consideration is the usefulness of elicited expectations in predicting prospective outcomes. Suppose that respondents have reasonably accurate expectations about the probability of future events. Then, as Juster (1966), Savage (1971), and Manski (1990), argue, numerical responses to probability questions should have more predictive power than do categorical responses to verbal expectations questions. (I will discuss this matter, which is of particular importance to election polling, further in the second section.)

These desirable features of probabilistic expectations data must be weighed against the possibility that respondents may not think probabilistically about uncertain events. Among cognitive psychologists, there has long been controversy about how humans internally represent their beliefs and their ability and willingness to express their internal beliefs as numerical probabilities. Ferrell and McGoey (1980) posed models in which individuals may have some difficulty expressing beliefs as numerical probabilities; nevertheless, they concluded that elicitation of numerical subjective probabilities is feasible. However, Zimmer (1983) argued that humans process information using verbal rather than numerical modes of thinking and concluded that expectations should be elicited in verbal, not numerical, forms.

Wallsten, Budescu, Zwick, and Kemp have (1993) reported that most respondents prefer to communicate their own beliefs verbally and to receive the beliefs of others in the form of numerical probabilities. This asymmetry is intriguing but only marginally relevant to the design of expectation questions. The relevant question is not what communication mode respondents prefer to use, but rather what modes they are willing and able to use. Wallsten et al. report that virtually all of their respondents were willing to communicate their beliefs numerically, should the situation warrant it. Certainly the experience of researchers using questionnaires to elicit probabilistic expectations has been that respondents are willing and able to communicate their beliefs in numerical probabilistic terms.

Experience with Probabilistic Expectations

The idea that probabilistic elicitation of expectations might improve on the traditional approaches of attitudinal research appears to have developed independently in cognitive psychology and in economics.

Elicitation of subjective probabilities has a long history in cognitive psychology. Psychologists have conducted many calibration studies assessing the accuracy of elicited expectations reports. Lichtenstein, Fischhoff, and Phillips (1982) review findings from calibration studies dating back to 1906. McClelland and Bolger (1994) update the review with findings from 1980 through 1994. Whereas the older studies mostly examined the accuracy of experts (e.g., weather forecasters' reported probabilities of precipitation), the more recent research typically analyzes the expectations of convenience samples of nonexperts, especially students in a cognitive laboratory. A body of research using probabilistic questions to elicit the risk perceptions of adolescents is described in Quadrel, Fischhoff, and Davis (1993).

In economics, probabilistic questioning appears to have originated with Juster (1966), who recommended elicitation of purchase probabilities for consumer durable goods. Market researchers were immediately attracted to Juster's proposal, and elicitation of purchase probabilities has since become a common practice in market research (e.g., Jamieson and Bass 1989). However, the idea that expectations might be elicited probabilistically from survey respondents did not draw serious attention within economics until the early 1990s, when economists began to reassess the discipline's long-standing self-imposed prohibition on the collection and analysis of subjective data.

Modules of probabilistic expectations questions have recently appeared in a growing set of national surveys developed primarily by economists. The longitudinal Health and Retirement Study elicits probabilistic expectations of retirement, bequests, and mortality from older Americans (see Juster and Suzman 1995; Hurd and McGarry 1995). The National Longitudinal Survey of Youth 1997 elicits probabilistic expectations of school completion, parenthood, arrest and incarceration, and mortality from American teenagers (see Fischhoff et al. 2000; Dominitz, Manski, and Fischhoff 2001). The Survey of Economic Expectations elicits probabilistic expectations of income, job loss, health insurance coverage, and crime victimization from a cross-section of Americans (see Dominitz and Manski 1997a, 1997b; Manski and Straub 2000).

Most of the research to date using probabilistic questions to elicit expectations has been conducted in settings unlike the short-interview, telephone survey format common to election polls. The expectations modules in economic surveys have mainly been embedded in long, omnibus questionnaires administered face-to-face to large, stratified random samples of households. The cognitive psychology research has been performed face-to-face with small convenience samples of subjects. Among the surveys to date that pose probabilistic expectations questions, the SEE appears most directly comparable in format to the major election polls. Hence, it is instructive to discuss SEE in some detail.

The Survey of Economic Expectations

SEE is a repeated cross-sectional survey administered since 1993 as a module in WISCON, a continuous national random-digit telephone survey conducted by the University of Wisconsin Survey Center. The WISCON core questions ask respondents about their labor market experiences, demographics, and attitudes, (procedures described in Dominitz and Manski [1997a]. Since 1994, the SEE module has been included in WISCON in the spring/summer and fall/winter of each year (May to July and November to January).[3]

The SEE questions elicit subjective probabilities of personal events that may occur in the year ahead.[4] Dominitz and Manski (1997a) and Manski and Straub (2000) have analyzed the cross-sectional and time-series distribution of responses to these questions:

Health Insurance: "What do you think is the percent chance that you will have health insurance coverage twelve months from now?"

Burglary: "What do you think is the percent chance that someone will break into (or somehow illegally enter) your home and steal something, during the next twelve months?"

Job Loss: "What do you think is the percent chance that you will lose your job during the next twelve months?"

Job Search: "If you were to lose your job during the next twelve months, what is the percent chance that the job you eventually find and accept would be at least as good as your current job, in terms of wages and benefits?"

Voluntary-Quits: "What do you think is the percent chance that you will leave your job voluntarily during the next twelve months?"

The survey also elicits one-year-ahead income expectations through questions of the form:

Income: "What do you think is the percent chance that your total income, before taxes, will be less than Y over the next 12 months?"

The responses to a sequence of such questions posed for different income thresholds Y enable estimation of each respondent's subjective probability distribution for next year's income. Dominitz and Manski (1997b) have analyzed the data on income expectations.

The item-response rates to the health insurance, crime victimization, and job expectation questions have been approximately 95%; the response rate to the sequence of income questions has been approximately 80%. There has until recently been something of a conventional wisdom that respondents asked to give probabilistic responses will likely use the values (0, 50, 100) and not exploit the refined reporting possibilities permitted by the 0–100 *percent chance* scale. However, contrary findings emerge in the SEE data. Most respondents do not round their responses to these values (0, 50, 100), but rather to the nearest multiple of 5. Respondents perceiving very low or very high probabilities of events provide yet more refined responses, with many reporting 1, 2, 98, or 99%.

A sense of the usefulness of SEE in addressing questions of interest to social scientists and policy researchers may be obtained in the recent Manski and Straub (2000) study of job insecurity. This article analyzes the responses of 3,561 persons interviewed from 1994 through early 1998 to the SEE questions eliciting expectations of job loss and job search. The responses to these two questions can be combined to form an index of job insecurity: the chance that a worker will lose his current job and not recover satisfactorily from this event.[5]

We found that workers vary considerably in their perceptions of job insecurity, with most workers perceiving little or no risk but some perceiving moderate to high risk. Expectations of job loss tend to decrease markedly with age, but so do expectations of a good outcome should a job search become necessary. The net result is that job insecurity tends not to vary at all with age. Subjective

probabilities of job loss tend to decrease with schooling, and subjective probabilities of good search outcomes tend to increase with schooling; hence, composite
job insecurity tends to decrease with schooling. Perceptions of job insecurity vary
little by sex, but substantially by race, the main differences being that subjective
probabilities of job loss among blacks tend to be nearly double those of whites.
Self-employed workers see themselves as facing less job insecurity than do those
who work for others. Worker perceptions of job insecurity peaked in 1995 and
have fallen since.

The success of the Survey of Economic Expectations does not necessarily
imply that probabilistic elicitation of voting expectations would be similarly successful. However, I do not see fundamental differences between the SEE questions
and voting questions of the form P1 and P2 I posed in the introduction. Hence,
the SEE experience suggests that probabilistic polling should be feasible in practice.

ELECTION POLLS

The previous section examined the merits of verbal and probabilistic elicitation
of expectations from the perspective of social science research. The data collected
in election polls are used in research, but they also serve the pragmatic objective
of predicting election outcomes. Probabilistic elicitation is particularly well-suited
to this purpose.

Two forms of verbal questions have been standard among pollsters, as illustrated by these questions concerning the year 2000 American presidential election:[6]

> *(CNN/USA Today/Gallup Poll, February 20–21, 2000, questions 5 and 5a)*
> Next, we'd like you to think about the general election for president to be held in
> November.
> Q1.   If Vice-President Al Gore were the Democratic Party's candidate and Texas
>   Governor George W. Bush were the Republican Party's candidate, who would
>   you be more likely to vote for [Al Gore, the Democrat (or) George W. Bush,
>   the Republican]?
>
> Q1A. As of today, do you lean more toward [Al Gore, the Democrat (or) George
>   W. Bush, the Republican]?
>
> *(Pew Research Center Survey, September 1–12, 1999, questions 8 and 8a)*
> Q2.   Suppose the 2000 Presidential election were being held TODAY, and the can-
>   didates Al Gore, the Democrat, and George W. Bush, the Republican. Who
>   would you vote for?
>
> Q2A. As of TODAY, do you LEAN more to Gore, the Democrat, or Bush, the
>   Republican?[7]

Questions Q1 and Q2 set up distinct scenarios and call for different types of answers. Whereas Q1 asks the respondent to think ahead to the election in November 2000, Q2 sets up a counterfactual scenario in which the election is held today (in September 1999). Whereas Q1 asks, "who would you be more likely to vote for," Q2 asks, "Who would you vote for?" A common feature of the two questions, as well as of Q1A and Q2A, is that they specify only the Democratic and Republican candidates, with no mention of possible minor-party candidates. Another common feature is that none of the questions mentions the possibility that the respondent may choose not to vote.

Neither of the previous forms of question is especially well-suited to predicting election outcomes. To see why, suppose that the Gallup and Pew questions are administered on the same date to large random samples of the population and that all sample members provide valid responses; these simplifying assumptions enable us to abstract from issues of missing or misleading data, statistical precision, and differential timing that may arise in actual polling. How might one use the responses to predict the vote share that candidates Gore and Bush will receive?

Gallup Poll (Q1)

Suppose that the Gallup survey is administered to a sample of potential voters. The discussion here focuses on question Q1, but similar considerations apply to Q1A. Let g denote the fraction of the sample who report that they are more likely to vote for Gore, and b the fraction more likely to vote for Bush. One may be tempted to use g and b as predictions of the vote shares for the two candidates, but there are several problems with this.

First, Gore and Bush supporters may vary in the probability that they will vote in the election. The Gallup organization recognizes this by reporting two sets of findings, one for currently registered voters and the other for a subsample of *likely voters*.[8] However, segmentation of the sample into two subsamples takes only a small step toward expressing the potential heterogeneity across sample members in probability of voting.

Another potential problem is that the Gallup question makes no reference to minority-party candidates. Some sample members may legitimately say that they are more likely to vote for Gore or Bush, yet actually be most likely to vote for another candidate, such as Nader. If minority-party candidates have support within the population, learning whether voters prefer Gore to Bush may not reveal their vote shares.

Perhaps the most basic issue is that questions of the Gallup form do not enable respondents to express uncertainty about their future voting behavior. Suppose, for simplicity, that all respondents vote and that no minority candidates will be on the ballot; hence, we may abstract from the two problems already discussed. Even in this idealized setting, responses to question Q1 do not reveal whether sample members will vote for Gore or Bush. They reveal only whether these persons perceive themselves as more likely to vote for one candidate or the other. Thus, persons who respond "Gore" are saying that the chance they will vote for Gore is at least 50% and the chance they will vote for Bush no more than 50%; analogous reasoning applies to persons who respond "Bush."

In Manski (1990), I showed that questions of the Gallup form logically imply only a bound of width 0.5 on the fraction of voters who would vote for each candidate. Consider Gore, the reasoning for Bush being analogous. The lower bound on the fraction voting for Gore occurs if all the sample members who respond "Gore" have 50% chance of voting for Gore and all those who respond "Bush" have no chance of voting for Gore. The upper bound occurs if all the sample members who respond "Gore" have 100% chance of voting for Gore and all those who respond "Bush" have 50% chance of voting for Gore. Suppose, for example, that the fraction of persons who respond "Gore" is 0.6. Then one can logically conclude only that the fraction who would vote for Gore is between 0.3 and 0.8.[9]

Of course, the circumstances required to yield the lower and upper bounds are extreme. In practice, the Gallup and other election polls have tended to be far more accurate in predicting vote shares than the logical bound of width 0.5 suggests. This suggests that the extreme patterns of voter expectations that yield the lower and upper bounds tend not to occur in practice. One should not, however, conclude that the argument yielding the bounds is empirically irrelevant. Polls sometimes show large movements over time in the fraction of respondents reporting that they are more likely to vote for one candidate or another. My reasoning in 1990 shows that such movements can easily occur if enough potential voters are close to "undecided," if they view the chance of voting for each candidate as close to 50%. The example earlier in this chapter involving Gore, Bush, and Nader illustrates this well.

Pew Poll (Q2)

The problems that arise in using the Gallup question to predict the election outcome apply to the Pew question as well. However, the Pew question also raises an additional issue: it does not ask respondents to predict their vote in November but asks them to say how they would vote if the election were held today.

In Manski (1990) I analyzed the structure of questions like the Gallup and Pew types and showed that a rational person need not give the same response to both. The Pew question poses a *forced-choice* scenario; it asks respondents how they would vote if they were forced to decide using only the information they possess at the date of the survey. The Gallup question elicits *intentions;* it asks respondents to think ahead and assess what they may learn about the candidates and other matters relevant to voting between the date of the survey and the date of the election.

To make the point, consider an election with candidates A and B. Suppose that a poll is conducted a week before candidate A is scheduled to undergo a major medical examination. Consider the situation of a voter who would prefer candidate A if he is found to be healthy but who would prefer his opponent if A is seriously ill. Suppose that, on the date of the poll, the voter believes there to be a 70% chance that the examination will find candidate A to be healthy. Then the voter should indicate 70% chance on voting for candidate A and 30% on voting for B; hence, the response to the Gallup question should be "A." Yet it may be entirely reasonable for the voter to respond "B" to the Pew question. Seeing a 30% chance of a poor medical outcome ahead, the voter might well decide that if he or she were required to vote today, the safe choice would be to vote for B.

Probabilistic Polling (P1 and P2)

Probabilistic polling questions such as P1 and P2 solve the problems generated by the Gallup and Pew questions, provided that respondents are able to formulate and express subjective probabilities with reasonable care. Question P1 elicits the probability that sample members will vote; P2 elicits the probability that they will vote for Gore, Bush, Nader, Buchanan, or another candidate, conditional on voting. Hence, it is straightforward to use the responses to predict the vote share that each candidate will receive.

Suppose that questions P1 and P2 are administered to a sample of size N. Divide the responses by 100, so they fall in the 0–1 probability scale rather than in the 0–100 percent chance scale. For each sample member $i = 1, \ldots, N$, let $R_1(i)$ denote the re-scaled response to question P1 and let [R2(Gore, i), R2(Bush, i), R2(Nader, i), R2(Buchanan, i), R2(other, i)] denote the re-scaled responses to P2. Then $R_1(i)$ is the probability that person i places on voting in the election, $R_1(i) \cdot R_2(Gore, i)$ is the probability of voting for Gore, $R_1(i) \cdot R_2(Bush, i)$ that of voting for Bush, and so on.

These subjective probabilities provide the basis for predicting vote shares. Let V denote the sample average subjective probability of voting in the election, let G denote the sample average subjective probability of voting for Gore, and B that of voting for Bush. That is,

$$V = \frac{1}{N} \sum_{i=1}^{N} R_1(i); \; G = \frac{1}{N} \sum_{i=1}^{N} R_1(i) \cdot R_2(Gore, i); \; B = \frac{1}{N} \sum_{i=1}^{N} R_1(i) \cdot R_2(Bush, i).$$

Then G/V and B/V predict the Gore and Bush vote shares based on respondents' self-assessments of their prospective voting behavior. Vote shares can similarly be predicted for Nader and other candidates.

A PILOT STUDY

There is much reason to think that probabilistic polling should improve on standard practices. The percent chance scale enables citizens to express uncertainty about their future voting behavior and enables analysts to aggregate voting expectations into predictions of election outcomes. Empirical experience with probabilistic questioning in other settings suggests that probabilistic polling should be practical and informative. Questions like P1 and P2 should be no more difficult to administer than the job expectations questions in the Survey of Economic Expectations. Respondents respond meaningfully to the SEE questions and likely would do the same for probabilistic polling questions.

Definitive assessment of the potential of probabilistic polling will become possible only as empirical experience accumulates. To begin this process, I performed a small pilot study in the weeks preceding the year 2000 American presidential election. Using conventional random-digit telephone sampling methods, an interviewer contacted fifty respondents in a northern suburb of Chicago and queried them about the upcoming election.[10] Appendix B provides the script of the interview session.

As detailed in the script, respondents were first asked to answer two standard polling questions drawn from the CBS-*New York Times* poll: question Q1 requests a verbal indication of the likelihood of voting, and Q2 asks respondents to name the candidate they would vote for if the election were held today. Next, the interviewer explains the percent chance scale and poses an introductory weather-forecasting question (Q3); this material is drawn directly from the Survey of Economic Expectations. Then respondents answer two probabilistic polling questions (Q4 and Q5); these are essentially the same as questions P1 and P2. Finally, background information on age, education, and sex is obtained in questions Q6–Q9.

Table 14.1 reports the responses. The table omits Q7 because all respondents stated that they had a high school diploma. Observe that the item response rates were 100% to all questions except Q3 and Q6. Two respondents did not provide a weather forecast and four did not state their age.

Juxtaposition of the entries for Q1 and Q4 shows how respondents answer questions requesting verbal and probabilistic measures of the likelihood of voting. The responses correspond well in a qualitative sense, as shown in table 14.2.

The really interesting finding is that probabilistic elicitation of the likelihood of voting reveals quantitative differences in expectations that verbal questioning misses entirely. It turns out that the thirty-six persons who state that they will "definitely" vote when responding to Q1 are not uniformly certain that they will vote. Responding to Q4, most of these persons predict a 99 or 100% chance of voting, but one (R-10) reports only an 80% chance of voting and another (R-14) an 85% chance. We also learn that the ten persons who state that they will "probably" vote in response to Q1 actually vary widely in the chance that they will vote. One member of this subgroup reports a 40% chance (R-24), one a 78% chance (R-32), and six a 100% chance of voting.

Juxtaposition of the entries for Q2 and Q5 shows how respondents answer questions requesting verbal and probabilistic measures of the prospects of voting for particular candidates. Again, the responses correspond well in a qualitative

Table 14.1 Pilot Polling Data

Respondent number	Likelihood will vote Q1	Candidate today Q2	Chance rain Q3	Chance will vote Q4	Chance Gore Q5a	Chance Bush Q5b	Chance Nader Q5c	Chance Buchanan Q5d	Chance other Q5e	Age Q6	College degree Q8	Sex Q9
1	def	Gore	—	100	100	0	0	0	0	62	Y	M
2	def	Gore	20	100	100	0	0	0	0	58	Y	F
3	def not	Nader	10	0	30	20	50	0	0	24	Y	F
4	def	Gore	15	100	100	0	0	0	0	45	Y	F
5	def	Bush	10	100	40	60	0	0	0	35	Y	F
6	def	Gore	20	99	95	0	5	0	0	48	Y	F
7	def	Bush	15	100	0	100	0	0	0	52	Y	F
8	prob	Gore	20	100	80	20	0	0	0	21	Y	F
9	def	Gore	—	100	100	0	0	0	0	62	Y	F
10	def	Bush	20	80	0	100	0	0	0	—	Y	F
11	def	Gore	20	99	100	0	0	0	0	53	N	F
12	def	Gore	20	90	80	0	20	0	0	49	Y	F
13	def	Gore	90	95	95	0	5	0	0	63	N	F
14	def	Gore	20	85	100	0	0	0	0	46	Y	M
15	def	Gore	25	95	85	4	10	1	0	65	Y	M
16	def not	Bush	15	0	20	80	0	0	0	25	Y	M
17	def	Gore	10	100	89	10	0	1	0	30	Y	F
18	def	Gore	15	100	100	0	0	0	0	47	Y	F
19	def	Gore	10	100	100	0	0	0	0	71	Y	M
20	def	Gore	10	100	100	0	0	0	0	75	Y	M
21	def	Gore	20	100	100	0	0	0	0	54	Y	F
22	def	Gore	2	100	100	0	0	0	0	53	Y	F
23	def	Gore	20	100	100	0	0	0	0	70	Y	F
24	prob	Bush	100	40	30	40	10	20	0	26	N	M

(continued)

Table 14.1 (continued)

Respondent number	Likelihood will vote Q1	Candidate today Q2	Chance rain Q3	Chance will vote Q4	Chance Gore Q5a	Chance Bush Q5b	Chance Nader Q5c	Chance Buchanan Q5d	Chance other Q5e	Age Q6	College degree Q8	Sex Q9
25	def	Gore	15	100	50	0	0	0	50	35	N	F
26	def	Bush	10	100	0	100	0	0	0	—	Y	M
27	def	Buchanan	10	100	0	50	0	50	0	85	Y	F
28	def	Gore	0	100	100	0	0	0	0	74	N	F
29	def	Bush	10	100	0	100	0	0	0	38	Y	F
30	def	Gore	0	100	100	0	0	0	0	71	N	F
31	def not	Bush	15	0	5	40	10	5	40	23	Y	F
32	prob	Nader	10	78	30	0	70	0	0	34	Y	M
33	def	Bush	15	99	1	97	1	1	0	45	Y	F
34	prob	Gore	25	100	100	0	0	0	0	53	Y	F
35	prob	Gore	10	100	100	0	0	0	0	51	Y	F
36	prob	Gore	20	100	100	0	0	0	0	44	Y	F
37	prob	Gore	10	100	95	0	5	0	0	46	Y	F
38	def	Bush	20	100	0	100	0	0	0	—	Y	F
39	prob	other	35	100	0	0	0	0	100	35	N	M
40	def	Gore	20	100	100	0	0	0	0	27	Y	F
41	prob	Gore	15	90	100	0	0	0	0	28	Y	F
42	def	Gore	5	100	100	0	0	0	0	28	Y	F
43	def	Gore	40	100	100	0	0	0	0	50	Y	M
44	def	Gore	0	100	100	0	0	0	0	52	Y	F
45	def	Gore	10	100	100	0	0	0	0	61	Y	F
46	def not	Gore	15	0	100	0	0	0	0	28	Y	F
47	def	Gore	15	100	98	0	50	0	0	56	Y	F
48	def	Gore	20	100	100	0	0	0	0	—	N	F
49	prob	Bush	15	86	0	100	0	0	0	37	Y	F
50	def	Gore	15	90	100	0	0	0	0	64	Y	F

Table 14.2 Likelihood of Voting

			Q4 Response (Percent Chance)			
	0	[1–10]	[11–50]	[51–90]	[91–99]	100
Q1 Response						
Definitely vote	0	0	0	4	5	27
Probably vote	0	0	1	3	0	6
Probably not vote	0	0	0	0	0	0
Definitely not vote	4	0	0	0	0	0

sense, as shown in table 14.3. Again, the really interesting finding is that probabilistic polling reveals quantitative differences in voting expectations that verbal questioning misses entirely. Thirty-three of the fifty respondents report a 100% chance that they will vote for the candidate they named in response to Q2, but five respondents report no more than a 50% chance of voting for this candidate. Respondents R-5 and R-24 seem the very model of the "undecided" voter. Both say "Bush" when asked how they would vote if the election were held today, but they then go on to express much uncertainty in their percent chance responses. R-5 reports Gore—40, Bush—60, while R-24 says Gore—30, Bush—40, Nader—10, Buchanan—20.

It would be foolhardy to make too much of one small pilot study of probabilistic polling. Nevertheless, I believe that it is fair to characterize the findings of this study as encouraging. If enough serious empirical research is performed in the years ahead, probabilistic polling may make a real contribution to prediction of the outcomes of future American elections.

Table 14.3 Candidate Preference

	Q5 Response for the Candidate Named in Q2 (Percent Chance)				
	[0–50]	[51–80]	[81–90]	[91–99]	100
Q2 Response					
Gore	1	2	2	4	26
Bush	2	1	1	1	6
Nader	1	1	0	0	0
Buchanan	1	0	0	0	0
Other	0	0	0	0	1

APPENDIX A: RELATED RESEARCH
ON PROBABILISTIC POLLING

Probabilistic polling is too simple and appealing an idea to have been thought of only once. From the time that I initially critiqued traditional polling questions in Manski (1990) through the recent period in which I drafted this chapter and performed its pilot study, I was unaware of related research. However, after this chapter was complete, I learned of a scattering of related studies analyzing data across the world.

Burden (1997) analyzed data collected in Ohio in 1986 and 1988 eliciting probabilities that persons would vote for particular candidates in upcoming state and federal elections. Hoek and Gendall (1993, 1997) elicited voting probabilities in elections in New Zealand. Maas, Steenbergen, and Saris (1990) analyzed probabilities of voting for particular parties Dutch voters reported in 1986. Earlier still, Meier (1980) and Meier and Campbell (1979) used a seven-point scale to elicit voting expectations. For many reasons, these isolated studies do not yield strong evidence on the relative merits of alternative modes of polling, but they are instructive. I discuss the two most recent studies in the following section. These should be of particular interest because their data are from experiments in which respondents were randomly assigned to different question formats.

Burden (1997)

The data were collected by telephone interview in the Ohio Political Surveys, conducted by the Ohio State University's Political Research Laboratory. The 1986 survey, performed in October, randomized 1,013 respondents to one or the other of these questions concerning the upcoming gubernatorial election:

> *Deterministic:* If the election for governor were held today, for whom would you vote? (Probe: The candidates are Richard Celeste, a Democrat, and James Rhodes, a Republican.)

> *Probabilistic:* Just as the weatherman talks about the percent chance of rain tomorrow, what is the percent chance, from 0 to 100, that you will go and vote? In the governor's election between Mr. Rhodes and Mr. Celeste, what is the percent chance that you will vote for Mr. Rhodes? And what is the percent chance that you will vote for Mr. Celeste?

The 1988 survey, performed in the summer, randomized 988 respondents to one or the other of these questions concerning the upcoming presidential election:

> *Deterministic:* As it now stands, George Bush, a Republican, will be running for president, as will Michael Dukakis, a Democrat. Who do you expect to vote for for president?

Probabilistic: As it now stands, George Bush, a Republican, will be running for President, as will Michael Dukakis, a Democrat. What is the percent chance you will vote for Bush? What is the percent chance that you will vote for Dukakis, the Democrat?

Analogous questions were asked concerning the U.S. senatorial election in Ohio that year.

In 1986 the deterministic and probabilistic questions inquired about different events. Whereas the former asked about voting if the election were held today, the set of probabilistic questions asked respondents to look ahead to the upcoming election. The format of the probabilistic questions is attractive in its use of "percent chance" wording and in its effort to separately elicit expectations of going to the polls and of voting for particular candidates. However, the wording of the candidate-specific questions is ambiguous as to whether persons should answer conditionally on going to the polls or unconditionally.

The 1988 versions of the deterministic and probabilistic questions are more comparable to one another but still somewhat problematic. Here, neither question separated the act of going to the polls from that of voting for a candidate. As in 1986, respondents may have interpreted the probabilistic questions as asking them to forecast their voting behavior either conditional on or unconditional on going to the polls.

Burden does not explicitly address these issues of comparability but notes the following: "Though the deterministic and probabilistic questions differ in some respects, the phrasings are as similar as possible and come from the same survey so that question wording artifacts will introduce minimal error" (p. 1157). Beginning his analysis, he finds that the response rates to the probabilistic questions compare favorably with those to the deterministic questions. Comparing the elicited voting intentions to the subsequent election outcomes, he reports that the two formats, deterministic and probabilistic, do equally well in predicting the fraction of the vote received by each candidate. Drawing conclusions from these and other analyses, he concludes: "Though the probabilistic measures are new, I conclude that they perform at least as well as their deterministic counterparts and in some cases a bit better" (p. 1165).

Hoek and Gendall (1997)

Data collection was performed in face-to-face interviews conducted in the two-month period prior to a multiparty election in New Zealand in 1993. Following the election, a second survey was conducted by telephone to learn respondents' actual voting behavior. The pre-election questions, whether deterministic or probabilistic, asked respondents to report how they would have voted "if the election had been held yesterday." These were the formats:

Deterministic: If this year's general election had been held yesterday, which party would you have voted for?

Probabilistic: If this year's general election had been held yesterday, please tell me how likely it is that you would have voted for the (fill in party name) candidate?

Hoek and Gendall measure probability on an eleven-value scale, attributed to Juster (1966), that jointly uses numerical and verbal expressions of probability. Each person was asked to use this scale to report the likelihood that he or she would have voted for each of four named parties or for an unnamed "other" party.

The deterministic version of the polling question does not permit the respondent to reply that he or she would have chosen not to vote at all, whereas the probabilistic question implicitly permits this possibility. In this respect, the probabilistic format is clearly superior to the deterministic one. However, the authors' use of probabilistic questioning to ask about voting in a hypothetical past election is much at odds with the forward-looking perspective that I have taken in this chapter and elsewhere. I cannot readily say how a person should respond to questions asking him or her to place probabilities on hypothetical past behavior, nor how such responses may be related to probabilities of voting in the actual upcoming election. (See Manski [1999] for general discussion of the problem of interpreting elicited probabilities of counterfactual events.)

Be this as it may, the authors report that the probabilistic responses were somewhat less accurate in predicting election results than were voting intentions elicited using deterministic questions. They attribute this finding to the failure of some respondents to understand the eleven-value scale. They particularly note that their mode of questioning does not inform respondents that the five probabilities reported for the candidates of different parties must sum to a value less than or equal to one. Given this deficiency of the question format, they conclude that their data "do not represent a clear test of the scale's predictive accuracy, since it is not possible to differentiate the level of error caused by respondent misuse of the scale from that associated with the scale itself" (p. 8).

APPENDIX B: PILOT POLL SCRIPT

Hello. I am calling in connection with a political polling research project at Northwestern University. I would like to ask you two types of questions about whether you expect to vote in the upcoming presidential election and, if so, for whom. The questions should take no longer than three minutes of your time. [wait for consent]. The purpose of asking the two different types of question is to learn how the manner in which election polls are conducted may affect their findings. I assure you that all responses will remain confidential and will be used solely for the purpose of research.

I would like to begin by asking two questions of the form used in one of the standard election polls, the CBS–*New York Times* poll. [The sequence in which candidate names are presented is randomized.]

Q1. How likely is it that you will vote in the 2000 election for President? Would you say that you will definitely vote, probably vote, probably not vote, or definitely not vote in the election for President?

Q2. If the 2000 election were being held today and the candidates were Al Gore, the Democrat, George W. Bush, the Republican, Ralph Nader, the Green Party candidate, and Pat Buchanan, the Reform Party, would you vote for Al Gore, George Bush, Ralph Nader, or Pat Buchanan?

Q2A. [If no answer in Q2, ask]: Well, as of today, do you lean more toward Al Gore, George Bush, Ralph Nader, or Pat Buchanan?

Thank you for your responses. Now I will ask questions similar in form to those in the nationwide Survey of Economic Expectations. These questions will permit you to more fully express your expectations about how you may vote. In particular, I will ask you about the PERCENT CHANCE of your voting for different candidates. The percent chance must be a number from zero to one hundred. Numbers like two or five percent may be "almost no chance," twenty percent or so may mean "not much chance," a forty-five or fifty-five percent chance may be "a pretty even chance," eighty percent or so may mean "a very good chance," and a ninety-five or ninety-eight percent chance may be "almost certain." The percent chance can also be thought of as the NUMBER OF CHANCES OUT OF ONE HUNDRED.

Q3. To get a feeling for the questions, let's start with the weather where you live. What do you think is the PERCENT CHANCE that it will rain or snow tomorrow?

Now, I would like you to think about the 2000 election for president. Recall that the candidates will include Al Gore, the Democrat, George W. Bush, the Republican, Ralph Nader, the Green Party candidate, and Pat Buchanan, the Reform Party candidate. Candidates of other parties may also be on the ballot.

Q4. What do you think is the PERCENT CHANCE that you will cast a vote for president?

Suppose now that you will vote for President. I will read five voting possibilities, and then ask you the PERCENT CHANCE that you would vote for each one. Please listen to the choices, allocating 100 percentage points total among all five:

Q5a. Al Gore, the Democrat

Q5b. George W. Bush, the Republican

Q5c. Ralph Nader, the Green Party candidate

Q5d. Pat Buchanan, the Reform Party candidate

Q5e. another candidate

To conclude, I will ask you a few background questions.

> Q6. What was your age at your last birthday?
>
> Q7. Do you have a high school diploma?
>
> Q8. [Ask if response to Q7 is "yes"] Do you have a degree or diploma from a college, university, vocational, or technical school?
>
> Q9. Sex [record without asking]

This ends the set of questions. Your assistance in this research project is much appreciated. Thank you.

NOTES

I have benefited from the comments of Susan Herbst and Jeff Manza. I am grateful to Jordan Heinz, who assisted in the design of the pilot poll and administered it to a sample of respondents.

1. At the beginning of October, those who leaned toward Gore included both the committed and the disenchanted Democrats, but a week later only the committed Democrats leaned toward Gore; thus the decrease from .52 to .40. At the beginning of October, the expected vote for Gore is $.40 + (.70)(.12) = .484$, but a week later it is $.40 + (.45)(.12) = .454$.

2. One may also question whether responses are intrapersonally comparable. That is, does a given respondent interpret verbal phrases in the same manner when asked about different events?

3. The WISCON survey's effective response rate (the ratio of completed interviews to potential residential phone numbers called) is a bit over 50%. The data for the 5,432 SEE interviews completed from 1994 through early 1998 have been archived by the Data and Program Library Service of the University of Wisconsin-Madison and are available on the web at http://dpls.dacc.wisc.edu/econexpect/index.html.

4. To familiarize respondents with the percent chance scale, the SEE module of expectations questions begins this way (Dominitz and Manski 1997a):

> Now I will ask you some questions about future, uncertain outcomes. In each case, try to think about the whole range of possible outcomes and think about how likely they are to occur during the next 12 months. In some of the questions, I will ask you about the PERCENT CHANCE of something happening. The percent chance must be a number from 0 to 100. Numbers like 2 or 5 percent may be "almost no chance," 20 percent or so may mean "not much chance," a 45 or 55 percent chance may be a "pretty even chance," 80 percent or so may mean a "very good chance," and a 95 or 98 percent chance may be "almost certain." The percent chance can also be thought of as the NUMBER OF CHANCES OUT OF 100.

5. Formally, let L denote the response to the job-loss question and S denote the response to the search-outcome question. Then L(100—S)/100 gives the percent chance that a worker will lose his job in the year ahead and subsequently not obtain a position of comparable economic value.

6. These Gallup and Pew questions are available on the Web, as follows: www.gallup.com/poll/surveys/2000/Topline000220/index.asp and www.people-press.org/sept99que.htm.

7. Question Q2A is posed only to respondents who refuse to answer Q2, or who respond "other" or "don't know."

8. The Gallup survey does not report findings for persons not currently registered to vote. The implicit assumption seems to be that such persons will not register later and vote. The Gallup Web site information says that *likely voters* are registered voters "deemed most likely to vote in the November 2000 General Election, according to a series of questions measuring current voting intentions and past voting behavior."

9. That is, $(0.6)(0.5) + (0.4)0 = 0.3$ and $(0.6)1 + (0.4)(0.5) = 0.8$.

10. Respondents were contacted during the three weeks preceding the November 7 election. The sampling protocol was for phone numbers in one local exchange to be dialed at random until fifty interviews were completed. In all, 272 phone numbers were dialed. These yielded 91 residential contacts, the remaining 181 numbers being either businesses, inaccessible, or disconnected. Thus, the interview response rate among contacted households was 50/91.

15

The Future of Polling

Relational Inference and the Development of Internet Survey Instruments

JAMES WITTE AND PHILIP E. N. HOWARD

New media technologies have generated much excitement about ways of improving communication between leaders and citizens. During the last election cycle, pundits announced the arrival of electronic democracy—a political environment in which public deliberation and the measurement of public opinion would be facilitated by multimedia technologies like the Internet. Along with electronic town halls and e-mail listservs, Internet surveys and polls have been hailed as new ways of conducting and measuring public deliberation. For many practitioners, these innovations are akin to those that replaced the magnifying glass with the microscope in the biologist's lab. Most of the major survey houses have recast themselves as interactive, multimedia polling agents with the ability to employ a widening range of stimuli to help elicit responses from subjects.

Internet-based survey and polling techniques also require reexamination of arguments against polling in general regardless of the mode of data collection. There is a long tradition of doubting polling sciences, and their generalizability, of the utility of defining a "public opinion," and of the reduction of individual opinion to commensurable inputs (Binkley 1928; Crossley 1937; Gosnell 1937; Katz and Cantrill 1937; Lohman 1988). Some criticize polling for reducing public opinion to a distillate of unrelated individual opinions based on snapshot responses to simple close-ended questions. Political ethnography has long recognized that public opinion is a social process frequently led by a few individuals with strong opinions and persuasive abilities (Mansbridge 1983; Herbst 1993). In this view, a sample design that "democratically" assigns equal weights to individual responses arithmetically ignores the relative social stature of respondents (Converse 1987). Traditional polling techniques placed this kind of social information outside the research frame of empirical study; it was considered auxiliary, if not immeasurable. However, the large and potentially diverse sample frame of the Internet has made it possible to expand the theoretical sample of "opinion leaders" and permits some Internet polling firms to claim to be able to measure opinion leadership by building a peer-review process into the survey design itself.

Other chapters in this collection have discussed polls and other tools of public opinion measurement. Here, we are specifically concerned with the role of contemporary survey methods and technologies in honing the science of opinion assessment and expanding the range of applications for the art of political polling. We begin with a brief discussion of Internet survey instruments and their advantages and disadvantages. A review of historical lessons learned in polling follows, leading to a discussion of the challenges presented by modern techniques. We highlight the methodological issues associated with sampling public opinion, emphasizing that the nonrandomness of most Internet surveys needs to be viewed in light of a realistic assessment of the randomness of other survey sampling methods, particularly telephone surveys.

In the next section of this chapter, we illustrate the significance of sampling techniques for Internet surveys, using data from Survey2000, a large-scale Internet Survey conducted on the National Geographic Society's (NGS) Web site in fall 1998. Over 80,000 individuals participated in the study worldwide, yielding more than 50,000 completed surveys. Respondents were asked a series of questions to determine patterns of individual mobility over the life course, attitudes toward community, patterns of social contact, and mutual assistance and questions about their musical, literary, and culinary tastes. Though the Survey2000 sample is basically a large convenience sample of visitors to the NGS web site, outreach efforts were conducted to diversify the sample. In fact, over 400 respondents indicated that the first time they had gone on-line was to complete the survey. Moreover, a number of the Survey2000 questions were based on existing survey instruments, most notably the General Social Survey (GSS), as a means to provide external benchmarks of the sample's representativeness. The chapter concludes by emphasizing that representativeness is the aim of all sampling techniques—random and nonrandom—and suggesting that a well-reasoned approach to relational inference is the key to generalization, regardless of the sampling technique employed.

AN INTRODUCTION TO INTERNET SURVEY INSTRUMENTS

There are several clear advantages to Internet survey instruments. Even some of the more traditional polling firms are staking their future on these new developments, renaming themselves and rethinking the way they do business. First,

1 they allow researchers to collect huge samples, some of hundreds of thousands of respondents. This makes it easier to purposively subsample special sections of the population on a range of variables, from demography, medical conditions, and mobility history to musical, literary, or culinary tastes. *2* Second, the instrument itself permits a range of interesting testing stimuli, allowing researchers to control a respondent's exposure to different media and the flow of information to the respondent, such that Internet survey instruments take on the better features of traditional qualitative research methods. Firms and lobbyists test entire commercials, product packaging, and political arguments on population segments. For example, one firm expects to help political consultants estimate when the public will call a candidate "too negative" by testing small populations for their reactions to entire campaign ads. Ideally, campaigns will be able to compose ads with a range of strong messages, and interactive surveys will help them pick the strong and aggressive, but not too negative ads. *3* Third, Internet survey instruments extract richer information from respondents. Traditional question types, new question types, and the quality of information from open-ended questions can exceed that from Computer-Assisted Telephone Interview (CATI) or personal interviews. This point is well illustrated by the literature section of Survey2000. Questions intended to measure respondents' knowledge of local literature were customized to include the names of authors associated with each respondent's state of residence, including current residence and past residence. Even a well-trained interviewer would be hard-pressed to follow the related questionnaire skip patterns. Similarly, when Survey2000 respondents were asked about their preference for particular music genres, they were not only told the name of the genre but were also given the opportunity to listen to a short audio clip representative of that genre.

4 Fourth, Internet techniques can quickly reconnect with respondents should follow-up be necessary, whereas both the time involved in the initial survey and any follow-up is often less lengthy than that of other methods. *5* Fifth, more complex experimental designs (e.g., testing for instrument or measurement effects) can easily be accommodated with Internet survey instruments. An experiment of this type will be conducted in Survey2001 using questions, about respondents' attitudes regarding endangered and threatened species. Following the model of the Survey2000 literature questions, it will ask respondents to indicate their support for preserving species associated with their state of residence. Moreover, while the standard question prompt also includes a photographic image of the species, randomly selected respondents will be presented the question without the image prompt. These questions concern the extent to which attitudes toward the environment are influenced by perceptions and emotions surrounding particular species rather than a consistent environmental attitude. The experimental component will consider the extent to which visual images increase the likelihood of inconsistent response patterns. *6* Sixth, the interactive potential of Internet surveys may lead respondents to feel more invested in the research. They tend to provide helpful critiques of the surveys, and as the media allows results to be quickly returned to respondents, they may revisit the project to learn about the results of the research in which they participated. Here, too, Survey2000 provides a useful example. A comment and suggestion e-mail icon was included on every page of the survey. During the ten-week data collection period, nearly 2,000 e-mail comments and suggestions were received, many constructively addressing the survey technology and content.

Disadvantage

1

However, there are also disadvantages to Internet survey instruments. First, the survey environment created at the terminal comes at the expense of a survey environment regulated by an interviewer. Although interviewer effects are known, it is less known if the environment in which an Internet survey instrument is administered affects response patterns. One of the advantages of having questions asked by a human interviewer is that the agent can gauge the degree to which the respondent is answering without prompting. Many of the new techniques for home surveying are designed to be innocuous, increasing the possibility that something in the environment, uncontrollable by the survey managers, may affect the respondent. A challenge for the future will be learning how to monitor and mitigate instrument and environment effects in new survey contexts.

2

A related concern raised about Internet surveys and polls is the possibility that interest groups might attempt to deliberately distort the outcome, encouraging members to vote "early and often" to ensure an outcome favorable to the group's position. Thinking about this concern in terms of stuffing "the ballot box," however, places it in perspective. Just as a minimum of standard election procedures make it difficult to manipulate a paper ballot, features common to all but the simplest of on-line surveys and polls are sufficient to thwart the electronic equivalent. Few on-line polls and surveys today consist of simple electronic documents that could be readily copied and anonymously submitted. Programming a certain level of interactivity into a survey or poll not only makes the instrument engaging, but also ensures that a live respondent, or at least a semi-intelligent program, is on-line to complete the instrument. To return to the paper ballot analogy, stuffing an electronic ballot box requires getting in line each time to submit a ballot. Clearly, an electronic survey or poll is not monitored by an election judge, who could spot repeat voters. However, identifying information (e.g., IP address, host name, browser labels, and so on, not to mention "cookies" stored on a respondent's computer) regularly exchanged as part of being on-line is available to identify and exclude efforts to overrun the instrument with many responses from a single source.

3

The most obvious potential limit of Internet survey methods concerns sampling, discussed at length in the following sections. At this point, however, one point is worth emphasizing: telephone samples, face-to-face survey samples, and Internet survey samples are all the products of considerable self-selection. Quotas and stratified sampling assure "representative" findings in terms of key demographic criteria, but high levels of respondent refusal conceal biases that remain embedded within demographic categories. However, in traditional survey methods, these concerns are largely ignored. These methods have acquired a taken-for-granted legitimacy that may never have been warranted, based primarily on avoiding three important lessons about mistaken sampling.

HISTORICAL LESSONS IN POLLING

In each political campaign, pollsters learn most from the errors of previous campaigns. Over time, pollsters have learned three basic lessons. Early on, the industry learned to improve techniques for sampling the right population, then they learned about the importance of sampling for interesting populations, and more recently they learned about the importance of sampling for a trendline.

The reader might recall the famous *Literary Digest* presidential election poll that predicted Landon's victory over Roosevelt in 1936. This poll had a sample size of more than 2 million, but still came to the wrong conclusion. The *Literary Digest* poll made no effort to assess the representativeness of its sample, and it clearly sampled the wrong people. But an oft-overlooked fact is that in 1920, 1924, 1928, and 1932, the *Literary Digest* used the same techniques to accurately predict the outcome of presidential elections. Beyond the truth that a large sample does not guarantee accurate results, a nonrandom sample does not amount to a recipe for invalid results. The most important lesson is that sampling must always be assessed; it can be random or purposive, *but it cannot be purposeless.*

In contrast to the *Literary Digest* debacle, the National Election Study came under attack for not sampling a population many people considered most interesting after the 1964 presidential election of Lyndon Johnson. One of the main new political forces of the time was the John Birch Society, and scholars interested in studying this radical new right-wing group were unhappy to find that the national sample included one member of the John Birch Society. In their defense, survey organizers argued that a perfect national sample would have at most two members of the John Birch Society, and that no other national survey had caught the rise of this conservative grassroots movement in the previous four years. Nonetheless, academics with good theoretical reasons for being interested in the John Birch Society were dissatisfied with a representative survey that failed to capture the impact of an influential political group (Converse 1987).

The practical restrictions of traditional polling techniques permit researchers to take a snapshot of respondent demographics, behavior, or preferences. Although two data points *can* make a trendline, they do not always. In 1980, pollsters correctly predicted a Reagan victory using snapshot data, but they did not construct a useful trendline, such that the margins of his victory were significantly underestimated. In the last few days before the election, there was a shift in popular support for Reagan that the polls did not catch. If the shift had been in the other direction, this polling error might have achieved the same infamy as the *Literary Digest* error.

MODERN TECHNIQUES, MODERN CHALLENGES

Telephone surveys, particularly with the introduction of CATI systems, transformed public opinion research. Today, however, telephone survey research has become increasingly problematic, most obviously due to low response rates. A concern over declining response rates is not new among survey researchers; however, recently this issue has also captured broader public attention with articles such as the November 1999 *New York Times* piece titled "Polling's 'Dirty Little Secret': No Response." A low response rate will increase the cost of a survey but does not necessarily undermine its validity. A real problem, however, occurs when nonresponse is not randomly distributed but is instead correlated with respondent characteristics. Weighting and statistical adjustment provide possible corrections when differences in response patterns are observed, but heterogeneity based on unobserved criteria is equally problematic. In addition, from a theoretical sampling perspective, the increasing prevalence of multiple phone lines raises a new question. This clearly breaks down the assumption of a one-to-one correspondence between telephone numbers and respondent households that has been the methodological mainstay of adherents of RDD (random digit dialing).

In the election of 2000, polls again proved their worth as a democratic institution in their own right by providing succinct, albeit simplified, measures of public preferences (Crespi 1989; Gallup and Rae 1940). The campaigns of all the major candidates, especially those who could afford good pollsters, devoted significant resources to assessing public policy priorities. Along with internalizing results and reshaping their platforms, political consultants also used polls to "prime" their candidate, to confirm his popularity, and to help them select which campaign ideas to emphasize (Jacobs and Shapiro 1994a). Organizationally, polling for the presidential candidates was conducted by trusted professional advisers with clear ideological affiliations with their teams. Poll results were used to demonstrate popularity, to evaluate and improve the effectiveness of candidate's media strategy, and to review and challenge media coverage. Internally, polling was also used by powers within campaigns to guide strategic decisions about campaigns and policy (Altschuler 1986; Jacobs and Shapiro 1995b).

Often viewed as a means of reading public opinion, polling clearly has also become a tool to shape public opinion. Good internal polling by the Bush presidential campaign in 1988 helped staffers to realize that public knowledge of what Dukakis stood for was minimal, so Republicans might define him to their advantage by creating a negative image of him (Richard 1994). Push polls, developed more as a way of planting ideas with specific publics than as a means of measuring preexisting opinion, have become a common phenomena. Most pollsters are embarrassed by this application of polling techniques, but they are still used. Even in the last ten days of the 2000 campaign season, stories emerged of a Republican push poll asking residents of New York if they would vote for Hillary Clinton, even if they knew she had accepted campaign contributions from an Islamic group with members who sympathized with the use of violence in the Middle East. Given that terrorist bombing of the *USS Cole* was still in the news, this tactic tried to associate Clinton with terrorist sympathizers under the guise of testing the resilience of Clinton supporters. The immense political implications of interpreting—or misinterpreting—exit polls were lived out during the presidential election of 2000. The politics of who called what for which campaign and for what reason, with little regard for estimable margins of error, will be debated for years to come.

Over the course of the 2000 election, Internet survey instruments allowed pollsters to refine the science of politics in three ways. First, traditional measures of political involvement—listing forms of political involvement, looking for respondent reaction to public issues and personalities—were greatly refined. Second, the strategic formula for legislative success developed by lobbyists increasingly employed these refined polling instruments. Lobbyists now claim to have growing insight into statistical relationships that connect public opinion, voter turnout, membership in political action groups, political volunteerism, donorship patterns, correspondence with legislative representatives, and legislative outcomes. The refined science of polling is now applied to both test and prod the progression of issues: from their conceptualization in the lobbyist's boardroom to the seeding of grassroots movements and the targeting of issue campaigns in specific congressional districts. Finally, political pollsters can now gather such detailed information and match this information with existing databases, so that they no longer offer demographic analysis to issue and candidate campaigns, but "psychographic" analysis that includes detail about voter sophistication and how people learn and process political information.

METHODOLOGICAL ISSUES IN SAMPLING PUBLIC OPINION

This section emphasizes polling issues associated with sampling, coverage, and nonresponse, that is, who is polled. However, the full range of methodological issues in research, including instrument, interview, environment and measurement effects, potentially take on a new cast in an on-line polling environment.

Who Is Polled: Sampling, Coverage, and Nonresponse in Telephone Surveys

Though there are a variety of types of errors associated with survey research, including coverage error, measurement error, instrument effects, interviewer effects, and nonresponse, issues associated with sampling error have clearly received the most attention from survey researchers. Not surprisingly, as Herbst (1993) points out, this is the type of error that survey researchers are best able to measure and quantify, though not necessarily the most serious type of error.

Beyond sampling error, other types of errors related to sample selection are no less serious in their consequences; however, they are more difficult to detect and remedy. For example, standard practices regarding sampling error rest on an assumption of probability sampling and complete and adequate *coverage* of the population of interest. Clearly Internet-based surveys and polls face their greatest challenge here, but one ought not assume that traditional survey techniques have at last resolved questions of coverage. Coverage refers to the extent to which a sampling design ensures that all individuals in a population have a known probability of selection into a sample. Simply thinking in terms of sample selection—ignoring the issue of nonresponse for the moment—questions of coverage have typically been treated as a tractable problem. Not everyone has a telephone and, to the extent that surveys and polls are interested in samples that represent all segments of the population, alternative data collection methods (e.g., door-to-door surveys) may be used to collect data from those who would otherwise not be contacted.

On the other hand, new telephone technologies and user habits (answering machines, call forwarding, cell phones, and multiline households) have raised a whole new set of concerns regarding coverage. A description of these concerns is presented in considerable detail in guidelines established by the American Association for Public Opinion Research (AAPOR 2000). Though some researchers follow the explicit guidelines, a cavalier approach to the problem is certainly more common. Simply think back to the last few times you were contacted by a telephone survey or poll. How often were you asked about the number of phone lines associated with your household or your use of call forwarding? Rarely, if at all? However, this information is essential to maintain the integrity of RDD sampling procedures. For example, studies conducted in 1997 and 1998 found that about one-third (31.3%) of households nationwide and about one-quarter of households (25.7%) in the Pacific Northwest have two or more telephone lines (Oregon Survey Research Laboratory 1998). Industry sources in another twelve-state region of the United States indicate that multiple line penetration is currently at 17% with another 6.5% of the households subscribing to calling features that associate multiple numbers with a single line. In addition, as one would expect, the prevalence of multiple phone lines was not randomly distributed but was positively correlated with income, education, and home ownership. Though these studies did not explicitly ask whether there was a unique number or a distinctive ring associated with each line, multiple phone lines pose a significant challenge to any RDD study that simply assumes a single selection port for each household. Moreover, in some areas where multiple phone lines are included as part of a local calling package, household members may themselves be unaware of the fact that their household is associated with multiple phone numbers.

Furthermore, once a sample has been selected, surveys and polls still need to confront issues associated with response and nonresponse. Some of these issues are definitional; for example, AAPOR (2000) distinguishes six different methods of calculating responses rates. The rate may vary, on the one hand, with whether one includes partial interviews with complete interviews in the numerator. On the other hand, it will vary based on the definition of the denominator, which contains partial and complete interviews as well as the number of noninterviews (refusals and break-offs) and cases of unknown sample eligibility. Not only is the line between partial interviews and break-offs necessarily arbitrary but also caller identification and answering machine technology have blurred the line between refusals and instances of unknown sample eligibility. Finally, the calculated response rate will also vary with the assumptions made about survey eligibility among households and individuals for whom there is insufficient information to establish eligibility.

To think about this from a practical perspective, consider the pool of randomly selected numbers needed to complete a telephone survey of a given size. For example, using equal probability sample selection methods and assuming a medium-length interview on a nonsensitive topic, nearly 7,000 randomly selected phone numbers would be needed to obtain 1,000 complete surveys.[3] In other words, on average, seven numbers yield one completed survey, so we can assume that significant nonrandom effects deplete the value of random selection because nonrandom instrument, interviewer, or environment effects must account for the remaining six incomplete surveys.

Focusing particularly on refusal rates as a key aspect of nonresponse, it is widely accepted that nonresponse is not random. Accordingly survey researchers and pollsters invest considerable effort in call-backs and conversions, prepaid incentives, and advance letters (Frey 1989, Dillman 2000, Singer, Van Hoewyk, and Mahar 2000). Interestingly, one recent experiment has found that while rigorous efforts were able to significantly boost response rates (from 36.0% to 60.6%), there were few differences in response patterns found primarily in demographic characteristics not in substantive areas (Keeter et al. 2000). Nevertheless, even with rigorous efforts, approximately 40% remain nonrespondents, and more than one in four of those who were contacted and eligible refused to be interviewed. Moreover, the apparent similarities between ready and reticent respondents does not preclude real and important differences between these groups and those who remain nonrespondents.

In sum, sampling error, coverage problems, and nonresponse bias are all ways in which traditional, telephone survey, and polling methods commonly fail to live up to the assumptions of probability sampling. In evaluating the potential of Internet-based methods, our point of comparison should not be the textbook ideal for those standard methods but rather everyday practices in the field.

Who Is Polled: Sampling, Coverage, and Nonresponse in Internet Surveys

Until now, Internet-based surveys and polls that seek to tap public opinion were necessarily limited because only about half of Americans have Internet access, while nearly one-third of those not on-line say they have no plans to gain access (Howard et al. 2001). Even though many of the Internet holdouts are older, it is unlikely that Internet market penetration will reach that of the telephone any time soon. Moreover, turning from the general population to the Internet population, there is no mechanism to specify members of the on-line population, for example, through e-mail addresses, that would be exhaustive and mutually exclusive to serve as the basis for a probability sampling procedure. In this regard, any discussion of sampling error is meaningless. Similarly, discussions of coverage and nonresponse are limited when one cannot define the size of the population or specify its members.

Against this backdrop, one ought to consider an important advantage of Internet-based polling methods: Internet-based methods can survey large numbers of respondents at relatively low costs. Internet-based polls are self-administered, so there are no variable interviewer costs, only fixed programming costs. Internet-based delivery, as compared to traditional postal delivery, is essentially free. Moreover, with an Internet-based system, the pollster need not consider the effect of sample size on data entry costs, as there are no data entry costs, or more accurately, these costs are borne by the respondents who enter the data in the course of completing the poll or survey.

It is easy to underestimate the benefits of increased sample size, if one forgets that polls and surveys are often interested in more than the overall outcome. More often than not, analysts are interested in subgroups in a population and not just the population at large. For analyses of this type, the potential advantages of Internet-based polls and surveys are striking. For example, the widely used GSS in 1993 had only 179 African Americans, while the GSS African American oversamples in 1982 and 1987 included 354 and 353 African American respondents, respectively. Even in 1996, when the GSS sample was doubled, African Americans number only 402. Survey2000, on the other hand, resulted in 538 surveys completed by African Americans at a fraction of the cost of the GSS. Although Survey2000 makes no claims to randomness, the diversity of its sample certainly adds richness. Moreover, this tradeoff needs to be considered in light of a realistic assessment of the extent to which traditional sampling methods are increasingly falling short of the assumption of randomness.

A Nonrandom Road to Representativity

The goal of a poll or a survey is to collect data on a sample that represents a population. Randomness does not guarantee representativeness; rather, it provides the means to quantify the level of confidence with which one can say that the sample *does not* represent the population. Moreover, across the social sciences, the random selection of research subjects is by no means the only approach to generalizability. If one were to discount all findings not based on a random sample, then one would be choosing to ignore much of the historical and comparative work that makes up a sizeable segment of the social science literature. Whereas survey researchers, pollsters, and demographers emphasize randomness nearly to the point of fetishism, others are more catholic in their approach. Trochim (2001) describes the random sample approach to generalizing as one of two primary approaches:

> I'll call the second approach to generalizing the Proximal Similarity Model. . . . The term proximal similarity was suggested by Donald T. Campbell as an appropriate relabeling of the term external validity. . . . Under this model, we begin by thinking about different generalizability contexts and developing a theory about which contexts are more like our study and which are less so. Notice that here, we can never generalize with certainty—it is always a question of more or less similar.

Like the notion of relational inference discussed at the end of this chapter, the proximal similarity model depends on a theoretically informed assessment of the nonrandom nature of a sample to avoid the pitfalls of a pure convenience sample. The *Literary Digest* polls made no effort to assess the representativeness of its sample, whereas Internet surveys such as Survey2000 explicitly incorporates items designed to measure the gradient of similarity. Such surveys collect data on standard demographic characteristics (e.g., gender, age, race, education, etc.). Combinations of these attributes for the sample can be compared to data collected by standard techniques. In addition, a proximal similarity framework may include other factors—such as attitudes and values toward community and cultural preferences—that cut across standard demographic variables. For this reason, a number of items used in Survey2000 come from the 1993 GSS to provide an external benchmark.

No matter how large the sample, size never guarantees representativeness. A Web survey such as Survey2000, which basically relied on a modified convenience sample, will not yield a random sample, and we will not "know" the selection probabilities for sample members. However, this *does not mean that the survey cannot yield representative social science data*. In fact, a sample of any size may be representative. Focus groups often include well under a dozen members; a single key informant may accurately represent an entire group. The advantage of a random sample design (where the intent is to use a random sample and then quantify the probability with which one's sample does or does not represent the population) is that sufficient sample size may be determined more exactly. Moreover, when one moves from sampling in theory to sampling in practice, a random design is no guarantee that the realized sample will be random. In the following section, we highlight results from two recent surveys to illustrate the significance of sampling strategies for Internet-based surveys.

THE INTERNET AND COMMUNITY: WHAT YOU SEE DEPENDS ON HOW YOU SAMPLE

The Internet itself has been one of the first areas explored using Internet survey techniques. At first glance, however, findings from these efforts are difficult to reconcile. On the one hand, a recent paper based on the Survey2000 data argues that "people's interaction online supplements their face-to-face and telephone communication, without increasing or decreasing it. However, heavy Internet use is associated with *increased participation* in voluntary organizations and politics" (Wellman, Haase, Witte, and Hampton 2001). By contrast, several months earlier, Norman Nie, political scientist and SPSS statistical software founder, made national headlines when he announced, "The Internet could be the ultimate isolating technology that further reduces our participation in communities even more than television did before it." Our contention is that these different findings can be traced back to each study's different approaches to sampling.

Although Survey2000 does not claim to be a random sample, Nie and others describe the InterSurvey sample as a national random sample of 4,113 American adults in 2,689 households. Respondents were provided with free Internet access and WebTV connections to facilitate the survey. In addition, "to avoid contamination of the results due to the fact that the study was itself conducted over the Internet, the results on Internet use presented in this study are based ONLY on the responses of participants who had Internet access prior and independent of the WebTV access installed by InterSurvey" (Nie and Ebring 2000). Even though the InterSurvey sample offered WebTV access to a random sample of individuals, there is no guarantee that those who accepted the company's offer to participate in the survey constitute a random sample. As in the case of a telephone survey, unobserved selection processes may dramatically alter the random character of the sample. For example, an individual with established and regular patterns of Internet use and on-line interaction would presumably be far less willing to adopt a new method of access than a less committed user. In short, just as those Internet users who frequent the National Geographic Society's homepage, which was the primary point of access for Survey2000, are not a perfect mirror of American society, so too those individuals who adopt WebTV as a means to access the Internet are not necessarily a random subset of Americans, even if they were randomly selected to be offered access.

To assess the distinctiveness of those who use WebTV to access the Internet, the subset of 359 Survey2000 respondents who were WebTV users will be compared to all other Survey2000 respondents. Table 15.1 indicates clear differences in social attitudes and engagement, as well as in political participation, between WebTV and non-WebTV respondents in the Survey2000 sample. For example, as shown in the top section of table 15.1, all Survey2000 respondents were asked whether they agreed or disagreed with three statements that indicate attachment to one's community. WebTV respondents were significantly less likely to agree with the statements that they felt close to their community or saw their community as a source of comfort. Meanwhile, WebTV respondents were significantly more likely to indicate that their daily activities did not create something of value for their community. When we compare non-WebTV respondents, these differences are not only statistically different but also each is of a magnitude of about 10%, suggesting real, substantive differences between the two segments of the sample.

Table 15.1   Differences in Social and Political Participation
between WebTV Users and Other Survey2000 Respondents

Social and Political Participation	WebTV Respondents (%)	Non-WebTV Respondents (%)
Agreeing with the statement:		
I feel close to other people in my community.	59.1**	68.6
My daily activities do not create anything worthwhile for my community.	41.3**	30.7
My community is a source of comfort.	59.8**	68.3
Index of social participation (mean value)[a]	3.6**	5.1
Political participation in the past 12 months:		
Signed a petition	65.0*	59.4
Attended a public/town or school meeting	29.5**	38.5
Wrote an elected official	32.6	35.1
Attended a political rally or speech	12.4*	17.2
Served on a local organization committee	12.7*	16.9
Served as a club or organization officer	17.7**	29.6
Worked for a political party	6.7	5.8
Wrote a letter to a newspaper or magazine	22.0	20.2
Gave a speech	15.6**	27.9
Was a member of a group for better government	17.2	13.8
Wrote a newspaper or magazine article	9.5*	13.2
Engaged in political discussion on the Internet	27.7**	20.2

Survey2000 data based on 359 WebTV respondents and 33,851 Non-WebTV respondents for value items, 367 WebTV respondents and 34,755 Non-WebTV respondents for the index of social participation, and 349 WebTV respondents and 32,745 Non-WebTV respondents for political participation items.
   [a] Index of social participation based on membership and active membership in 20 different categories of organizations and social groups.
   *p. < .05.
   **p. < .01.

The middle section of table 15.1 contrasts WebTV and non-WebTV respondents with regard to the mean value of an index of social participation for each segment of the sample. All Survey2000 respondents were queried about participation in twenty different types of groups or social organizations.[3] Further, respondents were asked to identify whether they were members or active members—an active member holds a leadership position, contributes money beyond regular dues, or regularly attends meetings. The index of social participation is the sum total of reported memberships, with active membership receiving double the weight of simple membership. As table 15.1 shows, WebTV respondents participated in significantly fewer organizations (1.5 fewer organizations on average) than non-WebTV respondents. Moreover, this finding remained robust with various specifications of the index of social participation (e.g., with log and exponential transformations of the totals, as well as with varied weights for regular and active membership). Regardless of the specification, the *t* statistic for the estimated difference never fell below 4, approximately double that needed to reject the null hypothesis at the conventional .05 level.[4]

The lower section of table 15.1 summarizes reported political participation in the past twelve months, also contrasting WebTV and non-WebTV Survey2000 respondents. In this instance, for four of the twelve reported forms of political participation, there is no significant difference between WebTV and non-WebTV respondents. Moreover, with regard to two forms of political participation (signing a petition and engaging in political discussion on the Internet), WebTV respondents are actually more involved than others in the sample. Nonetheless, for some of the more active and engaged forms of participation (attending public meetings, attending rallies and speeches, serving as local organization officers or committee members, giving a speech, or writing articles for newspapers or magazines), higher levels of participation occur among non-WebTV respondents than among WebTV respondents.

One plausible explanation for the differences between the WebTV and non-WebTV segments of the Survey2000 sample, as summarized in table 15.1, could be that the demographics of the two samples differ systematically. Indeed, we expect this to be the case; table 15.2 summarizes clear demographic differences between the two segments of the samples. WebTV respondents are significantly less likely to be women and are more heavily concentrated in the older age cohorts than non-WebTV respondents. Moreover, under a third of the WebTV respondents have a bachelor's degree or higher, whereas well over half the non-Web TV respondents have reached this level of educational attainment. Consistent with the observed age differences, WebTV respondents are also more likely to be employed and to live in households with children under the age of nineteen than non-WebTV respondents.

However, as table 15.3 indicates, the differences between WebTV and non-WebTV respondents extend beyond the demographic criteria commonly employed in the selection of a stratified sample. Table 15.3 reports the estimated coefficients obtained when the index of social participation is regressed on the set of demographic characteristics summarized in table 15.2, along with a variable indicating whether a particular respondent belonged to the WebTV segment of the sample. In table 15.3, we see that each of the demographic variables has a significant effect on the predicted value for the index of social participation. Participation in social organizations is higher among women than men. Membership is also greater among younger and older individuals than among individuals in the reference age group (25- through 34-year-olds). Compared to individuals with some college but no degree, respondents with lower levels of education participate at lower rates, whereas individuals with a bachelor's degree or greater participate at a higher rate. Furthermore, respondents engaged in full-time employment participate at lower rates than individuals who are employed part-time, are retired, or are in any other employment status. The index of social participation is also significantly higher among individuals living with children age 18 or younger. However, even after controlling for this set of significant de-

Table 15.2   Differences in Demographic Characteristics
between WebTV Users and Other Survey2000 Respondents

	WebTV Respondents (%)	Non-WebTV Respondents (%)
Female respondents*	39.3	48.9
Age cohort*		
16–19	2.9	7.0
20–24	5.3	9.6
25–34	22.3	25.0
35–44	20.5	23.4
45–54	22.9	20.8
55–64	12.2	9.6
65 and older	14.1	4.7
Educational attainment*		
High school degree or less	23.9	12.9
Some college but no degree	43.6	31.1
Bachelor's degree or higher	32.5	56.1
Employment status*		
Full-time employed	52.5	61.6
Part-time employed	7.8	14.7
Retired	18.9	16.4
Other (laid off, unemployed, military, homemaker)	20.8	7.3
Live with children 18 or younger in household*	15.8	29.4

Percentages for each type of respondent. Survey2000 data based on 359 WebTV respondents and 33,851 Non-WebTV respondents for value items.
*$p < .01$, for difference between types of respondents.

mographic characteristics, being a WebTV respondent has a strongly significant, negative effect on the index of social participation. Moreover, the effect size of the estimated WebTV respondent coefficient (-0.930) is not trivial. Larger than the effect of gender, employment status, and household composition, it is equal to roughly two-thirds the overall difference between the average WebTV and non-WebTV respondents, as reported in table 15.1.

Efforts to reconcile the different views of the Internet suggested by the InterSurvey study and Survey2000 illustrate just how little is known about using the Internet to gather survey data. Differences in sampling strategies are an easy and obvious explanation for these two different views of the impact of the Internet. However, given how little experience we have with Internet survey methods, which are so new that there has been little systematic study of their operation, we should be cautious about simply accepting the easy and obvious. Years of experience and detailed analyses with other modes of survey data collection (e.g.,

Table 15.3 Estimated Ordinary Least Squares Coefficients for Survey2000 Index of Social Participation Regressed on Demographic Characteristics and WebTV Respondent Status

Respondent Characteristics	Unstandardized Coefficient	Standard Error
Constant	2.351*	0.090
Female respondents	0.258*	0.045
Age cohort		
16–19	4.031*	0.118
20–24	0.919*	0.088
25–34 (reference category)		
35–44	0.940*	0.065
45–54	1.558*	0.066
55–64	1.889*	0.090
65 and older	2.487*	0.144
Educational attainment		
High school degree or less	−0.954*	0.220
Some college, but no degree (reference category)		
Bachelor's degree or higher	1.444*	0.167
Employment status		
Full-time employed (reference category)		
Part-time employed	0.853*	0.070
Retired	0.260*	0.116
Other (laid off, unemployed, military, homemaker)	0.462*	0.067
Live with children 18 or younger in household	0.880*	0.052
WebTV respondent	−0.930*	0.220

Survey2000 data based on 359 WebTV respondents and 33,851 Non-WebTV respondents for value items.

$*p < .01.$

face-to-face, telephone, paper-and-pencil self-administered) point toward a host of instrument and mode effects (cf, Dillman 2000). Similar issues probably affect the results of Internet surveys, such that it would be premature to attribute all differences between studies to sampling issues.

CONCLUSION: NEW TECHNOLOGIES, NEW METHODS, AND RELATIONAL INFERENCE

Internet-based survey instruments have the great advantage of widening the range of stimulus for respondents. However, survey designers hoping to take advantage of the new technologies must still face the challenge of building representative samples. From InterSurvey's WebTV sample to the Survey2000 on-line sample and the Harris Poll Online panel, which currently claims 7 million volunteer e-mail respondents, new technologies have made it possible to deploy increasingly creative and complex survey instruments and build enormous samples of respondents. For a growing number of Americans, Internet tools have become a significant conduit of their social life, allowing people to build their social networks by extending and maintaining friend and family relationships (Howard, Rainie, and Jones 2001). Pollsters are also looking at new ways to exploit Internet sociability to improve snowball samples through techniques such as affinity networks.

Further use of on-line surveys is inevitable, but researchers still need to think critically about the process of survey design, aware that representativeness, not randomness, is the important goal in sample selection. In coming years, wider and deeper Internet market penetration will mitigate sampling problems. In the meantime, however, researchers must remain aware of the implications of possible sample bias. For example, widespread use of on-line political polling may focus parties and platforms away from the needs of particular subsets of the population. Furthermore, instrument effects (e.g., question order, definition of response categories), which have been convincingly documented for other survey modalities, are virtually unexplored for on-line surveys and polls.[5] One also must keep in mind that "interviewer effects" (e.g., respondents' inclination to provide a socially desirable response) do not simply disappear because a survey is computer-mediated.

Perhaps the most intriguing issue for the future is how on-line surveying will move beyond the adaptation of traditional paper-and-pencil and telephone survey techniques to a new technology. On-line surveying raises the possibility of completely new approaches to data collection, particularly the use of engaging, interactive techniques to collect information in such a way that respondents may not even realize the extent of the data they are providing. However, as such techniques develop, researchers need to be reminded that their human subject and data confidentiality practices need to be updated.

On the issues of sampling reviewed in this chapter, Internet survey techniques necessarily raise a challenge to "business as usual" within survey research circles. If you read only within the quantitative survey research literature, you find a strong emphasis on the notion that validity is chiefly concerned with *external* validity. As whole, however, social science has a more expansive notion of validity that focuses on the extent to "which relationships between research operations, or the degree to which generalizations about higher order constructs can be made from research operations."[6]

Rather than thinking of a population as improperly sampled, pollsters and survey researchers should emphasize the extent to which valid conclusions may be drawn by *relational inference*—sensible inferences for a larger diverse population drawn from a well-known, controlled subpopulation, which may or may not have been randomly selected. For example, in Survey2000, the sample respondents are clearly better educated and better off than the general population. One may also assume that they are better informed and more likely to be familiar with a wide range of cultural influences. Within this sample, researchers have found important differences in cultural tastes and preferences that vary with geographical region. If one finds clear and significant differences in this sample, skewed as it is, then one can plausibly argue that similar and quite likely stronger regional differences are to be found among the population at large. Purposive sampling begins with the intent to select a specific sample relevant to the interesting research question at hand. Relational inference differs from purposive sampling in that it is guided as much by the relationships in the data as the purpose behind the study. The researcher is mindful of the characteristics of the sample obtained, and how the sample differs from the general population. The aim, as with much of social science outside the area of survey research, is to make tempered generalizations about the attributes of a larger population.

NOTES

1. Further detail on Survey2000, including information on obtaining the data, may be found in Witte et al. (2000).

2. An accessible and practical discussion of estimating sample size for telephone surveys may be found at http://www.surveysampling.com/ssi_home.html, the web site for Survey Sampling Inc., an industry leader in telephone survey sample selection.

3. Respondents were queried regarding the following types of groups: fraternal groups, service clubs, veterans groups, political clubs, labor unions, sports groups, youth groups, school service groups, hobby or garden clubs, school fraternity or sorority, nationality/ethnic groups, farm organizations, environmental groups, community/neighborhood groups, social advocacy groups, literary groups, art groups, discussion/study groups, professional/academic societies, religious groups, computer clubs, or any other groups.

4. In statistical terms, one of the likely consequences of the nonrandom nature of the Survey2000 sample is biased sample estimates of the population parameters. Standard corrections for bias of this type, including robust standard errors, inflate the estimated standard error, which is equivalent to requiring a larger test statistic to be able to reject the null hypothesis.

5. A notable exception is the Gilens chapter in this volume. In addition, Survey2001, a National Science Foundation follow-up study to Survey2000, includes several experimental components in its design, ranging from rather simple studies of the relative functionality of radio buttons and drop down menus to the impact of including photographic images of plants and animals in questions regarding endangered species. Most important, Survey2001 will also field a parallel telephone survey to assess the overall impact of Internet versus telephone-based data collection.

6. Mueller (1997) develops and tests a set of logistic regression models based on a nonrandom, purpose sample of German daily newspapers.

16

The Sovereign Status
of Survey Data

TAEKU LEE

I am invisible, understand, simply because people refuse to see me.
Like the bodiless heads you see sometimes in circus sideshows, it is
as though I have been surrounded by mirrors of hard distorting glass.
When they approach me they see only my surroundings, themselves
or judgments of their imagination, indeed, everything and anything
except me.

Ralph Ellison

The theory of the polls is essentially simplistic, based on a tremendously exaggerated notion of the immediacy and urgency of the connection of public opinion and events. The result is that sometimes we
seem to be interviewing the fish in the sea to find out what the birds
in the heavens are doing.

E. E. Schattschneider

The answer to the defining question of this volume—whether political institutions
are, and can be, responsive to citizens' preferences—depends intimately on
whether elites are pushing public opinion or being pulled by public opinion, as
several chapters have already noted. It also depends intimately on what we think
public opinion is and how we choose to measure it, as the chapters in this part
note. In this chapter, I suggest that these two pieces of the puzzle of democratic
responsiveness are themselves intimately linked to each other. More specifically,
I contend that a structural relationship between elites, polling organizations, political events, and the production of survey questions limits the ability of opinion
polls to render a decisive judgment about the elite or nonelite bases of the public's
political views.

The arguments in this chapter constitute part of a more comprehensive challenge to the conventional view of public opinion scholars that our political views
are shaped primarily by what elites say and do (see Lee 2002).[1] In this broader
challenge, I illustrate the dynamic interaction of elite, nonelite, and counterelite

influences on public opinion during the American struggle over civil rights and racial equality from the late-1940s to the mid-1960s. The civil rights movement is a critical test of elite theory, ironically enough, because several of the leading exemplars of the elite view—such as Edward Carmines and James Stimson (1989), John Zaller (1992), and Elisabeth Gerber and James Jackson (1993)—stake their claim on analyses and arguments about the civil rights movement.[2] Political elites do not always define the shape of public opinion because public opinion is deeply embedded and assumes multiple forms. Whether elites influence how ordinary individuals think and act depends fundamentally on the issue, which social groups and political institutions are invested in it, how the issue unfolds within specific historical and ideological contexts, and the like.[3]

I propose a more group-based, historically grounded, issue-specific account of mass opinion and test my propositions with survey data from 1956 to 1964. The survey results show that influences from black counterelites on racial policy preferences precede and predominate over the influences from mainstream partisan elites. They also show, contrary to findings from scholars like Carmines and Stimson (1989) and Edsall and Edsall (1991), that critical linkages between racial policy, partisanship, and social welfare liberalism find strong imprints in the 1950s and early 1960s, well before the putatively critical elite events of the mid-1960s. These findings mount a persuasive case against certain elite accounts. But they do not refute all possible versions of elite theory. We shall see in this chapter that the theoretical contested terrain exceeds the grasp of the available data: the case against elite accounts is not decisive largely because survey data during the civil rights movement are limited.[4]

More pointedly, I argue in this chapter that the incompleteness and inadequacy of survey data are a systemic shortcoming of opinion research, with troubling consequences for how we evaluate elite opinion theories. To make this case, I first demonstrate that survey data have come to predominate in our measurements and conceptualizations of public opinion. This sovereign status reverberates in the conceptual, normative, and empirical realms of opinion research: what we imagine public opinion to be, what role public opinion should play in democratic government, and what we can actually discover substantively about the nature and dynamics of public opinion. Relevant to the questions of democratic responsiveness, the ability of survey data to adequately discriminate between elite and nonelite influences on mass opinion depends on whether opinion polls accurately reflect (or even anticipate) the issues that engage the public at a given moment in time. In the dynamics of racial attitudes, this possibility is not merely theoretical: the production of survey items on racial attitudes—at critical junctures in the evolution of the civil rights movement—lags behind, rather than anticipates or mirrors, the events that engage the public. Survey data, used alone, are thus inadequate to the task of assessing elite theories.

I conclude by urging a more pluralistic approach to the study of mass opinion. Settling the score on debates about the civil rights movement or about the elite bases of public opinion may well require engaging multiple sources of opinion data. To make this more than merely a perfunctory plea, I briefly present the trade-offs entailed in using one possible alternative to opinion polls—written correspondences from ordinary citizens to their political representatives.

FROM PUBLIC OPINION TO SURVEY RESPONSES

Our academic and practical understanding of the term "public opinion" has come to rest on one point: the opinion poll. Of course, scholars have noted alternate modes of public political expression at other historical moments, ranging from festivals, strikes, riots, and discussions in French salons and English coffeehouses to straw polls, elections, and revolutions.[5] And with the relentless march of modern technology, ever newer forms of public expression are emerging, from radio and television talk shows, to "town hall meetings" and "deliberative polls," and, most recently, to "e-mail" groups and Internet "chat rooms." These active modes of public political expression, however, are generally studied outside the domains of opinion research—usually, under the rubric of "political participation," "voting behavior," "social movements," "media studies," "mass communications," and the like.

Today, both critics and practitioners of survey research recognize that poll data are singularly sovereign among possible measures of public opinion, and this indicator (poll data) is rather routinely conflated with its underlying construct (public opinion). Among critics, Susan Herbst (1995a, p. 90) notes, "These days we tend to believe that public opinion is the aggregation of individual opinions as measured by the sample survey. . . . This definition is now hegemonic; when most of us consider the meaning of public opinion, we can't help but think about polls or surveys."[6] Among practitioners, Philip Converse (1987, p. S14) notes that "it is exactly this kind of 'one person one vote' tally of opinions as routinely reported today by polls and surveys which has now become the consensual understanding of the world around as to a baseline of public opinion," and John Zaller (1992, p. 265) writes of "the survey responses that virtually everyone now takes as constituting public opinion."

This sovereign status is exemplified by the increasing reliance on survey data in social scientific research on public opinion. Stanley Presser (1984) and, building on Presser's data, Jean Converse (1987) show this increase in several social science disciplines between the time before World War II and 1980. Articles in sociology journals that use survey data increase more than threefold from about 18% in 1939 to more than 54% by the mid-1960s. In political science, the percentage of published work using survey data jumps from less than 3% in 1939 and 1940 to almost 20% by 1964 and 1965, and then to 35% by 1979 and 1980.[7] In *Public Opinion Quarterly* (*POQ*) (the preeminent journal of public opinion research), survey data comprise almost 28% of all articles from 1939 through 1940. This percentage doubles by 1964 and 1965, and rises to more than 90% by 1979 and 1980. In hindsight, it may appear odd to us that survey data did not comprise a greater percentage of articles in *POQ*

Table 16.1   *Public Opinion Quarterly* Articles on Race,
by Type of Opinion Data, 1937–1986

Year	Poll Data	Interview	Voting	Media	Other	% Poll
1937–46	1	0	2	2	2	14.3
1947–56	2	0	1	2	2	28.6
1957–66	5	2	5	0	1	38.3
1967–76	37	1	1	3	2	84.5
1977–86	17	0	0	1	0	94.3
1987–96	21	0	0	2	0	91.3

even in the 1940s and 1950s. Jean Converse (1987, p. 402) notes, however, that this progressive rise in the use of survey data in *POQ* "represented real change. *POQ* was not a journal of survey research at the outset. It had been established for the study of public opinion and thus drew articles on public relations, advertising, propaganda and censorship, radio, film, the press, and public opinion generally, many of which had little or nothing to do with surveys."

An alternative procedure to make the case about the dominance of survey data is to examine how public opinion about a particular issue is researched over time. Here, consider the study of racial attitudes.[8] Table 16.1 tabulates research articles in *POQ* on race by different sources of data on public opinion from 1937 to 1996. As with Converse's tabulation of *POQ* articles, table 16.1 shows that, in its first decade, research using survey data constituted only a small fraction (14%) of all *POQ* research articles on race and public opinion. The remaining articles in this period focus instead on alternate sources of opinion data, such as in-depth interviews, voting behavior, and media coverage. By 1967 to 1976, however, almost 85% of all research articles on racial attitudes in *POQ* are based in survey data, and by 1977 to 1986, the figure rises to 94%.

Table 16.1 also presages two central points in this chapter. First, a glance suggests that the rise of survey research on race lags behind the rise of survey research generally, especially around the period of the civil rights movement. Jean Converse (1987) finds that from 1959 to 1960, survey data comprise 58% of all articles in *POQ*. By comparison, table 16.1 shows that from 1957 to 1966, survey data comprise only 38% of articles on racial attitudes in *POQ*. Second, the rise in the absolute number of research articles on racial attitudes in *POQ* closely parallels the rise in civil rights activism. By implication, the production of survey items on racial attitudes also appears to closely parallel the rise in civil rights activism. That said, the study of racial attitudes (and the use of survey data to study racial attitudes) explodes most dramatically during the period from 1967 to 1976, several years after the height of the civil rights movement. These observations hint at a general relationship between the times when we gather survey data and when political events happen, which I revisit and develop in greater detail in the coming sections.

THE LIMITS OF SOVEREIGNTY

The exact path to the sovereign status of poll data and their virtual conflation with public opinion is likely contentious, and my purpose here is not to develop an exhaustive exegesis on how this evolution came about.[9] As I argue elsewhere (Lee 2002), unequivocal influences can be attributed to three factors: the close correspondence of polling to voting, the ascendance of scientific approaches to the study of public opinion, and the development of technological innovations like random sampling and CATI. Many critics of survey research implicate other forces: the logic of social control, the need to engineer democratic consent, and historical accident.[10] That said, the trajectories of liberalism, scientism, and technological change give us the rudiments of an account of how opinion polls achieved their preeminence over the last six decades.

In the remaining sections of this chapter, I examine some of the reverberations that result from that this dominant role of survey data. Ultimately, I argue that the presumed authority of survey data limits what we understand public opinion to be and how we evaluate elite opinion theories. The fact that opinion scholars almost exclusively use poll data does not in itself undermine the survey research program. The sovereign status of survey data may simply be a fortuitous historical contingency or, more forcefully, an outcome warranted by the simple fact that polls are the optimal way to measure public opinion. Criticisms of opinion polls persist, and in this section I consider three such criticisms—normative, ontological, and conceptual. In normative terms, the sovereign status of survey research threatens the vitality and autonomy of our political life. In ontological terms, the "public opinion" that opinion polls purport to measure simply does not exist. In more general form, essential characteristics of public opinion are lost when the construct is solely identified with one possible measure of it. In conceptual terms, opinion polls render a static, disjunctive, and individualistic notion of what is ultimately a dynamic, conjunctive, and collective phenomenon.

To begin, critics of survey research note that polls are far from a neutral mirror on society and that their historical origins and present dominion pose a sober threat to fair democratic representation. Jürgen Habermas (1989) and Benjamin Ginsberg (1986), for example, attribute the ascendance of survey research to the bureaucratic necessity of political states to "domesticate" the sentiments of their electorate. In doing so, the argument goes, such states effectively "manufacture" legitimacy and consent that might otherwise not exist.[11] Ginsberg famously argues that opinion polling is thus an instrument of political control, made powerful by the aura of objectivity and political neutrality conferred upon it by the public and politicians alike. For instance, in the context of the civil rights era, Ginsberg alleges that the National Advisory Commission on Civil Disorders—which conducted some of the first surveys that focus on African American mass opinion—effectively used the results of polling to manipulate public opinion and avoid any costly acquiescence to the demands of blacks in urban America.[12]

James Beniger (1986) further implicates what he calls the "Control Revolution," in which change is driven by and reinforces the need for information processing and social control. Opinion polls thus emerge as merely another "control technology." In particular, Beniger sees polls as a form of "market feedback technology" used to gather information to shape and influence mass consumption.[13] Softer shades of such sentiments, of course, can be found in earlier theorists such as James Bryce and Walter Lippmann. Even V. O. Key (1961, p. 3) notes that "governments must concern themselves with the opinions of their citizens, if only to provide a basis for repression of disaffection." Hence, the same tool that pioneers like Crossley and Gallup praised as enabling democratic representation can also be perceived as undermining it.

The intertwined historical trajectory of opinion polling and liberalism implies a particular conception of the democratic public and a particular conception of political representation. Perhaps the most relevant development in this regard since the eighteenth century has been the evolution of formal mechanisms for the expression and aggregation of citizens' political preferences. The "public" came to be embodied in a voting electorate and viewed as an aggregative ideal with the emergence of majority rule, the secret ballot, and liberal utilitarianism.[14] The easy analogy of surveys to an individualistic, "one person-one vote" model of democracy made surveys especially relevant and appealing. It also changed our understanding of public opinion itself, marking a sea change in the status of public opinion from the abstract domain of political theorists to the empirical substrate for survey practitioners.

With this shift to an aggregative, behavioral approach to public opinion, the normative appeals to opinion polls came to imply a particular conception of democratic representation. In Hanna Pitkin's (1967) classic distinction between Burkean trustees who represent by acting independently but in the best interests of their constituents and Millsean delegates who represent by following the direct mandates of their constituents, the appeal of opinion polls clearly nudges us toward the ideal of representatives as delegates.[15] Absent direct democracy of the sort advocated by the anti-federalists, Rousseau, or Aristotle, the liberal use of opinion polling was promoted by James Bryce, George Gallup, Archibald Crossley, and others as the best substitute. Polls would provide elected representatives qua delegates with continuous feedback on their constituents' preferences, and these preferences ought then to shape government output.

More pointedly, other critics question the ability of opinion polls to meaningfully measure public opinion at all. Herbert Blumer (1948, p. 543), an early and steadfast critic of opinion polls, warns against "the narrow operationalist position that public opinion consists of what public opinion polls poll. . . . What is logically unpardonable on the part of those who take the narrow operationalist position is for them to hold either wittingly or unwittingly that their investigations are a study of public opinion as this term is conceived in our ordinary discourse." The fatal flaw, according to Blumer, is that pollsters equate the findings of survey data—merely an instrument used to measure public opinion—with the object of inquiry itself.

Perhaps Blumer's contemporary on this point is the French sociologist Pierre Bourdieu (1979, p. 130), who makes the deliberately provocative claim that public opinion, in the "sense of the social definition implicitly accepted by those who prepare or analyze or use opinion polls, simply does not exist." Bourdieu indicts survey researchers on three counts of problematic assumption making: that everyone's opinion is equal; that, on a given issue, everyone actually holds an opinion; and that a consensus exists about what questions merit asking (and, by corollary, that surveys can know what that consensus is).[16] Thus, survey data—all other possible caveats notwithstanding—adequately measures mass opinion only if it accurately surveys what ordinary individuals are actually thinking about at a given moment.

Last, the study of public opinion through survey research is impugned by critics because it allegedly captures only a static, disjunctive, cognitively based, individualistic dimension of mass opinion that is at best tenuously linked to political action and social processes. Ginsberg (1986, p. 60) boldly asserts that "polling has contributed to the domestication of opinion by helping to transform it from a politically potent, often disruptive force into a more docile, plebiscitary phenomenon." The evidence on which critics draw to support this claim is that legislators who once relied on a diverse range of expressions of public opinion—local newspapers, visits with their constituents, letters from their districts, and interest groups—were now increasingly turning to opinion polls.

In an analysis of the emergence of the straw poll, Susan Herbst demonstrates that this shift is emblematic of a deeper shift in underlying conceptions of public opinion. In particular, Herbst (1995d, p. 99) notes a critical shift from public opinion as the product of groups (especially, political parties) to public opinion as "an aggregation of atomized, anonymous individuals." The paradoxical result is that public opinion ceases to be *public*. As Lynn Sanders (1999, p. 263) observes, "because of the analytic and measurement strategies of survey researchers, public opinion has become literally private and only figuratively public." Moreover, Bourdieu argues that politics involves conflicts in which citizens must take sides. Hence, Bourdieu distinguishes opinion as measured through polls from opinion that influences political action ("mobilized opinion") and argues that opinion research should focus on how individuals' opinions on an issue become mobilized and activated. These points echo Blumer's (1948, p. 543) assertion that public opinion is fundamentally a collective product "having its setting in a society and . . . being a function of that society in operation."

The cumulative effect of these critiques is that the exclusive reliance on survey data as a measure of public opinion may lead to an impoverished or inaccurate understanding of public opinion and its role in democratic regimes. The ascendance of survey research is accompanied by a shift in focus from public opinion as the subject of theoretical speculation to public opinion as the object of empirical inquiry. A casualty of this shift is that the normative and conceptual parameters of public opinion largely become presumed, rather than interrogated, and much to the neglect of alternate parameters of public opinion. With the growing dominance of opinion polls, survey researchers increasingly command authority over the substantive parameters of public opinion as well—over what, when, and how mass opinion is measured, analyzed, and interpreted.

SURVEY DATA AND ELITE OPINION THEORY

Survey researchers are not without rejoinder to these critics. The possibility that our contemporary conception of public opinion may be problematic—whether a bureaucratic invention, an instrument of state control, or simply a captive of the agenda control of survey researchers—does not, in itself, preclude an action or expression from being reliably categorized as an instance of public opinion. Blumer does not argue that public opinion cannot be operationalized, merely that such operationalization should not be conflated or confused with the underlying construct itself. And Bourdieu (1979, p. 124) himself suggests that "polls can make a useful contribution to social science if they are treated rigorously and with certain precautions."[17]

From the standpoint of the practice of survey research, many of the attacks levied against poll data can be accommodated, and have been. Survey researchers have examined non-respondents, included open-ended questions, clarified context effects such as question wording and question order, refined sampling techniques, interpreted race-of-interviewer effects, and incorporated uncertainty and heterogeneity of responses.[18] The progress in survey research techniques and the sheer accumulation of knowledge about what the public thinks have been so impressive that Eleanor Singer (1987, p. S1) begins her editor's introduction to the fiftieth anniversary issue of *Public Opinion Quarterly* with the bold proclamation of three words: "Blumer was wrong."

From the standpoint of theory, practitioners themselves have engaged in ontological skepticism about what opinion polls really measure. At least since the early works of Paul Lazarsfeld and his colleagues at Columbia University and Philip Converse and his colleagues at the University of Michigan, what we know about public opinion from survey research has provoked some thorny questions about the competence of the democratic public.[19] Today, the apparent political ignorance of the ordinary citizen is one of the most thoroughly documented and lamented facts about U.S. politics.[20] John Zaller and his contemporaries respond to this challenge by revising our traditional view that polls measure stable and coherent underlying attitudes.[21]

Zaller (1992, p. 35) abandons "the conventional but implausible view that citizens typically possess 'true attitudes' on every issue about which a pollster may happen to inquire."[22] In its place, he presents a more situational account of how people respond to polls and proposes that we use the more fitting terminology of "opinion statements" (instead of "public opinion") to describe what polls measure. Ordinary individuals may not necessarily be thinking about the topics in which pollsters are interested. And for this reason, not all individuals will express informed, intelligible responses to survey questions.[23]

These methodological and theoretical refinements surely yield a more apposite, adaptable view of how to use opinion surveys and what they tell us about public opinion. Yet accommodating such a revised view is not without risk, particularly so when we juxtapose the potential pitfall of relying exclusively on survey data with the critical consideration of elite opinion theory. If "true attitudes" do not exist, then we invariably broach the possibility that Ginsberg correctly implicates opinion polls as a tool for state control or that Habermas correctly diagnoses mass opinion as the product of elite manipulation.[24] Zaller (1992, p. 311) himself notes that one consequence of his modified view of "opinion statements" is that citizens "pay too little attention to public affairs to be able to respond critically to the political communications they encounter; rather, they are blown about by whatever current of information manages to develop the greater intensity."[25]

On this point, accepting a more adaptable view of "opinion statements" has consequences for whether we think that poll data can comprehensively measure the full gamut of public opinion. Opinion surveys hold de facto agenda control over what questions to ask, and when and how to ask them. Thus, the potential slippage between public opinion and survey data is negligible only if polling centers produce surveys that ask about the issues that actually engage the public at a given moment. In particular, if citizens do not always possess "true attitudes" on the questions that pollsters ask about, then likely there are matters on which citizens hold informed and intelligible opinions that pollsters *do not* ask about. As James Beniger (1983, p. 482) observes, "survey research does not arise from a need to speak one's mind . . . but rather from the need to find out what is on people's minds—whether they intend to speak them or not." In short, "public opinion," as gauged from survey responses, may differ crucially from "public opinion" revealed through political action.

Furthermore, the validity and reliability of opinion polls may depend not only on *whether* they ask the questions actually on the minds of ordinary individuals but also on *when* they ask them. If Roosevelt's victory in the 1936 election boldfaces the spectacular success of opinion surveys, then Truman's unexpected victory in the 1948 election footnotes the dramatic failure of opinion surveys. In the latter case, the media and the pollsters on whom they relied took Dewey's reasonably strong lead (five percentage points) into mid-October as sufficiently decisive to render a prediction in Dewey's favor. Yet they were caught off guard precisely because they failed to survey voter sentiments in the final weeks of the election, when public momentum was actively shifting from Dewey to Truman.

The consequence of this potential mismatch between survey responses and the public's underlying "true" opinion is that polls, used exclusively, may be insufficient to adequately discriminate elite from nonelite influences on mass opinion. Barring foresight or serendipity, pollsters may view an emerging issue as worth asking about *only after* receiving cues (elite or nonelite) that the issue is significant and salient at the level of mass publics.[26] In fact, if polling centers themselves depend on elite cues to decide which issues to ask about, this will predispose opinion research to confirm elite theories. Moreover, even if foresight and serendipity converge, survey research centers are often constrained by periodic administration (e.g., the biennial American National Election Studies), by fiscal constraints, and by the production time required to develop a survey instrument, pretest it, and send it out to the field. Except in experimentally designed survey settings or under fortuitous circumstances, surveys may well tap into the public's mind only after its gaze on a particular issue is engaged and transformed.[27] Thus, surveys may fail to capture nonelite influences on mass opinion (even if they exist) at precisely the time they occur. Not just a methodological point, this possibility bears important substantive implications.

THE PRODUCTION OF RACIAL ATTITUDE ITEMS

Take racial attitudes. Here, the question of whether opinion research leads or follows opinion change is embedded in a troubled history of academic research on race. In the nineteenth century, such research from biologists and social scientists (under the rubric of phylogeny, craniometry, and the like) effectively legitimated and perpetuated racist views of nonwhites and segregationist regimes like the Jim Crow South. In the aftermath of such dubious projects up until recent decades, moreover, social scientists either left race off their agenda or continued to examined it within revamped, but equally discreditable frameworks of analysis.[28] Walton, Miller, and McCormick (1995, p. 146) argue that

> American political science responded to this concatenation of developments with its own hands-off policy; and when political scientists . . . did take up the issue of race, they usually did so in terms that one can only describe as racist. Moreover, the solutions they sought for the race "problem" often turned out to be little more than justifications for segregation. In other words, political science was responding to realities and reflecting ideologies outside the walls of the academy.[29]

Thus, they implicate political science research on race as emblematic of the historical and political currents of its time, such as Social Darwinism and Jim Crow. "The sad fact," add Michael Dawson and Ernest Wilson (1991, p. 192), "remains that the study of African-American politics still is the stepchild of the discipline."

This "invisibility" of African Americans has been noted in survey research as well. Despite early bellwethers like Gunnar Myrdal's *An American Dilemma* (1944) and surveys conducted by the National Opinion Research Center (NORC, under the auspices of the Office of War Information [OWI]) in the 1940s, the polling community has been slow to conduct surveys on race relations. As Wade Smith notes, Myrdal's juxtaposition of the egalitarian principles of "the American creed" with inegalitarian, racist practices toward African Americans largely set the agenda for what survey research existed. Thus, researchers for the most part came to focus on the racial attitudes of white Americans, with the presumption that "blacks' opinions on racial matters were obvious" (Smith 1987, p. 443). Or, when the attitudes of African Americans were examined, it was done primarily *in relation to* the attitudes of white Americans. It is only recently, with surveys like the 1984 and 1988 National Black Election Studies and the 1993–94 National Black Politics Study, that there has been significant scholarly interest in the attitudes of racial minorities in themselves.[30]

Ira Katznelson (1973) and others controversially allege that the study of African American politics was pursued with a seriousness of purpose only after black insurgency in the 1950s and 1960s successfully pushed race on the American political agenda. This suggestion—that the production of data and research on racial politics lags behind and responds to actual political events—lies at the heart of my skepticism concerning survey data's ability to adequately test theories of opinion dynamics. We have already seen faint evidence for the possibility that survey research on racial attitudes actually follows important shifts in mass opinion, rather than mirrors or anticipates them. The percentage of increase in research on race in *Public Opinion Quarterly* using survey data appears to lag behind the increase in all *POQ* articles using survey data across comparable time periods.

As I intimated at the beginning of this chapter, survey questions on race and racial policy during the civil rights movement are somewhat incomplete and inadequate to the empirical tasks we want them to speak to. This point bears some elaboration. It is quite evident from historical accounts of the civil rights movement, for instance, that racial group consciousness, racial group conflict, and core political values are a central part of the story. Yet the first nationally sampled academic survey containing a battery of questions on racial group consciousness does not appear until the 1972 American National Election Study (ANES). Similarly, the first battery of items that we presently use to measure "core values" like equal opportunity and economic individualism do not appear in the ANES until 1984, well after the height of movement activism, after the allegedly critical period of the mid-1960s, and even after the tumultuous period of mass uprisings in inner cities and college campuses in the mid-to late-1960s.

That said, at the micro-level of individual questions, the production of poll data on racial politics appears to mirror events fairly well, at least at first blush. The earliest poll data on race are found in January and then again in October–November 1937, when the American Institute of Public Opinion (AIPO, subsequently, Gallup) asked the public about whether Congress should make lynching a federal crime.[31] The AIPO then asks the public in February 1941 whether the poll tax should be abolished. Then, on three separate occasions in 1948 (March, late November, and early December), the AIPO polled the public about views on President Truman's proposal to pass sweeping civil rights legislation. The first poll question that marks the onset of what we generally consider the civil rights movement appears in May 1954 (again, by AIPO) and concerned the Supreme Court's ruling on segregated schools, *Brown v. Board of Education of Topeka,*

Kansas. The AIPO asks this question again in April 1955, November 1955, December 1956, April 1957, December 1957, May–June 1959, and May–June 1961.

Two features characterize these early polls on racial politics. They all concern legislative issues and, by corollary, all such poll items are framed around elite politics. There are no questions on the Montgomery Bus Boycott. Even with events like the Little Rock crisis in 1957, the two poll questions concern public views on the actions of President Eisenhower and Arkansas governor Faubus. Even into the 1960s, most of the questions ask about the actions of political elites, like President Kennedy's decision to send U.S. marshals to Montgomery and the Supreme Court's decision that public accommodations (trains, buses, public waiting rooms) must be integrated. Thus, the timing of poll questions may closely parallel actual events prior to the onset of civil rights movement activism, but they do so primarily in response to elite politics.

There are some exceptions, but not until the 1960s. The AIPO poll in May–June 1961 also asked whether respondents had heard of the Freedom Riders and, if so, whether they approved of their actions. The same AIPO poll asked whether respondents believed that black insurgency through acts like lunch counter sit-ins and freedom rides were helping the cause of integration. An AIPO poll in August 1963 asked whether respondents had heard of the planned March on Washington and, if so, whether they supported or opposed such a public demonstration.[32] In each of these cases, polls were asking about events staged by movement activists *once the civil rights movement was well under way.* A similar relationship persisted as the activism proliferated into Northern cities and exploded in urban uprisings in the mid- to late 1960s. Polls by Harris (Brink and Harris 1964, 1966), the Survey Research Center (Campbell and Schuman 1968), and others follow quickly on the heels of these changes, but they are ultimately *reactive* to them.

Thus, the suggestion—that the production of poll data on racial politics lags behind the actual course of political events—remains. To examine the relationship between survey research into racial attitudes and the course of racial politics itself more closely, I enumerated all poll questions on race from 1937 to 1972. Figure 16.1 presents the results of this count aggregated over time.[33] These results strongly point to a time-dependent relationship between the rise of racial attitude items and the rise of civil rights on the national agenda. Racial attitude items, notably, track closely the unfolding civil rights movement—with the early rise of survey items in the mid- to late-1950s and an explosion in survey items by the early 1960s.

The production of poll questions on race do not always exclusively follow the insurgent activism of African Americans. Figure 16.1 prominently shows a significant interest in racial attitudes in 1942 and 1944, well before the putative onset of the civil rights movement. This anomaly is almost entirely the result of two surveys conducted by the NORC under the auspices of the OWI's Surveys Division. Credit for these early polls goes to the OWI, which needed accurate surveys of civilian sentiments and military morale, and to NORC founder Harry

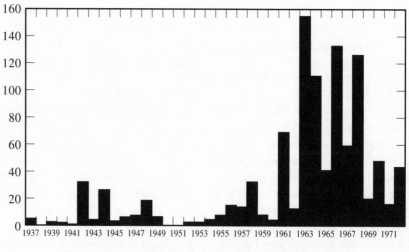

Figure 16.1 Number of Survey Items on Race, 1937–1972

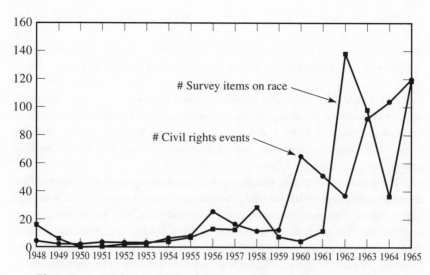

Figure 16.2 Movement-Initiated Events and Survey Questions, 1948–1965

Field, whose mission was to conduct academic research on issue domains that, left to the private sector, would be neglected.[34]

Figure 16.2 compares the rise in survey items on race to the number of events initiated by movement activism from 1948 to 1965. Here the visual evidence more directly demonstrates that opinion research follows the mobilization of mass politics vis-à-vis the civil rights movement. Jumps in movement activism between 1955 and 1956 are followed by jumps in survey items between 1957 and 1958, and again an increase in polling in 1962 trails behind an increase in movement activism between 1959 and 1960. With respect to elite opinion theories, the time series of events chosen is deliberately a *nonelite* measure of political events.[35] And the two events that appear to galvanize interest in polling on racial attitudes are clearly movement-initiated: the Montgomery Bus Boycott from late 1955 through 1956 and the lunch-counter sit-ins throughout the South in spring 1960.

If (very generous) allowances for the small number observations are permitted, this visual evidence can be put through a more rigorous statistical test. Specifically, the relationship between survey questions on race and civil rights movement–initiated events over time can be estimated by a simplified time-series (autoregressive distributed lag) model.[36] Put plainly, such a model estimates the number of racial attitude items in a given year as a function of the number of movement-initiated events in previous years—in this case, one, two, and three years prior—controlling for the carry-over effect of racial attitude items from previous years. The results from such a test are unambiguous. The number of movement-initiated events in a given year strongly predicts the number of racial attitude items the following year, controlling for the number of racial attitude items in the initial year. Though this is obviously underspecified as a general model of survey production, the number of movement-initiated events in a given year even appears to influence the number of racial attitude items two years hence.

TOWARD A PLURALISTIC APPROACH

My purpose in this chapter has not been to distill and defend a particular conception of public opinion as optimal. Rather, it has been to establish the sovereign status of survey data in the measurement and study of public opinion and then to uncover some essential tensions and important limitations that follow from that sovereign status. As I have shown, the claim that survey data are equated with the construct of public opinion is well-grounded: today more than 90% of research articles on racial attitudes, for example, rely on survey data. Moreover, I have argued that public opinion qua survey data bounds our conceptual, normative, and substantive understanding of mass opinion. Conceptually, public opinion qua survey data takes the form of the discrete and equally weighted responses of anonymous individuals within the survey setting. Normatively, public opinion qua survey data draws its rhetorical authority from an aggregative, majoritarian mechanism of democratic choice and a delegative system of representation. Substantively, public opinion qua survey data delimits our knowledge of the public's viewpoints: what they are, how they are formed, and when they are expressed.

These boundaries on public opinion hold some potentially critical implications for elite opinion theories. As I have argued, survey data used alone may not satisfactorily discriminate between theories of opinion dynamics. Because the production of survey items may follow the activation and transformation of mass opinion (rather than parallel or anticipate such changes), the relevant survey items may merit asking only after the fact. And, in fact, racial attitude items do appear to lag behind the mobilization of events in the evolving civil rights movement.

This limitation is especially relevant to a consideration of racial attitudes during the civil rights era in the United States. For one thing, equating public opinion with the political viewpoints of the voting electorate is dubious in a nation in which race and gender have historically been used as the grounds for an exclusionary conception of citizenship.[37] Metaphorically and in actuality, African American voices have been essentially invisible on the punch cards of opinion polls up until the 1960s. Significantly, the place for African Americans in the polls (both the voting booth and the opinion survey) was, in part, won outside of, and as a direct challenge to, the conception of democracy implicit in opinion polls.

Furthermore, because survey data potentially delimit a fairly narrow conception of public opinion (again, as the aggregation of individual viewpoints, measured anonymously and discretely), using survey data alone will rule out the more dynamic, active, and group-based manifestations of mass beliefs and sentiments. Such a broader conception of public opinion is especially relevant to the study of racial attitudes during the civil rights movement. As I have argued elsewhere (Lee 2002), social movements entail the dynamic interaction and mobilization of group interests—at least initially, outside of formal political channels. What is more, a more action-oriented, collective, deeply embedded conception of public opinion is especially relevant because it better describes African American political life.[38] Taken together, then, these points marshal a strong case for a pluralistic approach to opinion data and for research that uses multiple conceptions of mass opinion.

CONSTITUENCY MAIL AS PUBLIC OPINION

The spectrum of alternate conceptions of public opinion that we might choose to study is quite broad. In this final section, I consider one such alternate conception: letters that ordinary citizens write to their elected officials. Written contact with our elected officials—whether to ply political pressure on them, to gain favor or fortune, or simply to share intimate insights with a political celebrity—

has long been a cherished mode of expressing public opinion. Letters satisfy the precondition of *opinion*, in that these are neither random thoughts nor logical proofs but, on the whole, reasoned and deliberated expressions of one's personal beliefs and sentiments. Letters also satisfy the precondition of *public* opinion in that they are political views of some consequence. There is, prima facie, good cause to believe that citizen correspondences tell us something meaningful about public opinion. Yet the move away from survey data is still a risky one. Even if one concedes that alternative measures—from letters to public demonstrations to Internet chat rooms—aptly capture "public opinion," the empirical analysis of such expressions lacks the conceptual clarity or established guidelines of inquiry we enjoy with survey research.

A nascent step toward such conceptual clarity is to chart important differences between letter writing and survey response. First, various modes of public political expression—whether through surveys, letters, elections, uprisings, street corner soapboxes, inter alia—can be distinguished in terms of the incentives that motivate an individual to voice her opinion and the kind of information that such expressions convey to elite actors.[39] From the standpoint of the incentives, there are some important differences in the structure of decision making that differentiate polls from letters. For one thing, individuals cannot proactively *decide* to respond to a survey without first being (randomly) chosen to do so. Survey response occurs when a stranger knocks on the door or rings the telephone and you *do not* decline an interview.[40] By contrast, letter writing is a more proactive and collective form of political expression. More often than not, letter writing is evoked in the heat of political contest—whether during a political campaign, or a legislative session, or a social movement—or through social interactions that confer solidary and purposive rewards, from co-authored letters, petitions, mass mailing, organizational mail, not available from survey responses. Letter writing results from a diversity of motivations and institutional contexts, ranging from individuals who solicit gainful employment or government assistance on personal matters to organizations that advocate legislative change, government regulation, or juridical action.

These differences between survey responses and letter writing are also reflected in the information conveyed to elite political actors. In particular, different expressions of opinion tell political actors different things about the preferences of the polity along at least four dimensions of "publicity": (1) size, (2) coordination, (3) anonymity, and (4) salience. An opinion poll, literally, tells elite actors about the opinions of some 500 to 2,000 anonymous individuals. Figuratively, when that poll is randomly sampled from the country, it speaks for the entire nation as well. Further, while polling firms expend a great deal of institutional resources to organize interviewers and recruit a sufficiently large response, there is almost no coordination among respondents to speak of. Survey interviews are characteristically anonymous interactions, and the opinions expressed in polls are visible to political actors only as an aggregate conception (e.g., as the percentage of the electorate who support a particular candidate or policy). Finally, surveys—

vis-à-vis their claims to produce instantaneous tribunals from the general electorate—should enjoy a fairly high degree of political salience.[41]

With constituency mail, publicity is contingent on the form of correspondence. Letters from private citizens voice only the sentiments of a lone individual, while organizational mail and collective mail can purport to speak for a much larger "public." The level of coordination that letter writing signals to political actors also depends critically on whether it is a correspondence from an isolated individual or a more collective expression such as a petition, mass mailing, or organizational mail. The same kind of distinction carries over with anonymity: individual letters are generally anonymous to political actors, but more collective forms of letter writing are visible in their making. Last, letters from individuals are unlikely to be salient unless the volume is especially high or the correspondent is especially prominent. Yet individual letters are also often taken as a more valid indicator of the average constituent's "latent opinion" than mail from organizations or groups.[42]

This discussion of the incentives that motivate political expression and the information that this expression conveys to political elites gives us one demonstration of how letter writing differs from survey response. Yet another critical difference between correspondences and polls underlies this discussion. Namely, polls are a relatively standardized product. Opinion surveys may differ by polling firm, sample size, sampling frame, and the like, but the incentives facing survey respondents and the characteristics of publicity that elites read generally do not vary across polls. With letter writing, these characteristics are apt to vary across different contexts. The chorus of letter writers generally sing with an upward bias in socioeconomic status and a white bias in racial representation. Yet for a given issue, certain segments of the general public are likelier than others to care enough to actively voice an opinion. And at certain times, the nation as a whole may become activated and likelier to take up vocal forms of political expression. This context specificity hints at some distinctive analytical advantages to using constituency mail as an alternative to survey data.

At heart, letter writing varies across circumstances because it is a costly undertaking that requires a high degree of personal investment. Thus conceived, public opinion is not, as Walter Lippmann (1925, p. 92) observes, "the voice of God, nor the voice of society, but the voice of the interested spectators of action." As a result, such correspondences inform elite actors about the preferences of an active and attentive public. Constituency mail exists because ordinary individuals are compelled to voice their beliefs and sentiments on a given issue; opinion polls arise because pollsters are compelled to identify mass opinions, whether or not individuals care to express them.[43] In the end, a primary reason for caring about public opinion per se must be because our opinions make a strong claim on our likely actions. This is, to borrow V. O. Key's (1961, p. 14) oft-cited definition, the form of public opinion "held by private citizens which governments find it prudent to heed."

Constituency mail thus captures an expression of "activated mass opinion" where an issue is salient in the individual's mind and compels that person toward political action. In this regard, constituency mail more specifically captures the viewpoints of individuals who occupy a special place in public opinion theories. At least since Philip Converse's (1964) discussion of issue publics, politically engaged and activated citizens have occupied a middle stratum between conventional political elites and the largely inattentive general public. In that position, they are often conceived of as opinion leaders. So, constituency mail should tell us something about the nature and dynamics of what opinion leaders think. And if these engaged and activated citizens do in fact act as a critical bridge between elites and masses, then constituency mail should also tell us something about *how they lead*.[44]

By inference, constituency mail may also tell us something more generally about the nature and dynamics of mass opinion. Letter writers tell us about latent opinion: the potential (and potentially mobilizeable) opinions of a wider constituency above and beyond that of the correspondent. As such, analysis that tracks change in aggregate opinion among letter writers might offer an informative complement to existing studies of long-term aggregate shifts in mass opinion.[45] For instance, although elite opinion theories require that this middle stratum between elites and mass obey a strictly top-down, elite-driven chain of influence, the dynamics of letter writing might also be used to test for nonelite influences on mass opinion.

The test implication here is clear. If this middle stratum becomes activated or transformed on a particular issue in the absence of any elite cues to do so, nonelite influences are suggested. If letter writing is unmediated or results from counterelite mobilization, then mass opinion formation must to some extent be autonomous from elite influences. Moreover, such mobilization and activation in the absence of elite cues can also indirectly show how the categories of elite and mass become blurred during social movements as previously inactive, disinterested, or unmobilized individuals become mobilized and professionalized into careers of activism and political engagement.

Finally, as data, constituency mail is an especially rich and informative alternative to opinion polls. Letters tells us more than merely that individuals feel sufficiently invested on a given issue to contact their elected officials. In addition to the act of letter writing, the content of the letters themselves offers textual and contextual information on the correspondent's opinions and how he or she chooses to express them. Thus, constituency mail tells us more than other active modes of public political expression such as attending political rallies, riot participation, and voting. With letters, preferences are revealed both through political action and through content.[46]

Consequently, constituency mail clearly offers a qualitatively different kind of opinion data than that found in surveys. Survey response is typically negative and reactive. Individuals act by *not* declining an interview (often after multiple call-backs) and respond to a *fixed* agenda of (usually) close-ended questions. Letter writing, by contrast, is more positive and *proactive:* correspondents not only choose to express an opinion but also do so publicly and—within the limits of pen and paper—are *unbounded* in how that opinion is expressed. The supply of opinion polls begins with the interest, organizational capacity, and material resources (among other things) of polling firms. The supply of constituency mail, by contrast, begins with the interests, capacities, and resources of ordinary individuals. Because letters result in the first instance from a desire to speak one's mind, correspondents hold free rein not only over issue definition and issue position but also over how to structure that position—what language to use, which frames to conjure, what other issues to link to, and the like.[47]

Let me conclude by highlighting a final set of distinctions between survey response and letter writing. Specifically, letters reveal a dialogical, narrative, and rhetorical structure and an emotional intensity to public political expression. Like dialogue, letters are addressed *to* someone, and opinions are shaped by knowledge about one's dialogical partner. Like narrative, letters tell a story, and that story can be layered in multiple, interwoven justificatory dimensions that unfold before the reader. Like rhetoric, letters aim to persuade the reader on a particular issue. And, last, letters capture an intensity of opinion and emotional pitch not easily and not often measured in opinion surveys.

These are important features of public opinion often invisible to the survey researcher's eye. In this regard, a proactive, freely formed mode of expression like letter writing may divulge how activated mass opinion is formed and expressed during moments of political tumult and transformation like the civil rights movement better than survey response. I hope that this meandering passage into an alternate mode of measuring opinion data has illuminated some of the potential costs and benefits of a more pluralistic approach to opinion research. The proof, ultimately, is in actually *doing* opinion research in such a pluralistic manner. I attempt to do just that as part of my broader critique of elite opinion theory (Lee 2002).

NOTES

1. This chapter is adapted from chapter 3 of *Mobilizing Public Opinion* (Lee 2002).

2. Works that take an elite approach are too numerous and diverse to list here. See Lee (2002) for some representative cites.

3. In *Mobilizing Public Opinion*, I present an alternate account of "activated mass opinion" in which the public's views on political matters are nurtured and activated within multiple spheres of interaction. On an issue like race, public opinion is defined by a dominant, mainstream public at the center of political affairs and oppositional publics at the margins of this dominant public. By conceiving of mass publics as multiple and relational, both elite and nonelite influences on mass opinion are considered. In the civil rights movement, for example, the bottom-up insurgency of a black "counterpublic" turns out to play a critical role in raising the public's awareness on racial issues, mobilizing an active public voice on such issues, and pushing racial policy reforms onto the political agenda.

4. Another reason that the case against elite theory is not decisive is that many versions of elite theory do not exclude the possibility of nonelite, bottom-up opinion dynamics.

5. See, for example, Hobsbawm (1965), Tilly (1983), Herbst (1993, 1994).

6. Charles Tilly (1983, p. 462) goes even further, claiming that "nowadays we can consider the opinion survey a complement to, or even an alternative to, voting, petitioning, or protesting." The observation that the construct of public opinion was increasingly becoming conflated with one possible measure of that construct, opinion polls, can be found among early critics, most notably Herbert Blumer (1948), who cautions against the tautological construction in which "public opinion consists of what public opinion polls poll."

7. Brehm's (1993) compilation from 1986 suggests that the rise of research using survey data may well have peaked in the 1970s: 49.3% of articles from 1986 in the *American Sociological Review* and the *American Journal of Sociology* used survey data; 25.6% of articles from 1986 in the *American Political Science Review* used survey data. The evidence for the salience of polls in economic and psychological research is not as striking; the rise of survey data peaks sooner and plateaus at a lower peak than with sociology or political science.

8. Table 16.1 includes only *POQ* articles on race that present empirical results relating to public opinion—articles that discuss racial attitudes and politics in general terms (or, book reviews in *POQ*, e.g., that for Myrdal's *An American Dilemma*) are excluded from this table. In addition, the conception of "race" coded for in these articles is limited to black-white relations in the United States.

9. Much interesting work on that evolution already exists (e.g., see Ginsberg 1986; Gunn 1983, 1995; Herbst 1993; Peters 1995; Price 1992).

10. See, for example, Beniger (1992) and Sanders (1999). The most celebrated instance of the role of historical accident is the presidential election of 1936, in which a prominent *Literary Digest* straw poll inaccurately predicted sweeping victory for Alf Landon, while randomly sampled polls correctly predicted an easy victory for Franklin Delano Roosevelt (see Gallup and Rae 1940).

11. For Habermas, the term "public opinion" is reserved to describe an idealized conception that occurs only within a public sphere in which political discourse is characterized by rationality and deliberation. As such, "public" opinion is differentiated from "mass" opinion, which results from what he terms the "manufactured publicity" of ideas among a limited, elite group of political actors. For the masses, social psychological processes "liquidate" into an apparent consensus as "public opinion," which then legitimates the rule of the few.

12. For an excellent rebuttal to these critiques, especially Ginsberg's, see Converse (1996). As Converse notes, Ginsberg and others are never clear about the precise causal mechanism by which polls themselves would domesticate mass sentiments. Moreover, Converse points out that popular protest has not obviously declined since the advent of opinion polls and that ordinary citizens are not beyond giving their elites a "nasty surprise."

13. On the notion of controlling and shaping public sentiment, see also the collection of essays in Margolis and Mauser (1989).

14. See Herbst (1993), Gunn (1995), and Price (1992) on this point.

15. See also Manin (1997) on theories of representation.

16. Bourdieu's theoretical interest in the (non)existence of public opinion becomes more apparent in later works like *Distinction* (1986), where he emphasizes the downward class bias to survey nonresponse. Whether someone responds to a survey question depends, to Bourdieu (1986, p. 409), not just on whether the question asked has any import to the respondent but also on that respondent's "socially authorized and encouraged sense of being entitled to be concerned with politics, authorized to talk politics." As Bourdieu sees it, opinion polls thus legitimize and reproduce social hierarchies and muffle the unvoiced desires and needs of the politically dispossessed. See also Bourdieu (1990).

17. Even for a nonpositivist like the early Habermas, the question is as much about why researchers do not find a more precise term than "public opinion" as it is about the lack of such a notion itself. Moreover, authors like Herbst, Tilly, and Bourdieu, I would argue, implicitly or explicitly accept that there is an underlying observable "public opinion" that merits study. Finally, some of this ambiguity can be clarified by differentiating what opinion polls and the discursive rendering of "public opinion" signify from whether there is an underlying construct that merits empirical study. Take Herbst (1993), who in the section "Defining Public Opinion" offers the categories "aggregation," "majoritarian," "discursive/ consensual," and "reification" as definitions of the term. None of these categories actually describes what it is that survey researchers think they are measuring when they administer polls; rather, the categories describe particular meanings that interpreters of poll data or other political acts that might fall under "public opinion" attach to that act or praxis. Thus, Herbst's (1993, p. 92) choice "to avoid discovering the true meaning of the phrase, and simply grant that the definition is fluid" describes a different undertaking than that of survey practitioners.

18. See Lee (2002) for citations on each of these refinements of survey methodology.

19. See, for example, Lazarsfeld, Berelson, and Gaudet (1944); Campbell, Converse, Miller, and Stokes (1960) Converse (1964).

20. Delli Carpini and Keeter (1996).

21. Zaller's sensitivity to what surveys actually measure is captured well in the subtitle of an article co-authored with Feldman, "Answering Questions versus Revealing Preferences" (Zaller and Feldman 1992). In this regard, the understanding of what surveys measure is remarkably similar to Habermas's and Bourdieu's understanding, albeit from radically different normative presuppositions.

22. John Zaller (1992) comes the closest to a "paradigm statement" among contemporary elite accounts. For this reason, I focus on Zaller's particular account in this section, although the argument generalizes to other elite accounts as well. See Lee (2002, chap. 1).

23. This rendition on response instability is not solely due to Zaller, but jointly developed with Stanley Feldman. See Feldman (1989, 1991) and Zaller and Feldman (1992). A similar account is also developed in Chong (1996).

24. For an excellent discussion on the prospects for democratic deliberation in the face of response instability, see Kinder and Herzog (1993). Among other things, Kinder and Herzog resuscitate Dewey (1927) against both Converse (1964) and Lippmann (1922).

25. Although proponents of elite theories are wary of the potential for domination, they generally remain agnostic (e.g., Carmines and Stimson 1989), conclude that the elite influences and response instability pose no threat to democratic representation (Zaller 1992), or find inflections of collective rationality amid the apparent noise (Page and Shapiro 1992). Such positions often reflect theoretical priors rather than well-grounded empirical analysis, priors that are often grounded in the assumption that public opinion and survey data are equivalent. This is, of course, an oversimplification to which some noteworthy exceptions exist (e.g., Margolis and Mauser 1989; Lupia and McCubbins 1998; Jacobs and Shapiro 2000).

26. This possibility is also shown in the way elite domination is characterized. To continue using Zaller (1992, p. 313), elite domination is defined as "a situation in which *elites induce citizens to hold opinions that they would not hold if aware of the best available information and analysis.*" This definition is incomplete because it excludes some forms of elite domination. Zaller is primarily focused on the face of power describable in behavioral, pluralist terms, neglecting the kind of invisible, agenda-control face of power that Bachrach and Baratz (1962) describe, or the false consciousness that Lukes (1974) points out. Thus, the central point of elite domination for some—whether Gramscian hegemony or Haber-

masian manufactured publicity or Foucauldian power-knowledge—is not the completeness of information, but authenticity of interests.

27. See Gilens in this volume for examples of experimental survey work.

28. See Lee (2002) for citations.

29. Walton et. al. (1995) also note the importance of the racial composition of political scientists in transforming not only the amount of research into race but the analytic focus and substantive implications of such research (see also Barkan 1992; Harding 1993).

30. See Gurin, Hatchett, and Jackson (1989) and Tate (1993) for a description of the 1984 and 1988 NBES; see Dawson (2001) for a description of the 1993–94 NBPS. Smith (1987) notes two other surveys on the viewpoints of African Americans: the National Survey of Black Americans and the Three Generation Family Study. Smith also notes the over-samples of African Americans in the 1982 and 1987 General Social Surveys, but the knowledge of black mass opinion accessible in these surveys is limited to questions that are relevant to the full sample (i.e., including, and compared to, white Americans).

31. Support for such legislation is quite high: in the October–November poll, 75% of New Englanders, 79% of respondents from the Mid-Atlantic, and 57% of Southerners favored such a bill. The breakdown of respondents by race and region from available sources is limited. In most cases, African Americans are not polled in these early surveys.

32. In both cases, it is interesting to note a disjuncture between generally encouraging levels of support for racial egalitarianism but generally dismal levels of support for demonstrations for legislation favoring such principles. Of the 63% who had heard of "Freedom Riders," fully 64% disapproved of their activism; 57% of respondents from the same survey felt that the activism of blacks in the South was hurting their chances at integration; and of the 69% who had heard of plans for a March on Washington, 63% were unfavorable.

33. The following constitute the set of surveys and survey organizations counted: American Institute of Public Opinion (later the Gallup Poll), American National Elections Studies, Harris National Surveys, National Opinion Research Center, *New York Herald Tribune*, Opinion Research Corporation, Public Opinion Survey (conducted by AIPO), Quality of American Life Study (conducted by the Center for Political Studies), the Roper Organization (commercial polls and for *Fortune* magazine), the Survey Research Center at the University of Michigan, Survey Research Service (conducted by NORC), and Surveys of Consumer Attitudes and Behavior (conducted by the Center for Political Studies). The catalog of sources used to tabulate racial attitude items for figure 16.1 are cited in Lee (2002).

34. See Converse (1987) and Smith (1987). An important exception to this is the NORC's two pioneering studies of racial attitudes in 1942 and 1944. Converse also notes that the interpretation and publication of NORC's survey met resistance and that Southern Democratic outrage at the OWI pamphlet praising the endeavors of the black soldier (titled *Negroes and the War*) led in part to a cut in OWI allocations from the $8.9 million requisition to $2.7 million.

35. Data for the number of movement-initiated civil rights events over time are taken from McAdam (1982, p. 121). See also Burstein (1979).

36. See Lee (2002, Chap. 3) for more details on the time-series analysis.

37. See Keyssar (2000).

38. As Michael Dawson (1994, 2001) shows, for example, racial group identity and the sense of a collective fate strongly marks the political beliefs of African Americans.

39. This distinction is suggested by Rosenstone and Hansen's (1993) categorization of "personal" and "political" perspectives on political participation.

40. Thus, it is characterized as much by solidary incentives—social desirability, con-

formity, norms of cooperation, and the like—not to say no to someone's request for your time, attention, and honest viewpoints as it is by any incentives to act. One might also contend that significant purposive benefits accrue from something like contributing to the quest for greater knowledge, or that there are significant solidary rewards to seeing "your" poll's results in the newspaper.

41. The political salience of polls will, of course, vary with the kind of survey conducted, the reputation of the pollsters involved, how newsworthy the substantive findings are, and the like. Moreover, to the extent that electoral considerations dominate elite actors' political calculus, political salience should vary as a function of the constituency involved: a politically active public, an issue-centered public, a politically attentive public, the voting public, or the general public writ large. In addition, certain instances of political expression like riots and revolutions achieve political salience even without any direct electoral considerations to speak of (Price 1992; Fenno 1978).

42. That said, political actors can seldom afford to ignore such pressure mail.

43. Or, per Converse (1964), for that matter whether or not individuals hold intelligible beliefs and sentiments to begin with.

44. The term "issue public" itself can be traced before Converse at least as far back as Almond (1950). The notion of a pivotal activated segment of the mass public is also noted by Key (1961), Lippmann (1925), and others.

45. See, for example, Carmines and Stimson (1989), Page and Shapiro (1992), and Stimson (1991).

46. Letters can make no claims to surgically probe the sincere "attitudes" of the general public. We cannot infer that letters reflect true, underlying beliefs as expressed in the text of the letters per se, as the correspondents often write strategically. Rhetorically, strategic writers may choose metaphor, irony, hyperbole, even dissemblance in order to persuade, rather than sincerely translate thoughts and emotions into words. Opinion polls clearly hold a methodological advantage on this point, but there are ample grounds for skepticism as to whether surveys themselves can faithfully capture "true" attitudes or whether such a demanding notion as "attitudes" can even be sustained.

47. This proactive, freely formed characteristic is also what distinguishes letter writing from other possible measures of public opinion such as media content. The fact that the form and framing of letters is not screened or filtered is quite important, especially in a work that aims to challenge elite-driven theories of public opinion.

Part IV

CONCLUSION

17

The Value of Polls in Promoting Good Government and Democracy

HUMPHREY TAYLOR

Those who are critical of the influence of opinion polls on the political process in the United States might change their opinions if they considered the experience of countries where free, independent polls are rarely or never published. A recent United Nations Development Program (UNDP) report argues that bad government is the most important cause of poverty in developing countries. Most people's examples of bad government would include countries in which public opinion is not heard and has little influence and countries where unpopular governments "win" grossly unfair elections or steal them through fraudulent vote counting. Recent events in Latin America, the Caribbean, Asia, and Africa provide many examples of "emerging democracies" where opinion polls have let the voice of the people be heard and made it much harder for governments to steal elections. In these countries both preelection polls and exit polls are having a positive impact.

I recently returned from a visit to Haiti where I met with journalists, editors, business and community leaders, and four marketing and opinion research firms. My central thesis was that accurate and independent opinion polls make two important contributions to democracy and that this role is particularly important in emerging democracies—more so than in the United States, Canada, and in Western European countries with a strong democratic history and culture.

LETTING THE VOICE OF THE PEOPLE BE HEARD

The first important contribution of polls is to let the voice of the people be heard. In countries without polls (for example, in the Soviet Union before Gorbachev, or in China or North Korea today, or in Haiti until recently), there is really no way to know what the public thinks, feels, or believes about the government or about the issues and problems the government might address.

Opinion polls, while by no means infallible, are the only reasonably reliable way to measure public opinion, and only through the publication of polls can a society ensure that leaders and decision makers in government and the private sector know and understand what the public believes and wants.

Whereas governments and other leaders may or may not be helped to make better decisions by the availability of poll data, their having a good knowledge and understanding of public opinion is usually better for democracy than their not having it. Good information is better than misinformation.

Research that has shown that most people—including most political and business leaders—tend to discuss political and public policy issues with people who have opinions similar to their own (for example, in the United States Republicans talk more often to Republicans, and Democrats talk more often to Democrats). In the absence of polls, therefore, it is normal for most people, and most leaders, to be misinformed about public opinion and to believe that more people share their opinions than actually do so. During the 1999 impeachment process, many people in the minority who wanted to impeach President Clinton and remove him from office could not believe they were a minority, presumably because they did not believe the polls. Some, like Ariana Huffington, argued that we would be better off without polls.

The publication of polls in the media in countries where democracy is at risk often encourages the representatives of disadvantaged groups, of groups opposed to the government, and of groups without easy access to the media, to speak up for their interests. Polls therefore serve to balance the loud voices of special interests. Without polls, it is much easier for rich, powerful, and influential minorities to claim that they speak for the majority, when they do not.

MAKING IT HARDER TO STEAL ELECTIONS

The second major contribution of polls in new and emerging democracies is that they make it much harder for governments to steal elections. In dictatorships, whether communist, fascist, or military, it is common for dictators, or their "parties," to claim to have won almost 100% of the votes, and there is no way to determine how people actually voted. In many newly democratic nations, it is all too common for presidents and parties who were initially elected freely to prevent free elections from removing them from office. President Marcos of the Philippines and President "Papa Doc" Duvalier originally came to power in more or less free elections, as did many of the postcolonial leaders in Africa. From then on, they stayed in power by ensuring that—however unpopular they were—the official election results, which of course they controlled, showed that they had won.

In the Mexican presidential election of 1988, most people believed that Cuatemoc Cardenas defeated Carlos Salinas and that the official vote was fraudulent. Because there were no reliable preelection polls and no exit polls, there was no evidence to support a challenge to the official results.

Contrast this with the election of President Corazon Aquino in the Philippines, where the evidence of an independently funded exit poll (showing Aquino to be the clear winner) made it impossible for President Marcos to publish fraudulent election results and to claim that he had won. Nobody would have believed him.

Based on these experiences, I stressed to everyone I met in Haiti that free, independent, accurate opinion polls could make a substantial contribution to Haitian democracy. I urged the leaders whom I met to fund such polls. I urged the executives of the four marketing research firms in Haiti to persevere in their efforts to seek funding for more polls and to improve their methods. And I urged journalists to support opinion polls but also to be vigilant critics of the polls to ensure that they are not misled by fraudulent polls commissioned by those who seek to mislead or influence events rather than to inform the public.

CONDITIONS FOR FREE AND FAIR ELECTIONS

Many things are important to ensure free and fair elections. To the best of my knowledge, no countries fully meet all of these criteria; not the United States, where the system gives the people, companies, unions, and lobbying groups that fund political companies too much power; not Britain, where the overwhelming weight of the widely read national newspapers is almost always thrown strongly behind the Conservative Party; not in most new democracies, where, historically, the main radio and television channels are much more favorable to their governments than to the opposition parties; and not in France, Mexico, and many other countries, where governments have often used taxpayers' money to support their political campaigns.

However, there are obviously many countries where elections are *relatively fair and free*. It is a matter of degree. In some countries all, or most, of the following conditions for fair and free elections are met:

1. There is freedom of speech and freedom to run political campaigns without fear of harassment or intimidation.
2. There is freedom of the press, including print and broadcast media.
3. Opposition candidates and parties have reasonable access to the media, so that their campaigns can be heard.

4. The government does not control, dominate, or have unfair access to the media.
5. The media are not overwhelmingly tilted in favor of, or against, one candidate or party.
6. The constitution assures that there must be elections within some period of time.
7. It is easy for people to register to vote and to vote.
8. The votes are counted honestly and accurately.

Because there are few "new democracies" where all of these eight criteria are fully met, we need to add a ninth—that there be free, independent and reliable preelection polls and exit polls.

Whereas polls are, I believe, even more important in the "emerging democracies" to prevent governmental abuse of power, they are also crucial in the strongest and oldest democracies, and even governments even there have sometimes tried to manipulate or corrupt the opinion polls.

FEAR OF REPLYING HONESTLY TO POLLSTERS

My thesis, that free independent opinion polls strengthen democracy, is subject to one very important caveat. If those interviewed do not completely trust that the interviewers and the polling firms will protect the confidentiality of their replies, they may give answers that will not get them into trouble with the government.

Marty Gilens has described the Nicaraguan pen experiment initiated by Howard Schuman in which three different pens were used: a red-and-black pen with "Daniel Presidente" written on it, a white-and-blue pen with the letters UNO on it, and a red-and-white pen with no lettering. The "Sandinista pen" sample grossly overstated Daniel Ortega's lead, presumably because respondents believed the poll was being conducted by the ruling Sandinistas. The "UNO pen" sample produced a much larger vote for Chamono, the challenger, which closely matched the election results.

In the Mexican elections of 1994, Harris surveys using anonymous self-completion questionnaires inserted in a "secret ballot" box consistently produced fewer votes for the ruling PRI party when face-to-face interviews asked the same question, and the "secret ballot" results were more accurate.

THE MANIPULATION OF POLLS AND THE MEDIA

In the closing weeks of the 1972 U.S. presidential election, I was a witness to a bizarre attempt by the Nixon campaign to pressure the Harris Poll and influence our published numbers. Chuck Colson, one of the Nixon aides who later served time in prison because of Watergate, called to tell us that the peace negotiations with North Vietnam were at a very critical stage. The North Vietnamese, he assured us, were following the preelection polls very closely. If they saw Nixon's lead slipping, they would probably wait on the possibility of a McGovern victory. If Nixon maintained his big lead, there was a good chance North Vietnam would agree to peace terms before the election—he said. Tough pressure on a pollster. Fortunately, Nixon's lead did hold up, so we did not have to feel guilty for his failure to get a peace treaty before the election.

Unfortunately, attempts to manipulate and corrupt the polls are now a serious worldwide phenomenon. The spread of democracy and free elections around the world has brought a new generation of political leaders to power, who are learning a painful truth. What democracy giveth, it can also take away. Those who win by the ballot box can also lose by it. In short, freely elected governments are often defeated in the next free election. As a result, some of them are tempted to tilt the electoral playing field, to manipulate the press, to make elections less free and fair and, on occasion, to stuff ballot boxes and steal elections.

However, it is harder to steal elections if there are honest and accurate pre-election opinion polls and exit polls, which show someone else is well ahead. So governments, politicians, business interests, and even the media are using their power to manipulate and suppress the publication of honest polls.

To their surprise, many pollsters now find themselves in the unexpected role of defenders of civil rights and bastions of democracy. This puts honest pollsters at great risk from those who want to corrupt the political process. Those who play along with their governments get rich; those who do not may get badly hurt. The pressures they face make Nixon's attempts look like softball.

By way of example, consider Mexico. I have discussed these issues with several potential presidential candidates, senior members of the three main political parties, a senator, two governors, pollsters, and two very influential Mexican journalists. Most of them confirmed, and none of them denied, that all of the following had occurred in the last two years and are not uncommon:

- Many of the polls quoted in the media are wildly inaccurate, either because the poll numbers were changed or because these supposed polls were never actually conducted. Some poll clients are willing to pay handsomely for these phony polls.
- Honest, independent poll findings have been suppressed by the media because they would have displeased those with power.
- Polling firms that do not provide their clients with poll numbers they like (or are unwilling to change the real numbers to fictional ones) sometimes do not get paid.
- Contracts for multiple polls—for both the media and politicians—with honest polling firms have been cancelled because those with power did not

like the numbers from the early polls and the polling firms would not change them.

• Some courageous media executives have suffered because they published honest polls. This is not just hearsay; I have seen some of the cancelled contracts and the polls that were suppressed.

These attempts to mislead the public with phony polls and the censorship of honest ones are not unique to Mexico. I have heard similar reports from other countries in three continents. I have been told by Russian pollsters, for example, that it was almost impossible to have the media publish polls showing just how unpopular President Yeltsin was. Both the media and the pollsters were afraid of being punished by the government if they did that.

In fairness, I should note that similar abuses of poll and media manipulation have occurred in the United States and Europe. In a famous case in the 1970s, a French cabinet minister persuaded a leading French polling firm to reduce the number of people in a poll who were hostile to immigrants. In 1994, Frank Luntz, a well-known Republican consultant, persuaded the American media to run stories stating his polls found that 60% of the public supported every element of the Contract with America. Long after the election, it emerged that there were no such polls and Luntz was formally censured by the American Association of Public Opinion Research (AAPOR)—which has apparently had no impact on him or the use of his services by political candidates.

In Britain, in the early 1970s Labour leader Harold Wilson was guilty of a mean-spirited intervention that affected me personally. My firm, which I had recently sold to Louis Harris and Associates, had launched what I believe was the first regular poll jointly sponsored by a TV channel and a newspaper. (The CBS/ New York Times poll followed later.) Our ITN/Times (of London) poll was a great success. Both of our clients were delighted with it. But Harold Wilson was furious. How dare ITN, the news channel he trusted much more than the BBC, get into bed with the Times, then edited by William Rees-Mogg, whose editorials supported the (quite soon to follow) departure of Roy Jenkins and the "Gang of Four" from Labour?

So Wilson nobbled two ITN board members who persuaded the board to vote to end the Times/ITN Poll. As a result, a high quality, well-regarded—and truly independent—regular poll bit the dust.

After the 1972 election, President Nixon asked two of his top aides (Chuck Colson and Dwight Chapin) to "influence" the Gallup and Harris polls, particularly their data on Vietnam and Watergate. Fortunately, there is no evidence that Nixon succeeded: both polls showed the public swinging strongly against Nixon on both issues, and these polls may well have had some influence on critical congressional votes against Nixon, as well as the congressional hearing on Watergate.

EXAMPLES OF THE POSITIVE IMPACT OF POLLS

If that is the bleak side of the picture, there is plenty of good news about the positive impact of polls in strengthening democracy. In the last year, we have seen several examples of the important contribution that opinion polls can make to the democratic process.

In the presidential election in Senegal, the longtime president, Diouf, was shown by all of the several published preelection polls to be trailing the challenger, who is now President Wade. I have heard it argued that Diouf might well have stolen this election and declared himself reelected—as many people believe he did in previous elections—had there been no opinion polls.

In Zimbabwe, a country where political opposition is not good for your health, many people were astounded to learn that a recent opinion poll found that 56% of the public had such negative opinions of President Mugabe that they believed he should leave office right *now,* without waiting for another election. It was not this finding that was astounding; it was the fact that anyone dared to conduct this survey and publish the results. Certainly I was astonished, until I heard that the survey was conducted for, and released by, the South African–based Helen Sussman Foundation, which lies beyond the reach of Mugabe and his thugs, who have killed and beaten up his political opponents.

Peru and Venezuela are two other important examples of countries where polls have shown serious challenges to their authoritarian, if not dictatorial, presidents Fujimori and Chavez, respectively, from opponents who might otherwise have looked like no-hope candidates. Without the preelection and exit polls in Peru, Fujimori likely would have been declared the winner after the first round of voting.

The 2000 elections for the Yugoslav presidency may well be another example of polls helping to prevent election fraud. There were reports of several preelection polls showing President Milosevic well behind Vojislav Kostunica. Quite possibly, without these polls, Milosevic could have manipulated the vote count and declared himself the winner.

There is also better news from Mexico, where the 2000 elections were notably more free and more democratic than any previous elections there, and the polls that showed Fox ahead were a forecast of his victory. However, the preelection period also saw the publication of several polls showing the PRI candidate Labastida ahead; some political commentators believe that these were fraudulent polls financed and planted by the PRI. Since Fox's victory, Mexican pollsters have told me that they now feel completely free to publish their results without fear of pressure or intimidation.

For these reasons, the full and free right to conduct opinion surveys and publish the results—regardless of whether these annoy, embarrass, or irritate the political and business establishment—is one important measure of democracy. That is not to say that all poll results are beneficial to society. Polls provide information, just like economic data or political reporting. Polls have shown that the public sometimes supports draconian security measures that many people would consider serious violations of important human and civil rights. Polling data, like much other information, are value-neutral and can be used to achieve desirable or undesirable objectives. But, all things considered, good poll data, good science, and accurate news reporting are better than no data or bad data, bad science, or false news.

The relevance to the United States of these experiences of polling in other countries is that the publication of free, independent opinion polls is one of the protections we enjoy, which make the chances of abuse of power less likely.

BANNING OR PREVENTING THE PUBLICATION OF POLLS

Nevertheless, some thirty countries that call themselves democracies have banned the publication of election surveys for one, two, or more weeks prior to elections, on the grounds that they have a malign influence on voting behavior. These laws have been triggered by politicians' dislike of (some) poll results and their mistaken belief in a mindless bandwagon effect—not by any serious review of the real effects of polls.

The arguments against banning the publication of opinion polls include the following:

- Bans violate the freedom of the press (and are therefore unconstitutional in the United States and other countries where press freedom enjoys constitutional or legal protection).
- Bans prevent the public from having access to the best (albeit imperfect) information about public opinion, without inhibiting the freedom of governments, politicians, and the media to provide dishonest and misleading reports of public opinion.
- Bans prevent the voice of the public from being heard.
- Bans make it much easier for corrupt and dictatorial governments to steal elections and sustain very unpopular policies.

However, the role of opinion polls in promoting democracy and more honest election is not widely perceived or accepted. There are plenty of sincere critics of the polls and of politicians who, it is argued, pander to the polls. For example, Arianna Huffington in her new book, *How to Overthrow the Government*, attacks the polls and urges her readers to "say no to pollsters" by hanging up on them.

I once heard George Meany, the legendary union leader and former plumber, ask an audience of lawyers to consider whether they would prefer life in "a city without plumbers or a city without lawyers." A no-brainer! At first blush a city, or a country, without pollsters and polls may sound quite appealing. But wait a minute. Consider the evidence:

- If public opinion polls are dangerous to democracy, why do dictators, whether right wing or left wing, prevent the publication of polls in their countries?
- If the publication of free, independent, reliable polls is a problem, why do so many governments try, often successfully, to so intimidate the press, and the pollsters, that they are afraid to publish them?
- If large numbers of people with a particular point of view (Ms. Huffington's perhaps) were to follow her advice, their opinions would be under-represented in the polls. Is that what they want?

Unfortunately, Ms. Huffington's arguments may be used as justification by the thirty quasi-democratic governments around the world that have already banned the publication of polls for days or weeks before elections and others that would like to do so. Never mind that this is a form of press censorship. The effects of such bans have clearly been undemocratic. The public has been deprived of the most reliable and independent information on public opinion and could more easily be misled by the political, military, or business elites who commissioned and read their own private polls.

PANDERING TO THE POLLS AND PUBLIC OPINION

Many people in addition to Arianna Huffington have argued that politicians pander to the polls. But with or without polls, politicians have always paid close attention to public opinion, as some of the greatest presidents, from Lincoln to FDR, most certainly did. The silver-tongued populist Cleon pandered to Athenian public opinion in the age of Pericles 2,400 years before the first polls. But without polls, the chance that political leaders would misread public opinion is much greater. Is that really an improvement?

To argue in favor of the publication of the most accurate (albeit imperfect) and independent measures of public opinion is not to suggest that the public is always right, or that politicians should pander to public opinion to get elected. Public opinion data, like news or science, are essentially value-neutral. As a pollster, I often disagree with the views of the majority as published in our Harris Polls, but we publish them anyway.

Of course, Ms. Huffington is right to deplore the misuse of polls by some politicians and their consultants. President Clinton's decision, based allegedly on a poll commissioned by Dick Morris, to lie to the nation, his cabinet, and his wife about his relationship with Monica Lewinsky is indefensible. But do we believe he would have made the right decision, to tell the truth, had there been no poll? Furthermore, Morris's advice suggests a naivete, even stupidity, as to how to design and analyze such a poll. Clinton might not have been impeached had he ignored Morris's advice and told the truth. But with Dick Morris and Frank Luntz on our team, we pollsters obviously have an image problem.

Those who, like Ms. Huffington, attack the polls are, whether they realize it or not, arguing against the influence of public opinion. Perhaps they believe we should go back to a restricted franchise when only those citizens who were "qualified" to vote were allowed to do so.

Without public opinion polls, the deep pockets that finance, influence, and (Ms. Huffington, and many others, believe) corrupt our politicians and our government would have more, not less, power. The polls are often a strong counterbalance to the loud voices of the special interests whose political goals are different from those of the general public. Public opinion would sometimes not be heard if there were no polls.

As former British Prime Minister James Callaghan once wrote, "If you cannot trust the public with polls, you should not trust them with the vote." Knowledge of public opinion, whether well used or misused, is far better than ignorance, and those who attack, censor, corrupt, or intimidate the polls are the enemies of democracy.

18

The Semi-Sovereign Public

BENJAMIN I. PAGE

More than forty years ago, E. E. Schattschneider—the great advocate of responsible parties and governmental responsiveness to ordinary citizens—wrote about
the "semi-sovereign people" of the United States. He maintained that the public
can exert substantial control over government policymaking, particularly when
issues are made highly visible through conflict and when citizens are mobilized
by competitive, unified, programmatic political parties. Still, Schattschneider insisted that "public opinion about specific issues does not necessarily govern the
course of public policy." Instead, he argued, a "pressure system" dominated by
well-organized business groups often gets its way, particularly when the people
are not looking (1960, p. 133 and chaps. 2 and 8.)

I believe that the research reported in this volume largely confirms, or is
consistent with, Schattschneider's view of American politics. There is substantial
evidence of government responsiveness to public opinion, especially on high-
salience issues. But the evidence also indicates that there is considerable room for
interest groups, party activists, policymakers, and others to prevail against the
public on many issues. Often anti-popular policy decisions can be kept out of
the public spotlight or cleverly packaged to avoid offense. Sometimes public opinion can be manipulated. Moreover, the extent of responsiveness to public opinion
varies by type of issue and over time. Schattschneider's picture of a quite imperfect
democracy appears to be correct.

As we acknowledged in the introduction, we cannot hope in this book to

give definitive answers to all questions about how often and under what circumstances U.S. government policies respond to public opinion. To a rather surprising
extent, however, the different sorts of evidence presented in this volume—which
at times seem to be in sharp conflict—can actually be reconciled to form a single,
reasonably coherent view of public opinion and policy. Let me outline such a
view, bearing in mind that I will choose among findings and reinterpret some in
ways the authors may not approve.

HOW MUCH RESPONSIVENESS?

Statistical studies that explore connections between policies and poll-measured
public opinion have invariably found substantial covariation between opinion and
policy. This has been true for quite a variety of research designs. Assessments of
"consistency" between majority opinion and existing policies on various issues,
correlation or regression coefficients between policies and central tendencies of
opinion across the American states, measures of association between changes over
time in opinion and changes in policy have all indicated strong relationships.

It is important to recognize, however, that all such studies (including those
in which I have participated) have very likely overestimated the extent of responsiveness. All have been prey to varying combinations of sampling and aggregation
biases and specification errors, especially specification errors involving the omission of relevant variables and relationships that might have revealed the opinion-
policy relationship to be partly spurious or reciprocal. The very design of these
studies has ruled out, a priori, certain processes that are likely to occur in the
real world. Nearly all studies have excluded from the analysis a number of factors,
such as world events, mass media stories, and interest group lobbying and propaganda, that may directly affect both opinion and policy and create a spurious
relationship between the two. A number of studies have also excluded (or inad-
equately modeled) processes by which policymakers or policy itself may recip-
rocally affect opinion—"preparing" the public for new policies or selling those
policies after they are enacted—so that one-way estimates of the effects of opinion
on policy are exaggerated. Some have overaggregated the independent and dependent variables, producing excessively strong relationships.

The problems are most obvious in the earliest studies, which looked only at
bivariate relationships between opinion and policy (omitting all other variables)
and posited a purely one-way causal relationship, with opinion influencing policy
but not vice versa. Both Monroe (1979) and Page and Shapiro (1983), for example,
offer evidence that seems to support a "two-thirds rule": that government policy
tends to correspond with majority opinion, or to move in the same direction as
opinion changes, on about two-thirds (63% or 66%) of sampled issues. (Of
course, the finding that policy moves in the *opposite* direction from public opinion
about one third of the time might be taken as a sobering limit on public influence.) But neither study included any independent variables other than public

opinion in the analysis, so neither could test for possible spuriousness; and neither empirically ruled out a reciprocal relationship in which policy affected opinion. (Page and Shapiro's [1983, pp. 185–86] somewhat strained effort in that direction cast doubt on reciprocal influence in only about half the subset of cases considered.)[1]

Erikson, Wright, and McIver (1993), with their clever use of an across-state design, produced even heftier estimates of the effects of opinion upon policy. They found an estimated "true" correlation between state "opinion liberalism" and "composite policy liberalism" of fully 0.91 (p. 80), which remained nearly as high when controlling for demographic factors (wealth, urbanism, and education level; p. 85.) Beyond those demographics, however, they did not include independent variables that might produce spurious relationships between opinion and policy. State political parties, for example, were treated as part of the processes by which opinion affects policy, but not as possible shapers of opinion itself. The authors tried to rule out possible reciprocal influences of policy upon opinion through an instrumental-variables approach that yielded a big opinion/policy coefficient of 0.86 (p. 89), but the specification of exogenous variables was questionable. (The crucial "exogenous" factor of religious fundamentalism, for example, probably influences policy directly through organized lobbying, not just indirectly through public opinion—as posited—thus inflating the estimate of public opinion's impact; see pp. 67, 88.) Moreover, any gains in accuracy due to improved measurement and model specification may have been offset by losses due to excessive aggregation in both the independent and the dependent variables. All issues were compressed into liberal-conservative scales that muffled variations in responsiveness—and may have concealed substantial nonresponsiveness—across specific issues. Aggregation over time also permitted such processes as selective political migration to inflate the apparent effect of opinion on policy. That is, people may tend to move to states whose policies they like, rather than the states responding to their residents' policy preferences.

The tremendously influential time-series analysis of liberal-conservative trends in national domestic opinion and policy by Stimson, MacKuen, and Erikson (1995) made important methodological advances, but still very likely overstated the impact of public opinion on policy. It gained some leverage on the causal direction of the opinion/policy relationship by using a time-lagged independent variable ("domestic policy mood"), thus ruling out any reciprocal impact by policy itself (but not earlier action by policymakers or others) upon the opinion postulated to affect it. And partisan-composition-of-government independent variables were included in the analysis, which indicated that the party balance in Congress and the presidency—independently of public opinion, and itself only moderately affected by the public's policy preferences—has strong effects upon policy (a coefficient of .704 in the "global" regression, p. 556.) This constituted a substantial concession to critics of a "public opinion drives everything" view, because party-in-government effects do not merely reflect the policy preferences of each party's citizen identifiers; they undoubtedly also reflect the preferences (often distinctly contrary to public opinion) of party activists and money givers. Within the time-series model itself (though unexamined by the authors), therefore, exists the possibility of substantial elite influence upon policy of the sort discussed by William Domhoff in chapter 6, insofar as it operates through differences between the political parties (see Ferguson and Rogers, 1986; Ferguson, 1995).

There is room within the framework for a number of factors and processes unrelated to public opinion that may influence policymaking. But such factors were not explicitly modeled. They were not, in most cases, even mentioned. As a result, the authors ran the risk of being unfairly criticized for proposing precisely what they reject (in chapter 4 of this volume): a univariate or mono-causal model of politics.

The chief impression given by Stimson, MacKuen, and Erikson (1995)—and carried through in their later work reported here—is one of enormous, virtually unopposed influence of public opinion upon public policy. In their full global analysis, the coefficient for indirect (through parties-in-government) plus direct impact of "domestic policy mood" upon policy was estimated as a remarkable 1.094. That is, they found "about a one-to-one translation" of preferences into policy. The authors offered a striking image of politicians stampeding like antelopes at the slightest noise from public opinion (pp. 556–57, 559.) This, I believe, is seriously misleading.

A major problem, the same problem that has plagued nearly all quantitative research in this area, is the omission of independent variables that may affect both opinion and policy and create a spurious relationship between the two. Stimson et al. did not allow, for example, for the possibility of influence by corporations, interest groups, and elites upon both opinion and policy, working outside of (or through) *both* political parties. Yet William Domhoff, in chapter 7, offers several compelling historical examples of precisely that kind of influence, and he outlines plausible mechanisms (including an "opinion-shaping process" in which foundations, think tanks, and policy discussion groups propagate elite views through a large dissemination network) that could bring it about. Other scholars (e.g., Ferguson 1995, chaps. 1 and 2) have uncovered strong historical evidence of similar phenomena.[2]

For example, the apparent congruence of conservative Reagan-era policy changes with a rightward shift in public opinion helped drive Stimson et al.'s time-series statistical findings. But the causal connection is questionable. Most of American business (including firms that had formerly backed the Democrats) made a sharp right turn in the middle and late 1970s, coming to oppose government taxes, regulation, and social spending (Ferguson and Rogers 1986). This was followed by—and may have influenced—a shift in public opinion that is discernable but very faint: considerably weaker than is implied by the big change in measured "domestic policy mood." There was very little decline in Americans' overwhelming support for economic regulation and for government spending on Social Security, education, medical care, and the like (Page and Shapiro 1992, chap. 4). It seems at least possible that the subsequent sharp Reagan-era policy changes were caused chiefly by business lobbying, with public opinion acting only as a supplementary transmission belt or as an irrelevant sideshow. That is, the opinion-policy relationship may have been partly or wholly spurious.

Readers can miss the potential importance of omitted variables because Stimson et al.'s time-series model seems to account so well for everything it tries to explain. But that explanatory power, and the big part played in it by public opinion, depends heavily upon extreme statistical aggregation that greatly restricts the domain and range of variation in the independent and dependent variables. In effect, an extremely selected, refined, and crunched opinion variable does an excellent job of accounting for an extremely selected, refined, and crunched policy variable. This reveals an interesting and important tendency but does not necessarily tell us much about the whole big, messy realm of public opinion and policymaking in the United States.

The analysis begins by entirely ignoring many policy issues that do not fit onto a single, liberal-conservative dimension. All foreign policy is thrown overboard, and certain inconvenient domestic issues (e.g., crime and abortion) are excluded as well. Then public opinion is measured in a highly aggregated way. The recursive algorithm for computing over-time "domestic policy mood" from the selected public opinion items (as described in Stimson 1999, chap. 3 and appendices 1 and 3) in effect standardizes each item and extracts a weighted-average central tendency of over-time movement from them, weighting each item by its contribution to the "mood" construct. The result is then subjected to "exponential smoothing." The selection, weighting, averaging, and smoothing of opinion items guarantees that only a rarified summary of broad liberal-conservative tendencies will be preserved in the measure. All public opinion that moves differently from the general tendency—that moves faster, slower, crosswise, or idiosyncratically—will be ignored. Such disparate movements of public preferences on different issues are quite common and are often meaningful, reflecting issue-specific social and demographic changes, new information, political events, and the like (Page and Shapiro 1992). But we will not learn anything from this analysis about whether or not policy responds to them.

One sign of just how thoroughly compressed and averaged the public opinion "mood" measure is: less than a quarter (24% or 21%) of the "real variance" over time in standardized liberal-conservative indices from each selected domestic opinion item can be accounted for by some forty time-period dummy variables, which one might expect to pick up almost every bit of the variation due to overall shifts in mood (Stimson 1999, pp. 57, 59.) In other words, more than 75% of the over-time variance of public opinion, even in the liberal-conservative essence of the selected domestic items, can apparently not be accounted for by a general mood.[3]

On the policy side, too, the many policies that may move in contrary ways, or idiosyncratically, or just *more sharply* in a liberal or conservative direction than the average, are ignored or scrunched into a single, liberal-conservative "policy" or "policy activity" trend line. Little wonder that public opinion and policy, so measured, move in close harmony with each other.

There is yet another important, though subtle and often-ignored, way in which the Stimson et al. time-series analysis (and, indeed, nearly all quantitative work on this subject) restricts the phenomena to be accounted for. By focusing on *covariation* (over time or cross-sectionally) between opinion and policy, it neglects the question of whether or not the *level* of policy corresponds to what the public wants on the average issue or at a given moment in time.[4] For example, if corporations' lobbying led to a steady conservative tilt in policy by a uniform amount every year, this effect would not generally show up at all in regressions or other studies based on covariation. A perfect correlation of 1.00 between opinion and policy could conceal the fact that policy was always (by a constant amount) more conservative than the average American wanted. (That such a situation is not totally implausible is suggested by the frequent General Social Survey findings that many more Americans favor spending "more" than favor spending "less" than the current amount on education, medical care, and other domestic programs.)[5] This, along with overaggregation and omitted variables, means that considerable room is left outside, as well as inside, the model for anti-popular influences upon policy of the sorts that power elite theorists like Domhoff, "biased pluralism" theorists like Schattschneider, and others propose.

The new statistical and computer simulation work that Robert Erikson, Michael MacKuen, and James Stimson report in chapter 2 and in their recent (2001) book does not alter the model or the core statistical findings of their 1995 paper in any major way. It does extend and modify them in certain important respects: exploring negative feedback effects of policy on public opinion; bringing in trends in unemployment and inflation; distinguishing the old policy measures—rechristened "Policy Activity"—from "Policies" or fundamental laws; and taking explicit account of how Constitutional provisions (especially the separation of powers) complicate the policy-making process. But its main contribution is to work out the complex ways in which the pieces of their model interact and to show how disturbances to one variable can cascade through the whole system.

Certain modifications in their model take better account of real-world limits to the responsiveness of policy to public opinion. "Policy," as opposed to "Policy Activity," is found to react only slowly, incrementally, cumulatively to the public's preferences. Policy changes are slowed by the separation of powers and multiple veto points (modeled by multiplicative interactions among branches of government and a partial adjustment, "error correction" process), so that there can be about an eight-year delay in fully translating public preferences into policy. The importance of party control of government (and implicitly, therefore, the importance of party activists, investors, and money givers) is shown to be profound, and parties are shown to oversteer, regularly pushing their agendas further than the public wants. Small electoral changes that tip the balance of party control in Congress or the presidency can have sharp, knife-edged impacts upon policy activity. (This aspect of the model reminds one of the startling changes in policy activity, some of them quite contrary to the public's preferences, that followed the narrow Republican victories in election year 2000.) There is no talk here of a 1.094, "one-to-one" translation of public preferences into policy, nor of easily spooked politician-antelopes.[6]

Yet the overall impression is once again of public opinion as an extremely powerful force on policy. The modest-appearing finding that just over a third (0.36) of each year's "Policy Mood" change shows up in a global measure of next year's "Policy Activity" understates the estimated immediate impact of public opinion on some of the separate institutions of government. And we can see that the estimated total, direct plus indirect (through elections and party-in-government) effects of public opinion are larger still. Perhaps most striking of all is the estimate, within the error-correction model, that unmeasured public "Preferences" correlate at a solid .83 level with "Policy" (accumulated laws) eight years later. Similarly, the measured biennial "Policy Mood" correlates fully .89 with Policy changes over the subsequent eight years. The picture here is of a ship of state that oversteers a bit to the left and then oversteers a bit to the right, but in the long run holds true to exactly the course that the public wants.[7]

Once again, however, the model almost certainly overestimates the impact upon policy of public opinion, for the same old reasons. It still omits major factors—such as many sorts of external events, the mass media, politicians' talk, and corporate and interest group activity—that may affect both opinion and policy (opinion first) and produce a partly spurious relationship between the two. The analysis still rests on the highly aggregated, liberal-conservative measures of opinion and policy, ignoring—and excluding from the variance to be explained or do the explaining—movements in policy or opinion that cut across, contradict, shrink, or magnify a general liberal-conservative trend. The results are important and intriguing; they indicate a general tendency for summary liberal-conservative opinion "moods" and certain summary features of domestic policy to move together. But this does not tell us to what extent the whole set of different public policies is actually influenced by the public's preferences on each of those policies.

Let me comment briefly on Erikson, MacKuen, and Stimson's chapter 4 response to Jacobs and Shapiro. In that response, they seem largely to disregard the possibility that opinion-policy relationships are *spurious*: that public opinion has no real causal impact on policy, but only appears to do so because some third factor—perhaps interest groups, or politicians with their own agendas—independently affects both opinion and policy. (Indeed, they do not mention interest groups at all.)

Instead, Erikson, MacKuen, and Stimson focus on the possibility that politicians or other elites may influence public opinion, which itself then affects policy: that is, the possibility that public opinion acts as an *intervening variable* between some third factor and policy. They correctly point out that in such a case, public opinion would still have an important causal status as the proximate cause of policy change. (They suggest that politicians or others would bother influencing public opinion only if opinion had that sort of causal force, but this confuses actual with potential public influence. It neglects the possibility of spuriousness, in which policy shapers might defuse public opposition to their plans before it had any actual effect, or in which they might affect opinion only incidentally or even accidentally.) Their use of the appealing term "educate" to characterize such cases, however, seems to rule out the possibility of systematic misinformation or deception, which would not alter the causal picture (public opinion as an intervening variable) but might drastically change our normative reaction. Presumably, we would not want to celebrate as democratic a process in which elites grossly deceived the public and then bowed to the god of public opinion. Terms like "crafted talk" and the "deception" or "manipulation" of opinion not only address causal structure but also have normative connotations (particularly concerning the truth or falsehood of persuasive information) that Erikson, MacKuen, and Stimson do not address in chapter 4.

How Big Are the Biases in Quantitative Studies?

It is easy enough to point out that the quantitative estimates of public opinion's effect on policy are almost certainly biased upward. But it is much harder to figure out precisely how big the biases are.

In order to be more sure about how responsive policy is to public opinion, we will need more studies that take account of all the key variables, including the activities of interest groups and opinion shapers, and that allow for public opinion to be endogenous, in a variety of ways, to the policymaking process. It would be unrealistic to hope for a single, definitive coefficient summarizing opinion's impact, both because that impact is likely (in the real world) to vary markedly across issues, time, and other circumstances, and because each feasible type of research design suffers from inherent weaknesses that are bound to render all results less than definitive. Cross-sectional, multiple-issue studies face the daunting challenge of finding truly exogenous variables, in order to identify reciprocal effects among many potentially endogenous variables. Time-series studies must either be fragmented by issue or must overaggregate issues and lose the ability to analyze the effects of issue-specific variables and processes. Yet issue-specific case studies (unless and until many such studies cumulate) inevitably raise questions about generalizability. Quantitative studies of all sorts risk neglecting subtleties and factors that are hard to measure, including actors' private intentions, secret communications and agreements, under-the-table money, and the like, which may (or may not) play significant parts in policymaking.

Moreover, one fundamental type of sampling bias subtly, and almost inescapably, affects nearly all studies of opinion-policy links. We can study the impact of public opinion only to the extent that public opinion is measured. But opinion is measured—at least polls and surveys are conducted—only with respect to a relatively small and rather vaguely formulated subset of policy alternatives that pollsters and their clients are interested in investigating. This usually excludes any policy alternatives not currently "on the agenda" among policymakers (see chap.

16), and it excludes anything very detailed or obscure. To restrict in this way the range of policy that is studied, to consider only general tendencies of opinion on relatively high-salience issues, almost certainly leads to overestimates of the impact of public opinion on the whole range of actually existing policy choices.[8] Detailed examinations of policymaking can alert us to this problem by revealing the wide range of policy alternatives about which measured public opinion has nothing to say. But this invites the opposite error, of assuming that public opinion has no impact (by anticipated reactions, for example) when convenient measures of opinion do not exist.

Thus, we should continue to embrace methodological pluralism of the sort represented in this volume. We will need to pursue a variety of methods (definitely including observational and historical/archival as well as quantitative methods), each with significant strengths and significant weaknesses.

Still, even the presently existing, incomplete, quite imperfect research can begin to give us some idea of the extent of biases in the quantitative estimates of public opinion's impact. The trick is to pay serious attention to case studies, limited to one or a few policy issues, that include additional variables and/or that closely examine the details of the policymaking process.

Certain quantitative studies that limit their attention to a single policy issue over time have included independent variables in addition to public opinion. They generally find that adding the new variables lowers estimates of public opinion's impact. Hartley and Russett (1992), for example, found that from 1965 to 1990 the public's judgment that "too much" or "too little" was being spent on defense had a statistically significant but modest effect (a standardized coefficient of .261) upon subsequent annual changes in U.S. military spending. Soviet spending, lagged two and three years, had considerably more impact (coefficients of .357 and .503, p. 910).[9] If the study had included such additional factors as corporate lobbying, opinion shaping and Reagan policy influencing by the Committee on the Present Danger, and media hype over the Iranian "hostage crisis," it might have found a still more limited effect of public opinion upon the main policy variation in the data (the Reagan-era spike in spending).

The inclusion of analogous opinion-related variables that may affect other kinds of policymaking (unemployment rates, inflation rates, crime statistics, poverty levels, etc.) generally lowers estimates of opinion's impact by comparable amounts, even when indirect policy effects of those factors, through their impact on public opinion, are (as is proper) attributed to opinion.

Also helpful are detailed, "inside the black box" case studies of the policymaking process that consider public opinion along with other influences upon particular realms of policy. Such studies generally demonstrate that there is no instantaneous, knee-jerk responsiveness of policy to opinion. Far from it. Even though these studies, too, may suffer from sampling bias (they usually concern issues big and visible enough to interest researchers and readers, where public opinion is presumably at its strongest), they generally reveal messy, start-and-stop, incomplete effects of public opinion. Moreover, some of them provide important evidence of spurious opinion-policy relationships due to outside factors, including manipulation of public opinion (and independent influence on policy) by presidents and other policymakers.

Paul Burstein, for example, looking at some sixty years of policymaking on equal employment opportunities for minorities and women (see chap. 5), found that congressional action and inaction on major legislation has generally been quite consistent with public opinion, even when salience has been relatively low. On only one of ten major decisions (i.e., not ending affirmative action) did Congress clearly go against the public's preferences. Yet plainly many years passed in which opinion changes were not responded to, and countless small policy changes doubtless occurred without regard to public opinion.

More closely examining a single important piece of legislation, R. Kent Weaver (chap. 6) found that high-salience public disgust with the old AFDC program propelled action on some sort of welfare "reform," and that certain provisions of the 1996 legislation (e.g., work and training requirements; increased funding for child care) did indeed reflect the public's preferences. But other provisions (e.g., "hard" time limits without work guarantees) did not. Those who controlled the legislative agenda, namely, congressional Republicans, had considerable leeway under the rubric of "reform" to enact provisions without public support.

Again scrutinizing a single important legislative issue, chapter 8, written by Fay Cook, Jason Barabas, and me, indicates that accurately measured public opinion was certainly not a consciously articulated preoccupation among legislators, presidents, and experts as they discussed Social Security reform. To be sure, silence about public opinion could conceal quiet acquiescence to it, but the frequent misleading or downright erroneous references to poll results tend to cast doubt on this possibility.

More broadly, Steven Kull and Clay Ramsay, in chapter 10, summarize substantial evidence that many members of the foreign policy elite systematically misperceive public opinion about foreign policy. Many of the surveyed elites (including members of Congress) were quite convinced that "the American people"—or at least their own constituents—held isolationist opinions on foreign policy that they simply did not hold, including alleged opposition to the United Nations and aversion to peacekeeping operations. National survey evidence to the contrary seemed to cut little ice; even data from surveys of their own districts were sometimes dismissed out of hand. We need to know more about exactly why officials (especially elected officials) could be so out of touch with the citizens they are supposed to serve. One factor, no doubt (pointed out by Kull and Ramsay), is mythology about the supposed representativeness of Congress, the media, and interest groups as surrogates for public opinion. Further factors may include elites' reliance on "vocal publics" with quite unrepresentative views; their insulation from electoral punishment due to the relatively low salience of foreign policy issues; their location in safe, one-party seats; their need to please activists and voters in their party primaries; and the highly restricted turnout in congressional elections.

Particularly useful is the work by Lawrence Jacobs and Robert Shapiro (chap. 3), which reports on a detailed inside look at how the Clinton administration both reacted to and used or manipulated public opinion on health care reform. As in the welfare case, public discontent with the existing system pushed for *some* sort of change. But the administration did not simply respond to specific policy preferences of the public; instead, it created its own managed-competition scheme and used "crafted talk" to try (with limited success) to sell it to the public. Jacobs and Shapiro's detailed interview and archival evidence on administration efforts to manipulate public opinion raises a serious challenge to other scholars—many of whom have not allowed for such a possibility—to investigate whether and to what extent it occurs in other policy areas.

The review by Shapiro and Jacobs (chap. 10) of many foreign policy decisions and of the growing White House "public opinion apparatus" suggests that policy makers' efforts to manipulate public opinion—and to evade responsiveness to opinion—may be particularly frequent in foreign policy. And such efforts may have increased in recent years (see also Nacos, Shapiro, and Isernia, 2000.)

Qualitative case studies cannot, of course, assign precise numbers to the extent of upward bias in the multiple-issue, quantitative studies' estimates of opinion's impact on policy. But multi-issue quantitative studies themselves can begin to tell us something about the magnitude of bias from one particular source: the inevitable focus on the rather high-salience issues for which survey data are available. Within certain multi-issue studies, it is possible (while holding research methods and measurement techniques constant) to compare the strength of opinion-policy congruence on higher-salience issues with that on lower-salience issues.

Page and Shapiro (1983), for example, found congruent movement of policy and opinion on 73% of fifty-five issues about which opinion was highly salient ("don't know" responses were very infrequent), but only 56% of twenty-five issues of much lower salience. (Medium-low- and medium-high-salience issues were 61% and 70% congruent, respectively; p. 181.) That is, on the lowest-salience issues studied, policy actually moved in the *opposite* direction to public opinion close to half (44%) of the time. This suggests that the level of opinion-policy congruence in a hypothetical universe of "all" policy issues, including the even-lower-salience matters not subject to opinion surveys, would be quite low, well below Page and Shapiro's 66% "two-thirds rule."[10]

All in all, the research to date seems to me quite consistent with the view that the U.S. public is, at best, "semi-sovereign."

UNDER WHAT CIRCUMSTANCES?

When, and under what circumstances, does policy tend to respond more closely or less closely to public opinion? How and why does this come about? Research reported in this volume and elsewhere offers some insights into these questions.

Is there, for example, more responsiveness to public opinion on domestic issues than on foreign policy issues, which may be dominated by the president and executive branch? The evidence to date seems inconclusive. Page and Shapiro (1983, p. 182) found that policy moved in harmony with opinion slightly more often on the domestic issues than on the foreign policy issues they studied: 70% versus 62% congruence. But the difference was not statistically significant. And Monroe (1979, 1998) suggests just the opposite. Monroe found nondefense foreign policy to be consistent with public opinion on 84% and 67% of the issues in his two data sets, a substantially higher level of consistency than the averages for all issues of 63% and 55%, respectively (1998).

As we continue to explore foreign/domestic differences, we need to be alert to the possibility (highlighted by the work on presidential uses of public opinion that Shapiro and Jacobs report in chapter 10) that policymakers may have more success in the foreign than the domestic realm at influencing—educating or manipulating—public opinion to harmonize with intended or existing policies. Presidents and other officials have substantial information control and have been known to lie to the public during crises. If this is often the case, multi-issue studies like those I have mentioned may overstate their estimates of foreign policy responsiveness more than they overestimate domestic responsiveness, thereby distorting comparisons between the two.

Certain studies suggest, on the basis of rather large sets of issues, that responsiveness may also vary systematically across other policy domains. Particularly striking is Monroe's (1998) finding of extremely low levels of consistency—only 17% in the 1981–93 period—between public opinion and policy on issues of political reform.[11] The U.S. political system has proven highly resistant to such proposals as moving to popular (rather than electoral college) selection of presidents, easing registration and voting procedures, reducing the role of private money in elections, and the like that would increase the power of ordinary citizens in politics.

Also suggestive is Monroe's (1998) finding of slightly below-average consistency in recent years between opinion and policy on social welfare and economic/labor issues. This hints at support for William Domhoff's argument in chapter 7 that economic and political elites take the trouble to mold or defy public opinion mainly on issues of the greatest importance to themselves, presumably including major matters of taxation, spending, and economic regulation. But these data offer no more than a hint. Future research should test this proposition by systematic analysis of separate samples of issues that do and do not meet clearly specified criteria signifying high importance to elites. Such studies could proceed by quantitative or case-study methods (ideally both) but would have to encompass explicitly the possibilities of spuriousness and reciprocal influence often ignored by researchers yet central to the elite-influence argument.

The best-established finding about differences in responsiveness across types of issues probably concerns issue salience. As noted, Page and Shapiro's (1983) evidence indicates that policy tends to be much more in harmony with public opinion on issues of high salience than low. (Paul Burstein's interesting finding in chapter 5 of high consistency between opinion and policy even on relatively lower-salience equal opportunity cases does not really refute this tendency, since his lower-salience cases are still rather salient in absolute terms: all involve central provisions of major legislation.) This is very much in accord with E. E. Schattschneider's views concerning the "scope of conflict." When conflict is intense and widespread, when an issue is highly visible, when ordinary citizens are paying attention, citizens are more likely to prevail in policymaking. When politics is quiet, obscure, and out of sight, on the other hand, organized interests (especially corporate interests) are more likely to get their way (Schattschneider 1960, chaps. 1 and 2).

One methodological caveat: it is conceivable that the high-salience/low-salience contrasts in opinion-policy congruence may be an artifact of a tendency for opinion manipulation—rather than genuine policy responsiveness to public opinion—to be greater when the public is more fully engaged. Perhaps elites work harder to bring public opinion into line with what they want when the issues are crucial and the public's inclinations seem threatening. This possibility is less worrisome than the analogous problem with foreign/domestic policy contrasts, however, because foreign policy—in contrast to many high-salience domestic issues—regularly involves conditions especially conducive to manipulating public opinion. Foreign policy issues are often obscure, distant from everyday life, and the executive often enjoys a high degree of information control as well as substantial bipartisan deference from other elites. Still, we need to pin down high-versus low-salience distinctions using research techniques that better take account of possibly spurious or reciprocal relationships between opinion and policy.

What about differences in responsiveness to public opinion by different political institutions? Page and Shapiro (1983, p. 183) expressed surprise at finding higher levels of congruence with public opinion on state than on national policies. But their study may have magnified the extent of state responsiveness, as the state issues on which they had data were mostly important, nationally polled social issues (capital punishment, divorce, abortion) involving large, stable, high-salience opinion changes to which high responsiveness would be expected. Stimson, MacKuen, and Erikson (1995) found intriguing differences in connections between domestic liberal-conservative mood and policy activity by different institutions. Their estimated reduced-form coefficients (not controlling for party composition) ranged from 1.183 for the Senate and .850 for the House of Representatives down to .490 for the presidency and just .302 for the Supreme Court. Moreover, the mechanisms seemed to differ: House members apparently moved quickly to anticipate and avoid the voters' biennial wrath, whereas the Senate responded to public opinion mainly through electoral replacement (1995, 552–56).

Has policy responsiveness to public opinion varied over time? Lawrence Jacobs and Robert Shapiro in chapter 3 argue that the answer is "yes," based on research by themselves and others. Shapiro (1982) and Page and Shapiro (1983, p. 182) found varying levels of congruence between opinion change and policy

change in different historical periods, with peak (75%) congruence in 1969–79;
the New Deal period came in second at 67%, but after 1945 there was a slow,
steady decline in congruence to the 54% level of 1961–68, before the jump to 75%
in 1969–79. In a preliminary study of social welfare issues, Jacobs and Shapiro
found a drop in congruence in the post-1980 period. Monroe (1998), whose estimate of 63% consistency between policy and majority opinion in 1960–79 is
quite consistent with Shapiro's congruence estimates for that same period, found
a subsequent drop to 55% consistency in 1980–93.

As Jacobs and Shapiro acknowledge, the evidence for a recent drop in responsiveness is still preliminary and tentative; more research will be needed to
firmly establish or refute it. In case the finding holds up, however, Jacobs and
Shapiro (here and in their 2000 book) have offered some rather convincing explanations for the drop, including the sharply increased party polarization in
Washington and presidents' increased capability (through the institutionalized
"public opinion apparatus") to learn about public opinion and attempt to craft
talk that will evade or manipulate it. I would also emphasize, perhaps more
strongly than Jacobs and Shapiro do, three other factors that may have contributed to a decline in responsiveness to public opinion. First is the long-term erosion in the already limited membership and political power of organized labor
in the United States (see Goldfield 1987). Though often ignored, this is arguably
one of the most important facts about politics in the United States as opposed
to the rest of the industrialized world. Labor's decline has largely removed as key
political actors organizations representing the views of millions of ordinary citizens and countervailing the power of business corporations. Second, economic
globalization (increased trade flows, immigration, and, especially, capital mobility) has greatly enhanced the political power of business, by increasing the credibility of firms' threats to cut jobs or to flee abroad in reaction to popular but
costly taxing, spending, and regulatory policies (see Winters 1996.) Third, the
increasing circumvention of post-Watergate campaign finance reforms and the
ensuing flood of "soft money" into the electoral process have probably increased
the political power of moneyed minorities and decreased the influence of ordinary
citizens on policy (Drew 1999).

If the recent decline in responsiveness is real and if these factors have contributed to it—on top of the abysmally low voter turnout and the class-biased
political participation that have been with us for a long time (Burnham 1970;
Verba, Schlozman, and Brady 1995)—then to reassert popular control of government will be no simple matter.

HOW TO MEASURE PUBLIC OPINION

I have so far ignored the rather important question of how public opinion—
especially citizens' policy preferences—should be measured. Implicitly, I have accepted the mainstream view that polls and surveys do it best: that aggregations

Defense of Surveys

(medians, means, majorities) of responses to issue questions asked of representative national samples of citizens can rather accurately tell us what "the people" want their government to do. Surveys may not exactly be the *only* wheel in town. But no feasible, regularly available alternative method of measuring citizens' opinions and policy preferences seems to me to be superior.

Susan Herbst, in a series of books and articles (e.g., Herbst 1993) and in chapter 9, has vigorously challenged this view. Herbst has pointed out a number of deficiencies in polls: the danger, for example, that forced-choice, closed-ended questions will create the appearance of opinions where no opinions actually exist; the problem that responses can vary widely with different question wordings; the general failure of surveys to measure intensity of opinion; the risk that analysts of survey data on isolated individuals will ignore social contexts and social dynamics; and the empirical fact (supported by our work in chapter 8 and Kull and Ramsay's chap. 11, as well as by Herbst's chap. 9) that, in any case, many or most politicians disdain polls as inaccurate or irrelevant. Herbst has championed alternative or supplemental measures of public opinion, based on real-life conversations, which get at the texture of genuine attitudes; public meetings, actions, and demonstrations, which clearly signal intensity; and stands taken by interest groups and the media, which express real opinions by real people when polls may not be available (e.g., in a state legislative setting) or issues may be too complex or obscure for ordinary citizens to form attitudes about.

Similarly, Taeku Lee in chapter 16 thoughtfully reviews a wide range of normative, conceptual, and empirical critiques of polls, scoring some important points. For example, survey data certainly should not be conceptually confused with the construct of "public opinion" itself, which can take many forms and can be measured in many ways. The production of polls is indeed a political, largely elite-driven process, and polls may indeed often ignore or lag behind what is on ordinary citizens' minds, as they did in Lee's well-documented case of the civil rights movement. When survey data are not available, letters to public officials—interesting in any case for the insights they offer into the views of a set of highly attentive and active citizens—may give us useful glimpses of the views of the public as a whole, or at least help illuminate the dynamics of change in mass opinion (see Lee 2002).

Again, James Witte and Philip Howard in chapter 15 note that telephone- and personal-interview-based survey research has encountered increasing problems over time. Interview refusal rates, for example, have risen alarmingly, and the proliferation of multiple telephones within households has greatly complicated probabilistic sampling.

Herbst, Lee, and Witte and Howard raise a tangle of important issues that I will not attempt to analyze at any length here; Peter Miller deals with many of them in chapter 12 (see also Page and Shapiro 1992, esp. pp. 27–31). I will simply defend the pro-survey consensus on its two points of greatest strength: feasibility and representativeness.

As to feasibility, if we want to ascertain—in comparable fashion—the views of many different people on a particular issue, the most feasible way to do so is usually to ask them identical, specific questions about that issue. It can be enlightening to observe natural-setting conversations, letters, demonstrations, and the like, but such observations cannot generally provide the comparable information we need about everyone's views on a specific matter. Moreover, if we want to know the views of *millions* of citizens, it is not generally feasible to ask questions of everyone; much better to ask questions of a small but statistically representative sample.

2

Representativeness constitutes the prime advantage of surveys, both for the empirical purposes that Miller notes and for normative purposes. The sort of public opinion most relevant to democratic theory as I conceive it (granted, this is a liberal, individual-based democratic theory) consists of the aggregated policy preferences of *all* citizens, with each individual citizen *weighted equally*. I see universality and political equality as absolutely central to democracy. Properly designed and analyzed surveys can deliver a good, highly representative picture of what citizens as a collectivity think, free of the participatory biases inherent in other measures of public opinion (see Verba 1996). Yes, we have to be careful about selective (and untimely) question asking, the vagaries of question wording, effects of interview context, sampling complexities due to new telephone technology and altered ownership patterns, refusal problems, possible biases in "don't know" responses,[12] and so forth. These are serious problems, but they are not beyond our power to solve.

Indeed, as Humphrey Taylor points out in chapter 17—with a refreshing dose of comparative, outside-the-U.S. perspective—the existence of free, independent public opinion polls may be quite crucial to the establishment of political accountability and democracy. Polls make decision makers aware of what the public wants so that they can take public opinion into account. And accurate polls can expose (hence sometimes prevent) the stealing of elections.

Alternative measures of public opinion, in contrast to survey-based measures, are all subject to biases that tend to make them highly unrepresentative. Interest groups, for example, are notoriously unrepresentative of ordinary citizens. As practically every scholar since Mancur Olson (1965) has recognized, David Truman's broadly based "potential groups" have trouble forming because of free-rider problems. Actual groups tend to represent businesses, producers, and upper-income professionals much better than they represent workers, consumers, or middle-class people (Schlozman and Tierney 1986). Newspaper editorials and other media voices often express very unrepresentative political opinions. Demonstrators, letter writers, party activists, and the like tend to be quite unlike ordinary citizens in their views and demography, with higher incomes, more formal education, and more extreme opinions (Verba, Schlozman, and Brady 1995).

Herbst, like Kull and Ramsay, provides some important findings about how politicians and their staffers often rely for readings of "public opinion," upon these biased sources rather than on polls or surveys. (Again, we need to know more about exactly why they do so; besides nonavailability of pertinent surveys, one factor may be the electoral importance of unrepresentative activists, money givers, and organized groups.) But I have no doubt that, in terms of democratic theory, they *should* rely, whenever possible, on more representative survey measures. The normative features of survey-based measures of public opinion make poll data—and their relations to policymaking—well worth studying. Democratic theory has provided a major motivation for researchers who, in this volume and elsewhere, have investigated connections between public opinion and policymaking. Poll data necessarily play a central part in such investigations.

That said, it does not follow that existing poll data are perfect or cannot be improved. Several of our authors, in fact, have suggested highly promising improvements.

Charles Manski, for example (in chap. 14), proposes survey techniques to ascertain citizens' voting intentions in a fine-grained probabilistic fashion, rather than the usual dichotomous "Would you be more likely to vote for Bush or Gore?" or the crude verbal "How likely are you to vote? Very likely? Not too likely?" The preliminary evidence indicates that most citizens are able to ascribe a meaningful numerical probability figure to their likelihood of voting for a particular candidate or to their likelihood of voting at all. Probabilistic data promise to be particularly useful for predicting outcomes in elections with multiple candidates (e.g., third-party candidates like Ralph Nader) and for studying the determinants—both over time and across individuals—of higher and lower uncertainty about voting.

Similarly, James Witte and Philip Howard in chapter 15 describe some exciting actual and potential uses for on-line survey research. Internet-based surveys would seem to be especially promising for the study of small, specialized, dispersed population subgroups (e.g., members of the John Birch Society, fans of *National Geographic*), where conventional surveys—even telephone surveys with screener questions—would be far more expensive. And they are best suited for topics for which the vexing problems of nonrepresentativeness (due to differential access to computers, self-selection of respondents, multiple hits by individuals, and even organized campaigns to "flood" surveys) are minimal. I would not, however, expect on-line surveys to replace conventional sample surveys any time soon in ascertaining Americans' collective policy preferences.

In chapter 13, Martin Gilens crisply describes the great power of survey experiments (relying on differential treatment of random subsets of respondents, especially through CATI technology) to illuminate a wide range of substantive and methodological issues. Experiments on question wording, question context, the interview relationship, and survey modes can help us improve survey data and analysis by pinning down the precise impact of using such treacherous words as "welfare," and of priming respondents with cues about crime rates or foreign aid spending; relying on male versus female (or black vs. white) interviewers; using "secret ballots," mail surveys, or list techniques rather than straightforward personal interview questions on sensitive topics; and the like. But experimental

CONCLUSION

techniques can also illuminate substantive matters: interactions between methods and respondent characteristics (a tendency of liberals to conceal qualms about affirmative action in response to traditional questions; easier incorporation of new information into preferences by the already knowledgeable), and the crucial role of correct or incorrect information in forming policy preferences.

Information is also central to Kull and Ramsay's discussion in chapter 11 of public opinion concerning foreign policy. Not only do foreign policy elites often misperceive the state of public opinion but on some issues measured public attitudes that seem to fit an image of American isolationism are based on seriously erroneous information. Opposition to foreign aid spending, for example, appears to depend on gross overestimates of the amount of current spending (see also Kull and Destler 1999.) To the extent that poll-measured opinion is based on misinformation, of course, the normative status of those poll results comes into question, and we need to think about alternative measurement techniques such as those Kull has used and the experiments cited by Martin Gilens. We also need to think about how to improve our information system so that the collective public is exposed to the correct information it needs.

CONCLUSION

In an early book about public opinion and American democracy, V. O. Key Jr. (1961) wrote that popular governments "give . . . weight" to public opinion, but there is no "mechanistic articulation" between opinion and action, no "precise mirroring" of public opinion by government policy (pp. 411–12). To an extent that we can never be certain of, parallelism between opinion and policy results from influence on opinion by "government and other centers of political influence" that attempt to form opinion, rather than adjusting of policy to bring it into accord with public opinion (pp. 412, 423). In the end, public opinion is like a "system of dikes" that channel public action or fix a "range of discretion" within which government may act. These dikes rule out some policy alternatives as not worthy of serious attention and define other areas of "permissive consensus" within which action may be taken (p. 552; see also Sobel 2001).

I believe that the research reported in this volume is largely consistent with Key's formulations, just as it is largely consistent with E. E. Schattschneider's insistence that the American public is only "semi-sovereign." Ordinary citizens can have substantial influence upon policy, especially on high-salience issues for which the scope of conflict is broad, but on many issues (especially those of low visibility) autonomous public officials or a business-oriented pressure group system may prevail over the general public.

We have seen substantial evidence that policy often moves in harmony with public opinion. But we have also seen evidence that the extent of opinion-policy congruence varies with the degree of salience, the type of issue, and over time, with a distinct possibility that responsiveness has declined in recent years. And we have seen evidence that organized interests and policymakers themselves may sometimes shape public opinion rather than being moved by it.

The leading quantitative studies of opinion-policy links offer a number of important findings, but close scrutiny of those studies reveals a consistent tendency to *overstate* the impact of opinion on policy. Sampling and aggregation biases, as well as specification errors—especially the omission of variables that may influence both opinion and policy and generate spurious opinion-policy relationships, and failures to identify reciprocal effects of policy on opinion—afflict all these studies to varying degrees and seriously inflate their estimates of opinion's impact on policy. As a number of case studies confirm, the true relationship between opinion and policy is far from perfect.

If the empirical evidence does, in fact, support the views of Key and Schattschneider, and if we accept a populistic democratic theory that calls for close adherence of policy to the preferences of ordinary citizens, then the U.S. political system has a long way to go before it becomes fully democratic. And if our authors are right about the factors that impede responsiveness—such as increased party polarization in Washington, clever "crafted talk" by policymakers, economic globalization, and increasingly powerful political money, along with the separation of powers, the weakness of labor unions, the lobbying power of business and other organized interests, and restricted, class-biased political participation—then movement toward more democracy will require considerable political struggle.

NOTES

1. In self-defense, I should point out that Page and Shapiro (1983) carefully qualified their findings and disclaimed any notion that democracy worked perfectly in the United States. Still, it is also true that Shapiro and I have subsequently come to put a greater emphasis on the undemocratic, nonpopular influences on American politics, as we have perceived those influences to grow in importance.

2. Mark Smith's (2000) data indicating that business (as represented by the U.S. Chamber of Commerce) loses on a good many highly visible issues on which it takes a stand does not necessarily contradict this point. Such public stands may be taken more often on the (perhaps relatively infrequent) occasions on which business is already losing. Business victories may be more frequent and more important, even if less visible, than the defeats. In any case, Smith is more interested in variations in business success over time than in the level of success, which he considered hard to measure objectively (pp. 85–86).

3. True, the different time periods over which different poll items were fielded mean that standardizing each of them independently does not guarantee to calibrate them exactly to the postulated public "mood" over that period. Hence, one should not actually expect either the measured mood or the time-period dummy variables to account for 100% of the variation in individual items, even if the actual relationship were perfect.

The authors' estimate—using an eigenvalue analog—that "about half" of the variance in selected time series is common variance (see chap. 4, especially footnote 11) may come closer to the truth than the 24% or 21% figure that I suggest. But to neglect even half the variance in *selected,* standardized public opinion items is to neglect a lot. And again: the selection excludes all foreign policy, crime, and abortion items, as well as numerous short time series and isolated items that may be particularly unlikely to track a simple liberal-conservative mood.

4. An exception is Monroe (1979, 1998), whose "consistency" measure tries to assess discrepancies between the level of policies at a given moment and majority public preferences at that moment. But such judgments are necessarily difficult and subjective when (as is usually the case) opinion and policy are not measured on identical metrics.

5. If opinion and policy are measured on identical metrics, as is arguably true in Achen (1978), a constant deviation of policy from opinion should appear in the intercept term of a regression or in a simple arithmetic difference between the average values of the two variables. (See the intercept terms in Achen's [1978, pp. 490–94] estimates of "responsiveness," which do, in fact, suggest a degree of bias.)

6. The antelopes do, however, creep back—by way of an ambiguous reference—in chapter 4.

7. A simulation result not included in the final version of chapter 2 actually produced an example of "hyper-representation" in policy activity. When the authors moderately disturbed public opinion by every year (starting in 1977) adding 1.0 extra units of liberalism to the "Domestic Policy Mood," this disturbance worked its way through the political system, tipping control of Congress to the Democrats in 1984 and 1986, and having a rather prolonged impact on policy activity that was *larger* than the change in public opinion itself. The authors did not claim that such an effect would be typical, but it did follow from their model.

8. Burstein, Bauldry, and Froese (2001) make this point concrete by tabulating the vast number of issues on the legislative agenda, few of which are the subject of opinion polls, and by noting that most legislative activity is "virtually invisible" to the public. Studying a stratified random sample of policy proposals, they find responsiveness to public opinion to be very low, by conventional measures, though Congress seldom acts in direct opposition to the measured preferences of the public.

9. To be sure, measurement error in the opinion variable may have led the estimates of direct effects of Soviet spending to erroneously include some impact that actually occurred indirectly through public opinion and should be attributed, in the sense of proximate cause, to opinion.

10. See Burstein, Bauldry, and Froese (2001). Note that even the modest levels of opinion-policy congruence that Page and Shapiro (1983) estimated for lower-salience issues were presumably biased upward by that study's omission of nonopinion independent variables, by its partial failure to rule out reciprocal causation, and by the fact that it considered only cases in which *both* public opinion and policy moved significantly and measurably. (Not counted as instances of nonresponsiveness were cases in which public opinion did not move but policy did, or in which public preferences changed but policy did not.)

11. Within Monroe's (1979, 1998) research design, however, issues of political reform face a high hurdle for achieving consistency because they inherently involve substantial departures from the status quo. Measured policy consistency is much higher on opinion items that do not call for such departures.

12. Nonresponse and "don't know" biases are particularly threatening to the normative status of surveys, if the views of citizens with less political information (and often lower incomes) tend to be underrepresented (see Althaus 1998). But these biases may not be enormous. Althaus's simulation of "full information" preferences found an average of seven percentage points of change in marginal frequencies. By my calculation, however, a measured majority actually switched sides on only two of his forty-five issues (pp. 552, 555–57).

REFERENCES

Achen, Christopher H. 1975. "Mass Political Attitudes and the Survey Response." *American Political Science Review* 69: 1218–31.

———. 1978. "Measuring Representation." *American Journal of Political Science* 22: 475–510.

———. 1986. *The Statistical Analysis of Quasi-Experiments*. Berkeley: University of California Press.

Adams, Greg D. 1997. "Abortion: Evidence of Issue Evolution." *American Journal of Political Science* 41: 718–37.

Akard, Patrick J. 1992. "Corporate Mobilization and Political Power: The Transformation of U.S. Economic Policy in the 1970s." *American Sociological Review* 57: 597–615.

Aldrich, John. 1995. *Why Parties? The Origin and Transformation of Political Parties in America*. Chicago: University of Chicago Press.

Alesina, Alberto, and Howard Rosenthal. 1995. *Partisan Politics, Divided Government, and the Economy*. New York: Cambridge University Press.

Alexander, Herbert E. 1992. *Financing Politics: Money, Elections, and Political Reform*. 4th edition. Washington, DC: CQ Press.

Almond, Gabriel. 1950. *The American People and Foreign Policy*. New York: Harcourt.

Alston, Lee J., and Joseph P. Ferrie. 1999. *Southern Paternalism and the American Welfare State*. New York: Cambridge University Press.

Althaus, Scott L. 1998. "Information Effects in Collective Preferences." *American Political Science Review* 92: 545–58.

Altschuler, Bruce. 1986. "Lyndon Johnson and the Public Polls." *Public Opinion Quarterly* 50: 285–99.

Amacher, Ryan, and William Boyes. 1978. "Cycles in Senatorial Voting Behavior: Implications for the Optimal Frequency of Elections." *Public Choice* 33 (3): 5–13.

The American Association for Public Opinion Research (AAPOR). 2000. *Standard Defi-*

nitions: Final Dispositions of Case Codes and Outcome Rates for Surveys. Ann Arbor, MI: AAPOR.

Ansolabehere, Stephen D., James M. Snyder Jr., and Charles Stewart III. 2001. "Candidate Positioning in U.S. House Elections." *American Journal of Political Science* 45: 136–159.

Arnold, R. Douglas. 1990. *The Logic of Congressional Action.* New Haven, CT: Yale University Press.

Bachrach, Peter, and Morton Baratz. 1962. "The Two Faces of Power." *American Political Science Review* 56: 947–52.

Baker, Dean, and Mark Weisbrot. 1999. *Social Security: The Phony Crisis.* Chicago: University of Chicago Press.

Ball, Robert M. 1997. Testimony at Hearing 010. *The Future of Social Security for This Generation and the Next.* Washington, DC: Committee on Ways and Means, U.S. House of Representatives, March 6.

Balz, Dan, and Ronald Brownstein. 1996. *Storming the Gates: Protest Politics and the Republican Revival.* Boston: Little, Brown.

Barkan, Elazar. 1992. *The Retreat of Scientific Racism.* Cambridge: Cambridge University Press.

Barone, Michael, and Grant Ujifusa. 1995. *The Almanac of American Politics.* Washington, DC: National Journal Inc.

Bartels, Larry M. 1991. "Constituency Opinion and Congressional Policy Making: The Reagan Defense Buildup." *American Political Science Review* 85: 457–74.

Bauer, Gary L. 1995. *New Welfare Poll Shows Strong Support for Combating Illegitimacy.* Washington, DC: Family Research Council.

Baumgartner, Frank R., and Bryan D. Jones. 1993. *Agendas and Instability in American Politics.* Chicago: University of Chicago Press.

Beckett, Katherine. 1997. *Making Crime Pay.* New York: Oxford University Press.

Beckley, Gloria T., and Paul Burstein. 1991. "Religious Pluralism, Equal Employment Opportunity, and the State." *Western Political Quarterly* 44: 185–208.

Benford, Robert D., and David A. Snow. 2000. "Framing Processes and Social Movements: An Overview and Assessment." *Annual Review of Sociology* 26: 611–39.

Beniger, James R. 1986. *The Control Revolution.* Cambridge, MA: Harvard University Press.

———. 1992. "The Impact of Polling on Public Opinion: Reconciling Foucault, Habermas, and Bourdieu." *International Journal of Public Opinion Research* 4: 204–19.

Bennett, W. Lance. 1990. "Toward a Theory of Press-State Relations in the United States." *Journal of Communication* 40: 103–25.

Bennett, W. Lance, and Robert M. Entman, eds. 2001. *Mediated Politics.* New York: Cambridge University Press.

Berke, Richard L. 1996. "Poll Indicates Stable Ratings for President." *New York Times,* June 5, p. A1.

Bernstein, Aaron. 2000. "Too Much Corporate Power?" *Business Week,* September 11, pp. 145–49.

Berry, William D., Evan J. Ringquist, Richard C. Fording, and Russell L. Hanson. 1998. "Measuring Citizen and Government Ideology in the American States, 1960–93." *American Journal of Political Science* 42: 327–48.

Besharov, Douglas J. 1995. "A Monster of His Own Creation." *Washington Post,* November 2, p. A-31.

Best, Samuel. 1999. "The Sampling Problem in Studying Public Mood: An Alternative Solution." *Journal of Politics* 61: 721–740.

Bickers, Kenneth, and Robert M. Stein. 1998. "The Micro Foundations of the Tiebout Model." *Urban Affairs Review* 34: 76–93.

Binder, David. 1995. "Children Crusade against Proposed Republican Budget Cuts." *New York Times*, March 20, p. A13.

Binkley, Robert. 1928. "The Concept of Public Opinion in the Social Sciences." *Social Forces* 6:389–96.

Birnbaum, Jeffrey H. 1996. *Madhouse: The Private Turmoil of Working for the President.* New York: Times Books.

Bischoping, Katherine, and Howard Schuman. 1992. "Pens and Polls in Nicaragua: Analysis of the 1990 Preelection Surveys." *American Journal of Political Science* 36: 331–50.

Bishop, George F., and Bonnie S. Fisher. 1995. " 'Secret Ballots' and Self-Reports in an Exit-Poll Experiment." *Public Opinion Quarterly* 59: 568–88.

Bishop, George, Robert Oldendick, and Alfred Tuchfarber. 1978. "Change in the Structure of Amerian Political Attutides: The Nagging Question of Question Wording." *American Journal of Political Science* 22: 250–69.

Bloom, Jack M. 1987. *Class, Race, and the Civil Rights Movement.* Bloomington: Indiana University Press.

Blumenthal, Sidney. 1980. *The Permanent Campaign: Inside the World of Elite Political Operatives.* Boston: Beacon Press.

Blumer, Herbert. 1946. "The Mass, the Public, and Public Opinion." In *New Outline of the Principles of Sociology*, ed. Alfred McClung Lee. New York: Barnes and Noble.

———. 1948. "Public Opinion and Public Opinion Polling." *American Sociological Review* 13: 542–54.

Bond, Jon R., and Richard Fleisher. 1990. *The President in the Legislative Arena.* Chicago: University of Chicago Press.

Bourdieu, Pierre. 1979. "Public Opinion Does Not Exist." In *Communication and Class Struggle*, vol. 1, ed. Armond Matelart and Seth Siegelaub, pp. 124–30. New York: International General.

———. 1986. *Distinction: A Social Critique of the Judgment of Taste*, trans. R. Nice. Cambridge, MA: Harvard University Press.

———. 1990. *In Other Words: Essays Toward a Reflexive Sociology,* trans. M. Adamson. Stanford, CA: Stanford University Press.

Bradburn, Norman, and Seymour Sudman. 1988. *Polls and Surveys: Understanding What They Tell Us.* San Francisco: Jossey-Bass.

Branch, Taylor. 1998. *Pillar of Fire: America in the King Years, 1963–65.* New York: Simon & Schuster.

Breaux, John. 1998. Remarks at Hearing 013. *The Stock Market and Social Security: The Risks and the Rewards.* Washington, DC: Special Committee on Aging, U.S. Senate, April 22.

Brehm, John. 1993. *The Phantom Respondents: Opinion Surveys and Political Representation.* Ann Arbor: University of Michigan Press.

Brink, William, and Louis Harris. 1964. *The Negro Revolution in America.* New York: Simon and Schuster.

———. 1966. *Black and White: A Study of U.S. Racial Attitudes Today.* New York: Simon and Schuster.

Broder, John. 1996. "Decision Was Difficult for Clinton, Tough on Dole." *Los Angeles Times*, August 1, p. A16.

Brooks, Clem. 1994. "The Selectively Political Citizen? Modeling Attitudes, Nonattitudes, and Change in 1950s Public Opinion." *Sociological Methods and Research* 22: 419–52.

Brown, Michael K. 1999. *Race, Money and the American Welfare State.* Ithaca, NY: Cornell University Press.

Brownstein, Ronald. 1995. "Welfare Debate Puts Blame for Poverty Mainly on the Poor." *Los Angeles Times* (Washington edition), March 24, pp. A1, A8.

Bryce, James. 1895. *The American Commonwealth.* Vol. 3. London: Macmillan.

Bulmer, Martin, Keven Bales, and Kathryn Kish Sklar, eds. 1991. *The Social Survey in Historical Perspective, 1880–1940.* Cambridge: Cambridge University Press.

Burden, Barry. 1997. "Deterministic and Probabilistic Voting Models." *American Journal of Political Science* 41: 1150–69.

Burnham, Walter Dean. 1970. *Critical Elections and the Mainsprings of American Politics.* New York: W. W Norton.

Burris, Val. 1992. "Elite Policy-Planning Networks in the United States." *Research in Politics and Society* 4: 111–34.

Burstein, Paul. 1979. "Public Opinion, Demonstrations, and the Passage of Anti-discrimination Legislation." *Public Opinion Quarterly* 43: 157–72.

———. 1991. "Policy Domains." *Annual Review of Sociology* 17: 327–50.

———. 1992. "Affirmative Action, Jobs, and American Democracy: What Has Happened to the Quest for Equal Opportunity?" *Law and Society Review* 26: 901–22.

———. 1998a. "Bringing the Public Back In: Should Sociologists Consider the Impact of Public Opinion on Public Policy?" *Social Forces* 77: 27–62.

———. 1998b. *Discrimination, Jobs, and Politics: The Struggle for Equal Employment Opportunity in the U.S. since the New Deal.* Chicago: University of Chicago Press.

———. 1999. "Social Movements and Public Policy." In *How Social Movements Matter,* ed. Marco Guigni, Doug McAdam, and Charles Tilly, pp. 3–21. Minneapolis: University of Minnesota Press.

———. 2001. "Public Opinion and Congressional Support for Policy Change." Paper presented at annual meetings of the American Political Science Association, San Francisco, CA, August 29–September 1.

Burstein, Paul, Shawn Bauldry, and Paul Froese. 2001. "Public Opinion and Congressional Support for Policy Change." Paper presented at the annual meeting of the American Political Science Association. San Francisco, CA. August.

Burstein, Paul, R. Marie Bricher, and Rachel Einwohner. 1995. "Policy Alternatives and Political Change: Work, Family, and Gender on the Congressional Agenda, 1945–1990." *American Sociological Review* 60: 67–83.

Burstein, Paul, and Mark Evan Edwards. 1994. "The Impact of Employment Discrimination Litigation on Racial Disparity in Earnings." *Law and Society Review* 28: 79–111.

Burstein, Paul, and Susan Wierzbicki. 2000. "Public Opinion and Congressional Action on Work, Family, and Gender, 1945–1990." In *Work and Family: Research Informing Policy,* ed. Toby L. Parcel and Daniel B. Cornfield, pp. 31–66. Thousand Oaks, CA: Sage Publications.

Butler, David, and Austin Ranney, eds. 1992. *Electioneering: A Comparative Study of Continuity and Change.* New York: Oxford University Press.

Campbell, Angus, Philip E. Converse, Warren E. Miller, and Donald E. Stokes. 1960. *The American Voter.* New York: Wiley.

Campbell, Angus, and Howard Schuman. 1968. "Racial Attitudes in Fifteen American Cities." In *Supplemental Studies for the National Advisory Commission on Civil Disorders.* Washington, DC: United States Government Printing Office.

Cannell, Charles, Peter Miller, and Lois Oksenberg. 1981. "Research on Interviewing Techniques." In *Sociological Methodology,* ed. Samuel Leinhardt. San Francisco: Jossey-Bass.

Cantril, Hadley, and S. S. Wilks. 1940. "Problems and Techniques: Experiments in the Wording of Questions." *Public Opinion Quarterly* 4: 330–38.

Carmines, Edward G., and James A. Stimson. 1989. *Issue Evolution: Race and the Transformation of American Politics.* Princeton, NJ: Princeton University Press.

Charen, Mona. 1995. "High Ground on Welfare." *Washington Times*, March 22, p. A20.

Chong, Dennis. 1996. "Creating Common Frames of Reference on Political Issues." In *Political Persuasion and Attitude Change*, ed. Diana C. Mutz, Paul M. Sniderman, and Richard A. Brody, pp. 37–57. Ann Arbor: University of Michigan Press.

Cigler, Allan, and Burdett Loomis. 1983. *Interest Group Politics.* Washington, DC: CQ Press.

Clausen, Aage. R. 1973. *How Congressmen Decide: A Policy Focus.* New York: St. Martin's Press.

Clawson, Dan, Alan Neustadtl, and Mark Weller. 1998. *Dollars and Votes: How Business Campaign Contributions Subvert Democracy.* Philadelphia: Temple University Press.

Clinton, William J. 1998a. *Public Papers of the Presidents of the United States: William J. Clinton, 1993–2000.* Washington, DC: Government Printing Office, 2001.

———. 1998b. Remarks at the University of Illinois, Champaign-Urbana, January 28.

———. 1998c. Remarks on departure from Capitol Hill, February 10.

———. 1998d. Remarks at a roundtable discussion with Employees of Therma, Inc., San Jose, CA. May 1.

———. 1999a. Address before a Joint Session of Congress on the State of the Union, Washington, DC, January 19.

———. 1999b. Remarks at Brooke Grove Elementary School, Olney, MD, September 7.

Cohen, Bernard C. 1973. *The Public's Impact on Foreign Policy.* Boston: Little, Brown.

Cohen, Jeffrey E. 1997. *Presidential Responsiveness and Public Policy-Making: The Public and the Policies That Presidents Choose.* Ann Arbor: University of Michigan Press.

Colasanto, Diane. 1997. "A Proposal for a New Role and New Voice for AAPOR." *Public Opinion Quarterly* 61: 523–30.

Colwell, Mary A. C. 1993. *Private Foundations and Public Policy: The Political Role of Philanthropy.* New York: Garland Publishers.

Congressional Quarterly, Inc. 1992. *Congressional Quarterly Almanac 1991.* Washington, DC: Congressional Quarterly, Inc.

Converse, Jean. 1986. *Survey Research in the United States.* Berkeley: University of California Press.

Converse, Philip E. 1964. "The Nature of Belief Systems in Mass Publics." In *Ideology and Discontent*, ed. David Apter, pp. 206–64. New York: Free Press.

———. 1987. "Changing Conceptions of Public Opinion in the Political Process." *Public Opinion Quarterly* 51: S12–S24.

———. 1996. "The Advent of Polling and Political Representation." *PS: Political Science and Politics* 29: 649–57.

Converse, Philip E., and Michael W. Traugott. 1986. "Assessing the Accuracy of Polls and Surveys." *Science* 234: 1094–98.

Cook, Fay Lomax. 1979. *Who Should Be Helped?* Beverly Hills, CA: Sage Publications.

Cook, Fay Lomax, and Edith J. Barrett. 1992. *Support for the American Welfare State: The Views of Congress and the Public.* New York: Columbia University Press.

Cook, Fay Lomax, and Lawrence R. Jacobs. 2001. "Assessing Assumptions about Americans' Attitudes toward Social Security: Popular Claims Meet Hard Data." In *The Future of Social Insurance*, ed. Peter Edelman and Dallas L. Salisbury, pp. 82–110. Washington, DC: Brookings Institution Press.

Costain, Anne N. 1992. *Inviting Women's Rebellion.* Baltimore: Johns Hopkins University Press.

Cotter, Patrick R., Jeffrey Cohen, and Philip B. Coulter. 1982. "Race-of-Interviewer Effects in Telephone Interviews." *Public Opinion Quarterly* 46:78–84.

Couper, Mick. 2000. "Web Surveys: A Review of Issues and Approaches." *Public Opinion Quarterly* 64: 464–94.

Couper, Mick, Johnny Blair, and Timothy Triplett. 1999. "A Comparison of Mail and E-mail for a Survey of Employees in U.S. Statistical Agencies." *Journal of Official Statistics* 15: 39–56.

Crespi, Irving. 1989. *Public Opinion, Polls and Democracy.* Boulder, CO: Westview.

Crossley, Archibald M. 1937. "Straw Polls in 1936." *Public Opinion Quarterly* 1: 24–35.

Curtin, Richard. 1982. "Indicators of Consumer Behavior: The University of Michigan Surveys of Consumers." *Public Opinion Quarterly* 46: 340–52.

Curtin, Richard, Stanley Presser, and Eleanor Singer. 2000. "The Effects of Response Rate Changes on the Index of Consumer Sentiment." *Public Opinion Quarterly* 4: 413–28.

Dalton, Russell J. 1996. *Citizen Politics: Public Opinion and Political Parties in Advanced Western Democracies.* Chatham, NJ: Chatham House.

Dao, James, and Franklin Bruni. 2000. "Jabs Fly in Presidential Ring over Social Security's Future." *New York Times,* May 4. Section 4, Page 1

Davidson, Roger H., and Walter J. Oleszek. 1998. *Congress and Its Members.* 6th ed. Washington, DC: CQ Press.

Davis, James, and Tom Smith. 1994. *The General Social Surveys, 1972–1994, Cumulative File.* Chicago: National Opinion Research Center.

Dawson, Michael C. 1994. *Behind the Mule: Race, Class, and African-American Politics.* Princeton, NJ: Princeton University Press.

———. 2001. *Black Visions: The Roots of Contemporary African American Political Ideologies.* Chicago: University of Chicago Press.

Dawson, Michael C., and Ernest J. Wilson III. 1991. "Paradigms and Paradoxes: Political Science and the Study of African American Politics." In *Political Science: Looking to the Future,* vol. 1, ed. William Crotty, pp. 189–234. Evanston, IL: Northwestern University Press.

Delli Carpini, Michael X., and Scott Keeter. 1996. *What Americans Know about Politics and Why It Matters.* New Haven, CT: Yale University Press.

Destler, I. M. 1996. "Foreign Policy and the Public: Will Leaders Catch the *Full* Message?" *Brown Journal of World Affairs* 3 (Winter/Spring): 265–70.

Devroy, Ann. 1995. "House Republicans Get Talking Points." *Washington Post,* February 2, p. A9.

Dewey, John. 1927. *The Public and Its Problems.* New York: Holt, Rinehart, and Winston.

Dillman, Don A. 2000. *Mail and Internet Surveys: The Tailored Design Method.* New York: Wiley.

Domhoff, G. William. 1967. *Who Rules America?* Englewood Cliffs, NJ: Prentice-Hall.

———. 1970. *The Higher Circles.* New York: Random House.

———. 1990. *The Power Elite and the State: How Policy Is Made in America.* Hawthorne, NY: Aldine de Gruyter.

———. 1996a. Review of *Golden Rule: The Investment Theory of Party Competition and the Logic of Money-Driven Political Systems* by Thomas Ferguson. *Contemporary Sociology* 25 (March): 197–98.

———. 1996b. *State Autonomy or Class Dominance? Case Studies on Policy Making in America.* Hawthorne, NY: Aldine de Gruyter.

———. 1998. *Who Rules America? Power and Politics in the Year 2000.* Mountain View, CA: Mayfield Publishing Co.

———. 2002. *Who Rules America?* 4th edition. New York: McGraw-Hill.

Dominitz, Jeff, and Charles Manski. 1997a. "Perceptions of Economic Insecurity: Evidence from the Survey of Economic Expectations." *Public Opinion Quarterly* 61: 261–87.

———. 1997b. "Using Expectations Data to Study Subjective Income Expectations." *Journal of the American Statistical Association* 92: 855–67.

———. 1999. "The Several Cultures of Research on Subjective Expectations." In *Wealth, Work, and Health: Essays in Honor of F. Thomas Juster*, ed. James Smith and Robert Willis, pp. 15–33. Ann Arbor: University of Michigan Press.

Dominitz, Jeff, Charles Manski, and Baruch Fischhoff. 2001. "Who Are Youth At-Risk?: Expectations Evidence in the NLSY-97." In *Social Awakenings: Adolescents' Behavior as Adulthood Approaches*, ed. Robert Michael, pp. 230–57. New York: Russell Sage Foundation.

Dowd, Maureen. 1994. "Americans Like GOP Agenda But Split on How to Reach Goals." *New York Times*, December 15, p. A1.

Dowding, Keith, Peter John, and Stephen Biggs. 1994. "Tiebout: A Survey of the Empirical Literature." *Urban Studies* 31: 767–97.

Downs, Anthony. 1957. *An Economic Theory of Democracy*. New York: Harper & Row.

Dreiling, Michael C. 2001. *Solidarity and Contention: The Politics of Class and Sustainability in the NAFTA Conflict*. New York: Garland Press.

Drew, Elizabeth. 1996. *Showdown: The Struggle between the Gingrich Congress and the Clinton White House*. New York: Touchstone.

———. 1998. *The Corruption of American Politics: What Went Wrong and Why*. Secaucus, NJ: Carol Publishing Group.

Edelman, Murray. 1995. "The Influence of Rationality Claims on Public Opinion and Policy." In *Public Opinion and the Communication of Consent*, ed. Theodore L. Glasser and Charles T. Salmon, pp. 403–16. New York: Guilford Press.

Edsall, Thomas Byrne, and Mary D. Edsall. 1991. *Chain Reaction*. New York: W. W. Norton.

Eisinger, Robert M. 1996. *The Illusion of Certainty: Explaining the Evolution of Presidential Polling*. Ph.D. dissertation, University of Chicago.

Elling, Richard. 1982. "Ideological Change in the U.S. Senate: Time and Electoral Responsiveness." *Legislative Studies Quarterly* 7 (February): 75–92.

Ellwood, David T. 1996. "From Social Science to Social Policy? The Fate of Intellectuals, Ideas and Ideology in the Welfare Debate in the Mid-1990s." Evanston, IL: Center for Urban Affairs and Public Policy, Northwestern University, Distinguished Public Lecture Series.

Entman, Robert M. 1989. *Democracy without Citizens: Media and the Decay of American Politics*. New York: Oxford University Press.

———. 2000. "Declarations of Independence and the Growth of Media Power." In *Decisionmaking in a Glass House: Mass Media, Public Opinion, and American and European Foreign Policy in the 21st Century*, ed. Brigitte L. Nacos, Robert Y. Shapiro, and Pierangelo Isernia, pp. 11–26. Lanham, MD: Rowman and Littlefield.

Erikson, Robert S. 1978. "Constituency Opinion and Congressional Behavior: A Reexamination of the Miller-Stokes Representation Data." *American Journal of Political Science* 22: 511–35.

Erikson, Robert S., Michael B. MacKuen, and James A. Stimson. 2002. *The Macro Polity*. New York: Cambridge University Press.

Erikson, Robert S., and Kent L. Tedin. 2001. *American Public Opinion*. 6th edition. New York: Macmillan.

Erikson, Robert S., and Gerald C. Wright. 2001a. "Representation of Constituency Ideology in Congress." In *Continuity and Change in Congressional Elections*, ed. David Brady and John Cogan. Stanford, CA: Stanford University Press.

————. 2001b. "Voters, Candidates, and Issues in Congressional Elections." In *Congress Reconsidered*, 7th edition, ed. Lawrence C. Dodd and Bruce I. Oppenheimer, pp. 201–26. Washington, DC: Congressional Quarterly.

Erikson, Robert S., Gerald C. Wright, and John P. McIver. 1989. "Political Parties, Public Opinion, and State Policy in the United States." *American Political Science Review* 83: 728–50.

————. 1993. *Statehouse Democracy: Public Opinion and Democracy in American States*. New York: Cambridge University Press.

Erlanger, Steven. 1997. "Crowded, Ambitious Foreign Policy Agenda Awaits President in New Term." *New York Times*, January 19, p. L21.

Evans, Peter B., Dietrich Rueschemeyer, and Theda Skocpol, eds. 1985. *Bringing the State Back In*. New York: Cambridge University Press.

Farley, Christopher J. 1993. "Taking Shots at the Baby Boomers: A New—and Young—Breed of Social Activists Issue a Call to Arms." *Time*, July 19, pp. 30–31.

Feldman, Stanley. 1989. "Measuring Issue Preferences: The Problem of Response Instability." In *Political Analysis*, vol. 1, ed. James A. Stimson, pp. 25–60. Ann Arbor: University of Michigan Press.

————. 1991. "What do Survey Questions Really Measure?" *Political Methodologist* 4: 8–12.

————. 1998. "Structure and Consistency in Public Opinion: The Role of Core Beliefs and Values." *American Journal of Political Science* 32: 416–38.

Feldman, Stanley, and John Zaller. 1992. "The Political Culture of Ambivalence." *American Journal of Political Science* 36: 268–307.

Fenno, Richard F. 1973. *Congressmen in Committees*. Boston: Little, Brown.

————. 1978. *Home Style: House Members in Their Districts*. New York: HarperCollins.

Ferejohn, John, and James H. Kuklinski, eds. 1990. *Information and Democratic Processes*. Urbana: University of Illinois Press.

Ferguson, Thomas. 1995. *Golden Rule: The Investment Theory of Party Competition and the Logic of Money-Driven Political Systems*. Chicago: University of Chicago Press.

Ferguson, Thomas, and Joel Rogers. 1986. *Right Turn: The Decline of the Democrats and the Future of American Politics*. New York: Hill and Wang.

Ferrell, William R., and Paul J. McGoey. 1980. "Model of Calibration for Subjective Probabilities." *Organizational Behavior and Human Performance* 26: 32–53.

Fields, James M., and Howard Schuman. 1976. "Public Beliefs about the Beliefs of the Public." *Public Opinion Quarterly* 40: 427–48.

Fiorina, Morris. 1973. "Electoral Margins, Constituency Influence, and Policy Moderation: A Critical Assessment." *American Politics Quarterly* 1: 479–98.

————. 1974. *Representatives, Roll Calls, and Constituencies*. Lexington, MA: Lexington.

————. 1981. *Retrospective Voting in American National Elections*. New Haven, CT: Yale University Press.

Fischhoff, Baruch, Andrew Parker, Wendy de Bruin, J. Downs, C. Palmgren, Robyn Dawes, and Charles Manski. 2000. "Teen Expectations for Significant Life Events." *Public Opinion Quarterly* 64: 189–205.

Fiske, Susan T. 1986. "Schema-Based vs. Piecemeal Politics." In *Political Cognition*, ed. Richard R. Lau and David Sears, pp. 41–54. Mahwah, NJ: Lawrence Erlbaum and Associates.

Flacks, Richard. 1988. *Making History: The Radical Tradition in American Life*. New York: Columbia University Press.

Fleisher, Richard, and Jon R. Bond. 1996. "The President in a More Partisan Legislative Arena." *Political Research Quarterly* 49 (4): 729–48.

Fones-Wolf, Elizabeth. 1994. *Selling Free Enterprise: The Business Assault on Labor and Liberalism, 1945–1960.* Urbana: University of Illinois Press.

Fording, Richard C. 1997. "The Conditional Effect of Violence as a Political Tactic: Mass Insurgency, Welfare Generosity, and Electoral Context in the American States." *American Journal of Political Science* 41: 1–29.

Foyle, Douglas C. 1999. *Counting the Public In: Presidents, Public Opinion, and Foreign Policy.* New York: Oxford University Press.

Frey, James H. 1989. *Survey Research by Telephone.* Newbury Park, CA: Sage Publications.

Gallup, George H., and Saul F. Rae. 1940. *The Pulse of Democracy: The Public-Opinion Poll and How It Works.* New York: Simon and Schuster.

Gallup Poll. 2000. Available at http://www.gallp.com/poll/indicators.

Gamson, William A., and Andre Modigliani. 1987. "The Political Culture of Social Welfare Policy." In *Evaluating the Welfare State: Social and Political Perspectives*, ed. Richard D. Braungart, pp. 137–77. Greenwich, CT: JAI.

Geer, John G. 1996. *From Tea Leaves to Opinion Polls: A Theory of Democratic Leadership.* New York: Columbia University Press.

Gerber, Elisabeth R., and John E. Jackson. 1993. "Endogenous Preferences and the Study of Institutions." *American Political Science Review* 87: 639–56.

Gilens, Martin. 1996. " 'Race Coding' and White Opposition to Welfare." *American Political Science Review* 90: 593–604.

———. 1999. *Why Americans Hate Welfare: Race, Media, and the Politics of Antipoverty Policy.* Chicago: University of Chicago Press.

———. 2001. "Political Ignorance and Collective Policy Preferences." *American Political Science Review* 95: 379–96.

Gilens, Martin, Paul M. Sniderman, and James H. Kuklinski. 1998. "Affirmative Action and the Politics of Realignment." *British Journal of Political Science* 28: 159–83.

Ginsberg, Benjamin. 1986. *The Captive Public: How Mass Opinion Promotes State Power.* New York: Basic Books.

Glassman, James. 1998. Testimony at Hearing 012. *Enhancing Retirement through Individual Investment Choices.* Washington, DC: Committee on Commerce, U.S. House of Representatives, July 24.

Glynn, Carroll J., Susan Herbst, Garrett J. O'Keefe, and Robert Y. Shapiro. 1999. *Public Opinion.* Boulder, CO: Westview Press.

Goethals, G. R. 1986. "Fabricating and Ignoring Social Reality: Self-Serving Estimates of Consensus." In *Relative Deprivation and Social Comparison: The Ontario Symposium on Social Cognition*, Vol. 4, ed. C. P. Herman and M. P. Zanna, pp. 137–57. Hillsdale, NJ: Lawrence Erlbaum.

Gold, Howard J. 1992. *Hollow Mandates: American Public Opinion and the Conservative Shift.* Boulder, CO: Westview Press.

Goldfield, Michael. 1987. *The Decline of Organized Labor in the United States.* Chicago: University of Chicago Press.

Goldstein, Kenneth M. 1999. *Interest Groups, Lobbying, and Participation in America.* New York: Cambridge University Press.

Gorman, Hubert J. 1986. "The Discovery of Pluralistic Ignorance." *Journal of the History of the Behavioral Sciences* 22: 333–47.

Gormley, William. 1998. "Witnesses for the Revolution." *American Politics Quarterly* 26 (April): 174–95.

Gosnell, Harold F. 1937. "How Accurate Were the Polls?" *Public Opinion Quarterly* 2: 97–105.

Gould, Stephen Jay. 1981. *The Mismeasure of Man.* New York: Norton.

Goyder, John. 1987. *The Silent Minority: Nonrespondents on Sample Surveys.* Boulder, CO: Westview Press.

Graetz, Michael J., and Alicia H. Munnell, pp. 355–88. Washington, DC: Brookings Institution Press.

Graham, Thomas W. 1989. *The Politics of Failure: Strategic Nuclear Arms Control, Public Opinion and Domestic Politics in the United States, 1945–1985.* Ph.D. dissertation, Massachusetts Institute of Technology.

———. 1994. "Public Opinion and U.S. Foreign Policy Decision Making." In *The New Politics of American Foreign Policy,* ed. David A. Deese. New York: St. Martin's Press.

Gramlich, Edward M. 1997. Testimony at Hearing 011. *Concurrent Resolution on the Budget for FY98, vol. II: Proposal for Long-Term Reform,* pp. 91–174. Washington, DC: Committee on Budget, U.S. Senate, January 29.

Grassley, Charles. 1997. Remarks in Hearing 007. *2010 and Beyond: Preparing Social Security for the Baby Boomers.* Washington, DC: Special Committee on Aging, U.S. Senate, August 26.

Greenberg, Stanley B. 1996. *Middle-Class Dreams: The Politics and Power of the New American Majority.* Revised ed. New Haven, CT: Yale University Press.

Greene, William H. 1997. *Econometric Analysis.* 3rd edition. New York: Prentice-Hall.

Groves, Robert, and Mick Couper. 1998. *Nonresponse in Household Interview Surveys.* New York: Wiley-Interscience.

Gunn, J. A. W. 1983. *Beyond Liberty and Property: The Process of Self-Recognition in Eighteenth-Century Political Thought.* Kingston: McGill-Queen's University Press.

———. 1995. *Queen of the World: Opinion in the Public Life of France from the Renaissance to the Revolution. Studies on Voltaire and the Eighteenth Century,* vol. 328. Oxford: Voltaire Foundation.

Gurin, Patricia, Shirley Hatchett, and James Jackson. 1989. *Hope and Independence: Blacks' Response to Electoral and Party Politics.* New York: Russell Sage Foundation.

Habermas, Jürgen. 1989 [1962]. *The Structural Transformation of the Public Sphere.* Trans. T. Burger. Cambridge, MA: MIT Press.

Hacker, Jacob. 1997. *The Road to Nowhere: The Genesis of President Clinton's Plan for Health Security.* Princeton, NJ: Princeton University Press.

Hagel, Charles. 1998. Remarks at Hearing 013. *Stock Market and Social Security: The Risks and Rewards.* Washington, DC: Special Committee on Aging, U.S. Senate, April 22.

Hamilton, Richard F. 1972. *Class and Politics in the United States.* New York: Wiley.

Harding, Sandra, ed. 1993. *The "Racial" Economy of Science: Toward a Democratic Future.* Bloomington: University of Indiana Press.

Hargrove, Erwin. 1988. *Jimmy Carter as President: Leadership and the Politics of the Public Good.* Baton Rouge: Louisiana State University Press.

Hartley, Thomas, and Bruce Russett. 1992. "Public Opinion and the Common Defense: Who Governs Military Spending in the United States." *American Political Science Review* 86: 905–15.

Harvey, Andrew C. 1990. *The Econometric Analysis of Time Series.* 2nd ed. Cambridge, MA: MIT Press.

Harwood, John. 1995. "GOP, Given Power by Angry Voters over Welfare, Seeks a Compassionate Image in Reform Debate." *Wall Street Journal,* March 22, p. A18.

Hays, Scott P., Michael Esler, and Carol E. Hays. 1996. "Environmental Commitment among the States: Integrating Alternative Approaches to State Environmental Policy." *Publius: The Journal of Federalism* 26: 41–58.

Heard, Alexander. 1960. *The Costs of Democracy*. Chapel Hill: University of North Carolina Press.

Heclo, Hugh. 1978. "Issue Networks and the Executive Establishment." In *The New American Political System*, ed. Anthony King, pp. 87–124. Washington, DC: AEI Press.

———. 1994. "Poverty Politics." In *Confronting Poverty: Prescriptions for Change*, ed. Sheldon Danziger and Daniel Weinberg, pp. 396–437. New York: Russell Sage Foundation and Harvard University Press.

———. 2000. "Campaigning and Governing: A Conspectus." In *The Permanent Campaign and Its Future*, ed. Norman J. Ornstein and Thomas E. Mann, pp. 1–37. Washington, DC: AEI Press and Brookings Institution Press.

Heinz, John P., Edward O. Laumann, Robert L. Nelson, and Robert H. Salisbury. 1993. *The Hollow Core: Private Interests in National Policy Making*. Cambridge, MA: Harvard University Press.

———. 1998a. "The Public Opinion Apparatus and the Presidential Agenda." Paper presented at the annual meeting of the American Political Science Association, Boston, September 3–6, 1998.

Heith, Diane J. 1998b. "Staffing the White House Public Opinion Apparatus, 1969–1988." *Public Opinion Quarterly* 62: 165–89.

———. 2000. "Presidential Polling and the Potential for Leadership." In *Presidential Power: Forging the Presidency for the 21st Century*, ed. Robert Y. Shapiro, Martha J. Kumar, and Lawrence R. Jacobs, pp. 380–407. New York: Columbia University Press.

Henry J. Kaiser Family Foundation, Kaiser-Harvard Program on the Public and Health-Social Policy. 1995. *Survey on Welfare Reform: Basic Values and Beliefs; Support for Policy Approaches; Knowledge about Key Programs*. January.

Herbst, Susan. 1993. *Numbered Voices: How Opinion Polling Has Shaped American Politics*. Chicago: University of Chicago Press.

———. 1994. *Politics at the Margin: Historical Studies of Public Expression Outside the Mainstream*. Cambridge: Cambridge University Press.

———. 1995a. "On the Disappearance of Groups: 19th- and Early 20th-Century Conceptions of Public Opinion." In *Public Opinion and the Communication of Consent*, ed. Theodore L. Glasser and Charles T. Salmon. New York: Guilford Press.

———. 1995b. "Election Polling in Historical Perspective." In *Presidential Polls and the News Media*, ed. Paul J. Lavrakas, Michael W. Traugott, and Peter V. Miller, pp. 23–33. Boulder, CO: Westview Press.

———. 1998. *Reading Public Opinion: How Political Actors View the Democratic Process*. Chicago: University of Chicago Press.

Hibbs, Douglas. 1987. *The American Political Economy: Macroeconomics and Electoral Politics*. Cambridge, MA: Harvard University Press.

Hicks, Alexander. 1984. "Elections, Keynes, Bureaucracy, and Class: Explaining United States Budget Deficits, 1961–1978." *American Sociological Review* 49: 165–82.

Hilgartner, Stephen, and Charles L. Bosk. 1988. "The Rise and Fall of Social Problems." *American Journal of Sociology* 94: 53–78.

Hill, Kim Q. 1998. "The Policy Agendas of the President and the Mass Public: A Research Validation and Extension." *American Journal of Political Science* 42: 1328–34.

Hill, Kim Q., and Angela Hinton-Andersson. 1995. "Pathways of Representation: A Causal Analysis of Public Opinion-Public Policy Linkages." *American Journal of Political Science* 39: 924–35.

Hill, Kim Q., and Patricia A. Hurley. 1999. "Dyadic Representation Reappraised." *American Journal of Political Science* 43: 109–37.

Hill, Kim Q., Jan E. Leighley, and Angela Hinton-Andersson. 1995. "Lower-Class Policy

Mobilization and Policy Linkage in the United States." *American Journal of Political Science* 39: 75–86.

Himmelstein, Jerome L. 1997. *Looking Good and Doing Good: Corporate Philanthropy and Corporate Power.* Bloomington: Indiana University Press.

Hinckley, Ronald H. 1992. *People, Polls, and Policymakers: American Public Opinion and National Security.* New York: Lexington Books.

Hobsbawm, Eric J. 1965. *Primitive Rebels: Studies in Archaic Forms of Social Movement in the 19th and 20th Centuries.* New York: W. W. Norton.

Hoek, Janet, and Philip Gendall. 1993. "A New Method of Predicting Voting Behaviour." *Journal of the Market Research Society* 35: 361–371.

———. 1997. "Factors Affecting Poll Accuracy: An Analysis of Undecided Respondents." *Marketing Bulletin* 8: 1–14.

Holsti, Ole. 1996a. Foreign Policy Leadership Project. Durham, NC: Duke University and George Washington University.

———. 1996b. *Public Opinion and American Foreign Policy.* Ann Arbor: University of Michigan Press.

Hook, Janet. 1996. "GOP Pares Legislative Wish List in Run-Up to Elections." *Los Angeles Times* (Washington edition), July 8, p. A6.

Howard, Philip E. N., Lee Rainie, and Steven Jones. 2001. "Days and Nights on the Internet: The Impact of a Diffusing Technology." *American Behavioral Scientist* [forthcoming].

Huffington, Arianna. 2000. *How to Overthrow the Government.* New York: HarperCollins.

Hurd, Michael, and Kathleen McGarry. 1995. "Evaluation of the Subjective Probabilities of Survival in the Health and Retirement Study." *Journal of Human Resources* 30: S268-S292.

Inglehart, Ronald. 1990. *Culture Shift in Advanced Industrial Societies.* Princeton, NJ: Princeton University Press.

Iyengar, Shanto. 1987. "Television News and Citizens' Explanations of National Affairs." *American Political Science Review* 81: 813–31.

Iyengar, Shanto, and Donald P. Kinder. 1987. *News That Matters: Television and American Opinion.* Chicago: University of Chicago Press.

Jacob, Herbert. 1988. *Silent Revolution.* Chicago: University of Chicago Press.

Jacobs, Laurence R. 1992a. "Institutions and Culture: Health Policy and Public Opinion in the U.S. and Britain." *World Politics* 44: 179–209.

———. 1992b. "The Recoil Effect: Public Opinion and Policymaking in the U.S. and Britain." *Comparative Politics* 24: 199–217.

———. 1992c. *Health of Nations: Public Opinion and the Making of Health Policy in the U.S. and Britain.* Ithaca, NY: Cornell University Press.

———. 1993. *The Health of Nations: Public Opinion and the Making of American and British Health Policy.* Ithaca, NY: Cornell University Press.

———. 1995. "Politics of America's Supply State: Health Reform and Technology." *Health Affairs* 14: 143–57.

———. 2002. "Manipulators and Manipulation: Public Opinion in a Representative Democracy." *Journal of Health Politics, Policy, and Law* [forthcoming].

———. 2001a. "A Political and Conditional Theory of Candidate Strategy: President Nixon's White House Polling on Policy Issues and Candidate Image." Paper presented at the annual meeting of the American Political Science Association, San Francisco.

Jacobs, Lawrence R., James Druckman, and Eric Ostermeier. 2001b. "A Theory of Candidate Strategy: President Nixon's White House Polling on Policy Issues and Candidate Image." Paper presented at the annual meeting of the Midwest Political Science Association, April 19–22, Chicago.

Jacobs, Lawrence R., Ronald H. Hinckley, and Robert Y. Shapiro. 1999. "Detached Democracy: Americans See Lobbyists and National Interest as More Influential than Public Opinion." Minneapolis: Department of Political Science, University of Minnesota.

Jacobs, Lawrence R., Eric Lawrence, Robert Y. Shapiro, and Steven S. Smith. 1998. "Congressional Leadership of Public Opinion." *Political Science Quarterly* 113: 21–42.

Jacobs, Lawrence R., and Robert Y. Shapiro. 1992. "Public Decisions, Private Polls: John F. Kennedy's Presidency." Prepared for delivery at the annual meeting of the Midwest Political Science Association, Chicago.

———. 1993a. "Leadership in a Liberal Democracy: Lyndon Johnson's Private Polls and Public Announcements." Presented at the 1993 Annual Meeting of the Midwest Political Science Association, Chicago, April 15–17.

———. 1993b. "The Public Presidency, Private Polls, and Policymaking: Lyndon Johnson." Presented at the annual meeting of the American Political Science Association, Washington, DC, September 2–5.

———. 1994a. "Issues, Candidate Image, and Priming: The Use of Private Polls in Kennedy's 1960 Presidential Campaign." *American Political Science Review* 88: 527–40.

———. 1994b. "Public Opinion's Tilt against Private Enterprise." *Health Affairs* 12: 285–98.

———. 1994c. "Questioning the Conventional Wisdom on Public Opinion toward Health Reform." *PS: Political Science and Politics* 27: 208–14.

———. 1994d. "Studying Substantive Democracy: Public Opinion, Institutions, and Policymaking." *PS: Political Science and Politics* 27: 9–16.

———. 1995a. "Public Opinion and President Clinton's First Year: Leadership and Responsiveness." In *The Clinton Presidency: Campaigning, Governing, and the Psychology of Leadership*, ed. Stanley A. Renshon, 195–211. Boulder, CO.: Westview Press.

———. 1995b. "The Rise of Presidential Polling: The Nixon White House in Historical Perspective." *Public Opinion Quarterly* 59: 163–95.

———. 1996a. "The Annenberg Public Policy Center Poll Watch: The 1996 Presidential Elections." Unpublished report, November 4.

———. 1996b. "Presidential Manipulation of Public Opinion: The Nixon Administration and the Public Pollsters." *Political Science Quarterly* 110: 519–38.

———. 1997a. "The Myth of the Pandering Politician." *Public Perspective* 8: 3–5.

———. 1997b. "Pollwatch: The Media's Reporting and Distorting of Public Opinion toward Entitlements." Unpublished report, September.

———. 1998a. "More Social Security Bunk: UFO Stories." *New Republic*, 10 August.

———. 1998b. "Myths and Misunderstandings about Public Opinion toward Social Security." In *Framing the Social Security Debate*, ed. R. Douglas Arnold. Washington, DC: National Academy of Social Insurance.

———. 1998c. "The Politicization of Public Opinion: The Battle for the Pulpit." In *The Social Divide: Political Parties and the Future of Activist Government*, ed. Margaret Weir, pp. 83–125. Washington, DC: Brookings.

———. 1999. "Lyndon Johnson, Vietnam, and Public Opinion: Rethinking Realist Theory of Leadership." *Presidential Studies Quarterly* 29: 592–616.

———. 2000. *Politicians Don't Pander: Political Manipulation and the Loss of Democratic Responsiveness*. Chicago: University of Chicago Press.

———. 2001. "Source Materials: Presidents and Polling: Politicians, Pandering, and the Study of Democratic Responsiveness." *Presidential Studies Quarterly* 31: 150–67.

Jacobs, Lawrence R., Robert Y. Shapiro, and Lynn K. Harvey. 1998. "The Endogeneity of Self-Interest and Collective Interest in Public Opinion: The Case of Health Care Reform." Unpublished paper, Department of Political Science, University of Minnesota, Minneapolis.

Jacobs, Lawrence R., Robert Y. Shapiro, and Eli Schulman. 1993. "Poll Trends: Medical Care in the United States—An Update." *Public Opinion Quarterly* 57: 394–427.

Jaffe, Natalie. 1978. "Attitudes toward Public Welfare Programs and Recipients in the United States." In *Welfare: The Elusive Consensus*, ed. Lester Salamon, 221–28. New York: Praeger.

Jamieson, Linda F., and Frank M. Bass. 1989. "Adjusting Stated Intentions Measures to Predict Trial Purchase of New Products: A Comparison of Models and Methods." *Journal of Marketing Research* 26: 336–45.

Jencks, Christopher. 1985. "Methodological Problems in Studying 'Military Keynesianism.' " *American Journal of Sociology* 91: 373–79.

Jennings, M. Kent. 1996. "Political Knowledge over Time and across Generations." *Public Opinion Quarterly* 60: 228–52.

Jentleson, Bruce. 1992. "The Pretty Prudent Public: Post Vietnam American Opinion on the Use of Military Force." *International Studies Quarterly* 36: 49–74.

Jervis, Robert. 1997. *System Effects: Complexity in Political and Social Life.* Princeton, NJ: Princeton University Press.

Johnson, Haynes, and David Broder. 1996. *The System: The American Way of Politics at the Breaking Point.* Boston: Little, Brown.

Jones, Bryan D. 1994. *Reconceiving Decision-Making in Democratic Politics.* Chicago: University of Chicago Press.

Jones, Charles O. 1988. *The Trusteeship Presidency.* Baton Rouge: Louisiana State University Press.

Juster, F. Thomas. 1966. "Consumer Buying Intentions and Purchase Probability: An Experiment in Survey Design." *Journal of the American Statistical Association* 61: 658–96.

Juster, F. Thomas, and Richard Suzman. 1995. "An Overview of the Health and Retirement Study." *Journal of Human Resources* 30: S7-S56.

Kagay, Michael. 1991. "The Use of Public Opinion Polls by *The New York Times*: Some Examples for the 1988 Presidential Election." In *Polling and Presidential Election Coverage*, ed. Paul Lavrakas and Jack Holley, pp. 19–56. Newbury Park, CA: Sage Publications.

Kahn, Jonathan. 1997. *Budgeting Democracy: State Building and Citizenship in America, 1890–1928.* Ithaca, NY: Cornell University Press.

Kane, Emily W., and Laura J. Macaulay. 1993. "Interviewer Gender and Gender Attitudes." *Public Opinion Quarterly* 57: 1–28.

Katz, Andrew Z. 1997. "Public Opinion and Foreign Policy: The Nixon Administration and the Pursuit of Peace with Honor in Vietnam." *Presidential Studies Quarterly* 28: 496–513.

———. 1998. "Public Opinion and the Contradictions of President Carter's Foreign Policy." Unpublished paper, Denison University.

Katz, Daniel, and Hadley Cantril. 1937. "Public Opinion Polls." *Sociometry* 1: 155–79.

Katznelson, Ira. 1973. *Black Men, White Cities: Race, Politics, and Migration in the United States, 1900–30, and Britain, 1948–68.* Oxford: Oxford University Press.

Kau, James B., and Paul H. Rubin. 1993. "Ideology, Voting, and Shirking." *Public Choice* 76: 151–76.

Keeter, Scott, Carolyn Miller, Andrew Kohut, Robert M. Groves, and Stanley Presser. 2000. "Consequences of Reducing Nonresponse in a National Telephone Survey." *Public Opinion Quarterly* 64: 125–48.

Kelleher, Catherine McArdle. 1994. "Security in the New Order: Presidents, Polls, and the Use of Force." In *Beyond the Beltway: Engaging the Public in U.S. Foreign Policy*, ed. Daniel Yankelovich and I. M. Destler, pp. 225–52. New York: W. W. Norton.

Kernell, Samuel. 1986. *Going Public: New Strategies of Presidential Leadership*. Washington, DC: CQ Press.

———. 1993. *Going Public: New Strategies of Presidential Leadership*. 2nd ed. Washington, DC: Congressional Quarterly Press.

Kerrey, Robert. 1997. Remarks at Hearing 007. *2010 and Beyond: Preparing Social Security for the Baby Boomers*. Washington, DC: Special Committee on Aging, U.S. Senate, August 26.

Key, V. O. Jr. 1961. *Public Opinion and American Democracy*. New York: Alfred A. Knopf.

———. 1966. *The Responsible Electorate: Rationality in Presidential Voting, 1936–1960*. Cambridge, MA: Harvard University Press.

Keyssar, Alexander. 2000. *The Right to Vote: The Contested History of Democracy in the United States*. New York: Basic Books.

Kinder, Donald, and Don Herzog. 1993. "Democratic Discussion." In *Reconsidering the Democratic Public*, ed. George E. Marcus and Russell L. Hanson. University Park: Penn State Press.

Kinder, Donald R., and Lynn M. Sanders. 1990. "Mimicking Political Debate with Survey Questions: The Case of White Opinion on Affirmative Action for Blacks." *Social Cognition* 8: 73–103.

———. 1996. *Divided by Color: Racial Politics and Democratic Ideals*. Chicago: University of Chicago Press.

King, Anthony. 1997. *Running Scared: Why America's Politicians Campaign Too Much and Govern Too Little*. New York: Martin Kessler Books.

Kingdon, John. 1984. *Agendas, Alternatives, and Public Policies*. Boston: Little, Brown.

———. 1989. *Congressmen's Voting Decisions*. 3d ed. Ann Arbor: University of Michigan Press.

———. 1995. *Agendas, Alternatives, and Public Policies*. 2nd ed. New York: HarperCollins.

Kluegel, James. 1987. "Macro-Economic Problems, Beliefs about the Poor and Attitudes toward Welfare Spending." *Social Problems* 34: 82–99.

Kohut, Andrew. 1998. "Washington Leaders Wary of Public Opinion." Washington, DC: Pew Center for the People and the Press.

Krehbiel, Keith. 1991. *Information and Legislative Organization*. Ann Arbor: University of Michigan Press.

Krysan, Maria. 1997. "Privacy and the Expression of White Racial Attitudes: A Comparison across Three Contexts." Unpublished manuscript, Pennsylvania State University, University Park.

Krysan, Maria, Howard Schuman, Leslie Jo Scott, and Paul Beatty. 1994. "Response Rates and Response Content in Mail Versus Face-to-Face Surveys." *Public Opinion Quarterly* 58: 381–99.

Kuklinski, James. 1978. "Representativeness and Elections: A Policy Analysis." *American Political Science Review* 72 (March): 165–77.

Kuklinski, James H., Michael D. Cobb, and Martin Gilens. 1997. "Racial Attitudes and the 'New South.'" *Journal of Politics* 59: 323–49.

Kuklinski, James H., Paul J. Quirk, Jennifer Jerit, David Schwieder, and Robert Rich. 2002. "Misinformation and the Currency of Citizenship." *Journal of Politics* [forthcoming].

Kuklinski, James H., Paul M. Sniderman, Kathleen Knight, Thomas Piazza, Philip E. Tetlock, Gordon R. Lawrence, and Barbara Mellers. 1997. "Racial Prejudice and Attitudes toward Affirmative Action." *American Journal of Political Science* 41: 402–19.

Kull, Steven. 1999. "Expecting More Say: The American Public on Its Role in Government Decisionmaking." Washington, DC: Center on Policy Attitudes.

———. 2000. "Americans on Federal Budget Priorities." Washington, DC: Center on Policy Attitudes.

———. 2001. "Americans on Foreign Aid and World Hunger." Washington, DC: Program on International Policy Attitudes.

Kull, Steven, and I. M. Destler. 1999. *Misreading the Public: The Myth of a New Isolationism.* Washington, DC: Brookings Institution Press.

Kull, Steven, I. M. Destler, and Clay Ramsay. 1997. *The Foreign Policy Gap: How Policymakers Misread the Public.* College Park, MD: Center for International and Security Studies.

Kusnitz, Leonard A. 1984. *Public Opinion and Foreign Policy: America's China Policy, 1949– 1979.* Westport, CT: Greenwood Press.

Ladd, Everett. 1996. "The Election Polls: An American Waterloo." *Chronicle of Higher Education,* November 22, p. A52.

Laumann, Edward O., and David Knoke. 1987. *The Organizational State.* Madison: University of Wisconsin Press.

Lazarsfeld, Paul F., Bernard Berelson, and Hazel Gaudet. 1944. *The People's Choice: How the Voter Makes Up His Mind in a Presidential Campaign.* New York: Columbia University Press.

Lee, Taeku. 2002. *Mobilizing Public Opinion: Black Insurgency and Racial Attitudes in the Civil Rights Era.* Chicago: University of Chicago Press.

Levitt, Steven D. 1996. "How Do Senators Vote? Disentangling the Role of Voter Preferences, Party Affiliation, and Senator Ideology." *American Economic Review* 86 (June): 425–41.

Lewis, Justin. 2001. *Constructing Public Opinion: How Political Elites Do What They Like and Why We Seem to Go Along with It.* New York: Columbia University Press.

Lexis-Nexis Academic Universe. Available at http://web.lexis-nexis.com.

Lichtenstein, Sara, Baruch Fischhoff, and Lawrence Phillips. 1982. "Calibration of Probabilities: The State of the Art to 1980." In *Judgment under Uncertainty: Heuristics and Biases,* ed. Daniel Kahneman, Paul Slovic, and Amos Tversky, pp. 306–34. New York: Cambridge University Press.

Lindblom, Charles E. 1977. *Politics and Markets: The World's Political Economic Systems.* New York: Basic Books.

Lippmann, Walter. 1922. *Public Opinion.* New York: Macmillan.

———. 1925. *The Phantom Public.* New York: Harcourt Brace Jovanovich.

Lipset, Seymour Martin. 1996. *American Exceptionalism: A Double-Edged Sword.* New York: Norton.

Lipset, Seymour Martin, and Gary W. Marks. 2000. *It Didn't Happen Here: Why Socialism Failed in the United States.* New York: Norton.

Lohmann, Larry. 1998. "Whose Voice is Speaking? How Public Opinion Polling and Cost-Benefit Analysis Synthesize New Publics." The Cornerhouse Briefing #7.

Lott, John R., and Michael L. Davids. 1992. "A Critical Review and an Extension of the Political Shirking Literature." *Public Choice* 74: 461–85.

Lukefahr, Robert. 1994. Hearing 003. *Proposals for Alternate Investment of the Social Security Trust Fund Reserves.* Washington, DC: Committee on Ways and Means, U.S. House of Representatives, October 4.

Lukes, Steven. 1974. *Power: A Radical View.* London: Macmillan.

Lupia, Arthur. 1994. "Shortcuts versus Encyclopedias: Information and Voting Behavior in California Insurance Reform Elections" *American Political Science Review* 88(1): 63–76.

Lupia, Arthur, and Mathew D. McCubbins. 1998. *The Democratic Dilemma: Can Citizens Learn What They Need to Know?* New York: Cambridge University Press.

Lupia, Arthur, Mathew D. McCubbins, and Samuel L. Popkin. 2000. "Elements of Reason: Cognition, Choice, and the Bounds of Rationality." New York: Cambridge University Press.

Luttbeg, Norman R. 1968. "Political Linkage in a Larger Society." In *Public Opinion and Public Policy*, ed. Norman R. Luttbeg. Homewood, IL: Dorsey.

Maas, Kees, Marco Steenbergen, and Willem Saris. 1990. "Vote Probabilities." *Electoral Studies* 9: 91–107.

MacArthur, John R. 2000. *The Selling of "Free Trade": NAFTA, Washington, and the Subversion of American Democracy.* New York: Hill and Wang.

Maltese, John A. 1994. *Spin Control: The White House Office of Communications and the Management of Presidential News.* 2nd ed. Chapel Hill: University of North Carolina Press.

Manin, Bernard. 1997. *The Principles of Representative Government.* New York: Cambridge University Press.

Manley, John F. 1973. "The Conservative Coalition in Congress." *American Behavioral Scientist* 17: 223–47.

Mansbridge, Jane. 1983. *Beyond Adversary Democracy.* Chicago: University of Chicago.

Manski, Charles. 1990. "The Use of Intentions Data to Predict Behavior: A Best Case Analysis." *Journal of the American Statistical Association* 85: 934–40.

———. 1999. "Analysis of Choice Expectations in Incomplete Scenarios." *Journal of Risk and Uncertainty* 19: 49–66.

———. 2000. "Why Polls Are Fickle." *New York Times*, October 16, p. A27.

———. 2001. "Questionnaires: Assessing Subjective Probabilities." In *International Encyclopedia of the Social and Behavioral Sciences*, ed. Neil J. Smelser and Paul B. Baltes, pp. 134–157 Oxford: Elsevier Science.

Manski, Charles, and John Straub. 2000. "Worker Perceptions of Job Insecurity in the Mid-1990s: Evidence from the Survey of Economic Expectations." *Journal of Human Resources* 35: 447–79.

Manza, Jeff, and Clem Brooks. 1999. *Social Cleavages and Political Change.* New York: Oxford University Press.

Manza, Jeff, and Fay Lomax Cook. 2002. "A Democratic Polity? Three Views of Policy Responsiveness to Public Opinion in the United States." *American Political Research* 30 (in press).

Margolis, Michael, and Gary A. Mauser, eds. 1989. *Manipulating Public Opinion: Essays on Public Opinion as a Dependent Variable.* Pacific Grove, CA: Brooks/Cole.

Markoff, John. 1996. *Waves of Democracy.* Thousand Oaks, CA: Pine Forge Press.

Marmor, Theodore R. 1997. Testimony at Hearing 011. *Concurrent Resolution on the Budget for FY98, vol. II: Proposal for Long-Term Reform*, pp. 91–174. Washington, DC: Government Printing Office, Committee on Budget, U.S. Senate, January 29.

Martin, Cathie Jo. 2000. *Stuck in Neutral: Business and the Politics of Human Capital Investment Policy.* Princeton, NJ: Princeton University Press.

Mayer, William. 1992. *The Changing American Mind: How and Why Public Opinion Changed between 1960 and 1988.* Ann Arbor: University of Michigan Press.

Mayhew, David. 1974. *The Electoral Connection.* New Haven, CT: Yale University Press.

———. 1991. *Divided We Govern: Party Control, Lawmaking, and Investigations, 1946–1990.* New Haven, CT: Yale University Press.

McAdam, Doug. 1982. *Political Process and the Development of Black Insurgency, 1930–1970.* Chicago: University of Chicago Press.

McCarty, Nolan M., Keith T. Poole, and Howard Rosenthal. 1997. *Income Redistribution and the Realignment of American Politics*. AEI Studies on Understanding Economic Inequality. Washington, DC: AEI Press.

McChesney, Fred. 1997. *Money for Nothing: Politicians, Rent Extraction, and Political Extortion*. Cambridge, MA: Harvard University Press.

McClain, Paula D., and John A. Garcia. 1990. "Expanding Disciplinary Boundaries: Black, Latino, and Racial Minority Group Politics in Political Science." In *Political Science: The State of the Discipline*, ed. Ada W. Finifter, pp. 247–79. Washington, DC: American Political Science Association.

McClelland, A., and F. Bolger. 1994. "The Calibration of Subjective Probabilities: Theories and Models, 1980–94." In *Subjective Probability*, ed. G. Wright and P. Ayton, pp. 453–82. New York: Wiley.

McClosky, Herbert, and John Zaller. 1984. *The American Ethos: Public Attitudes toward Captialism and Democracy*. Cambridge, MA: Harvard University Press.

McCombs, Maxwell, and Donald L. Shaw. 1993. "Agenda-Setting Revisited." *Journal of Communication* 43: 58–128.

McCombs, Maxwell, and Jian-Hua Zhu. 1995. "Capacity, Diversity and Volatility of the Public Agenda." *Public Opinion Quarterly* 59: 495–525.

McDonough, Eileen. 1992. "Representative Democracy and State Building in the Progressive Era." *American Political Science Review* 86: 938–50.

Meernik, James, and Michael Ault. 2001. "Public Opinion and Support for U.S. Presidents' Foreign Policies." *American Politics Research* 29: 352–73.

Meier, Kenneth. 1980. "Rationality and Voting: A Downsian Analysis of the 1972 Election." *Western Political Quarterly* 33: 38–49.

Meier, Kenneth, and James Campbell. 1979. "Issue Voting: An Empirical Examination of Individually Necessary and Jointly Sufficient Conditions." *American Political Quarterly* 7: 21–50.

Mermin, Jonathan. 1999. *Debating War and Peace: Media Coverage of U.S. Intervention in the Post-Vietnam Era*. Princeton, NJ: Princeton University Press.

Meyer, Philip. 1990. "Polling as Political Science and Polling as Journalism." *Public Opinion Quarterly* 54: 451–59.

Meyrowitz, Joshua. 1985. *No Sense of Place: The Impact of Electronic Media on Social Behavior*. New York: Oxford University Press.

Miller, Peter V. 1984. "Alternative Question Forms for Attitude Scale Questions in Telephone Interviews." *Public Opinion Quarterly* 48 (4): 766–78.

Miller, Peter, and Charles Cannell. 1987. "Experimental Interviewing Techniques." In *An Experimental Comparison of Telephone and Personal Interviews: Vital and Health Statistics*, ed. Owen Thornberry, pp. 20–25. Series 2, No. 106. *Public Opinion Quarterly* 48: 766–79.

Miller, Warren E., and Donald E. Stokes. 1963. "Constituency Influence in Congress." *American Political Science Review* 57: 45–56.

———. 1966. "Constituency Influence in Congress." In *Elections and the Political Order*, ed. Angus Campbell, Philip E. Converse, Warren E. Miller, and Donald E. Stokes, pp. 351–72. New York: Wiley.

Molotch, Harvey. 1970. "Oil in Santa Barbara and Power in America." *Sociological Inquiry* 40: 131–44.

Monroe, Alan D. 1979. "Consistency between Public Preferences and National Policy Decisions." *American Politics Quarterly* 7: 3–19.

———. 1983. "American Party Platforms and Public Opinion." *American Journal of Political Science* 27: 27–42.

————. 1998 "Public Opinion and Public Policy 1980–1993." *Public Opinion Quarterly* 62: 6–28.

Morin, Richard. 1995a. "The 1992 Election and the Polls: Neither Politics nor Polling as Usual." In *Presidential Polls and the News Media*, ed. Paul Lavrakas, Michael Traugott, and Peter Miller, pp. 123–43. Boulder, CO: Westview Press.

————. 1995b. "Public Growing Wary of GOP Cuts." *Washington Post*, March 21, pp. A1, A6.

————. 2000. "Telling Polls Apart." *Washington Post*, August 16, p. A35.

Morin, Richard, and Mario Brossard. 1996. "Key Voters Are Fleeing House GOP." *Washington Post*, June 17, p. A1.

Morris, Dick. 1997. *Behind the Oval Office: Winning the Presidency in the Nineties*. New York: Random House.

Mueller, Carol. 1997. "International Press Coverage of Protests in East Germany." *American Sociological Review* 62: 820–32.

Mueller, 1973. *War, Presidents, and Public Opinion*. New York: Wiley.

————. 1994. *Policy and Opinion in the Gulf War*. Chicago: University of Chicago Press.

Murray, Shoon Kathleen. 1999. "The Reagan Administration's Use of Private Polls." Paper presented at the annual meeting of the American Political Science Association, Atlanta, September.

Murray, Shoon Kathleen, and Peter Howard. 2000. "Spending on Private White House Pollsters: Carter to Clinton." Unpublished paper, School of International Service, American University, Washington, DC.

Mutz, Diana. 1989. "The Influence of Perceptions of Media Influence: Third Person Effects and the Public Expression of Opinion." *International Journal of Public Opinion Research* 1: 3–24.

Myrdal, Gunnar. 1944. *An American Dilemma*. New York: Harper and Row.

Nacos, Brigitte L., Robert Y. Shapiro, and Pierangelo Isernia, eds. 2000. *Decisionmaking in a Glass House: Mass Media, Public Opinion, and American and European Foreign Policy in the 21st Century*. Lanham, MD: Rowman & Littlefield.

Nelson, Thomas E., R. A. Clawson, and Z. M. Oxley. 1997. "Media Framing of a Civil Liberties Conflict and Its Effect on Tolerance." *American Political Science Review* 91: 567–83.

Nelson, Thomas E., and Donald R. Kinder. 1996. "Issue Frames and Group-Centrism in American Public Opinion." *Journal of Politics* 58: 1055–78.

Neuman, Russell. 1989. "Parallel Content Analysis: Old Paradigms and New Proposals." *Public Communication and Behavior*, vol. 2. New York: Academic Press.

Nie, Norman, and Lutz Erbring. 2000. "Internet and Society." Stanford Institute for the Quantitative Study of Society, February 2000.

Nie, Norman H., Sidney Verba, and John R. Petrocik. 1979. *The Changing American Voter*. Enlarged ed. Cambridge, MA: Harvard University Press.

Norris, Pippa. 1995. "The Restless Searchlight: Network News Framing of the Post Cold-War World." *Political Communication* 12: 357–70.

Office of Management and Budget. 1999. *A Citizen's Guide to the Federal Budget: Fiscal Year 2000*. Washington, DC: Government Printing Office.

Oksenberg, Lois, Lerita Coleman, and Charles Cannell. 1986. "Interviewers' Voices and Refusal Rates in Telephone Surveys." *Public Opinion Quarterly* 50: 97–111.

Olson, Mancur Jr. 1965. *The Logic of Collective Action: Public Goods and the Theory of Groups*. Cambridge, MA: Harvard University Press.

Oregon Survey Research Laboratory. 1998. "Characteristics of Households with Multiple

Telephone Lines in Two Random Digit Dial Surveys." Oregon Survey Research Laboratory 1998 Annual Report, University of Oregon.

Ornstein, Norman J. 1996. "Enough Polls!" *USA Today*, Oct. 7, p. 17A.

Ornstein, Norman J., and Thomas E. Mann, eds. 2000. *The Permanent Campaign and Its Future*. Washington, DC: Brookings Institution Press.

Ostrom, Charles W., Jr., and Robin F. Marra. 1986. "U.S. Defense Spending and the Soviet Estimate." *American Political Science Review* 80: 819–41.

Page, Benjamin I. 1978. *Choices and Echoes in Presidential Elections: Rational Man in Electoral Democracy*. Chicago: University of Chicago Press.

———. 1994. "Democratic Responsiveness? Untangling the Links between Public Opinion and Policy." *PS: Political Science and Politics* 27 (March): 25–29.

———. 1996. *Who Deliberates?: Mass Media in Modern Democracy*. Chicago: University of Chicago Press.

———. 2000. "Is Social Security Reform Ready for the American Public." In *Social Security and Medicare: Individual versus Collective Risk and Responsibility*, ed. Shelia Burke, Eric Kingson, and Uwe Reinhardt, pp. 183–207. Washington, DC: National Academy of Social Insurance.

Page, Benjamin I., and Mark Petracca. 1983. *The American Presidency*. New York: McGraw-Hill.

Page, Benjamin I., and Robert Y. Shapiro. 1983. "Effects of Public Opinion on Policy." *American Political Science Review* 77 (March): 175–90.

———. 1992. *The Rational Public: Fifty Years of Trends in Americans' Policy Preferences*. Chicago: University of Chicago Press.

Page, Benjamin I., Robert Y. Shapiro, Paul W. Gronke, and Robert M. Rosenberg. 1984. "Constituency, Party, and Representation in Congress." *Public Opinion Quarterly* 48: 741–56.

Page, Benjamin I., and James R. Simmons. 2000. *What Government Can Do: Dealing with Poverty and Inequality*. Chicago: University of Chicago Press.

Patterson, James T. 1981. *Congressional Conservatism and the New Deal: The Growth of the Conservative Coalition in Congress, 1933–1939*. Westport, CT: Greenwood Press.

Peschek, Joseph G. 1987. *Policy-Planning Organizations: Elite Agendas and America's Rightward Turn*. Philadelphia: Temple University Press.

Peters, John Durham. 1995. "Historical Tensions in the Concept of Public Opinion." In *Public Opinion and the Communication of Consent*, ed. Theodore Glasser and Charles Salmon. New York: Guilford Press.

Piazza, Thomas, and Paul M. Sniderman. 1998. "Incorporating Experiments into Computer Assisted Surveys." In *Computer Assisted Survey Information Collection*, ed. Mick P. Couper, Reginald P. Baker, Jelke Bethlehem, Cynthia Z. F. Clark, Jean Martin, William L. Nicholls II, and James M. O'Reilly, pp. 167–84. New York: Wiley.

Pious, Richard M. 1979. *The American Presidency*. New York: Basic Books.

Pitkin, Hanna Fenichel. 1967. *The Concept of Representation*. Berkeley: University of California Press.

Piven, Frances F., and Richard A. Cloward. 1977. *Poor People's Movements: Why They Succeed, How They Fail*. New York: Pantheon Books.

———. 1993. *Regulating the Poor: The Functions of Public Welfare*. Updated ed. New York: Vintage Books.

Pogrebin, Robin. 1996. "Foreign Coverage Less Prominent in News Magazines." *New York Times*, Monday, September 23, p. D2.

Polsby, Nelson W. 1980. *Community Power and Political Theory: A Further Look at Problems of Evidence and Inference*. New Haven, CT: Yale University Press.

Poole, Keith T., and Howard Rosenthal. 1997. *Congress: A Political-Economic History of Roll Call Voting.* New York: Oxford University Press.

Popkin, Samuel. 1994 [1991]. *The Reasoning Voter: Communication and Persuasion in Presidential Campaigns.* 2d ed. Chicago: University of Chicago Press.

Potter, David M. 1972. *The South and the Concurrent Majority.* Baton Rouge: Louisiana State University Press.

Powell, G. Bingham. 2000. *Elections as Instruments of Democracy: Majoritarian and Proportional Visions.* New Haven, CT: Yale University Press.

Powlick, Philip J. 1991. "The Attitudinal Bases of Responsiveness to Public Opinion among American Foreign Policy Officials." *Journal of Conflict Resolution* 35: 611–41.

———. 1995a. "Public Opinion in the Foreign Policy Process: An Attitudinal and Institutional Comparison of the Reagan and Clinton Administrations." Paper presented at the annual meeting of the American Political Sciences Association, Chicago, September 1–4.

———. 1995b. "The Sources of Public Opinion for American Foreign Policy Officials." *International Studies Quarterly* 39: 427–52.

Powlick, Philip J., and Andrew Z. Katz. 1998. "Defining the American Public Opinion/Foreign Policy Nexus." *Mershon International Studies Review* 42: 29–61.

Prechel, Harland. 1990. "Steel and the State: Industry Politics and Business Policy Formation, 1940–89." *American Sociological Review* 55: 648–68.

Presser, Stanley. 1984. "The Use of Survey Data in Basic Research in the Social Sciences." In *Surveying Subjective Phenomena,* ed. Charles F. Turner and Elizabeth Martin, pp. 93–114. New York: Russell Sage Phenomena.

Presser, Stanley, and Howard Schuman. 1980. "The Measurement of a Middle Position in Attitude Surveys." *Public Opinion Quarterly* 44: 70–85.

Price, Vincent. 1992. *Communication Concepts 4: Public Opinion.* Newbury Park, CA: Sage.

Public Perspective. 1995. "People, Opinions, and Polls." 6 (February/March): 28–32.

Purdum, Todd. 1996. "Clinton Recalls His Promise, Weighs History, and Decides." *New York Times,* August 1, p. A1.

Quadrel, Marilyn, Baruch Fischhoff, and W. Davis. 1993. "Adolescent (In)vulnerability." *American Psychologist* 48: 102–16.

Quirk, Paul J., and Joseph Hinchliffe. 1998. "The Rising Hegemony of Mass Opinion." *Journal of Policy History* 10: 19–50.

Quirk, Paul J., and Bruce Nemith. 1995. "Divided Government and Policy Making: Negotiating the Laws." In *The Presidency and the Political System,* 4th ed., ed. Michael Nelson, pp. 531–54. Washington, DC: CQ Press.

Rasinski, Kenneth A. 1989. "The Effect of Question Wording on Public Support for Government Spending." *Public Opinion Quarterly* 53: 388–94.

Reich, Robert B. 1997. *Locked in the Cabinet.* New York: Alfred A. Knopf.

Reskin, Barbara F. 1998. *The Realities of Affirmative Action in Employment.* Washington, DC: American Sociological Association.

Richard, Patricia Bayer. 1994. "Polling and Political Campaigns." In *The Practice of Political Communication,* ed. Guido Stempel, pp. 25–38. Englewoods Cliffs, NJ: Prentice Hall.

Richman, Alvin. 1996. "The Polls—Trends: American Support for International Involvement: General and Specific Components of Post–Cold War Changes." *Public Opinion Quarterly* 60: 305–21.

Ringquist, Evan J., Kim Quaile Hill, Jan E. Leighley, and Angela Hinton-Anderson. 1997. "Lower-Class Mobilization and Policy Linkage in the U.S. States: A Correction." *American Journal of Political Science* 41 (January): 39–344.

Risse-Kappen, Thomas. 1991. "Public Opinion, Domestic Structure, and Foreign Policy in Liberal Democracies." *World Politics* 43: 479–512.

——. 1994. "Masses and Leaders: Public Opinion, Domestic Structures, and Foreign Policy." In *The New Politics of American Foreign Policy*, ed. David A. Deese, pp. 238–61. New York: St. Martin's Press.

Rivers, Douglas. 2000. "Probability-Based Web Surveying: An Overview." Paper presented at the Annual Conference of the American Association for Public Opinion Research, Portland, OR.

Rohde, David W. 1991. *Parties and Leaders in the Postreform House.* Chicago: University of Chicago Press.

Rose, Nancy E. 1994. *Put to Work: Relief Programs in the Great Depression.* New York: Monthly Review Press.

Rosenstone, Steven J., Roy L. Behr, and Edward H. Lazarus. 1996. *Third Parties in America: Citizen Response to Major Party Failure.* 2nd ed. Princeton, NJ: Princeton University Press.

Rosenstone, Steven J., and John Mark Hansen. 1993. *Mobilization, Participation, and Democracy in America.* New York: Macmillan.

Rugg, Donald. 1941. "Experiments in Wording Questions: II." *Public Opinion Quarterly* 5: 91–92.

Russett, Bruce. 1990. *Controlling the Sword: The Democratic Governance of National Security.* Cambridge, MA: Harvard University Press.

Russett, Bruce, and Thomas W. Graham. 1989. "Public Opinion and National Security Policy: Relationships and Impacts." In *Handbook of War Studies*, ed. Manus Midlarsky, pp. 239–57. London: Allen and Unwin.

Salisbury, Robert H. 1990. "The Paradox of Interest Groups in Washington: More Groups, Less Clout." In *The New American Political System*, 2d ed., ed. Anthony King, pp. 203–29. Washington, DC: AEI Press.

Salzman, Harold, and G. William Domhoff. 1983. "Nonprofit Organizations and the Corporate Community." *Social Science History* 7: 205–16.

Sanders, Jerry W. 1983. *Peddlers of Crisis: The Committee on the Present Danger and the Politics of Containment.* Boston: South End Press.

Sanders, Lynn. 1999. "Democratic Politics and Survey Research." *Philosophy of Social Sciences* 29: 248–80.

Sartori, Giovanni. 1970. "Concept Misinformation in Comparative Politics." *American Political Science Review* 64 (December): 1033–53.

Savage, Leonard. 1971. "Elicitation of Personal Probabilities and Expectations." *Journal of the American Statistical Association* 66: 783–801.

Schattschneider, E. E. 1960. *The Semi-Sovereign People.* New York: Holt, Rinehart and Winston.

Schlozman, Kay Lehman, and John T. Tierney. 1986. *Organized Interests and American Democracy.* New York: Harper & Row.

Schneider, William. 1995. "Ka-Boom! It's Another Contract!" *National Journal*, April 22.

Schultz, Charles L. 1995. Testimony at Hearing 004. *Privatization of the Social Security Old Age and Survivors Insurance Program.* Washington, DC: Committee on Finance, U.S. Senate, August 2.

Schuman, Howard. 1982. "Artifacts Are in the Mind of the Observer." *American Sociologist* 17: 21–28.

Schuman, Howard, and Stanley Presser. 1981. *Questions and Answers in Attitude Surveys.* San Diego: Academic Press.

Schuman, Howard, Stanley Presser, and Jacob Ludwig. 1981. "Context Effects on Survey Responses to Questions about Abortion." *Public Opinion Quarterly* 45: 216–23.

Schuman, Howard, Charlotte Steeh, Lawrence Bobo, and Maria Krysan. 1997. *Racial Attitudes in America*. Revised ed. Cambridge, MA: Harvard University Press.

Schumpeter, Joseph A. 1950. *Capitalism, Socialism, and Democracy*. New York: Harper.

Shami, Jacob, and Shamir, Michael. 1997. "Pluralistic Ignorance across Issues and over Time: Information Cues and Biases." *Public Opinion Quarterly* 61: 227–60.

Shapiro, Catherine R., David W. Brady, Richard A. Brody, and John A. Ferejohn. 1990. "Linking Constituency Opinion and Senate Voting Scores: A Hybrid Explanation." *Legislative Studies Quarterly* 15 (November): 599–621.

Shapiro, Robert Y. 1982. *The Dynamics of Public Opinion and Public Policy*. Ph.D. dissertation, University of Chicago.

Shapiro, Robert Y., and Lawrence R. Jacobs. 1989. "The Relationship between Public Opinion and Public Policy: A Review." In *Political Behavior Annual*, Vol. 2, ed. Samuel Long, pp. 149–79. Boulder, CO: Westview Press.

———. 1999. "Chapter 9. Public Opinion and Policymaking." In *Public Opinion*, ed. Carroll J. Glynn, Susan Herbst, Garrett J. O'Keefe, and Robert Y. Shapiro, pp. 299–340. Boulder, CO: Westview Press.

———. 2000. "Who Leads and Who Follows? U.S. Presidents, Public Opinion, and Foreign Policy." In *Decisionmaking in a Glass House: Mass Media, Public Opinion, and American and European Foreign Policy in the 21st Century*, ed. Brigitte L. Nacos, Robert Y. Shapiro, and Pierangelo Isernia, pp. 223–45. Boston: Rowman and Littlefield.

Shapiro, Robert Y., and Benjamin I. Page. 1988. "Foreign Policy and the Rational Public." *Journal of Conflict Resolution* 32: 211–247.

———. 1994. "Foreign Policy and the Public." In *The New Politics of American Foreign Policy*, ed. David A. Deese, pp. 216–35. New York: St. Martin's Press.

Sharp, Elaine B. 1999. *The Sometime Connection: Public Opinion and Social Policy*. Albany: SUNY Press.

Shelley, Mack C. 1983. *The Permanent Majority: The Conservative Coalition in the United States Congress*. Tuscaloosa: University of Alabama Press.

Shin, Annys. 1997. "Gen-X Rift over Social Security." *National Journal*, February 15, pp. 325–26.

Shogren, Elizabeth. 1996. "House and Senate Conferees Approve Welfare Overhaul." *Los Angeles Times*, July 31, p. A1.

Shoup, Laurence. 1975. "Shaping the Postwar World: The Council on Foreign Relations and United States War Aims." *Insurgent Sociologist* 5: 9–52.

———. 1977. "The Council on Foreign Relations and American Policy in Southeast Asia, 1940–1973." *Insurgent Sociologist* 7: 19–30.

Shoup, Laurence, and William Minter. 1977. *Imperial Brain Trust*. New York: Monthly Review Press.

Singer, Eleanor. 1987. "Editor's Introduction." *Public Opinion Quarterly* 51: S1-S3.

Singer, Eleanor, John Van Hoewyk, and Mary P. Maher. 2000. "Experiments with Incentives in Telephone Surveys." *Public Opinion Quarterly* 64:125–48.

Skidmore, Max J. 1999. *Social Security and Its Enemies*. Boulder, CO: Westview.

Skocpol, Theda. 1979. *States and Social Revolution*. New York: Cambridge University Press.

———. 1992. *Protecting Soldiers and Mothers*. Cambridge, MA: Harvard University Press.

———. 1995. "Response." *American Political Science Review* 89: 720–30.

Skowronek, Stephen. 1993. *The Politics Presidents Make: Leadership from John Adams to George Bush*. Cambridge, MA: Harvard University/Belknap Press.

Smith, A. Wade. 1987. "Problems and Progress in the Measurement of Black Public Opinion." *American Behavioral Scientist* 30: 441–55.

Smith, Eric R. A. N. 1989. *The Unchanging American Voter*. Berkeley: University of California Press.

Smith, Mark A. 2000. *American Business and Political Power: Public Opinion, Elections, and Democracy*. Chicago: University of Chicago Press.

Smith, Tom W. 1987. "That Which We Call Welfare by Any Other Name Would Be Sweeter: An Analysis of the Impact of Question Wording on Response Patterns." *Public Opinion Quarterly* 5: 75–83.

Sniderman, Paul M. 1993. "The New Look in Public Opinion Research." In *Political Science: The State of the Discipline II*, ed. Ada W. Finifter, pp. 219–46. Washington, DC: American Political Science Association.

Sniderman, Paul M., Richard A. Brody, and Philip Tetlock. 1991. *Reasoning and Choice: Explorations in Political Psychology*. New York: Cambridge University Press.

Sniderman, Paul M., and Edward G. Carmines. 1997. *Reaching beyond Race*. Cambridge, MA: Harvard University Press.

Sniderman, Paul M., and Douglas B. Grob. 1996. "Innovations in Experimental Design in Attitude Surveys." *Annual Review of Sociology* 22: 377–99.

Sniderman, Paul M., Louk Hagendoorn, and Markus Prior. 2000. "The Banality of Extremism: Exploratory Studies in Political Persuasion." Prepared for the annual meetings of the Midwest Political Science Association, Chicago.

Sniderman, Paul M., Pierangelo Peri, Rui J. P. de Figueiredo, Jr., and Thomas Piazza. 2000. *The Outsider: Prejudice and Politics in Italy*. Princeton, NJ: Princeton University Press.

Sniderman, Paul M., and Thomas Piazza. 1993. *The Scar of Race*. Cambridge, MA: Harvard University Press.

Sniderman, Paul M., and Sean M. Theriault. 1999. "The Structure of Political Argument and the Logic of Issue Framing." Unpublished manuscript, Department of Sociology, Stanford University.

———. 1996. "U.S. and European Attitudes toward Intervention in the Former Yugoslavia: Mourir pour la Bosnie." In *The World and Yugoslavia's Wars*, ed. Richard H. Ullman, pp. 145–81. New York: Council on Foreign Relations.

———. 1998. "Portraying American Public Opinion toward the Bosnia Crisis." *Harvard International Journal of Press and Politics* 3: 16–33.

———. 2001. *The Impact of Public Opinion on U.S. Foreign Policy since Vietnam: Constraining the Colossus*. New York: Oxford University Press.

Social Security Advisory Board. 1998. *Why Action Should Be Taken Soon*. Washington, DC: SSAB.

Social Security and Medicare Boards of Trustees. 1999. *Status of the Social Security and Medicare Programs: A Summary of the 1999 Annual Report*. Washington, DC: Government Printing Office.

Sorauf, Frank. 1988. *Money in American Elections*. Glenview, IL: Scott, Foresman.

Squire, Peveril. 1988. "Why the 1936 Literary Digest Poll Failed." *Public Opinion Quarterly* 52: 125–33.

Steeh, Charlotte, and Maria Krysan. 1996. "Affirmative Action and the Public, 1970–1995." *Public Opinion Quarterly* 60: 128–58.

Stein, Robert M., and Kenneth N. Bickers. 1995. *Perpetuating the Pork Barrel: Policy Subsystems and American Democracy*. New York: Cambridge University Press.

Stephanopoulos, George. 1999. *All Too Human: A Political Education*. Boston: Little, Brown.

Stevenson, Richard W. 2000. "The 2000 Campaign: The Issues; Bush to Advocate Private Accounts in Social Security." *New York Times*, May 1, p. 1.

Stimson, James A. 1991. *Public Opinion in America*. Boulder, CO: Westview.

———. 1999. *Public Opinion in America*. Rev. ed. Boulder, CO: Westview.

Stimson, James A., Michael B. MacKuen, and Robert Erikson. 1994. "Opinion and Policy: A Global View." *PS: Political Science and Politics* 27: 29–35.

———. 1995. "Dynamic Representation." *American Political Science Review* 89: 543–65.

Stokes, Donald E., and Warren E. Miller. 1966. "Party Government and the Salience of Congress." In *Elections and the Political Order*, ed. Angus Campbell, Philip E. Converse, Warren E. Miller, and Donald E. Stokes. New York: Wiley, 1966.

Stone, Peter H. 1995. "All in the Family." *National Journal*, October 28, pp. 2641–45.

Strickland, Ruth A., and Marcia L. Whicker. 1992. "Political and Socioeconomic Indicators of State Restrictiveness toward Abortion." *Policy Studies Journal* 20: 598–620.

Sullivan, John, James Piereson, and George Marcus. 1978. "Ideological Constraint in the Mass Public: A Methodological Critique and Some New Findings." *American Journal of Political Science* 22: 233–49.

Sundquist, James L. 1968. *Politics and Policy: The Eisenhower, Kennedy, and Johnson Years*. Washington, DC: Brookings Institution Press.

Sussman, Leila. 1963. *Dear FDR: A Study of Political Letter Writing*. Totowa, NJ: Bedminster Press.

Tanner, Michael. 1996. Testimony at Hearing 005. *Social Security Reform Options: Preparing for the 21st Century*. Washington, DC: Special Committee on Aging, U.S. Senate, September 24.

Tate, Katherine. 1993. *From Protest to Politics*. Cambridge, MA: Harvard University Press.

Teles, Steven M. 1996. *Whose Welfare?: AFDC and Elite Politics*. Lawrence: University Press of Kansas.

Tiebout, Charles. 1956. "A Pure Theory of Public Expenditures." *Journal of Political Economy*. 64: 416–24.

Tilly, Charles. 1975. *The Formation of National States in Western Europe*. Princeton, NJ: Princeton University Press.

———. 1983. "Speaking Your Mind without Elections, Surveys, or Social Movements." *Public Opinion Quarterly* 47: 461–78.

Toner, Robin. 1992. "New Politics of Welfare Focuses on Its Flaws." *New York Times*, July 5, sec. 1, p. 1.

Traugott, Michael. 2000. "Polling in the Public's Interest." *Public Opinion Quarterly* 64: 374–84.

———. 2001. "Assessing Poll Performance in the 2000 Campaign." *Public Opinion Quarterly* [forthcoming].

Trochim, William M. K. 2001. *The Research Methods Knowledge Base*. Cincinnati, OH: Atomic Dog Publishing Co.

Truman, David. 1945. "Public Opinion Research as a Tool of Public Administration." *Public Administration Review* 5: 62–72.

Tucker, William H. 1994. *The Science and Politics of Racial Research*. Urbana: University of Illinois Press.

U.S. Office of Management and Budget. 2001. *Budget of the United States Government, Fiscal Year 2002*. Washington, DC: Government Printing Office.

Verba, Sidney. 1971. "Conclusion." *Crises and Sequences in Political Development*, ed. Leonard Binder. Princeton, N.J.: Princeton University Press.

———. 1996. "The Citizen Respondent: Sample Surveys and American Democracy." *American Political Science Review* 90: 1–7.

Verba, Sidney, Kay Lehman Schlozman, and Henry E. Brady. 1995. *Voice and Equality:*

Civic Voluntarism in American Politics. Cambridge, MA: Harvard University Press.

Vogel, David. 1989. *Fluctuating Fortunes: The Political Power of Business in America.* New York: Basic Books.

Waksberg, Joseph. 1978. "Sampling Methods for Random Digit Dialing." *Journal of the American Statistical Association* 73: 40–46.

Wala, Michael. 1994. *The Council on Foreign Relations and American Foreign Policy in the Early Cold War.* Providence, RI: Berghahn Books.

Walker, Jack L. 1991. *Mobilizing Interest Groups in America: Patrons, Professions, and Social Movements.* Ann Arbor: University of Michigan Press.

Wallsten, Thomas, David Budescu, Anatol Rapoport, R. Zwick, and B. Forsyth. 1986. "Measuring the Vague Meanings of Probability Terms." *Journal of Experimental Psychology: General* 115: 348–65.

Wallsten, Thomas, David Budescu, Rami Zwick, and Steven Kemp. 1993. "Preferences and Reasons for Communicating Probabilistic Information in Verbal or Numerical Terms." *Bulletin of the Psychonomic Society* 31: 135–38.

Walton, Hanes Jr., Cheryl M. Miller, and Joseph P. McCormick II. 1995. "Race and Political Science: The Dual Traditions of Race Relations Politics and African-American Politics." In *Political Science in History: Research Programs and Political Traditions*, ed. James Farr, John S. Dryzek, and Stephen T. Leonard, pp. 145–74. Cambridge: Cambridge University Press.

Weaver, R. Kent. 2000. *Ending Welfare as We Know It.* Washington, DC: Brookings Institution Press.

Weaver, R. Kent, Robert Y. Shapiro, and Lawrence R. Jacobs. 1995a. "The Polls—Trends: Welfare." *Public Opinion Quarterly* 59: 606–27.

———. 1995b. "Public Opinion on Welfare Reform: A Mandate for What?" In *Looking Before We Leap: Social Science and Welfare Reform*, ed. R. Kent Weaver and William T. Dickens, pp. 109–28. Washington, DC: The Brookings Institution.

Webber, Michael J. 2000. *New Deal Fat Cats: Business, Labor, and Campaign Finance in the 1936 Presidential Election.* New York: Fordham University Press.

Weinstein, James. 1968. *The Corporate Ideal in the Liberal State, 1900–1918.* Boston: Beacon Press.

Weir, Margaret. 1998. "Wages and Jobs: What Is the Public Role." In *The Social Divide*, ed. Margaret Weir, pp. 267–311. Washington, DC: Brookings Institution Press.

Weissberg, Robert. 1976. *Public Opinion and Popular Government.* Englewood Cliffs, NJ: Prentice-Hall.

———. 1978. "Collective vs. Dyadic Representation in Congress." *American Political Science Review* 72: 535–47.

Wellman, Barry, Anabel Quan Haase, James Witte, and Keith Hampton. 2001. "Does the Internet Multiply, Decrease, or Increase Social Capital? Networks, Participation, and Commitment Online and Offline." *American Behavioral Scientist.*

West, Darrell, Diane Heith, and Chris Goodwin. 1996. "Harry and Louise Go to Washington: Political Advertising and Health Care Reform." *Journal of Health Politics, Policy and Law* 21 (Spring): 35–68.

West, Darrell, and Burdett Loomis. 1999. *The Sound of Money: How Political Interests Get What They Want.* New York: W. W. Norton.

Whalen, Charles W., and Barbara Whalen. 1985. *The Longest Debate: A Legislative History of the 1964 Civil Rights Act.* Washington, DC: Seven Locks Press.

Wilt, Evan. 1998. "Vote Early and Often." *American Demographics.* December.

Wines, Michael. 1994. "Washington Really Is in Touch. We're the Problem." *New York Times*, October 16, sec. 4, p. 1.

Winters, Jeffrey A. 1996. *Power in Motion: Capital Mobility and the Indonesian State*. Ithaca, NY: Cornell University Press.

Wiseman, Frederick. 1972. "Methodological Bias in Public Opinion Surveys." *Public Opinion Quarterly* 36 (1): 105–8.

Witte, James, Lisa Amoroso, and Philip E. N. Howard. 2001. "Method and Representation in Internet-Based Survey Tools: Mobility, Community, and Cultural Identity in Survey2000." *Social Science Computing Review* 18: 179–95.

Wittkopf, Eugene R. 1996. "What Americans Really Think About Foreign Policy." *Washington Quarterly* 19: 91–106.

Wlezien, Christopher. 1995. "The Public as Thermostat: Dynamics of Preferences for Spending." *American Journal of Political Science* 39: 981–1000.

———. 1996. "Dynamics of Representation: The Case of U.S. Spending on Defence." *British Journal of Political Science* 26: 81–103.

Wood, B. Dan, and Angela H. Andersson. 1998. "The Dynamics of Senatorial Representation, 1952–1991." *Journal of Politics* 60 (August): 705–36.

Woodward, C. Vann. 1951. *Reunion and Reaction: The Compromise of 1877 and the End of Reconstruction*. Boston: Little, Brown.

———. 1966. *The Strange Career of Jim Crow*. Oxford: Oxford University Press.

Wright, Gerald. 1989. "Policy Voting in the U.S. Senate: Who Is Represented?" *Legislative Studies Quarterly* 14: 465–86.

———. 1994. "The Meaning of 'Party' in Congressional Roll Call Voting." Paper delivered at the annual meeting of the Midwest Political Science Association, Chicago, April 14–16.

Wright, Gerald C., and Michael Berkman. 1986. "Candidates and Policies in United States Senate Elections." *American Political Science Review* 80: 567–88.

Wright, Gerald, Robert S. Erikson, and John P. McIver. 1987. "Public Opinion and Policy Liberalism in the American States." *American Journal of Political Science* 31: 980–1001.

Wyden, Ron. 1998. Remarks at Hearing 013. *Stock Market and Social Security: The Risks and the Rewards*. Washington, DC: Special Committee on Aging, U.S. Senate, April 22.

Yankelovich, Daniel. 1991. *Coming to Public Judgment: Making Democracy Work in a Complex World*. Syracuse, NY: Syracuse University Press.

Yankelovich, Daniel, and I. M. Destler, eds. 1994. *Beyond the Beltway: Engaging the Public in U.S. Foreign Policy*. New York: Norton.

Yankelovich, Daniel, and John Immerwahr. 1994. "The Rules of Public Engagement." In *Beyond the Beltway: Engaging the Public in U.S. Foreign Policy*, ed. Daniel Yankelovich and I. M. Destler, pp. 43–77. New York: Norton.

Zaller, John R. 1992. *The Nature and Origins of Mass Opinion*. New York: Cambridge University Press.

———. 1996. "The Myth of Massive Media Impact Revived: New Support for a Discredited Idea." In *Political Persuasion and Attitude Change*, ed. Diana C. Muntz, Paul Sniderman, and Richard Brody, pp. 125–44. Ann Arbor: University of Michigan Press.

Zaller, John R., and Dennis Chiu. 1996. "Government's Little Helper: U.S. Press Coverage of Foreign Policy Crises, 1945–1991." *Political Communication* 13: 385–405.

———. 2000. "Government's Little Helper: U.S. Press Coverage of Foreign Policy Crises, 1945–1999." In *Decisionmaking in a Glass House: Mass Media, Public Opinion, and American and European Foreign Policy in the 21st Century*, ed. Brigitte L. Nacos,

Robert Y. Shapiro, and Pierangelo Isernia, pp. 61–84. New York: Rowman and Little-field.

Zaller, John R., and Stanley Feldman. 1992. "A Simple Theory of the Survey Response: Answering Questions versus Revealing Preferences." *American Journal of Political Science* 36: 579–616.

———. 1994. "Strategic Politicians, Public Opinion, and the Gulf War." In *Taken by Storm: The News Media, U.S. Foreign Policy, and the Gulf War*, ed. Lance Bennett and David Paletz, pp. 250–74. Chicago: University of Chicago Press.

Zimmer, Alf. 1983. "Verbal vs. Numerical Processing of Subjective Probabilities." In *Decision Making under Uncertainty*, ed. Roland W. Scholz, pp. 159–82. Amsterdam: North-Holland.

INDEX